I0831784

J.R.D. TATA

Oswald A.J. Mascarenhas is J.R.D. Tata Chair Professor in Business Ethics at XLRI, Jamshedpur. Reach him at ozzie@xlri.ac.in

Doris D'Souza is professor of Business Ethics and Sustainability at XLRI. Reach her at dorisdsouza76@gmail.com

E. Abraham is the former Director of XLRI. Reach him at abraham@xlri.ac.in

J.R.D. TATA

ORATIONS ON BUSINESS ETHICS

~*Edited by* OSWALD A.J. MASCARENHAS,
DORIS D'SOUZA & E. ABRAHAM~

~*Foreword by* J.J. IRANI~

Published by
Rupa Publications India Pvt. Ltd 2019
7/16, Ansari Road, Daryaganj
New Delhi 110002

Sales Centres:
Allahabad Bengaluru Chennai
Hyderabad Jaipur Kathmandu
Kolkata Mumbai

Editorial Consultant: Dr Payal Kumar (FPM, XLRI)

ISBN: 978-93-5333-568-7

First impression 2019

10 9 8 7 6 5 4 3 2 1

'We do not claim to be more unselfish, more generous or more philanthropic than other people. But we think we started on sound and straightforward business principles, considering the interests of the shareholders, our own, and the health and welfare of our employees—the sure foundation of our prosperity.'

—Jamsetji Nusserwanji Tata

Contents

About J.R.D. Tata

Jehangir Ratanji Dadabhoy Tata's life and leadership of Tata Sons was not far from the philosophy of J.N. Tata, a man he admired the most. The philosophy was to strive for inclusive growth through sustainable business models. Although JRD may have never liked to be compared, he took Jamsetji's philosophies as his guiding principle throughout his years of nurturing and nourishing a unique business conglomerate. JRD once explained to his biographer, R.M. Lala, why he regarded Jamsetji so highly. He said, 'Jamsetji was a man of great intelligence, a man of extraordinary vision. There are some intelligent people, but they have no sense at all of the future. Jamsetji had that sense.'

Emulating the ideologies of Jamsetji, JRD's efforts were often directed towards nation-building. In his board meetings with fellow directors, JRD often raised the question, 'What does a nation need?' When he took over as chairman of Tata Sons, the group had fourteen companies. When he completed his fifty-year-long journey at the helm of the Tatas on 26 July 1988, there were ninety-five enterprises which the Tatas had either started or had a controlling interest in. JRD took over as director of the Tatas in 1926, when he was only half the age of the other Tata directors. His ascension to the role of chairman was in 1938 and by far, he was the youngest member of the board. Distinguished figures like Homi Mody, Ardeshir Dalal and Sorabji Saklatvala were already present on the board. Apart from directors, he also had to ally with senior executives like Sir Jehangir Ghandy, 'Kish' Naoroji and P.A. Narielwala. Bringing these senior and very distinguished figures together to work in perfect harmony was JRD's job, which, except for a few bumps, he managed with great flair.

His style of leadership was based on consensus. He said in his biography, *Beyond the Last Blue Mountain*, 'When I have to make a decision, I feel I must first make sure that the superior knowledge of my advisers confirm the soundness of my decision; secondly, that they would execute my decision not reluctantly, but be convinced about it; thirdly, I see myself in Tatas as the leader of a team who has to weigh the impact of any decision on other Tata companies, on the unity of the group. I think this policy has paid off.'

Under his chairmanship, the group expanded into chemicals, automobiles, tea and information technology. He chose to break away from the prevalent Indian business practice of having members of one's own family run different operations, and instead, JRD pushed to bring in professionals. He turned over a new leaf; the Tata Group became a business federation where entrepreneurial talent and expertise were given weightage. JRD's life was a stunning display of integrity and vision, far ahead of his times. He considered his leadership of the Tata group and his dedication to the cause of India as complementary, and he brought to the two undertakings a rare dignity and a sense of purpose. He touched the lives of countless others—rich and poor, manager and worker—as he became the embodiment of the principles and philosophy of the House of Tata.

JRD was born in Paris in 1904 to R.D. Tata, a business partner and relative of Jamsetji Tata and his French wife Sooni. JRD, the second of five siblings, was educated in France, Japan and England, before being drafted into the French army for a mandatory one-year period. JRD then desired to pursue engineering from Cambridge, but R.D. Tata summoned his son to India. He soon found himself in the midst of a business career in a country he was far from familiar with. Born out of his love for aviation was his first big adventure in business. In 1929, JRD became one of the first Indians to be granted a commercial pilot's licence. In 1932, Tata Aviation Services, the forerunner to Tata Airlines and Air India, took to the skies. The first flight in the history of Indian aviation lifted off from Drigh Road in Karachi, with JRD at the controls of a Puss Moth aircraft. However, Air India was later nationalized by the Jawaharlal Nehru government. It was a decision JRD had fought against with all his might.

The Tata Group, in the hands of this ingenious and enterprising leader, accomplished new heights and became one of the most trusted brands. His unceasing quest to make the world a better place, earned him several prestigious awards. He was awarded India's highest civilian honour, the Bharat Ratna, in 1992, for his selfless service towards humanity. He was the proud recipient of The Tony Jannus Award (1979) and the Edward Warner Award of the International Civil Aviation Organization in Canada (1986). Although JRD was showered with honours, he never yearned for them. On being told that the Indian government was thinking about giving him the Bharat Ratna, he is reported to have said, 'Why me? I don't deserve it. The Bharat Ratna is usually given to people who are dead or it is given to politicians. I am not prepared to oblige the government on the former and I am not the latter.'

He and his wife Thelma—whom he married in 1930—did not have any children, but JRD always appeared most comfortable with kids. He was a figure of modesty and generosity to whoever he came in contact with. Self-effacing, wistful and endearing are some of the adjectives that one would associate with JRD. When JRD breathed his last in a Geneva hospital on 29 November 1993, it could be truly said that an epoch had ended. A message from his former company, Air India, was the most befitting obituary of all:

'He touched the sky and it smiled.
He stretched out his arms
And they encircled the globe.
His vision made giants out of
Men and organizations.'

A Note from XLRI*

E. ABRAHAM

The unique contribution that Mr J.R.D. Tata has made to the Indian industry, the national economy and to management education, has always been with a certain ethical perspective, social concern and integrity in dealing with people. The establishment of a foundation for business ethics in Mr Tata's name would be the best recognition of this admirable facet of Mr Tata's life and character.

Living in close proximity to the two largest companies of the Tata family, we experience their constant and unobtrusive support, and also the support of other member companies of the Tata group.

Business ethics is not so much a concept but a culture or an environment in which industry and commerce can flourish. What we have done today is to give formal recognition to this idea and launch an effort to bring it to the notice of our countrymen.

*Delivered on 4 March 1991 by E. Abraham, Director, XLRI (1989–1994, 2008)

Foreword

J.J. IRANI

Adam Smith wrote *The Wealth of Nations* way back in 1776. This was not a book on economics as a source of wealth. It spoke about moral principles as the source of wealth. Adam Smith was a British moral philosopher; not an economist. He spoke about ethics as a way of life, for corporate advantage. According to the Ethics Resource Center, Washington DC, companies that are dedicated to doing the right thing, have a written commitment to social responsibility, and act on it as a way of life, are consistently more profitable than those who do not.

If your company is ethical and socially responsible, it won't automatically make you rich and successful, but it will definitely pave the way for you to become so. Ethics + competence = success is a winning equation. This is the equation of ethics for corporate advantage. On the other hand, companies that continually attempt to test the edge of ethics inevitably go over the edge. Shortcuts, deception, cheating and cutting corners test the edge of ethics and never pay off in the long run. People and organizations always lose in the long term when they live without ethics and guiding moral principles.[1]

Business and industry ethics is not just a concept or construct, a category or structure of thought, or even a theory or abstraction, but a concrete, challenging way of life for corporate executives to think and act legally, ethically, morally and spiritually in the turbulent markets of today. This commemorative volume on J.R.D. Tata illustrates this truth and strategy.

We need strong corporate ethics at all levels. Luk Bouckaert (2015) forcefully argues that a spiritual approach to business ethics is badly needed. Without a sense of greater intrinsic motivation, business ethics will be reduced to an instrument for reputation and risk management, while any genuine moral commitment will be lost. Corporate ethics is an invitation to look up and see the rest of the world in its stark reality and do something about it.[2]

We define and study corporate ethics and morals as lived, experienced and shared dynamic systems of socially accepted and morally universal values, principles, standards and rules that can spiritually empower our life and society, our markets and our world. While ethics deals with shared social values, and business ethics studies lived and shared values in buyer-seller exchanges, corporate executive ethics centres on governance values and principles that power corporate decisions and choices, strategies and implementation processes that have corporate-wide consequences, and often, industry-nation-wide ramifications. Accordingly, the twenty-seven speeches on ethics that constitute this volume in memory of J.R.D. Tata seek to explore and analyse corporate decisions and choices, especially in the context of contemporary turbulent markets ridden with risk, uncertainty, chaos and ambiguity, which, when further infected by buyer-seller information asymmetries (BSIA), can lead to corporate fraud, corruption, bribery and money laundering.

Such socially violent market conditions constantly challenge corporate executives, business practitioners, academicians and students of business today, and this volume provides a multidimensional approach to this challenge. It trains and empowers corporates to brave this turbulent yet opportunity-laden world with sound moral principles, standards and rules drawn from major ethical theories of deontology, teleology, distributive justice, corrective justice, ethics of human dignity, compassion, virtue, trust, critical thinking, rights and duties, moral reasoning, judgment and justification, and ethics of corporate moral and social responsibility.

We live in turbulent times. Poverty, inequality, youth unemployment and climate change are among the challenges we are facing. In businesses, CEOs have gone from being symbols of aspiration to objects of intense scrutiny. Even the younger, 'cooler' entrepreneurs, the kick-starters of the shared economy, are now being asked questions about the impact their companies have on society.

Trust has become the ultimate currency. We are at a critical juncture. According to last year's Edelman Trust Barometer, 64 per cent of people globally expect CEOs to lead on social change rather than waiting for government intervention. And a significant 84 per cent expect CEOs to influence policy debates on social issues. Overall, trust in business (52 per cent) remains higher than global trust in government (43 per cent).

Millennial consumers are driving this trend; 40 per cent of those polled by the Deloitte Millennial Survey 2018 believe that the goal of businesses should be to 'improve society'. This is seriously worth pondering. By 2020, millennials will make up 40 per cent of all consumers, influencing about $40 billion in annual sales.

Increasingly, companies are going beyond compliance. Nearly 90 per cent of the world's biggest companies are reporting on their sustainability performance, using metrics established by the GRI (The Global Reporting Initiative, established in October 2016). Nearly 9,933 companies from 160 countries are currently members of the UN Global Compact—an initiative launched to align business strategy with social goals, and to support Sustainable Development Goals. Corporate responsibility is going mainstream.[3]

Ethisphere Institute is a leader in defining the standards of ethical business practices. Ethics Quotient (EQ) framework has been used by Ethisphere Institute to rank companies. The EQ framework is based on the following parameters: a) ethics and compliance programme; b) corporate citizenship and responsibility; c) culture of ethics; d) governance; and e) leadership, innovation and reputation.

In 2018, Tata Steel was recognized, for the sixth time, as the most ethical company in the world in the category of 'Metals, Minerals and Mining' by Ethisphere Institute. Ethisphere Institute awarded similar recognitions to Tata Steel in 2012, 2013, 2015, 2016 and 2017. Tata Steel has been recognized worldwide as one of the most ethical companies. T.V. Narendran, global CEO and managing director of Tata Steel, said, 'It's a privilege for us to be receiving this recognition for the sixth time. It is also a befitting reminder to continue upholding the legacy of leadership with trust that underlines our business philosophy.'

One of society's abiding needs is to develop, nurture and mature its leaders. Organizations do not live on earnings alone, but they do live by their leaders and their followers. Vision is the basis for the best kind of leadership, especially ethical and moral leadership. Today, more than ever, leadership is more an art than a science, more a lived project than an academic programme. Ethical leadership is more an ethical imperative than an organizational quality, more a desperate need of the day than a pious wish of the future. Moral leadership is more an urgent calling than a job, more a professional clarion call for integrity than an organizational performance drive.[4]

'Today's best leaders,' says Max DePree, 'are *attuned to the needs and ideas of their followers* [emphasis added], and even step aside at times to be followers themselves.' Genuine leadership reveals how to hold people accountable and give them space to reach their potential; to see the needs of employees and those of the company as the same; to inspire change and innovation; and to work effectively with creative people.[5] 'I am still learning about leadership at the age of eighty-three. I am happy to tell you that becoming a better leader is a job that never ends.' 'Leadership is something we never completely understand.'[6]

It's becoming increasingly evident that the world's most pressing problems cannot be resolved by governments or civil society alone. It's time for businesses to pitch in. From reducing environmental impact to contributing to healthier societies and fighting forced labour, companies can achieve tremendous results if they balance profit and purpose. With the growing trend of investors and consumers buying into companies that deliver positive social change alongside financial returns, the tendency for big business to adopt impactful social missions looks set to continue. The question is: How many business leaders will have the courage to step up to the plate? The business of changing the world is in corporate hands.[7]

It is my honour and privilege to introduce this volume. The twenty-sixth oration on ethics herein is mine—it captures my close association with and inspirations from J.R.D. Tata over the quarter of a century that I have known him and worked under him. This book indirectly celebrate the ethical, moral and spiritual leadership of J.R.D. Tata during the fifty-four years he governed the Tata House. It beckons us to continue our journey of spiritual and corporate leadership wherever we are and in whatever we do—because that task and sacred journey never ends.

REFERENCES

1. Mascarenhas, Oswald A.J. (2018), *Corporate Ethics for Turbulent Markets: The Market Context of Executive Decisions*, UK: Emerald Publishing.
2. Bouckaert, L. (2015), 'Spirituality: The Missing Link in Business Ethics,' in Zsolnai L. Ed., *The Spiritual Dimension of Business Ethics and Sustainability Management*, Springer, pp. 15-26.
3. Zappulla, A. (2019), 'The Future of Business? Purpose, Not Just Profit,' *Thomson Reuters.* Available at https://blogs.thomsonreuters.com/answerson/the-future-of-business-purpose-not-just-profit/
4. Mascarenhas, *Corporate Ethics for Turbulent Markets* (2018).
5. De Pree, M. (1992/2008), *Leadership Jazz-Revised Edition: The Essential Elements of a Great Leader*, Manhattan: Crown Business.
6. Ibid.: xv; 173.
7. Mascarenhas, *Corporate Ethics for Turbulent Markets* (2018).

Introductory Address*

SAROSH J. GHANDY

Jamshedpur is a city of pioneers. Its citizens are accustomed to setting new records and starting processes that eventually do their country proud. Therefore, there is a real danger that the setting up of a foundation for business ethics may be perceived as a mere expansion of a management curriculum. Lest we succumb to such an oversight, may I mention that even though the Harvard Business School has invested an enormous amount of money for such a purpose, it continues to be embarrassed, year after year, for its inability to translate money into a programme to effectively promote ethics. Can a campus that teaches the art of making money encumber itself with the excess baggage of ethics?

With God's grace and Mr Tata's support, XLRI has ventured to give its answer in the affirmative. It is my privilege to share the course of events that has brought this good fortune to our campus.

The Problem—to Honour the Honourable!

For quite some time we have felt that XLRI must find a way to extend its recognition of Mr Tata, for the monumental contributions he has made to the industry and industrial life in India. Our rationale was that his contributions are so substantial as to merit special recognition. Little did we anticipate the dilemma that was soon to confront us.

The man we had set out to recognize, had already been adopted by the Indian Air Force as the honorary air vice-marshal!

India, his country, had already honoured him with the Padma Vibhushan!

---

*Introductory address at the inauguration of the XLRI–JRD Tata Foundation in Business Ethics on 4 March 1991. Delivered by Sarosh J. Ghandy, Resident Director, Telco, Jamshedpur; and Chairman, Board of Governors (1981–1993), XLRI

France, the country of his birth, had made him a Commander of the Legion of Honour!

The Vatican had made him a Knight Commander of the Order of St. Gregory the Great!

The Federal Republic of Germany had adorned him with The Knight Commander Cross of the Order of Merit!

And the American Institute of Aeronautics and Astronautics had bestowed upon him its most prestigious award, the Daniel Guggenheim Medal, for his pioneering work in civil aviation.

It was not merely a problem of finding a place on his chest to pin yet another medal. The real problem lay in our presumption that it was possible to confer further recognition on him. Men such as J.R.D. Tata are phenomena that lend their lustre to institutions which turn to them. But the reverse does not really hold true.

J.R.D. TATA AND XLRI'S MISSION

A second problem remained for us to solve. We had to choose the nature of the support for which we would turn to Mr Tata. This called for introspection. What is unique about the mission of XLRI? What is the message for which we would like to point to Mr Tata and say, 'Look dear alumni, this is how your alma mater wants you to be.'

The mission of XLRI is unmistakably directed towards the superordinate goal of ethics and social justice clearly enunciated in the prospectus of the Institute, as you would see it in this extract:

> XLRI hopes to contribute to the orderly growth and progress of the nation towards a more prosperous, just and humane society. In promoting professional management, through its educational, training and research activities, the Institute wants to emphasize a humane approach to work and management, along with technical competence, managerial excellence, indigenization of management practices, special concern for the 'weaker sections of society and dedication to social and ethical responsibility.'

This commitment of the Institute is also demonstrated by it being the first, and for long the only, management institute in the country to introduce and sustain a course on business ethics.

Mr Tata, on the other hand, is decidedly the living example of the idealist's dream of a 'good businessman.' But it is not so well known that this 'goodness' is by no chance a product of circumstances. Neither is it the result of the proverbial 'Honesty is the best policy.' It has been chiselled by his conscious commitment to highest standards and has been sculpted by an act of his will. Refer to this quotation from Mr Tata on how he viewed his mission when he set out in his career:

'In 1938, my colleagues, all much senior to me, in a moment of mental aberration, elected me as the chairman of Tata. I resolved to dedicate myself and the firm, to the task of carrying on Jamsetji Tata's vision of a politically free and economically strong India and to play a worthy role in its development.'

J.R.D. TATA, EXEMPLAR OF ETHICS

We found it extremely fortunate that through Mr Tata, the XLRI could find a living expression of the ethical component of its own institutional mission. We are indeed fortunate that he found us deserving to use his name for the foundation we wanted to set up for the promotion of business ethics.

We next approached all the Tata companies to give us the financial strength that would constitute the tangible component of this project. It is with deep gratitude that I acknowledge the fact that the generosity of the Tata companies has been exceeded only by their promptness in contributing to the building of the corpus of the foundation.

This foundation will set up a Chair for Business Ethics, which will confer from time to time, an award of high distinction on men of eminence in business ethics, and it will also organize an annual oration on business ethics.

When Mr Tata began his career, he measured money in thousands and lakhs.

But now, he allocates money by hundreds of crores. He began his career with worries about where the money would come from. Now, his concerns lie with where the money should go. He is a creator of wealth who fosters the concept that wealth should be held in trust for the people.

On the 6th of August, 1990, the *TIME* magazine published an interview with Mr Tata. The title they gave to the interview was—PROFIT IS NOT A DIRTY WORD.

1

Ethics and Business Success

J.R.D. TATA*

When Sarosh Ghandy and Father Abraham first approached me with the proposal to set up a foundation for business ethics at the XLRI, I applauded the idea, but questioned the suggestion that it should be named after me. I told them that, while throughout my career I had upheld the need to maintain high ethical standards, Jamsetji Tata had established them long before I came on the scene. For, as far back as 1895, when Jamsetji opened an extension of the Express Mills, he said, 'We do not claim to be more unselfish, more generous or more philanthropic than other people. But we think that we have started on sound and straightforward business principles, considering the interest of the shareholders as our own, and the health and welfare of the employees as the sure foundation of our prosperity.'

After Jamsetji Tata's death, his sons, who inherited the responsibility of guiding the firm, maintained the traditions and principles which he had so clearly established. Jamsetji was, of course, also a great humanitarian and philanthropist and the wealth gathered by him and his sons in a hundred years of industrial pioneering formed but a small fraction of the amount by which they enriched the nation; for, after their death, the whole of that wealth was held in philanthropic trusts for the people and used exclusively for their benefit. Thus, the cycle was complete. What came from the people has gone back to the people many times over.

I merely did what I could to ensure the continued adherence

*Oration delivered on 4 March 1991.

of the Tata Group of Companies, including those created after the founder's death, to the principles and traditions he had established. I, therefore, felt it would be more appropriate to name the foundation after Jamsetji Tata. However, my arguments were overruled by XLRI's board of governors.

WHY A FOUNDATION FOR BUSINESS ETHICS?

The question may be asked, why a foundation for business ethics needs to be created at this time to advocate the maintenance of high business ethics in the industrial life of our country. Those like myself, who have lived many more years than most, can recall the era when the need to advocate high ethical standards in business did not arise, as such standards were already being reasonably adhered to. There was no noticeable corruption in those days—tax evasion, the creation and use of black money and bribes were hardly heard of. Alas, conditions have indeed changed, and I have often asked myself—what were the main causes responsible for the deterioration in business morality and for the unethical business practices which have become so prevalent in our country today?

It may be noted, in passing, that the need for corrective actions against corruption and other unethical practices arose in other countries also, notably the USA, where legislation aimed at curbing corrupt practices was introduced many years ago; business schools established courses in business ethics as a regular subject of study and many companies laid down ethical guidelines for their management and staff.

REASONS FOR GROWTH OF CORRUPTION

What are the main reasons, as I see them, for the growth of corruption and unethical practices in our country over the past few decades?

Consider, first, the business environment as it existed during the first decades of this century. The highest emoluments in government jobs were then ₹4,000 a month, paid to high court judges and secretaries to government at a time when the purchasing value of the rupee was 40 to 50 times its present worth and taxes were largely non-existent—or so low as hardly to be felt. There were no obstacles then to what could be paid to the company chairman, managing directors or corporate managers. Yet, I remember a British director of the Tatas recalling the fact that when he first came to India, he could maintain a horse for ₹10 a month.

When India became independent, one of the first things our government did in the name of socialism was to reduce the emoluments of its senior-most employees to ₹3,500 per month from ₹4,000. This reduction was also imposed on the private sector, ignoring the fact that the continuing loss of the purchasing power of the rupee had already achieved the desired objective of lowering the officers' income. On the other hand, the emoluments of lower-paid employees in the administrative services and public sector companies continued to be steadily increased, largely in response to union pressures.

Under the government's and politicians' interpretations of socialism, government—or Parliament at its behest—drastically increased tax rates and created what came to be known as a *license-and-permit raj*, under which a host of controls, rules and regulations were imposed, seriously affecting the progress of business and industry. The marginal income tax was raised to the absurdly high level of 97.75 per cent, which together with the wealth tax then introduced, often exceeded the income being taxed.

Inevitably, as universally experienced, when taxes become oppressive or expropriatory, honesty and morality tend to disappear. Tax evasion, the creation and use of black money and other dishonest means of accumulating or saving tax-free money became the order of the day, as they are today.

The exercise of controls and the collection of taxes were necessarily entrusted to members of the bureaucracy giving them, and in the process, the tremendous economic power to say yes or no or the equally oppressive power to delay decisions—all of these—became vulnerable to the influence of money.

It can thus be seen that the severe degradation of honesty and character, experienced in the past fifty years or so, originated largely in wrong and harmful socio-economic policies adopted by successive governments and parliaments in the name of socialism—or rather, their own false interpretation of socialism. Fortunately, this system has now been discredited all over the world, and in many instances, discarded—even in countries where it virtually became the equivalent of religious conviction.

Unfortunately, in our country, the changes required in economic and fiscal policy for such reform are taking place slowly and hesitantly. Understandably so, since the powers and even the earning capacity of the bureaucracy would inevitably be reduced due to this. Many of the old principles and policies, therefore, continue to harm the economic progress of the country.

PUBLIC MISTRUST OF BUSINESS

The most important and damaging cause of suspicion and hostility towards private enterprise in our country has been the fact that the ethical standards adopted in the past by some elements in business and industry have not been as high as they should have been—and, in some cases, have been atrociously low. Immense damage has been caused to the image of private business and industry during the last fifty years or so through the depredations, misdeeds and conspicuous expenditure of a few individuals heading large enterprises who, in their pursuit of wealth, profit and self-aggrandizement, have wantonly disregarded the public interest. I have been dismayed and saddened at the number of the more fortunate people in our country, who, seemingly oblivious of the threat to their own good fortune and survival, continue not only to indulge in unethical self-enrichment but also flaunt their illegal gains by ostentatious living and conspicuous spending.

There has indeed been a need to rekindle old principles and ethical values which, alas, have too often been ignored or neglected in recent years in the belief that quicker profits and greater accumulation of wealth would be the result. Our own experience in Tatas has shown that this is a false belief.

2

Establishing and Maintaining an Ethical Business Climate*

JOSEPH M. SCIORTINO

It is common knowledge that J.R.D. Tata, the patriarch of the Tata Group of Industries and the doyen of Indian industrialists, is known throughout India and abroad for his integrity of character and commitment to high standards of business. I am not surprised, therefore, that the nation should have bestowed on him its highest award—the Bharat Ratna or 'Jewel of India'.

It is highly commendable that the Tata companies should want to share their ethical convictions with others by establishing at XLRI a foundation for business ethics in the name of their doyen. I am told that this foundation funds a chair in business ethics, provides for an annual oration on the subject and a periodical award to a business person for outstanding ethical commitment. What a wonderful gift to give to the people of India and the business community of this fine country!

I do not consider myself to be an ethicist; neither am I a moral theologian, nor an expert on ethics. I am merely the chief executive of a large company doing business in a very tough economic environment, struggling to meet the expectations of corporate management and the stakeholders of our corporation, while maintaining a spirit of decency in our company and a pleasant environment for our employees. That is a big assignment! It is not easy, in today's competitive environment, to be honest, ethical and to live by the Golden Rule (to treat others as you would want to be treated.)

---

*Oration delivered on 28 February 1992.

WHAT IS SYSCO?

The Sysco Corporation is a relatively new company founded in 1969 by nine entrepreneurs led by a visionary, who saw the potential growth in the 'eating-away-from-home' business. He convinced his colleagues (these nine individual entrepreneurs) to pool their assets and merge their companies into Sysco Corporation, so that they would be positioned to service the eating-out industry on a nationwide basis. Apparently, he was right on target, for the corporation has had a compounded growth of 18 per cent over the past twenty years, and has become an $8-plus-billion giant. Sysco is, by far, the number one supplier to the foodservice industry in the United States. It is nationwide and covers all of the major markets servicing the foodservice business. Revenues last year exceeded $8 billion—about ₹21,000 crore—and while we are a long way from dominating the industry, we have achieved the enviable position of being the unqualified leader. With some humility, Sysco is the model of what a food service distribution company should be. Our market is comprised of restaurants, hotels, hospitals, schools and other places which serve food. It is a huge market! Its potential represents approximately $100 billion (₹2,60,000 crore), and is fast approaching a point of development where one dollar of every two dollars spent on food in the United States is spent away from home.

The two Florida Sysco companies for which I am responsible represent approximately 6 per cent of Sysco's total volume. This year alone, they will generate in excess of $500 million in revenues. We have 850 employees and cover about three-fourths of the state's geography. Sysco's management style permits each of the operating chief executives to run his or her company autonomously. It is a very important part of Sysco's management philosophy and recognizes that each of our companies is quite different, and is located in a market that, in many cases, is totally different. This approach has been successful for Sysco.

MY BACKGROUND

Prior to joining Sysco, I was with a major multinational food manufacturing company, which I joined after completing graduate school. My entire business experience has been in the foodservice industry. I started with the company as a salesperson in New Orleans, Louisiana, in 1957 and when I left in 1976, some nineteen years later, I was general manager of the foodservice division, and close to achieving my career goal of divisional vice president. Fortunately, an irreconcilable conflict in management style, coupled with some moral/ethical differences with the divisional vice president, caused me to leave the company and seek my fortunes with Sysco Corporation. That has proven to be a *very* good choice.

I grew up in Louisiana in the southern USA in a rural community. My father was a grocer and my *very* early training as a young boy in the grocery store had a profound impact on my personal ethical development. In those days, *very* little was prepackaged, so we had to package and weigh everything for our customers. As a young boy, one of the severest reprimands I ever received was for sloppily weighing products. I can remember my father telling me how important it was to always weigh our products carefully and that if we ever err, it should be in the customer's favour, never in the store's favour. To give a little more is okay, but never less than what they are paying for. My father was a *very* honest and respected businessman who later became the mayor of our town.

Another example of early ethics development occurred as a 'prep school' student at age fifteen. I was a football player and our team travelled across the southeastern United States playing other prep schools. We had a good team. Some members of the team appropriated towels from hotels in our travels. I can remember going home from school for summer vacation and among my personal belongings, I had a hotel towel. My mother asked where I got the towel. I told her I picked it up on one of my football trips. She said, 'I don't want it in my house', 'it doesn't belong to us' and 'I want no part of stolen property'. I can't remember exactly what I did with that towel that summer, but I do remember feeling embarrassed about the situation, and I couldn't wait to get rid of it. I never stole another hotel towel.

My family was devoutly Catholic and sent me to parochial schools. It was there that my moral formation took place, in the family and in the school system. I mention this because this is where ethical development typically begins, in the home and in early education and the family environment.

WHAT IS BUSINESS ETHICS?

What does it mean to be ethical? What is business ethics? Dr Albert Schweitzer, famous humanitarian and missionary doctor, gave this definition in a 1952 Paris speech: 'In a general sense, ethics is the name we give to our concern for good behaviour. We feel an obligation to consider not only our own personal well-being but also that of others and of human society as a whole.' Confucius had one word that served as a rule of practice for one's life. 'Reciprocity'. Jesus told us to 'love one another as I have loved you.' He also said, 'Love the Lord your God with your whole heart, your whole mind and your whole soul and love your neighbour as yourself.' There is the ever-popular Golden Rule: 'Do unto others as you would have them do unto you.' The Bhagavad Gita expresses a similar sentiment. Although all of these are stated differently, the message is basically the same. Ethics is a study of what constitutes good and bad human conduct, including related activities and values. It has to do with fulfilling the relationships we have with people. When you apply this study in a business context, it is called business ethics.

Our personal lives cannot really be separated from our business lives even though there are some of us who think they can. They *try* to leave their ethics at the office door in the morning and pick them up again at night.

The issue of 'ethics in business' has become one of the most challenging issues confronting the corporate community. Major corporations throughout the US are vigorously addressing the challenge. One manifestation has been the widespread development of 'codes of ethics' and 'statements of values' in business organizations.

AN EARLY ETHICAL CHALLENGE

One of my greatest early challenges in ethical behaviour came shortly after I joined Sysco in Florida. The founder of the company, who was also one of Sysco's founding directors, had apparently maintained some of the habits he acquired as the sole proprietor of his company. Every Saturday morning, he would back his station wagon up to the company's dock and load it up with groceries. These groceries were supplied by brokers and suppliers. They viewed it as a 'cost of doing business' with the company. The message he was sending to all of the employees in the company, who witnessed his behaviour every week, was that it was acceptable for people to appropriate company products for their personal use.

Consequently, our theft losses were astronomical! One of my first tasks was to advise the broker and the supplier community to discontinue the practice of requesting groceries for personal use. The next task was to advise our employees that it was no longer acceptable to appropriate products for their own use and that those caught doing so would be terminated. Next, I circulated a policy that no product was to leave the premises without my approval. All automobiles would be checked on departure by the security guards, including those of the company president and its senior chairman. As a result, our theft losses were greatly reduced.

I learned very early that employee ethics directly reflect those of the leader, and if the chief executive is misbehaving, employees will do likewise. I hasten to add that this man wasn't a bad man: he just forgot somewhere along the way that he sold his company to the corporation, which gave him stock in exchange for his company's assets, and he was no longer the sole owner. Therefore, he couldn't help himself to the company's assets as he had done prior to selling his company to Sysco.

ETHICS—A LONG JOURNEY

Establishing an ethical climate in a company is a lot like starting a long journey; it begins with the first step. When you see an opportunity to change unethical behaviour, you have to do it at that point in time. Eventually, over a period of time, your company will become an ethical company. It is an 'ongoing process'! It never stops! The challenges are always there. It is not something that you achieve and then forget about. You have to keep building one step at a time.

Sysco South Florida has approximately 110 salespeople. These salespeople call on the hotels and restaurants, show new products, present marketing programmes and write their orders. In our early stages of development, when our environment was not right and we were struggling to make money and become professional, we were vulnerable to competitive raids on our salesforce. Competitors would lure our good people away by offering them huge salaries and guarantees and cars, and all sorts of perks. In some instances, our people would leave. This was distressing, particularly after having invested thousands of dollars training these people in sales and marketing techniques. So, we developed a 'no-compete contract', which curtailed competitive raids on our talent. Our competition quickly followed the no-compete contract system. Today we have created a climate which (though unwritten) establishes that if either company hires another's salesperson, they will not work in the same territory, calling on the same accounts. Occasionally we hire a competitor's sales people, but we don't want them to bring proprietary information from their previous employers about the company's customers and pricing.

There are still companies who do not play by the same rules and who will, in a minute, hire one of our marketers by promising them the Taj Mahal to get them to work for their company. This is particularly true now that Sysco has the most professional and best-trained salesforce in the marketplace. 'No-compete contracts' have proven to be a major deterrent to 'employee piracy' and have been adopted by most distributor companies.

An effective programme of corporate ethics requires the involvement and commitment of personnel at all levels. This participative element can be achieved only by programmes that work through the various levels of management and involve all work groups.

NEED FOR COMMITMENT BY ALL

Commitment to ethical behaviour by all of the company's employees is very important. When the company has total commitment, it is more likely to be an ethical company. Conversely, to merely publish a code of ethics and not attempt to get commitment will not achieve the management's ultimate goal—to be an ethical company. One of the ways I have attempted to get total commitment from all employees is to make available copies of the company's Mission Statement to all of them. The first sentence of that statement says, 'Sysco Food Services of South Florida, a dynamic and innovative company, is dedicated to satisfying its diverse and constantly growing customer base while maintaining the highest legal, moral and ethical standards.'

Each of our employees may have a copy of this, which they sign, along with the signatures of the divisional vice president and the company president. They can frame it, post it appropriately in their offices or cubicles and make themselves aware of what we all stand for. Not all of our employees have availed themselves of this opportunity, but many have, and I consider that to be a major step towards getting total commitment.

While no code of ethics can cover all situations, explicit standards can be helpful to guide the judgments and conscience of people as they make specific decisions. Many companies give special attention to areas of particular vulnerability. Companies generally require personnel to sign documents, periodically certifying compliance with company standards.

For example, employees of Sysco Corporation may not receive gifts from anyone with whom the company has a business relationship, unless the value of such a gift is less than $50, or the gift can be consumed or fully utilized in a twenty-four-hour period. Employees may not accept vacation packages, hotel accommodations, trips or other services of value from anyone with whom the company has a business relationship, unless the employee has been appointed as the company's representative by the president. Furthermore, a corporate officer or a division president may not accept vacation packages, hotel accommodations, trips or other services of like value from anyone with whom the company has a business relationship.

Many times, our suppliers attempt to incentivize our purchasing agents, merchandisers and marketing people to either favour their brands or to make purchases disproportionately greater than their needs. In many cases, it is not to the company's advantage. This policy statement details the types of incentives which are acceptable for people in our purchasing departments. It also causes the top executives of the company to be very careful about being seduced by exotic trips or other inducements. As I recall, it was Sysco's outside directors who initiated the policy that Sysco's subsidiary officers not be allowed to accept manufacturer trips or any other incentives which might influence the way they do business.

CODES OF ETHICS—AN EXAMPLE

Typically, areas covered in 'codes of ethics' usually include fundamental honesty, adherence to law, product safety and quality, health and safety in the workplace and conflicts of interest. Also, issues like employment practices, fairness in selling and marketing practices, financial reporting, supplier relationships, pricing, billing and contracting, trading in securities and using inside information, and payments to obtain business can also be found in some codes. Acquiring and using information about others, security, political activities, protection of the environment and intellectual property are also starting to show up, as companies become more aware of their obligations in the environmental issue.

We had a most interesting situation in our company recently that involved many of the above. An articulate and educated salesperson from a competitor came to us with an interesting proposition. He controlled a very large multi-unit chain account for the competitor. His problem was that his company couldn't adequately service the account. Therefore, the account was considering making a change. He felt that he could bring the account to Sysco if we hired him. We were talking about a piece of business that approximated $20 million (₹52 crore). For sure, he had our attention. One of my senior managers and I called on the account and determined that they were serious about making a distributor change. Their present supplier simply couldn't handle their business. The people we talked to obviously had the authority to make the decision to change. We were very careful to point out that our mutual contact was being considered for employment with Sysco. We also indicated that we were not interested in knowing what their programme was with the competitor because we felt we could provide superior service at a reasonable price. It became apparent that they were interested in our mutual friend's well-being and suggested that we hire him. (We found out why, later!)

Over the course of the next few weeks, he resigned from his previous employer and came to work for our company. After orientation, we assigned him the task of handling some of our accounts. Then some interesting developments occurred when we asked him to sign our policy on business conduct. It became apparent that he was involved in some very questionable business practices. For example, the executive chef had a fishing boat and the young man was supplying him customers (to fish with the chef) at a cost of $500 per trip. The chef was a part-time charter-boat-captain and our new salesperson was his procurer of customers. The customers were our suppliers. These suppliers were 'asked' to spend a day on the chef's fishing boat to get to know him better so that they might sell him their products. This venture provided the chef with a supplemental income that amounted to thousands of dollars.

Concurrent with that fast-breaking development, came the request for some computer equipment. It seems he was maintaining all of the account's records of purchases from suppliers who offered programmes for rebates. He was keeping these records on a personal computer and had established a 'sub-corporation' for the purpose of receiving these rebates. Only the director of purchasing had access to these rebate monies. In other words, he had set up a fund for the private use of the director of purchasing, involving extraordinary sums of money that should have been going to the corporation.

We quickly determined after only a few weeks that this young man did not need to be working for our company. He was terminated. We suggested that he try a different business and straighten his life out. At present, he is a broker and seems to be trying to clean up his act. In the meantime, we are selling the account on a local basis and bypassing the unethical people at the corporate office.

THE COSTS OF A LACK OF ETHICS

You can lay down the clearest guidelines and adopt the most straightforward Mission Statement, and some people will still make mistakes and/or break the rules. This could cause major problems and be very costly for the corporation or its subsidiaries or both.

For example, my counterpart in the Houston Sysco company was served with a grand jury subpoena. Apparently, one of his employees had been charged with conspiring with a competitor to rig the bid pricing for one of the Texas schools' systems. Sysco Food Services of Houston immediately decided that if one of its employees had participated in an improper activity, the company would not knowingly accept the benefits derived from such an activity and would instead, on its own initiative, make restitution to any injured customers. Letters of this intent were mailed by Sysco Corporation to thirty of the public-school customers. Senior officers of Sysco Corporation, and the CEO of the Houston subsidiary, called on the school districts to confirm that restitution would be made. At the time these visits were made, the local company had no idea what its total liability exposure might be. In addition to announcing its intention to make restitution, the company took remedial internal steps: the person involved was excluded immediately from the bidding process and a new system of 'checks and balances' was installed. The person involved was subsequently terminated and his immediate supervisor 'retired'. These steps were taken to prevent any future improprieties or even the appearance of improprieties. In addition, the Sysco Corporation established an antitrust compliance programme for all of its companies, which included the viewing of an educational film, the distribution of an anti-trust compliance manual and the presentation of seminars by the corporate general counsel. These special activities supplemented a pre-existing corporate policy statement regarding ethical conduct and lawful behaviour.

The employee involved in this activity eventually pled guilty to a criminal act. Later on, the company also pled guilty to one count alleging that it had conspired to rig bids for certain Texas school bids. This one unethical act, which was in direct violation of corporate policy, caused great embarrassment to Sysco Corporation and its officers, who, as a group, are some of the most ethical people in business. It also proved to be very costly to the corporation, resulting in fines and expenses exceeding $4 million. Most devastating of all was the investigative phase, which virtually consumed the company's top management's time for months.

Unethical behaviour can be very costly, as my counterpart in Houston found out and through no fault of his own.

EXCELLENCE NEEDS VALUES

In the book *In Search of Excellence,* Tom Peters and Robert Waterman write, 'Every excellent company we studied is clear on what it stands for and it takes the process of value shaping seriously, In fact, we wonder whether it is possible to be an excellent company without clarity of values and the right sorts of values.'

At the Woodstock seminar on business ethics at Georgetown University in Washington, D.C., which consisted of business people, academicians and theologians, it was concluded:

1. Ethical behaviour cannot be assured simply by writing and distributing an ethical code of conduct. Ethical behaviour results rather from a continuing process of doing the sort of actions which are listed and included in the checklist.
2. Since ethics is a constant, living, interpersonal process, we need always to be working at it. If it is not improving, it is deteriorating.
3. The process of ethical behaviour can no longer be assured by an authoritarian fiat or a command from the top. People today prize their freedom and individuality too highly for a mere issuing of commands to be effective. Individuals must freely agree with, and commit themselves to the principles and values that the corporation stands for.
4. Agreement is an exercise of intelligence. Therefore, values which

are proposed must be reasonable. Commitment is a matter of free choice, and therefore, values which are proposed must be desirable.

5. It is within the climate of a corporation that certain values are recognized by the membership to be reasonable and desirable. The climate grounds and supports the values. It also supports the membership of the corporation in their observance of these values if the climate does not penalize people for behaving ethically, but instead, praises, rewards and promotes them for this behaviour even when there is a financial cost.
6. The creation of an ethical climate is the indispensable means, therefore, for promoting ethical behaviour in a modern corporation.

Every time I think we're making progress towards achieving an ethical climate, I get a rude awakening. Our company does a tremendous amount of business with the cruise ships which are based out of Miami and cruise the Caribbean. It is a whole new industry that has grown up in South Florida. Cruises are one of the great tourist attractions in our area. Our company services seventy cruise ships which call on South Florida ports. One of these cruise lines has a purchasing director who is one of the most demanding and difficult human beings anybody could ever work with. But, he is definitely a big factor in the marketplace. I will give you some idea of how demanding this man is. One of our suppliers shorted us on a delivery of raisin bran muffins recently. We were five cases short for one of his ships. Most customers, under similar circumstances, would ask, 'What else do you have? Ship us blueberry muffins or plain bran muffins.' This man's attitude was, 'I don't care where you find them, locate five cases of raisin bran muffins and have them on the dock at 3 p.m. today.' So, we had an account executive search a number of grocery stores and buy all the raisin bran muffins he could find, and take them to the ship.

Anyhow, one day when we apparently didn't live up to his service expectations, he telephoned my VP of business development and left a message on his phone mail which scorched the telephone line. He used expletives that you don't even hear in bar rooms and pool halls any more. I thought, this is it! He's finally pushed me to the breaking point. I don't care if we do any more business with this man and his company, I am not going to expose our people to his type of abuse again. I even apologized to my secretary for having asked her to transcribe his phone mail message.

I sent a letter to the owner of the cruise line and included a transcript of the phone mail message. I reminded him that he went to great efforts, by his many philanthropic endeavours, to portray an elegant image for his cruise line—and that this man's actions were counterproductive. A few days later, I got a call from the cruise line's VP of purchasing. He acknowledged that the letter had been received. His attitude was that 'in the heat of battle, boys will be boys.' There was 'a lot of pressure associated with running a cruise line, and making sure that all the ships were properly provisioned, and that he probably just lost his cool.' To him, it really wasn't that big a deal. Then came the real shocker! He said (in effect), 'People who live in glass houses shouldn't throw stones. Your employees are not all that perfect either.' He then proceeded to tell me that one of our people had been exchanging pornographic materials with one of his people, until they put a stop to it. I responded disbelievingly. He assured me it was true and he made copies of the materials and sent them over to me by courier so I could see for myself. I can't tell you how embarrassed I was when I got this material. My first impulse was to fire the employee. After some very careful study, I concluded that she was a very trusted employee who had been with the company a long time. She was just 'being cute' with one of her friends over at the cruise line. She was sternly reprimanded, however, and warned that if anything like this ever happened again, she would be terminated. I then had our VP of the cruise division call the cruise line and tell them what actions had been taken with the guilty employee. He was surprised at both the way we reacted, and the speed with which we reacted.

Strangely enough, we are doing more business with that cruise line than before and on a more tolerable basis. Our 'adversary' has not raised his voice above a whisper. He is actually being nice to our people. We could just as easily have lost the account.

THE BIGGEST ASSET—PEOPLE

People are the most important asset that we have in our company. Even though we are a big company, we are 'family-oriented', and it is our belief that if we treat our people well, they will treat our customers well. We will be successful and all the stakeholders will be happy. While we are a profit-oriented company, we do not extract profits at the expense of our people. I could never knowingly let anyone abuse our people and would take the risk of losing an account rather than permit this to happen. Fortunately, I work for a corporation which supports this type of thinking.

So, developing and maintaining an ethical business climate is a constant challenge. It is never ending! It is always changing!

ROLE OF THE CEO

I want to give you a list of some of the things that I feel a CEO can do to move the corporate climate towards a more ethical resolution. If you would like to see a mechanical list of ethics efforts, I recommend *The Business Roundtable Report of Corporate Ethics.* It is a prime business asset and it's free. You can order it from the Business Roundtable in New York. It contains many ways companies use to influence ethics.

There are some other things that you can do to move the ethical development process along. First, use your charisma and example. Remember, your people are looking to you and they are thirsty for moral guidance. Secondly, take a careful look at your strategic decisions, because everything else in the organization will rest on them. If you have good strategies, if your purpose is the provision of value and you've found ways to do that, it's easy to be ethical. You can market honestly! You can care about people! Remember, you can make money being ethical. Thirdly, you provide the link between the concerns of your company and the larger concerns of society. Fourth, to feed the corporate sense of responsibility, give employees a sense of identity with local community organizations. The corporate good deed efforts get people involved in things outside the corporation and tells your people that 'volunteerism is okay.'

My perspective of management broadened immensely as a result of having attended the first conference on Business Vocations in Chicago in November 1989. In my previous thirty-three years, it had never once occurred to me that managing a business could be a vocation.

The word 'vocation' is normally thought of in spiritual dimensions and means 'a calling.' Usually it is a call to serve God as a priest or religious person. In the everyday world of commerce and industry, amid planning and controlling costs, and profit margins and competition, it is not typical to think of one's work as a vocation. And yet, I found out it can be. In doing so, it helped to bridge the gap between my faith and the place where I work. Interestingly, I discovered others viewed their work from a vocational perspective.

In their book *In Search of Excellence,* Peters and Waterman have a very powerful message: 'Successful companies are whole, holistic, holy, spiritual companies. All of the excellent companies have an overriding concern for the whole person, the employees, the suppliers, the customers, and other stakeholders.'

'Work must provide more than a paycheck,' writes John Nesbitt and Patricia Aburdene in *Re-inventing the Corporation*. We wanted to express ourselves and our values, to make a difference in society and to fit harmoniously with other priorities, family health and spirituality.

I think that business ethics is one expression of spirituality in work.

The late Robert Greenleaf of AT&T promoted the concept of 'servant leadership.' The genuinely successful business leader, he demonstrated, is the servant leader or steward.

CORPORATE STEWARDSHIP

Some business people are beginning to reclaim the concept of stewardship by adding 'corporate stewardship' to the title. Stewardship implies that a business looks out for all of its stakeholders—its employees, its shareholders and its community.

The recent scandals on Wall Street and the downturn in the economy have taught us that selfishness leads to ruin, not only in the next life, but in today's economy as well. It is applying this concept of 'stewardship' to my own company which adds this so-called spiritual dimension to the workplace. Let's define what a steward is. A steward is one who is put in charge of a specific function or asset and is expected to maintain this function or asset effectively. The steward's role is basically the same as a manager's or a CEO's. The translation is an easy one. Managers are, in effect, stewards.

Every culture has its own moral, religious and spiritual base. For me, being a Christian Catholic, my model is Jesus. Probably one of Jesus' greatest teachings was what scripture writers refer to as the 'Parable of the Talents.' As a businessman, I think of it as the world's earliest teaching on return on investment. I believe that in His divine wisdom, He was giving lessons 2,000 years ago that are just as applicable today as then. Jesus told the story of a businessman with much property and assets who was going away on a business trip. Sort of like the one that I am on here. He called in his three chief assistants and gave each of them some assets to manage in his absence. To the first he gave five, the second three, and the third one. He told them, 'Let's see how well you manage these assets and when I return, if you've done a good job, I'll increase your responsibilities and your earnings.' (This sounds like an exercise in 'management by objectives.') When he returned some weeks later, he called each of his managers in for a report on their progress. The first managed his assets well and increased them 100 per cent. The second managed well and doubled the value of his assets, but the manager who had only one small asset to manage was more concerned about his tough-minded boss and was afraid to take risks, so he played it *close.* He didn't advertise, he didn't promote, he exerted *all* of his energies at preserving his capital base. Consequently, he had no growth.

The parable goes on to say that the owner was very appreciative of the two managers who doubled their assets. He promoted them and gave them greater responsibilities and greater compensation. The manager who didn't do very *well* was terminated. His assets were reassigned to the manager who had the greatest growth.

The message is very clear to me: God expects a return on investment. He expects his stewards to be productive. He expects us to use our talents and to use them wisely. In fidelity to our mission, in service to others.

Stewardship makes each of us responsible for ensuring the best, the most productive and the most equitable use of the resources that we own, or for which we have responsibility. Let's consider, briefly, some of the ways that we can be stewards and managers of our companies.

Stewardship of people includes the care and development of our employees, our investor/owners, our client-customers, our suppliers, and even at times, our competitors. Being a good steward of people means making tough decisions while keeping the welfare of all concerned in mind. In our company, we work very hard to be good stewards of our people. We pay them *well;* we do comparative analyses of other companies to make sure that our wages are competitive, we constantly study various benefit programmes to make sure that most of the contingencies in our employees' lives will be accounted for. We offer an excellent benefits programme which costs 40 per cent of base compensation and includes everything from hospitalization and medical coverage to paid vacations and pension plans for their retirement. Recently, we added a 401k plan (a retirement savings plan), a nice tax-free benefit. This plan permits employees to contribute up to 15 per cent of their income per year on a payroll deduction plan. The company adds 50 per cent to the employee contribution, providing the company meets its profit goals. After our first year, 56 per cent of the employees were enrolled. Sysco also offers its employees an employee stock purchase plan which permits employees to deduct up to 5 per cent of their income on a payroll deduction plan with which they can purchase Sysco stock at a 15 per cent discount. We encourage employees to become stockholders. We want them to enjoy a sense of ownership in the company. Forty-eight per cent of all eligible employees in Miami are stockholders of Sysco Corporation. For managers who accomplish their major accountabilities, the company offers an attractive stock option programme, which permits substantial wealth accumulation with tax benefits throughout their careers with Sysco. Sysco looks out for its people.

Sysco is pleased to have one of India's native sons working in our merchandising department as director of international procurement. Rukmaker Rau is a native of Madras (Chennai now) and a graduate of the University of Chicago Business School. He is a great asset to our company and a close personal friend as well.

Stewardship for our customers involves providing customers with the finest products and services available at competitive prices. Sysco's greatest asset is our customers and we manage that asset with great care.

Incidentally, SYSCO is an acronym for 'Systems and Services Company.' To give you an example of our service capabilities, orders that are written for our customers and entered into our computer by 5 p.m. on any given day are processed that same evening and delivered the next day with a 99 per cent fill rate. The industry average is 95 per cent. This commitment to customer service is responsible for Sysco's compounded sales growth rate of 18 per cent for the past twenty years.

Sysco's involvement in community affairs takes many shapes and forms. We encourage all of our people to be active in various volunteer community benefit activities. I was personally involved in bringing the Daily Bread Community Food Bank to Florida. The food bank is a distribution centre which processes surplus, damaged and out-of-date foods (excess produce, blemished products, etc.) and redistributes them to approximately five hundred charitable agencies which feed the hungry and poor of South Florida. We started out with one food bank ten years ago and today there are three. We have delivered to the community fifty million pounds of food that would have been discarded or destroyed.

INVOLVEMENT IN THE COMMUNITY

I was also one of the founding directors of a shelter for runaway children in South Florida, Covenant House. Many of our employees and suppliers are also involved in charitable activities. Our most recent undertaking is a one-to-one tutoring service, sponsored by the company, which teaches adults to read. We believe that we must put back our time, talent and money into the community.

By delivering the compounded growth rates that we talked about earlier, we take very good care of our stockholders. Sysco stock is trading at one of the highest multiples of all the companies in the food industry, twenty-six times earnings. Our stockholders are happy with that performance.

Being a good steward of products and services means the best quality, safety and price possible. Probably one of the greatest concerns we have at the present time is concern for the environment. Many of our customers are concerned about garbage disposal. There are major product developments underway to supply packaging that is biodegradable and not damaging to the environment. Styrofoam cups are being replaced with paper cups. Various detergents and chemical products are being manufactured and modified to make sure that they are not polluting the environment. Garbage disposal is a major challenge. There is so much garbage that we are creating mountains along our interstate highways by burying garbage.

SOCIAL RESPONSIBILITY—TEN TRENDS

The January issue of *Business Ethics* magazine contains an excellent article entitled 'Is Business Waking Up?'

It defines ten trends towards social responsibility in the '90s. You will find these interesting.

Number 1: The Pursuit of Happiness

Well educated, talented individuals are 'cashing out' by taking their hard-earned dollars and climbing down from the corporate ladder and seeking more satisfying experiences. This does not mean that money is no longer important. Time and freedom are dominating the new lifestyles. Twenty-five million Americans are now working at home, part-time or full time, and entrepreneurial activity by seekers of the good life is at an all-time high. To avoid losing this valuable talent, companies are offering more flexible schedules, telecommuting opportunities and other ways for employees to recharge their batteries when their energy reserves run low.

Number 2: The Greening of the Corporation

Business is becoming more sensitive to environmental concerns. The 'responsible care initiative' launched by the chemical manufacturers association shows great promise, as does the famous Monsanto pledge to cut toxic air emissions by 90 per cent by 1992. The Valdez oil spill in Alaska did much to force companies to rethink their priorities, and Green Cross' life cycle assessments are helping businesses rethink not only their manufacturing by-products, but the waste management consequences of their products as well. Many large and small corporations like Exxon, Walt Disney and Patagonia have created a new position, Vice President of the Environment.

Number 3: Individuals Can Make a Difference

This notion is being played out all over the country by executives, entrepreneurs and managers, and assembly line workers, who are donating their time and skills to help the underprivileged. Volunteerism is at an all-time high. I mentioned our company's literacy programme earlier.

Number 4: Peace Seems to Have Broken Out All Over

For the most part, the Cold War is over. Whether or not we get a peace dividend, the breakup of the Soviet Union and the Warsaw Pact will surely change the way the mammoth defence industry does business. President Bush's announcement that he wanted to cut $20 billion from the defence budget signalled the beginning of a major shake-out among weapons manufacturers.

Number 5: Companies are Marketing the Good Cause

Environmental packaging is the best example. Trash bag companies are falling all over one another to proclaim their product the most biodegradable. Burger King is putting their burgers in brown bags made from recycled paper. Avis is selling rental cars by telling us it's better to do business with an owner. Ashland Oil has charming TV vignettes about their scholarship programmes; McDonald's is letting us know that they hire workers with mental disabilities. Everybody these days seems to be sponsoring the Olympics. All of these practices seem to be catching on.

Number 6: Companies are Practising Family-friendly Policies

Many companies have responded with family-friendly policies such as flex time, onsite child care centres, elder care arrangements, parental leave and telecommuting. Kodak and Bausch and Lamb have opened day-camps for their employees' children. Women now make up more than half of the USA's workforce. Child care remains the biggest issue for young families. Caring companies are putting together joint ventures such as the one IBM, American Express, All-state and two smaller companies are pursuing at Charlotte, North Carolina. They constructed a $2 million (194 child care) facility which exceeds state standards. It is used by employees as well as the public.

Number 7: The Era of Reaganomics is Over

Congress, legislators and courts are moving quickly to fill the regulatory vacuum left by a decade of unbridled capitalism. The new Clean Air Act, Americans with Disabilities Act, the 1990 Nutritional Labeling and Education Act, and new rules on TV advertising to kids, tell us that deregulation is a thing of the past. We expect to see closer cooperation between industry and government in years to come.

Number 8: A More Cooperative Workplace

The trend in the workplace is towards more open-minded management. Companies are finding that it is much cheaper to keep workers happy than to hire and train replacements. Companies are finding that to succeed with quality programmes, management and labour need to cooperate more closely than ever before to achieve their mutual goal, which is customer satisfaction.

Number 9: We Are Entering the Age of the Vigilante Consumer

This is an era in which doing business will have more and more to do with building relationships rather than marketing products. The public wants to know what's in a product; how it was tested, who produced it and under what working conditions. They even want to know where the package will go once it's discarded.

Number 10: Humanizing the Machine

Major efforts are being waged to redirect technology towards socially responsible goals. Computer bulletin boards are helping to democratize large corporations by allowing employees to send direct messages to the CEO and the communications revolution will soon spread to millions more people, making them richer, freer and better informed. Cellular phone systems can be set up in much less time than landline systems. The cost of an earth to satellite connection has dropped from $500,000 to $150,000 in the last five years. This means wider access to the global market place and expanded opportunities for responsible trade. The most innovative companies are riding the crest wave of technological advances, keeping an eye towards humanizing the workplace and the market place.

The trends described here should give you a sense of both what's here today and what will be arriving tomorrow. Some, we hope, will even provide a path towards appropriate responses. The rest is up to us.

A recent two-page advertisement written by Warren Buffet, interim chairman of the scandal-plagued Salomon, Inc., appeared in the *Financial Times* on 30 October 1991. It stated, 'An atmosphere encouraging exemplary behaviour is probably even more important than rules, necessary though these are. During my tenure as Chairman, I will consider myself the firm's chief compliance officer and I have asked all 9,000 of Salomon's employees to assist me in that effort. I have also urged them to be guided by a test that goes beyond rules. Contemplating any business act, an employee should ask himself whether he would be willing to see it immediately described by an informed and critical reporter on the front page of his local newspaper. There to be read by his spouse, children, and friends. At Salomon, we simply want no part of any activities that pass legal test but that we as citizens would find offensive.'

When a wise old business counsellor was asked how to improve profits, his answer was very simple, 'If you pursue profits as a goal, they will continue to elude you, but if you seek to be the best you can in all that you do, you will surely find them.'

I had an opportunity to put this philosophy to work recently in a real-life conversation with my son, John, who will be graduating from the University of Chicago Law School in June. John shared with me a dilemma: he had two interesting job offers, one with a major firm in Houston, Texas, with a very attractive compensation package, and the other with the United States Department of Justice's antitrust division, paying about half as much. He wanted to go to work with the Justice Department because he felt his immediate involvement would be much greater, the work much more interesting and the experience beneficial for his legal career. My advice to him was that he should always strive to do (for a living) what he enjoyed doing. That way he would give it his best effort and would enjoy his work. The money would eventually follow. He has chosen to go to work for the Justice Department.

Just as we pass on a legacy of honesty and integrity to our children, we have the same obligation to pass our corporate ethical traditions on to our successors in management. The Tata Group's efforts in this regard are noteworthy and commendable.

3

Business Ethics—Some Reflections*

BAKHTAWAR LENTIN

Lord Palmerston once told Queen Victoria that he was the best-loved man in England and Prince Albert the most hated, and therefore they were two ends of the same stick. This, as you know, provoked the Royal rebuke, 'Lord Palmerston, we are not amused.'

Similarly, business ethics also encompasses two ends of the same stick. One end of the stick can be a positive assertion that in business, values and ethics are very much alive. The other end of the stick can equally be a vibrant question mark.

There are occasions when it becomes more than a moral duty to speak one's mind—it becomes a pleasure. Therefore, as I go along, should business ethics become more of a vibrant question mark than an assertion in the positive, it is because I believe that what must be said is best said plainly or not said at all. I shall, therefore, speak plainly, and now is as good a time as any. In business, ethics may broadly be put into five slots, not necessarily in the sequence I present.

1. Ethics towards each other in private businesses,
2. Ethics in governmental ventures,
3. Ethics towards the consumer,
4. Ethics towards workers, and
5. Ethics, in general.

Under all these heads, if you, in all conscience, can give yourselves a ringing answer in the affirmative, then indeed in business, there is

*Oration delivered on 27 January 1993.

ethics. However, if you, in all conscience, cannot, then some soul-searching is called for. And who can do that best, but businessmen themselves?

'THE OLD ORDER PASSETH, YIELDING PLACE TO THE NEW'

In his *Le Morte d'Arthur*, Alfred Lord Tennyson said: 'The old order passeth, yielding place to the new.' Like Palmerston, Tennyson too, was prophetic.

In today's context of business, what is the old order? And, pray, what is the new?

There was a time, and that too not so long ago, when the word 'ethics' was an understood thing. It was taken for granted in all walks of life, amongst all right-thinking people. And the vast majority of the people were right-thinking people.

Such was the old order. The universality of comprehension of this word, 'ethics', and its application were the hallmarks of business in this country. I need hardly remind you that the stalwarts of yesteryear, like Jamshetji Tata, were household words. They are so, even today. They stood for rectitude, integrity and vision. They commanded respect. They do so, even today.

Such was the old order.

But time took its toll. All of this changed. And the old order yielded place to the new. In this new order, right-thinking people of the old order are considered antiquated and regarded as misfits; just as those of the new order would have been regarded by the old order as grasping and unscrupulous.

Today, the word 'ethics' means different things to different people, at different times, and in different circumstances. The universality of comprehension has disappeared—but not completely, thank God. For that saving grace, the credit must go to such of you who today hold aloft the stance of rectitude from the past.

Unfortunately, by and large, the expediency and exigency of the moment are the axes on which the wheel of ethics turns.

So we descend from past glory to the present ignominy, where the end justifies the means, howsoever degenerate be the means.

It is ironic there should have prevailed a better sense of ethics under an alien rule than prevails under our own.

The good old dictionary defines 'ethics' as 'moral principles of code in human behaviour.' I prefer the Biblical equivalent: 'Do unto others what you would have others do unto you.'

THE DEVIL'S COMMAND

This Biblical exhortation has, by and large, been brutalized into the devil's command—do unto others what you would NOT have others do unto you.

Today, by and large, it is this dogma of the devil which is practised, and has been honed into a refined art comprising doublespeak and double-dealing, double-crossing and triple-crossing—no holds barred.

The old order hath indeed passed yielding place to the new.

It is by the general reputation of a country that business ethics in it, or for that matter in any country, must be judged and lauded—or condemned—regardless of the integrity of a few. Therefore, it must be hollow consolation to those amongst you who still adhere to the old sense of values and ethics, when many of your peers do not.

It is this science of doublespeak, of double-dealing, double-crossing and triple-crossing, perfected to a fine art, that has made a mockery of values and ethics as once understood and is eating into the very vitals of business and industry in this country.

George Bernard Shaw once said, 'Poverty is the worst of crimes. So get ye wealth, no matter how.'

I readily agree that there is indeed no 'crime' worse than poverty. I will also agree with the 'get ye wealth' part of it, but not with the rider that Shaw adds, 'no matter how.' That was a piece of Shawian cynicism, to equate which with Shawian wisdom is to lay unction to the business conscience. There is, in this new order, nothing so unbecoming to a businessman as a non-conformist conscience.

I now pause to look around and ask: How did this general degeneration start? What is it due to? Oneupmanship? Overweening greed for money and more money? Political patronage? Just plain dishonesty? Or, is it a combination of some or all of these?

To find an exact answer is as difficult as trying to pinpoint where exactly one colour of the rainbow ends and an other starts. You see the rainbow as a whole, in its entirety. This is how business ethics must be seen. And seen thus, it does not compare with the seven glorious colours of the rainbow.

From the Olympian heights, the battles between labour unions are shrugged off as events of the lower order. But when mighty captains of mighty industries descend to levels unbecoming, they do credit neither to themselves, nor to the industries they captain, nor to the concept of ethics in business and industry as a whole.

In the ultimate analysis, it does not matter who is right and who is wrong, or who is convinced he is in the right or that he has been wronged. Linen is best washed in private, within cloistered walls, around the negotiating table. And who can do that better than the mighty captains of mighty industries themselves...

RAPACITY AND POLITICAL PATRONAGE

Rapacity and political patronage make for a heady mix. It is also a lethal mix. Not so long ago, this lethal mix manifested itself in a deep and complex conspiracy which spanned all walks of business and industry, from banking and finance to insider trading in stocks, maniacal trading in securities, calculated leakage of information, and kick-backs and needless and mindless speculation on the stock exchanges.

And when the bubble burst, all scurried for cover in an unseemly display of what the Americans would call 'passing the buck'.

The old order hath indeed passed, yielding place to the new.

GOVERNMENT'S ROLE IN CORRUPTING ETHICS

The function of government is to govern. When government—in a moment of rashness—ventures into the highly specialized fields of business, commerce and industry, and worse still, when it stifles individual enterprise and makes a monopoly of itself, the result is a disaster of far-reaching consequence and national proportions.

Any form of private monopoly is a form of tyranny. Any form of governmental monopoly is the worst tyranny of all.

When the government sets its face against private monopoly, it is right in doing so. But it is double-faced when the same government takes a business, enterprise or industry under its monopolistic wing, supposedly in the public interest. The public interest, instead of being catered to and safeguarded, is sacrificed to governmental ineptitude and monopolistic arrogance with an all-round decline in standards, values and ethics.

Nationalization, supposedly for the public weal, is actually governmental rapacity.

Nationalization of any business or any industry in any part of the world has done no good to the business or the industry nationalized, or to the exchequer of the nation concerned.

Attlee nationalized civil aviation, and the exchequer was in the red. Margaret Thatcher corrected that mistake with no loss to the exchequer. We too nationalized civil aviation; we are yet to correct that mistake.

The perpetuation of the Nehruvian fetish of nationalization, thereby eradicating competition, is the greatest stumbling block before this nation's progress.

When banks were nationalized, it was said to be a step in the right direction and for the public benefit. The public weal must prevail over private woe, was the reason proclaimed. It was indeed a step in the right direction—if diversion of public money towards political ends is a step in the right direction.

But how has the public at large benefitted? Not at all. Bank nationalization—as indeed any form of nationalization—has resulted in a paradox. Instead of public weal prevailing over private woe, it is political weal which prevails over public woe. Values and ethics are sacrificed.

In no other country in the world is there any word or concept equivalent to what in this country is called 'loan melas'—funfairs where loans are doled out at political behest against all canons of banking and banking practice—and loans have even been wiped out at an exorbitant cost to the public exchequer. It is no secret that nationalized banks are forced to give such loans. Ducks and drakes is played with public money—yours and mine—though happily, more yours than mine.

When political power is thus used for doling out largesse, it is an abuse of that power and a misuse of public money—the most blatant form of corruption and a violation of the most elementary norms of banking. Nationalized banks are not charitable institutions. Our political masters think they are. Values and ethics are sacrificed to political expediency and subservience.

Let it be faced squarely and honestly that bank nationalization has been a disaster at the national level, and for the common man, even elementary customer service has not been available. Some months ago, there was a power failure in the Fort area. My wife went to a nationalized bank. She found the footpath overflowing with the bank staff, idling away. They were outside because they said they could not work inside without electricity and air-conditioning.

My wife also had some work in another bank nearby. That was a non-nationalized bank; she went there, and everyone was in his or her appointed place. There was no air-conditioning and no electric lights; they were working by candlelight, as if nothing had happened.

When power was restored, she went back to the first bank. She told them how the other bank was working by candlelight. She received the unbelievable answer, 'Yes, but that is not a nationalized bank.'

Little wonder that against the growing public demand for denationalization of banks and public sector units (PSUs), resistance comes from within the banks and the PSUs themselves. This should, by itself, be an eye-opener as to whose benefit nationalized institutions operate for.

Then come hasty, mindless and alarming governmental pronouncements that there will be no denationalization.

I say, just as a man who is afraid to die is unfit to live, so a government which is afraid to act is unfit to govern.

Any form of nationalization eradicates private enterprise and competition. Any form of nationalization is a disservice to the nation, and a fraud perpetrated on the people. When you are the master of all you survey, values and ethics can become very inconvenient.

ETHICS PERCOLATES FROM THE TOP

A sense of values and a sense of ethics in any walk of life—and more so in business—must percolate from the topmost levels to the lowest. And they will, if the people at the top have them. Otherwise, they cannot. The result then is ineptitude, indifference, lack of motivation and irresponsibility. Such is the new order.

If you, at the highest levels, have contempt for values and ethics, you cannot expect your subordinates to do better. Such is the new order.

In business and industry, values and ethics must also encompass the sphere of employer-employee relationships.

Jamshedpur is said to be a model township. Workers are housed, cared for and looked after, and their children educated.

I suppose, that is what values and ethics in employer-employee relationships are all about.

But Jamshedpur is not representative of the story everywhere.

Unfortunately, employer-employee relationship is an area fraught with mutual suspicion, mistrust, intolerance and even hatred.

However, I do subscribe to the suspicion that many of your balance sheets are window dressing and that your books of accounts are intended to suppress more than they are expected to reveal.

Authenticity comes from veracity and not from some audit stamp. Even the most experienced chartered accountants are not expected to be detectives.

It is said businessmen keep four sets of books: one for tax purposes, the second for their partners, the third for themselves and the fourth for their wives. I do not know if all this is correct, but the last does appear to be an exaggeration.

Employers accuse workers of irresponsibility and rapacity. Workers accuse their employers of downright dishonesty. Both sides take extreme positions. Perhaps for both, the truth lies somewhere in between; for, as the hackneyed saying goes, there is no smoke without fire.

In this area of employer-employee ethics, I go a step further.

The worker must be made to feel that he is not some expendable commodity; that the undertaking he works for is as much his own as his employer's; that he has a personal stake in the venture. Unless he is assured of this, he will regard his employer as a parasite living by the sweat of the workers' brow. Of such are revolutions made, and workers have nothing to lose but their chains.

You may, in self-created smugness, think you are sitting pretty on top of the world on your hallowed thrones. You are not. You are sitting on the edge of a volcano which can erupt any time. It is known that workers have taken over entire undertakings and even perhaps run it better than their erstwhile masters.

PARTNERSHIP OF LABOUR

Perhaps it is time you start thinking in terms of collectivism. Or, if I might coin a phrase, 'partnership-ism.' Make the workers your partners. It is only then that they will be assured that they are not some expendable commodity; that the undertaking they work for is as much theirs as yours; that they have a personal stake in the venture and will not regard you as a parasite living by the sweat of the workers' brow. The modalities can be worked out. Common sense dictates that once they become your partners, who could they go on strike against? Surely not against themselves.

This, I suppose, to many of you would be heresy.

In Japan some time ago, workers in a large industrial establishment made certain demands. They were summarily rejected. So the workers resorted to a quaint way of protest. No strikes. No slogans. No abuse. No physical violence. No go-slow. No work-to-rule. They registered their resentment in a manner which hurt Japanese pride. They went about their work as usual, but with black armbands, mourning their employer's demise of values and ethics. This shamed the management so much that within no time negotiations started and a mutually satisfactory solution was reached. And, of course, off came the black armbands.

Compare this to what would happen in a similar situation here. The employer would regard the workers with cynical contempt, and the worker could wear his armband till hell froze over.

Just as you shall not hold your workers to bondage, they shall not hold you to ransom.

QUALITY AND SERVICE

If I have been critical of governmental enterprise, private enterprise must also take its fair share of criticism, *vis-à-vis* the consumer. Most of the commodities manufactured today are mass produced—from a pin to a tractor. This is as it should be. But what is lacking in general is something else—quality control and after-sales service worth the name. In a quest for quick profits, the consumer is taken for a merry ride.

Mind you, I am not against anyone making a profit. I do not consider 'profit' to be a dirty word. Only a fool would not want to make a profit, and only an incompetent cannot make one. But to do so at the cost of quality and at the expense of the consumer is profiteering. To equate profiteering with making a profit is like the devil prostrating himself before the altar of Christ.

As Oscar Wilde put it, you know the price of everything and the value of nothing.

FOOD AND DRUG ADULTERATION

Food adulteration, drugs adulteration and manufacture of spurious drugs, unheard of in the old order, have become part of the daily existence of the common man—mayhem and murder on a gigantic scale, organized into a regulated business. Human lives have become irrelevant.

This is the new order.

Not very long ago, I had to study the food and drug laws of several countries—the UK, France, Germany and the USA, and, of course, our own Drugs and Cosmetics Act, 1940. This I will say... Ours is a well thought out and a well-formulated piece of legislation; and as a piece of legislation, it is superior to similar legislations in many other countries.

Yet, our Drugs and Cosmetics Act has, for practical purposes, not achieved the degree of success it deserves. To put it bluntly, it has failed. Why has it failed? The Act is neither defective, nor are the courts anxious to acquit the culprits. But there needs to be a bureaucratic will, and the motivation to adhere to the provisions of the Drugs and Cosmetics Act on the part of those whose duty it is to adhere to them.

Outside the Old Bailey in London, there is—or at least there was—a legend which read:

Protect the children of the poor
and punish the wrongdoer.

Unfortunately, administrative lackadaisicalness to enforce the Drugs and Cosmetics Act and even rampant corruption are clearly reflected in the evidence presented in court, and must consequently result in a reluctant judicial acquittal on the basis of such evidence presented.

ETHICS COME FROM WITHIN

Values and ethics are not imbibed from legal and judicial precedents. They must come from within. The king can make you a knight, but he cannot make you a gentleman.

What today is endemic is a sense of insensitivity. From a nation of beggars, we are on the way to becoming a nation of thieves, anarchists and murderers.

In this tragic transition from the old order to the new, it is unfortunate, and even unfair, that the God-fearing amongst you must also pay the price for your godless peers.

The old order must re-assert itself over the new. The time is now. Tomorrow may be too late. The old order and the new order are like the two ships of Oscar Wilde:

Like two doomed ships that pass in storm
We had crossed each other's way;
But we made no sign, we said no word.
We had no word to say.

I do not agree that the past is dead and buried. I say the past is, in its very presence, alive. I, therefore, say: look to the past, so that we can, for the future, correct our mistakes of the present.

HOPE FOR THE FUTURE

Something is dead in each of us, but what is not dead is hope. Somerset Maugham once said, 'The stars never shine more brightly than when reflected in the muddy waters of a wayside ditch.'

It is in the reflection of the muddy waters of this wayside ditch of rapacity and deceit, intrigue and hypocrisy that I see the stars of the future shine brightly. I see the land of Gautama Buddha.

I see the vision of the man this nation calls its Father. I see his teachings and ideals returning to us, and with them the values and ethics that were once forsaken. I see the wheel turning full circle and the new order passing back to the old. I see a great and glorious nation rising like a phoenix from the ashes, and taking its rightful place in the comity of nations, where there is freedom and prosperity and self-respect.

And so, in God's unbounded mercy, it shall come to pass.

4

An Interpretation of Conscience in Business Life*

KENNETH E. GOODPASTER

> *'The claims of morality, as they operate in human life, present on the face of it a very different appearance from the claims of policy or purpose. They come as a recognized obligation to do or not to do, which is often seen to involve the temporary surrender or restriction of a desire in itself innocent, of a perfectly legitimate purpose. All serious moralists have had to recognize this very obvious and familiar contrast.'*
>
> –J.L. Stocks (British philosopher, 1930)

INTRODUCTION

My reflection on conscience in business life today has two main parts: First, I will describe what I believe is a basic stimulus for our topic—an 'occupational hazard' of business life, and second, I will defend a basic response to this stimulus—integrating the moral point of view (or conscience) into management decision-making.

A PARABLE AND PATHOLOGY

A dozen years ago, I was pleased to recommend to the editors of the Harvard Business Review an essay entitled *The Parable of the Sadhu* by Bowen McCoy, for the first Harvard Business Review Ethics Prize. The award was for a practitioner-written reflection on the

---

*Oration delivered on 11 February 1994.

relationship between ethics and business. Not only did this essay win the prize and merit the publication it was given, it was subsequently adapted by WGBR in Boston as a half-hour video that has for years been used in classrooms and training rooms to initiate discussions of leadership and ethical values.

THE SUMMIT AND THE SADHU

I have elsewhere gone into some detail in analysing McCoy's essay.[1] For present purposes, I simply wish to call attention to a fundamental problem that the story helps us to identify. 'Buzz' McCoy was the managing director of Morgan Stanley & Company. He and his anthropologist friend named Stephen decided to go mountain climbing in the Himalayas as a six-month sabbatical 'soul search' in 1982. After thirty days of climbing, as they neared the snowy 20,000-feet summit, they were presented (by the climbing group ahead of them) with an unconscious sadhu who was dying of exposure. McCoy was willing to give the sadhu some blankets and food, but insisted on moving ahead due to threatening weather conditions. Stephen, however, felt obliged to do something to help the sadhu to safety, which he attempted during the next several hours. Ultimately, Stephen left the sadhu beside the trail—with remorse and anger—and rejoined McCoy.

McCoy reflected later that 'in some ways, I never left home.' He does not know to this day whether the sadhu lived or died. But he acknowledges candidly that he missed an opportunity to get what he went on the journey to find in the first place—perspective, balance and spiritual growth. He explains (but does not excuse) his moral failure in terms of several factors: superordinate goals, lack of explicit attention to shared values before the climb, failure to respect the sadhu as an equal and a tendency to 'pass the buck' when responsibility interfered with the achievement of urgent and risk-laden objectives.[2]

McCoy described these true events as a parable because he thought the story had the potential to offer a lesson of lasting value. In this case, the lesson has to do with the mesmerizing effects of goals and purposes—the fact that they can distort our judgment at critical moments unless disciplined by clear values.

AN OCCUPATIONAL HAZARD

Some years ago, I named the 'syndrome' that McCoy exhibited on the mountain, teleopathy—the unbalanced pursuit of purpose.[3] I argued that teleopathy is the single most significant stimulus to which business ethics is, and must, be a practical response. It is at the normative core of business ethics as a discipline.[4] While not a physical or mental illness—like heart disease or depression—teleopathy would, I believe, be as central in any diagnostic manual of ethics as heart disease and depression are in their respective manuals. The principal symptoms of teleopathy can be described under three headings: fixation, rationalization and detachment. A few words about each are in order.

Fixation: The difference between determination, courage, perseverance and tenacity (each a virtue to be applauded in persons and organizations), and addiction, dependency, or fixation (which are not to be applauded) is profound. When determination is celebrated, we are confident that the person owns the goal. When fixation is lamented, we sense that the goal owns the person. The difference between 'management by objectives' and being managed by one's objectives is considerable. Investing in goals beyond our capacity for critical judgement is—in the language of philosopher Immanuel Kant—treating the self as a means, not an end. The unworthy somehow becomes master, as history reminds us in accounts of slavery and idolatry.[5]

In this connection, we might be reminded of something Father Anthony De Mello, wrote a few years back. He used the word 'attachment', but he might well have used the word 'fixation' in the same context:

> You may have your preferences for drum or violin or piano; no harm in these, for a reference does not damage your capacity to hear and enjoy the other instruments. But the moment your

> preference turns into an attachment, it hardens you to the other sounds, you suddenly undervalue them. And it blinds you to its articular instrument, for you give it a value out of all proportion to its merit. When you see this you will feel a yearning to rid yourself of every attachment. The problem is, how? Renunciation and avoidance is no help, for to blot out the sound of the drum once again makes you as hard and insensitive as to concentrate solely on the drum. What you need is not renunciation but understanding, awareness.[6]

Awareness, I believe, is critical to avoiding teleopathy, both in individuals and in organizations. And corporate awareness, as we shall see, includes regular open dialogue about the company's obligations to its many stakeholders, and a process for making such dialogue influential in decision-making.

Rationalization: The human psyche seems attuned to the problem of fixation at some fairly deep level—both individually and institutionally—else, how can we explain the persistence of denial and 'reinterpretation' so characteristic of drug addicts and other fixated actors? The New Zealand climber who passed the sadhu on the mountain said, 'How irresponsible of him for being here, half-dressed like this, at 18,000 feet!' Now, it is possible that the sadhu was irresponsible, but he was unconscious and there was no reason to assume that he was irresponsible—without communicating with him. Other explanations for his plight were quite possible. So why 'irresponsibility'? Was this not a form of rationalization, making abandonment easier?

Two types of rationalization dominate the landscape in the context of business and work life: loyalty (appealing to fiduciary obligations to shareholders in the face of market competition) and legality (appealing to the permissibility of a behaviour or policy within the constraints of the law). Each provides an excuse for questionable business behaviour, though not always plausibly.[8]

Detachment: Repeating the fixation-rationalization 'loop' becomes a self-reinforcing habit. This habit leads eventually to a kind of callousness, what some observers have called a separation of head from heart.[9] Competitiveness and goal-seeking eventually drive out compassion and generosity, making more serious compromises easier as time goes on. A kind of isolation from moral responsiveness sets in, dignified by metaphors like 'jungle', 'toughness' and 'real world'. The detached organization, like the detached individual, loses the ability to connect its behaviour to the larger human picture. The division of labour becomes the division of responsibility, and the division of responsibility becomes the fragmentation or dilution of responsibility beyond recognition. Cigarette companies insist that responsibility means responding to the market, no doubt a form of simultaneous rationalization and detachment.

I was reminded of the present-day reality of teleopathy by a November 1993 *Fortune* magazine cover story. The former managing director of McKinsey and Company remarked about the kinds of professionals his company sought to hire: 'The real competition out there isn't for clients, it's for people... And we look to hire people who are first, very smart; second, insecure and thus driven by their insecurity; and third, competitive.'[10] We see from this example that teleopathy can afflict organizations as well as individuals.

Individuals may be selected by an organization precisely because they are afflicted, or they may become afflicted as a result of their regular active participation in such an organization. The value of teleopathy in employees is no doubt the greatest when the organization itself is driven by the pathology. It becomes a matter of ethical congruence between person and organization. The other side of this coin is that organizations may 'contract' teleopathy because of certain key individuals' managerial values. Karl Marx seems to have believed that the capitalistic system itself was fundamentally hostage to something like this pathology, inevitably infecting institutions and individuals within it.[11]

Summary: Teleopathy, then, is a moral condition in which the unbalanced pursuit of purpose manifests itself in three symptoms: fixation, rationalization and detachment. Teleopathy is, in my opinion, the most significant stimulus to which business ethics in this century has been a response. It is the principal occupational hazard of business leadership in a market economy. And its consequences on the lives of individuals, companies and society at large can be devastating: alienation, stress, unreasonable demands on work time, loss of creativity and loss of community.[12] If the disease is multi-levelled in this way so, we might suspect, is its prevention or cure. Awareness, mentioned earlier, can and must include individual, organizational and even societal dimensions.

RESPONSE AWARENESS IN THE PURSUIT OF PURPOSE

Avoiding teleopathy as an occupational hazard of capitalistic institutions will call for a new outlook on general management. Winston Churchill is supposed to have said, 'First we shape our institutions; then they shape us.' It is possible that we might create a capitalist culture that, even though democratic, could drive us away from a union of work and spiritual growth. Consider the meditation of Pope John Paul II in his recent encyclical, *Centesimus Annus:*

> In singling out new needs and new means to meet them, one must be guided by a comprehensive picture of man which respects all the dimensions of his being and which subordinates his material and instinctive dimensions to his interior and spiritual ones. If, on the contrary, a direct appeal is made to his instincts—while ignoring in various ways the reality of the person as intelligent and free—then consumer attitudes and lifestyles can be created which are objectively improper and often damaging to his physical and spiritual health. Of itself, an economic system does not possess criteria for correctly distinguishing new and higher forms of satisfying human needs from artificial new needs which hinder the formation of a mature personality... Thus a great deal of educational and cultural work is urgently needed, including the education of consumers in the responsible use of their power of choice, the formation of a strong sense of responsibility among producers and among people in the mass media in particular, as well as the necessary intervention by public authorities.[13]

In an increasingly global marketplace, our convictions about core human values and virtues urgently need to be clarified and strengthened. Now is the time for both Western and Eastern democracies (and both developed and developing nations) to join in the kind of dialogue that can forge such shared convictions! Otherwise, we diminish ourselves as producers and consumers. [14]

MORAL DEVELOPMENT: FROM PERSON TO ORGANIZATION

The Swiss psychologist, Jean Piaget, distinguished three stages in the development of a child's individuality, personality and autonomy. At first, the child pursues his own wants and desires with no regard whatsoever to those around him. At some point, this self-centredness is transformed into a kind of rule-governed compliant mentality, in which conscience becomes an external constraint on wants and desires like an authority or a peer group. As we know, this ethic of rules and authorities is eventually challenged in the name of deeper values and convictions that can lead to either violent or nonviolent confrontation. Mature conscience, Piaget believed, emerges in the wake of self-centred and rule-governed mindness.

The life of a corporation is similar in some ways to the life of an individual, and this may have a bearing on the way we think about business responding to the stimulus described at the beginning of the chapter. What I called teleopathy is rather like the 'pre-moral' stages of child development. The unconstrained or constrained (but in either case unbalanced) pursuit of purpose is the most significant obstacle to adulthood, but also the most significant obstacle to a healthy organization and a healthy market economy. Corporations that are fixated on economic objectives without restraint—rationalizing a lack of concern for the well-being of many stakeholders (employees, customers, and local communities)—must become aware of this fact and find a collective conscience. They must put into place internal safeguards against blindness and detachment. Just as surely, corporations caught up in the worship of market competition and government regulation as excuses for ethical indifference must discover new policies and practices for humanizing their decision-making.

We are not talking here about a sentimental social ideal, a luxury of affluent countries and organizations that can 'afford' to be ethical. The challenge is much more compelling. For on its outcome turns the future of peaceful global commerce, the hope of developing democracies, and the avoidance of economic, and eventually political, warfare within and between countries. Communism has demonstrated its economic and political weaknesses dramatically in the last five years. It remains for modern capitalism to convince us that it is capable of a more human demeanour and worthy of a significant level of trust.

VIRTUES, BALANCING AND AWARENESS

Balancing of a pursuit of purpose, since it cannot mean simply disconnecting from the purposes of business, altogether indifferent to the energetic impulse that formulates and implements competitive strategy—must mean fostering in an organizational culture what Aristotle called virtues.

In view of the 1980s popularity of books like *In Search of Excellence* by Peters and Waterman and the 1990s popularity of *The Seven Habits of Highly Effective People* by Stephen Covey, we might be forgiven for speculating about whether traditional moral philosophy is finding its way into contemporary management literature. The indicators are real and plentiful. We may be discovering anew that the shortest distance between two points is not a straight line—that the successful pursuit of purpose is not necessarily the *single*-minded pursuit of purpose.

Table 1

Cardinal Virtue or Habit	Prevention of Teleopathy	Salient Stakeholders	Illustrative Applications	Managerial Implementation
Prudence: Attention to long-term comprehensive decision perspectives	Avoids fixation on 'us', 'here', and 'now'	Wide-ranging, but primarily owners or investors, employees and communities	Environmental awareness, bribery temptations, leadership succession	Planning structure, incentive systems
Temperance: Attention to spiritual and higher-order goods and services	Avoids fixation on material detachment from fully human	Customers and employees primarily, but also competitors, among others	Fair competition; responsible marketing to needs, not just wants	Control systems employee, consumer audits
Courage: Rising above sole reliance on market pressure and legal compliance; need for responsible risk	Avoids denials and rationalization in the name of surrogates for conscience and 'others do it'	Again wide-ranging but primarily owners, investors, employees and communities	Strong board membership, diverse staff composition, internal whistleblower protection	Leadership development programmes; rewards for initiative, individual spirit
Justice: Attention to distributive as well as aggregate productive results, to process as well as to overcome	Avoids fixation on self-serving ends; rationalization at the cost of weak	Employees, customers and communities primarily, but also shareholders and competitors	Fair competition of employees, job security, consumer product safety and quality tax honesty	Regular audits of affected stakeholders; representative voices

Consider the four core ('cardinal') virtues that have, for 2,000 years, served as a foundation for moral theory and practice: prudence, temperance, courage and justice. Each of these core habits or virtues can be present in an individual, an organization, and broadly in an entire society. Each relates rather directly to current challenges in business ethics. And each offers a way to balance, not eliminate, the pursuit of purpose. Table 1 presents a brief analysis of each virtue as it might play a role in organizational decision- making—balancing the pursuit of purpose and increasing corporate awareness.

Business leaders who understand the importance of these organizational virtues will take their companies' social consciences in hand, avoiding tempting appeals to competitive dilemmas and other familiar excuses such as 'If I don't sell this dangerous product or permit this hazardous waste, someone else will!' or 'Corporate responsibility in this industry is suicidal in the absence of effective laws governing all the players, domestic and foreign!' or 'We need jobs more than regulation, environmental protection and employee entitlement.' Perhaps the essence of responsible management lies, as De Mello suggested, in appreciating the art of orchestration—of affirming multiple values.

INSTITUTIONALIZING AND SUSTAINING CONSCIENCE—IS IT HAPPENING?

There is some evidence in the United States that this challenge is being heard by business. What do we see when we survey the landscape? That American firms, often predictors of European and Asian business trends, are shifting their management philosophies. Some companies have taken up the challenge in explicit and impressive ways. They have set out to orient, institutionalize and sustain a set of moral values that define their corporate cultures and clarify the boundaries regarding market forces and legal compliance. And there are other signs:

- The *Fortune* magazine regularly publishes its list of 'most admired companies,' emphasizing corporate responsibility to employees, environment, communities and customers, in addition to shareholders and law. Companies highly value their inclusion in the list, and this is only one of many such recognition lists. The Business Enterprise Trust, headquartered in California, presents an annual series of awards to small and large companies that exhibit striking virtues. The awards include case studies and video narratives depicting the activities in question—all made available to US business schools.

- The American Law Institute has recently included in its statement of corporation law a significant provision to the effect that corporations can and should depart from the profit motive in response to the 'reasonable ethical expectations of the community.'
- Laws in nearly 80 per cent of American states charge business boards of directors with obligations to 'multiple constituencies'—not just the shareholder constituency—and they protect directors from shareholder actions when other constituencies can be shown to be at risk.
- Business schools, both graduate and undergraduate, are increasing the attention given to corporate responsibility, not just corporate efficiency and productivity, in their curricula. Accrediting institutions, like the American Association of Collegiate Schools of Business (AACSB), make this a condition of approval.
- Finally, the US Federal Sentencing Guidelines, formulated in 1991, are now gaining a prominent place in the consciousness of senior executives—for they mandate serious penalties for companies that do not have in place an ethics awareness and legal compliance programme that is well-defined and credible. For those who do, reduced penalties are provided for, using a multiplier between zero and one, depending on the quality of the programme.

All of these facts combine with existing social and legal pressures to enhance the responsibility of business decision-making and they point to a new wave of corporate consciousness that is healthy.

At the same time, of course, there is an increase in the number of indictments for white-collar crime and routine exposures of wrongdoing among the most widely known large corporations. The signs (alas!) are not unequivocal. It is naive to assert that virtue is rationally irresistible if properly understood—as if it were the latest in a long line of undiscovered competitive strategies. In the concluding section of this chapter, I will discuss some recent efforts to expand awareness and international corporate support for ethical standards.

THE VULNERABILITY OF VIRTUE—WAYS TO SUPPORT CORPORATE ETHICAL AWARENESS AND BEHAVIOUR

So far, we have been discussing primarily 'intra-corporate' (individual and organizational) approaches to corporate conscience, approaches focused on management education and internal sources of management influence. But there are other approaches that are necessary if corporate conscience is to receive the cultivation that it needs to survive.

The insufficiency of market forces and limited legal jurisdiction has become apparent to most business leaders who seek fundamental trust-relationships with their various stakeholders: employees, customers, investors, suppliers, competitors and communities. The globalization of business carries with it a growing call for a shared set of business ethics. For while unilateral responsibility is admirable, not infrequent, and sorely needed, it is also fragile.

In a provocative *Harvard Business Review* article titled 'Why Be Honest if Honesty Doesn't Pay?', authors Amar Bhide and Howard H. Stevenson examine the rhetoric and the reality of business ethics and conclude that without institutional support and encouragement, virtue is vulnerable. 'We all know of organizations, industries, and even whole societies in which trust has given way either to a destructive free-for-all or to inflexible rules and bureaucracy,' they write, 'Only our individual wills, our determination to do what is right, whether or not it is profitable, save us from choosing between chaos and stagnation.'[15]

INTER-CORPORATE AND EXTRA-CORPORATE STRATEGIES

It is common to invoke what we might call 'extra-corporate' strategies for corporate responsibility—essentially, government regulation of business as a surrogate for conscience. The efficiency costs of externalizing conscience in this way are many—not to mention the fact that we only remove our problem by one step when we look to the virtue of a public sector institution to secure the virtue of a private sector one. Another approach is to work through 'inter-corporate' channels (industry agreements and cross-industry agreements whose signatories pledge adherence to specific sets of ethical principles and policies.)

The Minnesota Centre for Corporate Responsibility, housed at the University of St Thomas in Minneapolis, has developed a document called *The Minnesota Principles*, which has become the basis for dialogue not only in the US, but also in Europe, Japan, China, Africa and (we hope) South America. The motivation for this effort was initially to help companies headquartered in Minnesota to get clearer and more consistent ideas about what they stand for in international business activity.

This initiative has given rise to a second effort, by an international group of business leaders meeting in Switzerland, to formulate *The Caux Principles*, a set of moral guidelines which incorporate the Minnesota Principles into a document with an even wider degree of participation and consensus on corporate responsibility.

The Caux Roundtable, an association of executives from Japan, Europe and the United States who meet each year in Caux, Switzerland, believes that the world business community can and should play an important role in improving economic and social conditions. As a statement of aspirations, the Caux Principles do not pretend to mirror everyday reality, but they are a means to express a world standard against which corporate performance can be held accountable. In the end, members seek to begin a process that identifies shared values and reconciles differing values. Their goal is to articulate a perspective on business behaviour that is acceptable to, and honoured by, all countries.

The Caux Principles are rooted in two fundamental ethical ideals: the Japanese concept of 'kyosei' and the more Western concept of 'human dignity'. Kyosei means living and working together for the common good—in a way that enables cooperation and mutual prosperity to coexist with healthy and fair competition. 'Human dignity' refers to the sacredness or value of each human person as an end, not simply as a means to others' purposes or even—in the case of basic human rights—to majority prescriptions.

It is my belief, having had the privilege of working on the drafting committees of these international groups, that the most stable long-term response to the hazard of teleopathy includes a community of business organization in addition to an educational system that emphasizes individual and managerial conscience. The response to a multi-levelled hazard must itself be multi-levelled, as I have already suggested. [16]

Let me conclude as I opened, with a quotation to set the stage for dialogue. The Preamble to the Caux Principles (13 January 1994) contains a powerful reminder of the primary motivation of the entire document, and a useful summary for this paper:

> The mobility of employment and capital is making business increasingly global in its transactions and its effects. Laws and market' forces in such a context are necessary but insufficient guides for conduct. Responsibility for a corporation's actions and policies and respect for the dignity and interests of its stakeholders are fundamental. And shared values, including a commitment to shared prosperity, are as important for a global community as for communities of smaller scale.
>
> For all of the above reasons, and because business can be a powerful agent of positive social change, we offer the following principles as a foundation for dialogue and action by business leaders in search of corporate responsibility. In so doing...we afford the legitimacy and centrality of moral values in economic decision making because, without them, stable business relationships and a sustainable world community are impossible.

REFERENCES

1. Goodpaster, *Ethical Imperatives and Corporate Leadership,* in Andrews, ed., *Ethics in Practice* (Harvard Business School Press, 1991).
2. McCoy, Bowen, *The Parable of the Sadhu, Harvard Business Review* (September–October 1983).

3. 'Telos' (tele) in Greek meaning 'goal, target, 'purpose' and 'pathos' (Paqos) meaning 'disease, sickness.'
4. The unbalanced pursuit of purpose can take either of two basic forms: an unconstrained form, in which no boundaries or barriers are recognized by the person or group pursuing the purpose in question. The objective is sought relentlessly, we might say. A more constrained form of teleopathy, however, pursues purposes while recognizing certain specific boundaries or barriers (such as market forces and law), but is relentless within the narrow context of these specific constraints. The unconstrained form is perhaps easier *to* identify in practice, yet rare, because it is so extreme. The second variety of teleopathy is more subtle and perhaps more common, since it presents the appearance of being 'constrained'-—a surrogate not a substitute, for being 'balanced.' Harvard philosopher Robert Nozick, *Anarchy, State and Utopia* (NY: basic books, 1974, p29), reflected on the difference between pure goal directed views and views that insist on 'side-constraints,' but he sees instinctively that there can be problem with any goal-directed view.

   A *goal-directed* view with constraints added would be: among those acts available to you that don't violate constraints C, act so as to maximize goal G. Here, the rights of others would constrain your goal-directed behaviour. I do not mean to imply that the correct moral view includes mandatory goals that must be pursued, even within the constraints. This view differs from one that tries to build the side-constraints C into the goal G. The side-constraint view forbids you to violate these moral constraints in the rights (the constraints) in order to lessen their total violation in the society (p.29).
5. Examples of the 'harvest' of fixation in business life are as plentiful as they are in the government sector. When NASA safety recommendation against launching the Challenger in 1986, leading to fatal results, we saw a pattern not unlike corporate scandals during the 1980s (General Electric, E F Hutton, Dow Corning, Sears Roebuck). Examples in India are no doubt also ready-to-hand, but I leave these to you.
6. Anthony DeMello, *The Way to Love: Last Meditations*, 1993, posthumous.
7. Saul Gellerman, author of 'Why "Good" Managers Make Bad Ethical Choices' (*Harvard Business Review* 1987), argued that the common denominator in white collar crime during the last decade was

rationalization in its many forms. When conscience 'can't take no for an answer', it finds a way not to ask.

8. And each corresponds rather directly to the conditional types of fixation distinguished earlier: market and law.
9. Maccoby, Michael, *The Gamesman* (Simon and Schuster, 1976).
10. Ron Daniel, former Managing Director, McKinsey & Co., *Fortune,* 1 November 1993, p. 72.
11. 'This feature of teleopathy—its nested interactions among units of analysis from individuals to whole cultures—makes it particularly salient in the context of spirituality in the workplace. I have called this the Moral Fractal principle.' See Goodpaster, *Toward an Integrated Approach to Business Ethics, Thought* (Fordham University, 1985).
12. Instead of fixation on goals that are limited, urgent, etc., we might suggest a more dispassionate posture, broad and long term. Instead of rationalization, an attitude of impartiality, exemption from conventional norms. Instead of detachment of head from heart, an assimilation of the two that essentially avoids the distinction in theory and in practice. But De Mello's perspective quoted earlier reminds us that this solution lands us in as difficult a place as attachment itself—in a neutral posture no closer to personal, organizational, or societal balance than before.
13. John Paul 11, *Centesimus Annus* (May 1991).
14. The Minnesota Centre for Corporate Responsibility, housed at the University of St. Thomas, has recently developed a document called *The Minnesota Principles.*
15. *Harvard Business Review,* September–October 1990, p.325.
16. The 'General Principles' of *The Caux Principles* (Minneapolis, 13 January 1994) help to clarify the spirit of 'kyosei' and 'human dignity', while its more specific Stakeholder Principles offer practical ways to apply these ideals to policies and operations.

5

Development and Ethics: A Jesuit Perspective*

PETER-HANS KOLVENBACH

Mr Tata has demonstrated that one could run a successful and profitable organization without compromising on one's ethical stand. Presiding over Tata Steel, Air India and Tata Sons, throughout his career he upheld the need to maintain high ethical standards.

The American Jesuits of the Maryland Jesuit Province who came to Jamshedpur in 1948, besides setting up other centres of education, health, development and religious formation, also established the Xavier Labour Relations Institute to provide education and guidance to the workers, to the industries and to management. Their pioneering efforts were characterized by their unequivocal commitment to the mission of XLRI, namely, 'to imbue the managers, present and future, with social and ethical responsibility, special concern for the weaker sections of society and dedication to work and social justice.'**

Through its forty-six years of history, the Institute has upheld a high ethical standard and consistently inculcated it in its students and in the managers who come here for management development programmes.

XLRI has, from the beginning, introduced 'Corporate Social and Ethical Responsibility' as one of the core courses of its curriculum, and most business organizations that have recruited XLRI's graduates

*Oration delivered on 18 October 1995.

**Mission Statement of XLRI

agree that the students have been influenced in their thinking and attitudes by this course.

The Institute has gained credibility before the academic and business world, at home and abroad, in this matter of education for ethics in business. We consider this aspect of ethical education, of social concern (the poor being the point of reference), so vital to the presence and service of the Jesuits at XLRI, that had it been missing in the core curriculum, there would be no justification for their being here at all.

When the Jesuit General Congregation, the highest policy-making body of the Society of Jesus, met at the beginning of this year in Rome, it expressed its stance in the modern world. It said:

> Our Jesuit mission touches something fundamental in the human heart: the desire to find God in a world scarred by sin, and then to live by his Gospel in all its implications. This, the instinct to live fully in God's love and thereby to promote a shared, lasting human good, is what we address by our vocation to serve faith and promote the justice of God's Kingdom... This faith in God is inescapably social in its implications, because it is directed towards how people relate to one another and how society should be ordered.*

In the Jesuit vision of the world and of business and commerce, ethics and ethical behaviour are not mere intellectual abstractions; they are part of our commitment to life.

Throughout the 455 years of its history, the Society of Jesus has paid a price, a heavy price, in order to affirm its stand on ethics and its option for justice. Down the ages, in every country where the Society of Jesus has been present, heroic witnesses like Edmund Campion in England, Rupert Mayer in Germany and Miguel Pro in Mexico have fearlessly laid down their lives to stand for truth and justice. In our own day, in EI Salvador, six Jesuits, professors in the Jesuit University, were brutally silenced because in their teaching, research and publications—especially in the areas of economy and social analysis—they stood uncompromisingly on the side of the poor,

*GC 34 1.1, 11-12. Servants of Christ's Mission

and tirelessly proclaimed ethical and social values in production, business and distribution of the goods of the earth.

WHAT DOES ETHICS IN BUSINESS MEAN?

The Context

The term ethics in business conjures up different images for different people. However, all would agree that it concerns an attitude of mind and heart that governs our interactions with one another and in the market place.

The market place today is characterized by certain specific traits. Production, trade and commerce manifest a general tendency to move away from control of one form or another, be it political or ideological, and to assert their own autonomy and mechanisms. And so, competitiveness and the quest for quality have become the norm. Ownership has shifted from land and property to management and information. Economic activity is recognized as an integral aspect of human dignity.

In his encyclical letter *Centesimus Annus,* Pope John Paul II makes this observation:

> The modern business economy has positive aspects. Its basis is human freedom exercised in the economic field, just as it is exercised in many other fields. Economic activity is indeed but one sector in a great variety of human activities, and like every other sector, it includes the right to freedom, as well as the duty of making responsible use of freedom. But it is important to note that there are specific differences between the trends of modern society and those of the past, even the recent past. Whereas, at one time, the decisive factor of production was the land, and later, capital... Today, the decisive factor is increasingly man himself: that is his knowledge, especially his scientific knowledge, his capacity for interrelated and compact organizations, as well as his ability to perceive the needs of others and to satisfy them. *

*Centesimus Annus p.32

CREATING WEALTH: ETHICAL IMPLICATIONS

In our attitude to wealth and to the business of making and creating it, I think we ought not to be apologetic about admitting that, in order to distribute wealth equitably in society, it is necessary to create it. Rev John Mahoney, Dixon Professor of Business Ethics and Social Responsibility at London Business School, convincingly states:

> Developing the earth's resources to produce goods and services to satisfy the needs and aspirations of the increasing millions of its inhabitants does not merely add value in economic terms. It enhances the value and quality of human living, by expanding human freedom and culture, and by providing a social environment in which human dignity too can develop and prosper. Within this line of reflection, the business of creating wealth in and for society is then seen to, is a positive and constructive occupation for men and women.

Having affirmed that, let me at once, without entering into details, emphatically state that if on the one hand, the generation of wealth in the world has been considerable, on the other hand, this wealth has been distributed in a very unbalanced and unequal manner. If one believes the World Bank, the rich one-quarter of the world's population consumes by itself three-quarters of the total production. As a result, three-quarters of humanity have, for their use, only one-quarter of the production. Consequently, the riches produced are not where the people are: the population explosion is not taking place where economic development is unfolding. Hence, we have increasing poverty of the masses and a situation between the rich nations and the poor ones that is increasingly explosive, which reveals itself, among other things, in the insoluble problem of displaced persons, immigrants and refugees, who move toward the countries that are better off or more developed.

However, this is a question not merely of inequality between demographic development and economic development. At the very core of the generation of wealth, a split is growing between finance and economy. The capital that could and ought to have been invested in restoring the balance in the world's economy and in local development is placed instead in the market for financial speculation on stocks and bonds and currency, out of greed for more profit than would be gained from the healthy economic effort of production.

TWO ATTITUDES

In the face of these two approaches, there are at least two attitudes possible. One could be called, 'Business is business.' That a people without means of development never rises above its state of underdevelopment is inevitable. This is the law of the economic mechanism. The fact that the stock market attracts more capital than does investment in industry is fatal when profit is more important and more assured. Again, this is a law of the market place. At least in the short haul, this attitude seems to be economically the most profitable.

In the other attitude, there enters into play the element that is properly ethical. The attitude is based on the refusal to consider economy exclusively for itself in the conviction that economy ought to be at the service of human society and that in the long haul, such concern is in the interest of economy itself. The inequalities between riches for some people and poverty for the masses, between speculative finance and productive economy, are ultimately explosive and are in no way in the interest of healthy economic growth.

While recognizing the *raison d'etre* of 'business ethics,' the business person sees in economy the well-being of human society as he conducts himself not as a mere technician of the market, but as a professional who is a human being—responsible for, and in solidarity with, all other human beings.

In an address to business persons and economic managers, John Paul II has pointed out,

> The degree of well-being which society today enjoys would be unthinkable without the dynamic figure of the business person, whose function consists of organizing human labour and the means of production so as to give rise to the goods and services necessary for the prosperity and progress of the community.

This means that persons in management face, each day, hard choices on which depend not only the well-being of the private profit of their firms, but also the well-being of many others. In this way, they are not simply called to a career or a job, but to look upon their professional work as a vocation with a broader vision of managerial responsibility.

For that reason the two outlooks mentioned above, considered in the perspective of business ethics, evoke two challenges: first, that no one can ever own capital resources absolutely as if misery did not exist, or control their use without regard for others—especially the needy and the human society as a whole.* Secondly, the use of financial resources solely in pursuit of short term profits can stunt the production of needed goods and services, because investment is crucial for the long-term viability of human society.**

The Christian vision of man gives a theoretical basis of this understanding of the use of financial resources. The human person as a steward of creation has received the whole world to develop and to put its fruits at the service of all. The more faithful the person is in fulfilling this mandate, the greater the person's appreciation by the Lord.

ECONOMIC LIBERALIZATION IN INDIA: ETHICAL QUESTIONS

India has made giant strides in developing its commerce and trade. It has reached out to global markets and made Indian goods and services available on a competitive basis. India's industry has gained worldwide recognition through the awarding of ISO certificates, and has produced goods that can meet the demands of any customer. If these developments are to result in the tangible growth of the wealth of the whole nation and the well-being of all without exception, this way of productivity and profitability should be pursued vigorously.

In this context, permit me to raise two questions.

First, when we speak of poverty and welfare, of development

---

*Summa Theologica II, II, q. 55

**Economic Justice for All, p. 56-57

and economic progress, what indeed is our point of reference and comparison? Probably we often think of the western model, as if it were the only valid ideal towards which every developing nation must naturally, inevitably, move. Yet, we know from experience that this model of production and consumption leads to unbalanced, uncontrolled exploitation of the earth, and finally to the destruction of the ecology. Can we discover a model whose central preoccupation would be the quality of human life and harmony with the whole of creation—an attitude that is so inherent in the Indian ethos?

That would provide us with an alternative model, a different point of reference, to understand what really are poverty and riches, progress and welfare. We need to constantly ask ourselves: What exactly are we looking for in our legitimate fight against poverty and misery? What would be the viable medium between the two extremes of deprivation on the one hand, and consumerism on the other?

Secondly, India's effort to open itself to the world economy points to a globalization, a complex economic network behind every product. Our world has been reduced to one single system. But what kind of system? It is a system born out of close bonds of a growing inter-dependence, which determines our way of living, our lifestyle, our thinking and our values. The domestic and global inequalities that we witness have their roots no doubt in economic reasons primarily. But, obviously, other factors are involved—of a political, social and cultural nature—all of which further heighten global interdependence, whose negative effects, if not addressed concertedly, will inevitably lead to an unhappy economic and cultural domination of a large number of poorer nations by a few economic giants—in fact, to a new form of colonialism. Thus, the globalization process can adversely affect, in particular, poor nations that lack the resources to protect and nurture their specific cultures. This growing globalization—quite fascinating, since it certainly brings with it several advantages—is not being adequately addressed at the political level, to ensure a reduction of international inequalities in matters of riches and power.

The world is indeed becoming a global village, and some

longstanding sources of conflict are disappearing. But also the gap between the rich and the poor societies keeps growing, and could lead to new international tensions. Where indeed is that global mechanism, that central organization, which could effectively monitor and manage these international tensions?

As far as India is concerned, I think these are actual and serious concerns, but not yet recognized as such by those who have the responsibility to tackle them, because understandably these people are looking for a quick solution to the more urgent economic problems.

ETHICS IN BUSINESS MEANS RESPECT FOR HUMAN DIGNITY

Recently, we have become increasingly aware of some other dimensions of ethics in business. Respect for the human person created in the image of God underlies the growing international consciousness of the full range of human rights, which include:

> ...economic and social rights to the basic necessities of life and well-being; personal rights such as freedom of conscience and expression and the right to practice and share one's faith; civil and political rights to participate fully and freely in the process of society; and rights such as development, peace, and a healthy environment. *

The growing awareness of these rights has given voice to people of all nations and cultures. In a special way, the workers in factories and on shop floors demand their right to be heard in policy-making, planning and execution of their enterprises.** Many governments have responded favourably to this call for participative management.

Pope John Paul II affirms this principle when he says,

> ... Total recognition must be given to the human conscience which is bound only to the truth, both natural and revealed. The recognition of these rights represents the primary foundation of

---

*GC 34. 1.1.1.,6. Our Mission and Justice

**Thomas Donaldson, *The Ethics of International Business*, Oxford University Press, 1989

> every authentically free political order, or for that matter every free enterprise.*

Writing in 1939, Mahatma Gandhi stated,

> Democracy must, in essence, mean the art and science of mobilizing the entire physical, economic, and spiritual resources of all the various sections of the people in the service of the common good of all.**

I applaud the efforts of XLRI in joining hands with managers of serious repute in setting up and developing the National Network of Human Resources Development. Creating a climate for a healthy and cooperative interaction in every organization is a must. I am confident that with the increased implementation of the Human Resource Development practices, the rights of employees will be safeguarded, productivity increased, and the overall atmosphere will be an ethical one.

It was never easy to maintain the principle that the dignity of the human person is above capital and profit. If the respect for human dignity is the criterion to measure all aspects of economic activity, this implies that the human person, human labour and human needs can never be made mere instruments to accomplish socio-economic targets. Technology and economy have undoubtedly increased the quality and welfare of life; yet more than ever, the human person is vulnerable to the manipulation of market publicity and strategy. Hence arises the necessity of business ethics that not only promotes the fulfilment of basic human needs, but also protects human society against the most evident form of moral non-development, namely, greed. We must never allow a country to become materially rich, but spiritually poor.

Another aspect of respecting the individual person is the recognition of the due process of law. Father Tome, in his book *Business Ethics*, lists the 'right to due process of law' as one of the

---

*CENTESIMUS ANNUS. n. 49

**Quotes of Gandhi. P. 196

fundamental rights of a citizen.*

The recent efforts made by the Government of India in updating the law concerning labour is a step in the right direction. The vigorously flourishing trade union movement, the independent judiciary and respect for law continue to keep India a young and vibrant democracy.

One of the fundamental rights formally and legally guaranteed to every citizen in the present world, and *a fortiori*, to every worker, is the right to express one's opinion, especially in the context of business.

However, where inequality prevails, this right is often more effectively utilized by those who enjoy privilege or power. The deprived and the marginalized are rarely able to express their rights. And so the strong become stronger, the weak weaker. Developed countries always hold the initiative, imposing their views and systems. The weaker nations are condemned to compromise and to comply with what the strong nations dictate.

While this inequality at all levels prevails, the obligation to provide the necessary means that the needy should have is the single most urgent economic claim on the conscience of human society. To enable all persons to share in, and to contribute to, the common good, the prevailing inequality demands a special commitment to the powerless and the needy.

I have seen the freedom with which workers in India express their divergence from management through peaceful and non-violent means so as to enable them to become active participants in the life of society. The powerlessness of the needy wounds the whole community and the wounds will be healed by greater solidarity with them from all, without pitting one group against another.

Individuals and organizations have raised their collective voices to decry instances of injustice against the poor and the weaker sections of Indian society. They have also taken stances against deforestation, industrial pollution, food and drug adulteration, forced displacement of persons and families from their traditional habitats, dumping of

---

*Richard T De George, *Competing with Integrity in International Business*, Oxford University Press 1993

banned materials and medicines—all of which gives us hope that, as the poet Rabindranath Tagore prayed, into that heaven of freedom this country will soon awake.

ETHICS IN BUSINESS MEANS CONTRIBUTING TO THE DEVELOPMENT OF A GLOBAL OPINION

The marvellous gifts of God, the communication media, have helped to shape the way in which we think, feel, judge, and act. The global village that has been created by the network of communications requires responsible persons who can shape global opinions. Increasingly, organizations and industries are becoming sensitive to the formation of such opinions as they affect their business, not just at their home base, but throughout the world. Access to the media of communication, freedom to voice divergent views, and absence of monopoly over these media are necessary.

Talking about this aspect of industrial peace, Pope John Paul II in his encyclical, *Centesimus Annus,* wrote:

> Just as within individual societies it is possible and right to organize a solid economy which will direct the functioning of the market to the common good, so too there is a similar need for adequate intervention on the international level. For this to happen a great effort is to be made to enhance mutual understanding and knowledge, and to increase the sensitivity of consciences.*

The recent efforts at making the means of communication easily available even at the rural levels, and giving access to channels of communication over the airwaves, have made it possible for individuals, workers and citizens, to have access to the global opinion-making process.

These are some of the ways in which I find ethics in business could be practically implemented.

*CENTESIMUS ANNUS 11.52

MESSAGE TO THE INDUSTRIALISTS AND MANAGERS

Whenever I read of the rapid strides that you, the industrialists and managers, have achieved in a very short time, I feel very happy. You have not only successfully withstood the onslaught of multinational corporations, but have proven yourselves competent partners in the global market.

Your organizations, such as the Confederation of Indian Industries, the Associated Chambers of Commerce, and the Federation of Indian Chambers of Commerce and Industry, have worked together to project a consistent image of your country and her potential. The acquisition of ISO certificates has proven your commitment to total quality management.

I appeal to you to recognize your own individuality and maintain your position without compromise. Make your own the sentiments of Mahatma Gandhi when he said:

> I do not want my house to be walled in on all sides and my windows to be stuffed. I want the cultures of all the land to be blown about my house as freely as possible. But I refuse to be blown off my feet by any. I refuse to live in other peoples' house as an interloper, a beggar, or a slave.*

*Quotes of Gandhi. p. 28

6

Business Ethics: Commandments of Truths, Sacrifice, Integrity and Trusteeship*

TARJANI VAKIL

Let me begin by recounting a story. It happened a few years ago, soon after the demise of the Pope. In Heaven, as he was being conducted to his new home, he was joined by a businessman. They had just started talking to each other when an Archangel arrived with their new house keys. The businessman was surprised to see the Pope being directed to a block of neat but small apartments, while he was directed to the gates of a rather opulent bungalow. Sure that there was some mistake, he pointed out to the Archangel that the other person was the Pope, not him. The Archangel replied, 'Oh, we know that. You see, we already have over two hundred Popes here. You, on the other hand, are the first businessman.'

Humour aside, what are business ethics? Or, is 'business ethics' a joke or an oxymoron? Ethics, as the Oxford Dictionary will tell you, are 'the moral principles by which a person is guided...the rules of conduct recognized in...human life.' Business ethics is, therefore, the rules of conducting business. Less rigorous views, however, judge ethicality by conformance to sets of rules, rather than the moral purity of motivation.

BUSINESS ETHICS IN THE WEST

Business ethics draws largely upon utilitarian theory to judge actions by their effect on the greatest good of the greatest number. However,

*Oration delivered on 25 October 1996.

based on how the 'number' is defined, there are at least two schools of thought in the West regarding the extent to which business should consider the ethical implications of business acts.

One school, which is usually called the 'shareholder school', based on the concept of the shareholder as owner, believes that as long as an action is legal, business has no justification to consider implications other than its effects on shareholder value. Here, those actions are ethical which benefit the greatest number of shareholders.

Against this view, the other school holds that a business must consider the effects of its actions on all who are affected by them. These are potentially—in addition to its shareholders—its employees, customers, suppliers, bankers and the government, and community at large, which could include even its competitors. This extended group of people affected by business decisions have come to be called stakeholders, in contrast to the professed owners, the shareholders.

The mainstream approach to business ethics in the West is ultimately concerned with the consequences of a given action for the profitability of the firm, albeit in the long-term. It justifies actions that do not increase short-term profits by pointing out their long-term benefits.

A company's responsibility for its employees and the environment, above and beyond what can be justified by this strategic regard for ethics, is limited to its legal obligations. Ethical action can thus be described as being based on *'enlightened self-interest'.*

THE INDIAN TRADITION

The Indian tradition encompasses three broad principles which can be said to guide the evaluation of action in Indian philosophy. The first is a sense of duty or dharma. Along with the Gita, the first two commandments in the Taittiriya Upanisad enjoin us to speak the truth, fulfil our obligations, and avoid negligence. The second is a spirit of sacrifice and sharing. The third commandment enjoins integrity. Another school of Indian thought that has received the most attention to date is Gandhiji's concept of 'Trusteeship' as applied to business. In his words:

> 'If one has come by a fair amount of wealth...
> by means of trade and industry, he must know that
> all that wealth does not belong to him. What belongs
> to him is the right to an honourable livelihood.'

A small incident from the Mahabharata serves to indicate the depth of the tradition which Gandhiji draws upon. During the period when the ownership of the kingdom of Hastinapura was being debated, Duryodhana once asked, 'Why is not my claim to the throne legitimate? If my father, Dhritarashtra, had not been blind, he would have been king instead of Pandu. Then wouldn't I have been heir to the kingdom, instead of Yudhishtira?' Vidura replied, 'A son is entitled only to inherit what belongs to the father. The kingdom does not belong to the king. He only holds it in trust for his people.' Gandhiji believed that the notion of trusteeship should evolve voluntarily among businessmen and that it should not be necessary to impose it by fiat. A management consultant in the US propagated the concept of Gandhian trusteeship: 'In the twenty-first century, the organizational model that will work is the service model—service to customers, shareholders and employees. The task of the management is to balance the benefit and the leadership has to adopt the "trusteeship" concept.' This is where Gandhian values come into play. One of the core values espoused by Gandhi is a focus on responsibility, not rights. The second is leadership by example. The third is truth, integrity and moral values guiding all aspects of decision-making in both personal and public life.

> My focus is on espousing the Gandhian concept of leadership, heroic in its commitment to moral principles and service rather than one driven by the acquisition of power and leadership and one that harnesses the ideals in all of us, appeals to what is best in us and moves us to a better quality of life.

This philosophy seems to be catching on, perhaps because it offers different kinds of solutions in an age of increasing cynicism, decaying moral values, corporate greed and an erosion of trust in institutions including the family and the government. It is a scenario in which the teachings and values of Gandhi have more relevance than ever before.

In the recent past, social involvement by business has, for the most part, taken the shape of public philanthropy. This has included the building of temples, hospitals and educational institutions. A few examples of such activities would include the Birla Temple in Calcutta; the Shree Vivekananda Research and Training Institute set up by Excel Industries in Mandvi, which is very much in the spirit of trusteeship; the L&T Welfare Centre in Bombay; the Tata Institute of Fundamental Research; and the Voltas Lifeline Express that has been running on Indian tracks for over a decade.

Occasionally, such public spiritedness, combined with business necessity, has extended to building entire townships, an early example being this very city of Jamshedpur.

To some extent, the provision of such facilities has been in response to the failures in public administration. But to a large extent, it has also been driven by the desire of Indian businessmen to contribute to the community. For the public sector units in India, such actions have also formed part of their mandate as governmental institutions.

It is also heartening to find examples of unusually ethical behaviour within the practice of day to day business. When Tata sold Tata Oil Mills Company to Hindustan Lever (HLL), there were press reports which said that the Tatas had accepted a lower price from Hindustan Lever as opposed to competing bidders, because it thought that its erstwhile employees would be best treated under HLL's care. Such reports testify to the standing of the Tatas as concerned employers.

In another example, ACC, some time ago, discovered a batch of cement below their requisite standard. It immediately launched an effort to trace and recover this batch of cement. Furthermore, even where concrete made from this cement was of acceptable quality, ACC insisted on paying for the demolition of foundations built using this cement.

Similarly, Marico, the makers of Parachute oil, discovered a harmless tint in the oil from one of its production lines. The company withdrew the batch from the market, shut down the production line, but kept the workers on payroll and involved them in the investigation of the cause. In short order, the workers located the cause, rectified it and resumed production.

But these companies have reaped benefits too, intended or otherwise. In the case of Tata, this is reflected in its ability to retain and attract talent, in an era where employee knowledge may be the ultimate competitive advantage. ACC's care for the consumer and Marico's concern for its consumers and workers has also paid off handsomely in terms of their brand image and customer loyalty. In cases such as these, harmonizing business with obligations to the community and employees has also helped the company's bottom line.

It is important to underline that the justification for such behaviour, in the Indian tradition, does not come from its contribution to profitability, but from the rightness of the actions themselves. It is interesting to find that today, notices of voluntarism and distributive justice are being introduced into the current Western thought and debate on business ethics.

At another level, the European Foundation for Quality Management (EFQM) and the Malcolm Baldrige Awards for Excellence recognize active community engagement or societal responsibility of business among the parameters of excellence in quality. Incidentally, the EXIM Bank has, along with the Confederation of Indian Industry (CII), introduced in India a Business Excellence Award in 1995 much on the lines of EFQM.

Unfortunately, not all trends in Indian history have been conducive to the development of ethical business.

Over the last fifty years, the government has played a significant role in the economic development of India. Much has indeed been gained in the process. One of the more pernicious though unintended efforts of the license raj, however, was to breed an unethical attitude to business and encourage graft and corruption. The economic growth of a company often depended not on its efficiency, or on the market, or on its relations with its constituents, but on the extent of its contacts with the government and the political leadership. These contacts were often nurtured in a mutually degrading but re-enforcing atmosphere of shoddy work, payoffs and kickbacks. Fortunately, today, the situation is changing for the better in view of competition, which is a feature of a market economy.

THE SEARCH FOR INTERNATIONAL BUSINESS ETHICS

Ethics today occupies centre stage in discussions of international business. I believe strongly, for reasons I will outline shortly, that the reasons for this prominence are inextricably linked to the changes in today's business environment, and that ethics will not go the way of other management fads. The challenge before us is thus to address these issues squarely, and further, to contribute to their understanding, drawing upon our country's abundant history, our rich multicultural heritage, and our deep and perceptive philosophical tradition. This tradition pushes us to try and reconcile the apparent variance in different international viewpoints and coalesce them into unified business ethics.

The earlier discussion comparing Western and Indian ethics makes it clear that there already exists a substantial measure of agreement. Both cultures, perhaps for different reasons, have stopped concentrating on short-term profits and begun to consider the impact of business activities on various constituent groups.

Businesses in the West have also begun to take a greater role in the community via arrangements such as the Percent Club in the UK, which enjoins corporations to donate a small percentage (typically one half of one per cent) of their profits to community building activities. In the US, companies such as Rank Xerox, for instance, have a Social Leave Programme, which allows employees to take time off for community projects. Alternative corporate organizations, like the Society for Democratic Integration in Industry—of which the John Lewis Partnership is a prominent member—are alive and flourishing in the US.

Such initiatives are very close to the concept of trusteeship discussed in the Indian context above. To the extent that they are driven by 'enlightened self-interest' rather than by a sense of duty, it may not satisfy the strict demands of Indian ethical norms, but such behaviour is eminently acceptable—even laudable—both in the West and here in India, as part of the endeavour to reach those heights. Any true effort to reach them has to be inclusive and universal.

If I may quote from Swami Vivekananda's Teachings, 'The work of ethics has been and will be...not the destruction of variation, but to recognize the unity in spite of all these variations... The one aim of...the highest ethical codes that mankind has discovered up to the present time is to make for that sameness.'

To discover this unifying theme, it is important to try and understand the changes that have brought the discussion on business ethics to its current state. The permanence of these changes is also the reason why I believe strongly in the endurance of business ethics as a management concern.

THE ROLE OF GLOBALIZATION AND SIZE

The most important change that has affected our perceptions of ethics is, I believe, the phenomena of globalization. As in many other fields, this phenomenon is changing the rules of business. In the field of acceptable business practices, it has done so by confronting business norms developed in one culture with the environment of another. In addition, like all other reputations, a reputation for ethical integrity is extremely transferable, both in its pursuance and in its absence. As companies begin to operate in different political and social environments, they have to be sensitive to the fact that their practices in one environment may impact their reputation in other areas, with different bases for judgment.

The special problem with developing international business ethics is that it requires judgments on similar issues to be made across dissimilar environments. The very fact that ethical decisions are made in a given context implies that similar issues may be decided differently in two different environments. It then becomes incumbent upon the business to provide adequate justification as to why this should be so. As Indian companies become global, they are going to face these problems.

Globalization also interacts intimately with size, which is another reason for the rise into prominence of business ethics. The growing international presence of the individual firm has increased its size to a level that was not common before. Less than a handful of countries today are as big as the biggest multinationals. The more influence business has, or appears to have, the more interest there will be in how the influence is being used. This size and its attendant potential for influence bring these businesses under close scrutiny. This, in turn, makes it critical for these companies to conduct their relations with other entities in a manner that is free from reproach. Bigger firms are especially responsible, since, as industry leaders in terms of establishing appropriate conduct, their ethical codes percolate to the other firms in the industry.

THE ROLE OF INTELLECTUAL WORK

The changing nature of work is another growing force towards ethics in the workplace. When, in an unethical organization, an employee is repeatedly confronted with discrepancies between word and action, he becomes cynical about the company's values. He is likely to transfer the same cynical attitude to his work. When he is expected not to take the company's pronouncements on ethics seriously, why should he pay any more attention to its values of quality? It is extremely difficult to counter such attitudes by monitoring at a time when work is becoming increasingly intellectual. The only remedy is to provide a challenging environment—an ethical environment that encourages the fuller development of the human spirit. Only when an employee is proud to be a member of the organization to which he belongs, will he give of his best, voluntarily and enthusiastically.

Business ethics, which address the above issues, should be sensitive to different cultures, be applicable to large organizations, and have respect for the individual.

But the task of developing such ethics is not easy. To illustrate the difficulty in internationalizing ethical standards, consider the disagreements over the social clauses in the Maastricht Accord, popularly known as the European Social Chapter. Even within a relatively homogenous society such as the European Community, there has been substantial disagreement, particularly between the UK and the Continent on the necessity for uniformity in working environments, but also among other members on the Continent on the interpretation and applicability of specific clauses. It is true that no country in the European Union, the UK included, disputes the values behind the Social Charter, but almost all have something to say about the manner in which such values can inform the workplace. Of course, workers must be consulted, but are work-councils the only way it can be done effectively? Does the phrase 'working environment' cover family leave policies?

Such obstructions do not stop the search for a uniform ethical code, which continues apace. Based on the concept of human dignity, the idea of living together for the common good to ensure mutual prosperity as exemplified in the Japanese doctrine of *kyosei*, and partly on the Minnesota Principles developed by the Minnesota Centre for Corporate Responsibility, business leaders from three continents—the US, Europe and Japan—adopted the Caux Round Table Principles for Business in 1994. They laid out seven general principles including protection and improvement of the environment, support for multilateral trade agreements, respect for international and domestic trade union rules, avoidance of illicit operations, sensitivity towards the integrity of the culture of the consumers, and fostering open markets for trade and investment. All of the above are by and large, unexceptionable, but all are equally open to interpretation.

At another level, individual companies with multinational operations, like Digital, Honeywell and Levi Strauss, have developed codes of conduct for themselves which they seek to apply universally.

The special problem with developing international business ethics is that it requires judgments on similar issues to be made across dissimilar environments. But a beginning can definitely be made, starting with the common elements.

WHAT SHOULD BE DONE?

Eventually, after all is said and done, even if it becomes possible to agree upon an international code of ethics, it will still have to be implemented and practised. More importantly, in the interim, we must continue to conduct ourselves ethically, according to our own codes. How can that be accomplished?

Can ethics be taught? Maybe not, but perhaps it can be learnt. This process must be conducted at various levels. It must inspire the workplace and business schools. As Harvard found out while developing its Leadership, Ethics and Corporate Responsibility Programme, the teaching of ethics requires everyone to be on board, and it requires everyone to be educated. Foremost, it requires an understanding of the self-awareness of the students and faculty. To accomplish all this, Harvard Business School undertook an extensive survey of its students, and retrained its entire faculty on how to integrate ethical issues with the existing course structure, develop cases with an ethical component, and establish a core curriculum within the programme. The process took time—and is still ongoing—but the crucial aspect was the involvement of all concerned.

Will this programme make Harvard Business School graduates more ethical in their behaviour? That is difficult to say. But it will certainly enable them to better recognize the ethical implications of their actions. The ultimate action will depend on the individual, the context and the incentives faced by the decision-maker.

Workplace values have a large role to play in these incentives. First, there should be a clearly articulated corporate code that defines the core beliefs on which the firm will not compromise. This puts everyone on notice, whether inside or outside, as to what the values of the corporation are. But without supporting action, this is a hollow statement. Each decision of the company should reflect these beliefs. It is no use to say that the best person will be selected for the job, and then award it to the under-qualified nephew of the Chairman. Nor does it help if the company ethics statement stridently declares that it will not tolerate corruption, and then follows up by financing a resort holiday for the government official in charge of awarding contracts.

Ethics are inculcated in people by percept, by repeated examples. Management has to lead from the front. People come to believe that the company stands by its policy, if they see it walk away from business rather than behave unethically. Employees behave according to the code, if they perceive that such behaviour is valued. Is the worker who stops the production line rather than allow substandard work to go through, rewarded for paying attention to quality or reprimanded for stopping production? Answers to such questions will determine whether the code will succeed. Such sincerity and widespread adherence can only be achieved through commitment and communication. Commitment throughout and communication all over—from the very top to the newest recruit. This requires continuous effort and training. Everyone has to be reminded repeatedly how important it is to the company that its conduct be above reproach. The conduct of ethical business is not an annual training session; it is a daily regimen. Only in such an environment can an ethical code flourish.

CONCLUSION

In the end, it is important to recognize, along with Bertrand Russell, that 'all ethics, howsoever refined, remains more or less subjective.' A unifying set of international business ethics may just be another Holy Grail. But in the journey to search for the Grail, we have learnt and shall continue to learn more about the manner in which we conduct ourselves. This applies to all of us here—industrialists, educationists and students seeking their destiny in the real world. If we, as enlightened human beings, can today commit to practising what we believe—and remain open to sharpening our commitments—the journey will be its own reward.

7

Ethics in Media*

CHRIS FROST

MEDIA IN A DEMOCRATIC FREE MARKET SOCIETY

Media ethics is an important subject that is very topical at the moment back home and in many other parts of the globe following the sad death of Princess Diana. The press, in particular, was condemned widely for its perceived harassment and intrusion on the privacy of the princess, and there were many calls for a clampdown on media freedom in the UK. Consequently, I would like to look today at the media's role in a democratic, free market society.

Questions of ownership and control in the media have become more important in the era of the multinational company with its emphasis on profit at the expense of the needs of the citizens of any particular country: so-called cultural imperialism. The debate surrounding these questions often threatens to overshadow the more fundamental debate over how journalists behave ethically whilst trying to provide readers with unsullied information and proprietors with profits.

DEFINITION OF TERMS AND ASSUMPTIONS

It is worth checking, before I go into detail, what we mean by certain terms.

Media, as defined by media studies, has a very wide definition that can be considered as covering any area of human activity which

---

*Oration delivered on 17 January 1998.

involves message transmission, whether for information, persuasion, control or entertainment.

I have defined media as any transmission method that allows the publication of news to a broad and simultaneous audience, that is to say, newspapers, magazines, TV, radio and the internet.

In a Western-style, liberal, democratic free market, the purpose of the media is usually accepted as being to inform, educate, entertain and, in the case of non-public sector media, make a profit, usually by direct sales, space-selling or sponsorship.

I will also assume that there is nothing wrong with profit-making by the media in a free market economy, not because this point is undebatable, but because I want to deal with the status quo as we find it in your country and mine, assuming that most people in both are reasonably happy with a market economy.

FREEDOM OF SPEECH AND OPINION

The media around the world is regularly criticized for the work it produces. As a general principle in a free democracy, most people accept that there should be a free press examining the way the world works and the way the people within it are behaving. Whether you see the media as a mirror reflecting what is happening or a lens allowing us to focus on areas of particular interest, or even a spotlight illuminating this section over that, there is a general view that this is important work. But people also become angry at what they see as invasive treatment of either themselves or others. They want the media to use searchlights, but not on them or on people they consider important.

Our rights and obligations as citizens, to freedom of speech and access to certain information, should apply as equally to the media as they do to private citizens. The radical British lawyer, Geoffrey Robertson, has described journalism as, '...the exercise by occupation of the right to free expression available to every citizen.'[1] The press in the UK and many other countries has always resisted attempts to make them different in any way to the ordinary citizen, partly because if the media were to have special privileges, it might be expected to have special obligations. This is not the case everywhere though, and in some European countries, journalists have special rights including rights of access to information unavailable to the general public.

Freedom of speech and opinion is an absolute. Either you have it or you don't. If freedom of speech is removed in even the smallest part, it is removed almost in its entirety. Of course if I were to damage someone's reputation, then it is only reasonable that they should be able to lay suit against me for damages. When we move into the area of publication, where a person's freedom of speech can reach a wide audience, other safeguards are often felt to be required by society to prevent damage to other rights, such as the right to reputation and the right to be considered innocent until proven otherwise by a properly constituted court of law. Any right brings with it the duty to use it responsibly. But otherwise, the free press is an extension of freedom of speech and freedom of opinion. As English Utilitarianist John Stuart Mill put it, 'The time, it is to be hoped, is gone by, when any defence would be necessary of the 'liberty of the press' as one of the securities against corrupt or tyrannical government.' [2]

NEED FOR FREEDOM OF EXPRESSION

It is as confusing as it is concerning that many people in Britain, and indeed several other countries, seem to have forgotten or ignored the importance of a free press and freedom of speech and now support censorship against specific matters. In a Times Mirror survey taken in 1994, only a worryingly low 52 per cent of Britons said they supported a free press—the lowest of all the countries surveyed. Yet despite this small majority, 77 per cent of respondents in Britain favoured censorship to discourage terrorism, an even higher figure than those who would welcome censorship to restrict portrayals of explicit sex (72 per cent). Many might say this is because of the high levels of terrorism in the UK, yet both Spain and Italy, which face similar problems, had much lower numbers of respondents calling for censorship (62 per cent and 42 per cent). It is disappointing to see so many people support censorship on a political matter.

It is, of course, extremely important in a liberal democracy that all citizens have the right to express their views freely to audiences large and small. One cannot test the decision-making process in a system that requires all citizens to make decisions about policy, even if only through elected representatives, if the citizens required to make those decisions are not given the opportunity to inform themselves, build up belief structures and test them against those of other people. Where the people are entitled to pursue their beliefs, they should have the right to debate those views openly with whomever they wish. Your forthcoming elections will emphasize that point for all of you as you rely on the media to bring you the points of view of various politicians and political parties.

John Stuart Mill justifies the need for freedom of expression in his essay 'On Liberty'. In it, he says that there four distinct grounds for justifying freedom of expression:

> First, if any opinion is compelled to silence, that opinion may, for all we can certainly know, be true. To deny this is to assume our own infallibility.
>
> Secondly, though the silenced opinion may be an error, it may, and very commonly does, contain a portion of truth; and since the general or prevailing opinion on any subject is rarely if never the whole truth, it is only by the collision of adverse opinions that the remainder of the truth has any chance of being supplied.
>
> Thirdly, even if the received opinion be not only true, but the whole truth unless it is suffered to be, and actually is, vigorously and earnestly contested, it will, by most of those who receive it, be held in the manner of a prejudice with little comprehension or feeling for its rational grounds.
>
> And not only this, but fourthly, the meaning of the doctrine itself will be in danger of being lost, or enfeebled, and deprived of its vital effect on the character and conduct; the dogma becoming a mere formal profession, inefficacious for good but cumbering the ground, and preventing the growth of any real and heartfelt conviction, from reason or personal experience.[3]

If we are to live in equality, then we must all have access to education and information, and the media is one way of achieving that.

This is the platform on which the media builds its right to publish, its determination to have the same rights (no more, no fewer) as the ordinary citizen to find information, consider it, analyse it, comment on it and debate it.

If we were to accept the principle that there are certain people in society who do not have the right to speak and be heard, or who are limited in what they may write or speak about, it is only a small step to gagging anyone whose opinions are not welcome by the ruling group. To suggest otherwise is to live in ignorance of or indifference to the evidence presented by scores of tyrannical governments around the world who have imprisoned journalists, political opponents and others who have broadcast opinions that were not welcome.

So, despite a clear complacency about democratic freedoms in a number of democratic countries, they are essential to the style of government that we all seem to favour whether by choice or apathy and because of this, the journalist needs to take care that he or she does not step over the invisible mark that divides the responsible exercise of freedom of expression from a licence to print scandal—often enough to give governments the excuse they need to change editorial choice into censorship.

There are, of course, bound to be some limits on the information provided by news sources in even the freest of societies. Protecting the honour of citizens, preventing excessive invasions of privacy and intrusion, protecting the innocence of those facing court proceedings are all rights protected under the UN Charter and, if only for this reason, citizens expect State support for their rights. Most countries have laws of defamation and some have privacy laws. The defamation laws in Britain date back to King Alfred, who used to have the tongues of slanderers cut out.

FREEDOM OF EXPRESSION IN CERTAIN POLITICAL SYSTEMS

Political systems which do not require the participation of the majority of citizens through the ballot box do not need the hazards of a free media. A free media is a potential voice of dissent likely to cause disruption in a society which is not involved in choosing how it is governed. It is easy to justify its suppression on the basis that it only causes discontent, and without a vote, why do the people need to know what is going on?

Controlling the media allows only good news about the government to be disseminated. It also eradicates much of the ethical debate because few, if any, of the ethical problems facing journalists in free media arise in a constrained or non-existent media. If a journalist is limited in the sources he or she can use; is instructed by the authorities on what to write, how to write it, and then how it should be used in whatever media they work for, then the debate is not about ethics but about definitions—is that person a journalist at all? Without media freedom, the journalist's reason to behave in a way that brings direct moral conflict no longer exists. There can still be professional misbehaviour, but this would be a purely functionalist argument. With the journalist purely as entertainer or propagandist, the ethical debate becomes simple. The good journalist really becomes someone who gets their work in on time, and that work is well-written according to the brief provided by the political masters. There are no other ethical considerations, because there is no freedom of expression and no mission to inform.

Only if democratic decision making is genuinely required, does a fully free media also need to exist as a reliable source of information, comment and analysis, feeding the citizen's right to know so that they can arrive at properly informed decisions through some democratic process. Journalists can only behave in a way which could be construed as immoral: intrude, breach people's privacy, or agonize over this dilemma or that if they have a justification—and surely the only justification to publish such material is freedom of expression and the citizen's right to know.

Because of the importance of the freedom of expression, the media is very good at hiding its true purposes away from the general public. It is able to take a lofty stand. If they were in the business of, say, producing machine parts, there would be little to debate. Are these parts of sufficient merit to justify their price? If so, a deal is done and, one hopes, a profit is made for the manufacturer. No one expects a manufacturer to make parts for some loftier purpose than profit.

Yet the true objective of the commercial media is to make a

profit whilst it informs the public. Already we see conflicts in the central purpose of the media. Are there other problems because of this conflict? Of course there are. We know there would have to be.

PURSUIT OF INFORMATION AND PEOPLE'S PRIVACY

Let us start by looking at how the media, in its pursuit of information, often invades people's privacy.

'A society which permits individuals to choose how they are to lead their lives is one which will recognize the choice of privacy,' a UK government consultation paper on the infringement of privacy announced in July 1993.

Invasion of privacy is the issue that probably most concerns the public. It is certainly the issue that has underlined all major debates in the UK press over the past ten years or so.

Privacy is recognized by psychologists as a basic human need; a drive almost as powerful as sex, hunger and thirst. Many a person has taken their own life rather than live with having their private life exposed to the world. We all need a small private area somewhere which is our own. It need not contain anything shameful (although for most of us there is probably something of which we are not proud), but it does need to contain secrets; secrets shared only with those we choose, those we trust. We need to be in control of the flow of information of our private selves.

It is often said that information is power, but it is just as true that control of information is power. I am not a more powerful person than my neighbour because I have a certain piece of information, but I may well be a more powerful person because I know how to obtain that piece of information.

Some cultures believe in keeping names private. In all societies, names have some power. In the UK, when dealing with strangers, we expect to be called by our surname and probably a title. Only when we get to know the people involved would we use our forenames. Amongst intimates, of course, we might even have a nickname.

We use privacy in our social dealings as a token of faith and fair dealing. When introduced to strangers we will talk pleasantly about the weather, the traffic and other areas of inconsequential nonsense. Often sneered at as small talk, many people claim that they abhor it. Yet, it is clearly an essential social tool in the building of relationships. It allows us to measure up the other person before we move on to revealing elements of ourselves which are more intimate and not generally available for public consumption. We use gradual sharing of our privacy as the price for a growing bond with the other person; there are several levels of this relationship. Private details of work we might exchange with colleagues depend on the nature of our relationship. Personal family details would be exchanged with relatives depending on their closeness, whilst sexual details are retained mainly for those with whom we have sexual relationships.

If we are using self-inflicted invasions of our privacy as the price of our place in our circle of friends and acquaintances, we can hardly be surprised if people react badly to having their privacy invaded uninvited—particularly if that invasion goes straight to the really intimate details as the tabloids so often do. The problem isn't so much the invasion, but the control. This is why people will often allow their story to be published for money. Money can also be used as a token to establish our place in society, so one thing of value has been exchanged for another and the person selling their life has retained control of the transaction.

Because intimate revelations are tokens which people use to 'buy' our friendship, they have currency and we are always interested to hear of people's intimate affairs. This explains our desire to learn about other people, as this knowledge helps shape our view of society and its boundaries of behaviour.

COMMODITY THEORY OF INTIMACY

Charles Fried wrote of the 'Commodity Theory' of intimacy which argued that close relationships 'involve the voluntary and spontaneous relinquishment of something between friend and friend, lover and lover. The title to information about oneself conferred by privacy provides the necessary something...intimacy is the sharing of information about one's actions, beliefs, or emotions which one does not share with all, and which one has the right not to share with anyone.'[4] This needs to be considered in the context that the information itself does not necessarily have any specific value. I share personal information with my doctor, my banker and my tailor but this does not make me intimate with them, partly because I share only specific information that is necessary for them to do their job. It is no surprise that the morals of their job rely heavily on confidentiality. The spread of private information I volunteer to an intimate helps make it clear that they are special. But it is also the fact that the information is given as an expression of intimacy. The other person now has the same relation of control over the information, a position of trust if you will, to keep that information confidential.

This could explain why we become angry if we find a close friend has passed on 'confidential' information to someone else. Not that we are concerned about the other person knowing, but that there has been a breach of trust. Julie Inness believes that the act of love or liking is a component of privacy as well, 'The act of sharing information, either actively or passively, is intimate only if it is understood to take its meaning and value from our love, liking or care.'[5] This may be the case but it is not necessarily fully understood as part of the contract. Many celebrities reach and maintain their status by sharing information about themselves with the media and, therefore, with the public. It is a deal they are prepared to make, because the information they release is, as I have already explained, not particularly secret and the selling of it for celebrity status is called sensible PR. Unfortunately, many readers do not make this connection and feel they have a relationship of loving or liking with the celebrities which extends far beyond reality because the latter shared information, even though this sharing is only one way and does not involve any expression of intimacy. Readers, therefore, expect and demand more such intimacies and a media intent on making profit can often be keen to provide them.

Since celebrities are also role models, we look to them as major boundary shapers. This is why many of the fiercest rows about privacy in the UK have involved the royal family. Their marriages and love lives have been laid bare for our inspection under the guise of public interest and many people have rightly asked whether the press has gone too far, too often. Your own political leaders and film stars face similar intrusions for similar reasons. Writing a universal law for journalists to protect a person's privacy whilst maintaining the media's right to freedom of opinion is very difficult. There are too many variables around the circumstance of each invasion to allow for hard and fast rules. Clifford Christians advocates three tests for the journalist:

1. Decency and fairness is non-negotiable.
2. 'Redeeming social value' should be used as a criterion for deciding when to invade privacy.
3. The dignity of the person should not be maligned in the name of press privilege.

But because we have not accepted the full right to free expression of the media, we need to look at some of the moral problems and responsibilities that come with this awesome freedom.

MORAL PROBLEMS AND FREEDOM OF EXPRESSION

The media must have some right to invade a citizen's privacy if we are to maintain the right to freedom of expression, justified by the public's right to know about something being done privately by someone that is against the general or specific interests of society. It has to be accepted that those in positions of responsibility, from politicians to police officers and civic officials, are answerable for their positions of trust to the people who elected or rely on them. The public, therefore, has some right to know what they are doing with those positions of trust. If a politician has promised to clamp down on corruption, yet is himself taking bribes, then we deserve to know. If a police officer has sworn to uphold the law without fear or favour, then we deserve to know if he is taking bribes to free criminals. But are we entitled to expose the police officer for having an affair with someone who is not his wife? It could depend on who it was. Either way, the media has to decide whether it is right to invade that police officer's privacy.

The Nordic Conference on the Right to Privacy (1967) came to the conclusion that 'the Right to Privacy is the right to be let alone to live one's own life with the minimum degree of interference.' But what can we mean by 'minimum' in a society which supports a free press?

There have been a number of attempts to introduce privacy into the law of the UK over the years, but all have failed to make it to the statute book. Unless journalists exercise the privilege of the free press with care, one will eventually succeed, taking with it Britain's free press.

TRUTH AND ACCURACY

Another area of ethical dilemma is truth and accuracy. Sources of information are often not as accurate or as certain as we or journalists might like.

A police chief involved in a major incident may issue to journalists information that has not been checked and, therefore, could be inaccurate, because he or she wants to show the media that he or she is doing a good job. Those in authority learn very quickly that the nature of news means that a story is soon forgotten, taking false or misleading statements with it into oblivion. Everybody in the news wants to show themselves in a good light and so is likely to distort the story in some way, even if unconsciously. Again the journalist must use his or her judgement to try to spot the leaps of faith by the source of information and put them in the right context.

Most people buy into information systems because they want high-grade information, not just entertainment, and any media outlet that wishes to maintain its market would do well to justify the veracity of its sources.

This does not mean that the media never deals in inaccurate information. One of the prevailing dilemmas for the journalist is whether to publish stories about rumours. Publishing such a story gives it credence, but often the rumour is already widely known and believed and so requires the record being set straight. Very often consumers need to know about information that they cannot be certain is truthful. Much political reporting is of this sort. If one politician says that poor teachers are at fault for our ill-educated children whilst another says it is a lack of resources and a third says our children are actually the best educated in the world, it cannot be a surprise if a journalist reports the story of a row between politicians only briefly mentioning their points of view. The only thing we can be certain is true, is the row. The rest lies in the field of opinion, usually based on untested facts and one-sided statistics. It would be foolish, and indeed dangerous, for journalists to pretend they could provide sufficient accurate information for the consumer to come to a firm conclusion. It is important, however, that we know a debate about education has been started. Indeed, one consistent UK political argument of the '80s and '90s has been about the standard of teaching and the efficacy of the so-called new methods as opposed to traditional methods. Many professors and lecturers in education have spent their careers developing and testing new theories of education only to see them dismissed in a thirty-minute speech by an education secretary on the run-up to an election as the modern nonsense responsible for the failure of education in the UK.

No journalist is going to be able to track down in detail all the theories, and see whether the literature bears out the education secretary's view or not. They can, however, look at the obvious inconsistencies in the speech and use that as the basis of the story. In other words, a good story would be about the new methods of education and why the secretary of state has allowed them to be used for so many years and now, ignoring the advice of the experts, is hoping to use them to excuse the poor state of education over which the government had presided for so many years. Whilst it would be accurate to report just the secretary of state's speech, it would not be entirely truthful to report that and only that. A journalist has a duty to set such a report in a context for the consumer.

Accuracy is a word which causes more confusion in journalism than anything else. People expect the media to be accurate so that they can convince themselves that their model of the universe, formed in part by the information the media feeds them, is accurate.

Yet a considerable measure of that universal model will be formed from information that is not accurate or even truthful. Each person's model of the universe will be built around presumptions, assumptions and information that we actually know is either wrong or, at least, unproven. Whilst a consumer is looking for accuracy, there are other criteria which are just as important. There is no point in a reporter being absolutely accurate six months after the event. This would mean sacrificing timeliness to accuracy—the province of the academic. Whilst the journalist must do all he or she can to minimize mistakes, distortions and untruthfulness, he or she must also be aware that time is an important component of this type of information gathering.

INACCURATE INFORMATION: VALUABLE?

Suppose I were to learn, from a radio report, that the road I usually take to drive home from work is blocked because, as police have reported, a lorry has shed its load. I would be interested in this report and listen closely to gather all the knowledge that I could. I might learn that the load is unlikely to be cleared for several hours and, therefore, the road would remain blocked. I could then decide to take a different route home, or if this were not possible or was inadvisable, I might decide to stay in town and work late. Either way, it would not worry me if I later learnt that, in fact, the road was blocked because a car had broken down, rather than a lorry, unless that updated information meant that the road was cleared much faster than would have been the case if the original story had been correct, thus invalidating my decision process. Since my purpose in having the information is to use it as the basis for a decision to take a detour before being caught in the traffic jam, it does not matter much that the reason for blockage is not fully accurate.

Because of the way we treat information, not only do we occasionally accept inaccurate information, we actually need it. Making mistakes can be an important part of news reporting. Whilst news media should aim to produce truthful information, it is as important that they get the information out quickly. Accurate information too late is of little value in news terms. Journalists, however, need to be honest about making mistakes. If you were asking me the time and I said, 'It's such and such o'clock,' I might be wrong by a few seconds or even minutes. I would be accurate if I said it was between 7.00 a.m. and midnight, but that would be of little value to you. Much better to risk being inaccurate and give you a time that is useful.

If a journalist has taken every care to ensure that the information is as truthful as possible and is properly sourced so that the reader is able to decide how far they can trust the information, the journalist has surely dealt with the consumer fairly, even if the consumer's hopes of completely accurate information have not been fulfilled.

Readers expect that the information they are being fed is properly sourced, so journalists have a moral obligation—not to try to guarantee accuracy of information, but to ensure the reader/viewer is made aware of the sourcing of the story. The task of belief in the source (and, therefore, the information) lies with the consumer. It is the practitioner's job to give them the information they need to make a rational decision, and not to take that decision for the consumer.

None of this is to imply that accuracy is not a value to be cherished—it is an attempt to argue that accuracy by itself is not enough. Journalists need to aim for wider values of truth-telling than mere accuracy allows.

OBJECTIVITY: DEFINITION

Objectivity is another value that, it seems, is highly prized and desired by consumers and journalists.

Often consumers complain that journalists are not impartial or objective, whilst many journalists are convinced that not only should they be objective, but they should be objective. We need to define some terms here before we go any further, as there are a number of words here often used interchangeably by people who should know better. Bias, comment, slant, objectivity, neutrality, balance, impartiality, fairness, prejudice and opinion are all concepts that we need to discuss in relation to truth.

OBJECTIVE TRUTH AND JOURNALISTIC IMPARTIALITY

Objective truth and journalistic impartiality may, at face value, seem to be admirable ideals and may also seem to be one and the same thing. I intend to show that not only are they different and not especially desirable, but probably completely unattainable.

When we talk about objective truth, we should be aware that there are several assumptions here:

1. That there is such a thing as objective truth in the abstract.
2. That the truth is capable of being reported objectively in a theoretical sense.
3. That the truth is capable of being reported objectively in a practical sense.
4. That what consumers actually want is objective truth in any case.

Many philosophers have argued about whether there is such a thing as objective truth. These arguments can take in everything from the 'do I exist' question to the meaning of reason, and if you wish to exercise your brain more fully than I intend, these can be found in any good library. However, just by using intuition or pragmatism, we can usually arrive at some accepted objective truth. 'There are words in English printed on this page' is a statement unlikely to cause any reaction more significant than a cautious nod of the head. There seems little cause for argument. There is a page, there are words, those who read English will recognize those words and their use is consistent with English grammar and usage. We do not need to continue any argument about their existence, my existence or your existence because if either of us were to doubt the existence of any of the three, there would not be much point in continuing the presentation of evidence.

Bias or slant: The dictionary describes bias as prejudice. Its origin is from the game of bowls where the lop-side construction of the ball gives bias—a twist in the path it follows. Bias, as I use it in this book, can be assumed to mean the deliberate slanting of a story to favour one side of the argument rather than another on the grounds of personal choice of the writer.

Balance: The idea that the journalist can and should present equally the two sides of an argument.

Comment: An explanatory remark or criticism according to the dictionary. Comment in journalistic terms can range from the expert opinion of a correspondent, whether that be in sport or politics, to the unwanted insertion of unsupported views.

Objectivity: To make external to the mind, not subjective. In journalistic terms, many mean it to say that the journalist should not intrude his or her subjective feelings or views into an objective report. That which is objective cannot and should not contain that which is subjective.

Neutral or impartial: Taking neither side; impartial. This does not exclude subjectivity but expects the journalist to stand aloof from decision making.

Prejudice: Preconceived opinion. This differs from bias in that bias may slant a story without there being a preconceived idea. Prejudice is more likely to determine what information is gathered for a story while bias more likely to determine how it is written and used.

Fairness: Just, equitable. Giving all sides of the argument a fair hearing.

The words now stand for themselves and your ability to understand what the words appear to represent is an objective truth—a reality which is hard to question. My part in the existence of those words is now irrelevant. The only objective truth is that they are there for you to understand.

There are those who would argue that this alone is an argument for there being no objective truth. The transfer of any involvement by me in the message to the understanding by you, means that the truth of the existence of the message contained in the page and words is entirely subjective. The truth of the existence of the message, assuming there to be one, has changed by being understood by you. But this is to ignore the physical evidence of the page and the print which can also be seen by others, even if they interpret the message in another way. In other words, is there any objectivity in my meaning of the words and your understanding of the words, or only in the imprint of the words themselves on the page?

We can say pragmatically and with evidence that the page exists. If other people exist, we can prove to them that the page exists by showing it to them.

However, that is the last objective truth we can show them. You cannot prove that the understanding you take from this page and these words is the understanding I intended to give them or the same as the understanding someone else has. I hope that those understandings will be very similar, otherwise I have failed in my task as a communicator of ideas. But I would be foolish to think that I would have been able to transfer exact and identical understandings of a complex issue through anything I could write. I can only help present a perspective that would allow you to come to a closer understanding of how I view what is happening.

TRUTH LIKE A ROUNDABOUT

Truth can be seen to be a little like a roundabout in a fairground. It has an objective truth, there is evidence for its existence; we can see it and touch it and hear it. But for its riders, the view and perspective is constantly changing, despite the unchanging nature of the roundabout itself. Our choice of position on the roundabout will alter our experience. Sitting on the horses on the inside will provide a different view than to those riding the outer ring; those riders will see different things. Young riders will have a different experience to their more mature fellows, whilst the novice will experience a thrill half-forgotten by the experienced rider. Meanwhile, the ride operator, diffidently chewing gum and standing by the controls in the centre, has an entirely different experience. Ask any of those people what it is like on a roundabout and the tales would be true, accurate, but entirely different.

There is an objective truth in that there is a roundabout, but that is not enough to tell us what a roundabout is. We need the evidence of the riders and operators in order to allow us to experience the full reality of roundabouts and this is what we want, because the truth about roundabouts cannot be told by a detailed examination of the scratched and rusted horses standing idle at dawn in a dusty trampled field. A roundabout is a thing of bright lights, loud music, laughter, speed, excitement and fun. It is also a thing to make money, to pack away at the end of the day in a trailer that has sharp edges and scratchy corners with bolts that refuse to undo.

The roundabout exists, but can I even begin to give you an objective and all-encompassing truth; tell you of the full range of iconic images that exist in so many consciousnesses? Surely not. It is beyond the skill of any reporter to do more than trigger some of the many elements of truth involved in such complex realities.

Many journalists believe that the good journalist should hold up a mirror to the world to allow the viewer to see things as they really are. But—as advice to journalists—this has two flaws. None of us see things in mirrors as they really are. We view ourselves according to our own prejudices. The arrogant see a gorgeous creature smiling back whilst those with lower self-esteem may see a drab, ugly or over weight reflection.

It also assumes that the reporter adds no distortions or unconscious changes to the mirror. This is unlikely. Journalists are more like painters. They may not deliberately remove a wart or minimize the grey hair, but they will concentrate more on one feature than another. It also assumes that journalists are involuntary witnesses of events, gathering news from outside to present to the world. But as Theodore L. Glasser points out, this is one of the major mistakes of modern journalism, the view that news is something independent and external to the journalist. 'This is the essence of objectivity,' says Glasser, 'and this is precisely why it is so very difficult for journalism to consider questions of ethics and morality. Since news exists "out there" apparently independent of the reporter—journalists can't be held responsible for it. And since they are not responsible for the news being there, how can we expect journalists to be accountable for the consequences of merely reporting it?'[7]

Journalists not only decide what is news, but also what part of the story they should report. The journalist is never in the position of being able to present the whole picture, even if that were desirable. Anyone who has carried out in-depth research knows that no matter how deep you dig, there is still more to know. Additional matters are drawn into the growing whirlpool of understanding because they might impact the matter you are studying. The same is true in journalism. If a journalist is covering a plane crash, how much detail would he or she need to know about plane manufacture, safety-testing procedures, production of aviation fuel, airport procedures, the private lives of every passenger and crew member, the method of training pilots and crew, the private lives of the accident investigators and so on?

The journalist has to draw a line somewhere, or no copy would ever be filed. The instant a journalist decides that he or she has enough information to file a story, objectivity is out of the window; the editing process has started and subjectivity is in. With newspapers and broadcast stations perpetually short of space, with time pressing on the reporter and the importance of getting the story as quickly as possible, there are a range of physical and practical problems which will prevent objective reporting. Reporters have to decide who they will speak to, and editors have to select what to publish in order to meet deadlines and publish newspapers and produce news programmes.

OBJECTIVITY AND STATUS QUO

Theodore L. Glasser throws further light on the problems of objectivity. He believes, 'Objectivity in journalism is biased in favour of the status quo; ...against independent thinking; it emasculates the intellect by treating it as a disinterested spectator. Finally, objective reporting is biased against the very idea of responsibility; the day's news is viewed as something journalists are compelled to report, not something they are responsible for creating.... Objectivity in journalism effectively erodes the very foundation on which rests a responsible press.'[8]

So according to Glasser, objectivity actually works against the consumer's interests and is, therefore, not what the consumer needs.

Should it be what the consumer wants? No, for all the reasons I have given. The reader needs as many views from the roundabout as is possible to get—not one view claiming to cover all.

And, of course, deciding what to put into a story is not always all there is to worry about. Sometimes, of course, stories are suppressed because they do not suit the purpose of the media outlet carrying them. Murdoch's Astra satellite, for instance, famously limited its news service from the BBC in order to continue transmitting to China and other parts of the Far East.

SUMMING UP

So journalists have to worry about privacy, truth, accuracy, objectivity, impartiality and suppression when they are considering how to report the news. But the news is only a part of the media. I know I set out to look only at the news media, but even here it is realized that the major profits are to be made in entertainment—and as I also said earlier, in a free market, surely there should be the right to make a profit? So whether the entertainment is suitable items placed alongside a news service or whether the two become hopelessly intertwined, we have to accept that when the needs of shareholders and proprietors need to be considered as strongly as, or even more strongly than, those of readers or sources, the risk is that the journalist will aim to please the reader to increase circulation to please the editor and the proprietor.

This can be done by making stories more entertaining: building stories up to make them more exciting, playing with the truth to add drama, becoming more invasive to expose more of the private lives of the rich and famous. The juicier the information, the more saleable it is. And so the media moves away from covering the issues to exposing people's private lives, not to inform, but to entertain—all justified in the honourable name of 'freedom of expression.'

Of course, companies have the right to make a profit in a free market economy, and it would not be sensible to fight for the right to vote, the right to freedom of expression, without pursuing the right to freely sell your labour or capital.

In theory at least, competition should spur companies and journalists on to do a better job; to cover a subject more thoroughly and more accurately so that the media will be more attractive to the consumer. Of course, in practice, the easy way to draw more consumers is to make stories more sensational, to spice them up with salacious detail; to have brighter, more intrusive pictures, shriller, more colourful design. Also, it is often easier to buy up the competition and ensure a monopoly market than compete in real terms.

A newspaper has as much right to sell the information it has invested money to gather, as a company has the right to sell goods it has invested resources into manufacturing. But when consumers cannot verify the quality of information and when the media further exploits the lives of others in order to boost sales, it risks damaging the very thing it pretends to be upholding: freedom of expression. If we are to have free media, they must be free to investigate and yet still free to make a profit.

Figuring out how to prevent the excesses of the pursuit of profit being used as a reason to remove the freedom of the media, and with it the freedom of expression, is vital for a true democracy.

REFERENCES

1. Robertson, G (1983). *People Against the Press.* Quartot Books: London.
2. Mill, JS (1991). *On Liberty and Other Essays* (with an introduction by John Gray), Oxford UP Oxford.
3. Ibid.
4. Fried, C (1968). 'Privacy' *Yale Law Journal* 77: 480.
5. Inness, J.C. (1992) *Privacy Intimacy and Isolation*, Oxford University Press, New York.
6. Christian, C et al (1991) *Media Ethics: Case and Moral Reasoning*, Longmans New York.
7. Glasser, T (1992) *Objectivity and News Bias* in Cohen, Elliot (ed) *Philosophical Issues in Journalism*, Oxford University Press.
8. Ibid.

8

Business Ethics: The Bitter-sweet Ambrosia*

SURESH KRISHNA

I would like to begin by quoting from an ancient Tamil poem. This poet was a Tamil prince who lived in 150 BC. He was a Pandian prince. He was born in my hometown, Madurai, and his name was Ilam. In those days, princes used to be sent for trade and commerce outside India. They went to Thailand, Cambodia and Indonesia to trade; they went with traders so that they could understand what business was all about. So when they became king, they would not look at businessmen as outcasts. They would understand what business was all about.

But this prince was so erudite that he became a poet at the very young age of fifteen or sixteen, and was honoured by being admitted into a select association of poets. Unfortunately, the young prince died in one of his voyages before he reached the age of twenty. His name then aptly became *Kadalul Maaindha*, which meant 'the prince who died at sea.' He wrote many poems, but only one survives in Tamil literature. It is a wonderful poem, because it shows that the human values of honesty, integrity and ethics are timeless. It has nothing to do with our present world, but everything to do with human nature.

The short poem translates into:

This world lives
because
some men
do not eat alone,
not even when they get

---

*Oration delivered on 16 October 1998.

the sweet ambrosia of the gods;
they've no anger in them,
they fear evils other men fear
but never sleep over them;

give their lives for honour,
will not touch a gift of whole worlds
if tainted;
there is no faintness in their hearts
and they do not strive
for themselves
Because such men are,
the world is.

(*Kadalul Maaindha Ham Peruvazhidhi*; circa 150 BC).

There is no doubt that the industrial community is an important part of society. It creates wealth, skills, employment and goods. Despite its contribution, the industrial community in our country it is at best tolerated and at worst made to feel alienated. Before independence, the industrial community had identified itself with society by supporting the national cause of freedom. Important business leaders gave liberally of their time, energy and resources to a cause which was of national importance. Many business leaders who thus took part in the national struggle were respected members of society and were held in high esteem. The fact that Gandhiji stayed at Birla House was an accepted norm of society's respect for industry.

After independence, business lost its links with the national vision and except in pockets, failed to identify itself with mainstream aspirations. Business became increasingly regulated, protected and licence-oriented, which in turn made businessmen more self-seeking and preoccupied with devising ways of beating the system.

Any perceived alienation from society is a matter of grave concern. In the long term, business can only survive and grow if it enjoys the respect and confidence of society. It must be seen to be fulfilling an important need, to be worthy of trust. It is true that business enterprises must make profits, but they must not be perceived to be doing so at the cost of society. If there is a certain perception in society, born of a misconception that automatically places the burden of guilt on business, then it is the source—the misconception—that we must eliminate.

We live in the nervous '90s, amidst a rising wave of helpless concern about business, about economies, about mindless violence and generally the deteriorating state of the world we live in. Many experts and leaders, even of opposing political persuasions, seem to agree on one thing: a worldwide economic crisis is imminent, if not already upon us.

This crisis is most readily associated with declining investor confidence in currencies and markets and thus in business itself. Within a single month, we have read headlines about the greatest banking failure in Japan since the War; a 7 per cent loss in the US Dollar in a single day; and a ₹700 crore erosion in deposits in organizations that seemed like the last word in reliability in India.

No further elaboration is needed, I believe, to emphasize the erosion of faith in ethics or morality or standards of conduct (for they are all synonymous) in business the world over.

Yet, I said nothing could be more appropriate than ethics in business as a theme. This is because no time is more right than now. This is not blind optimism on my part. This view is based on the fact that, ultimately, a business must learn to earn the respect of people and society before it can hope to make a profit.

The most frequent comment about ethics in business is that it is a contradiction in reality: a phrase that people pay lip service to. Nonetheless, if one considered the matter in depth, it would be obvious that the very foundation of all transactions, exchange, and commerce is an assumption that the other party would act dependably and in the spirit of the contract.

What does ethics actually mean? At once, several issues spring immediately to mind:

- Is ethics about the goals of business or about the means and projects adopted?
- Is it about the individual or the organization as a whole?

- Is it personal or can it be institutionalized?
- Is it transitory—relative to time and place—and not universal, lasting or fundamental?

Clearly, if ethics is entirely flexible, it is difficult to say anything definite on the subject. On the other hand, there are many instances where there is a widespread agreement—as in the Barings disaster—that unethical practices were indeed involved.

What constitutes ethical conduct in business? When does it lead to irreconcilable conflicts and dilemmas? These are questions that must trouble each one of us at some point.

We'll look at this in three parts:

a) Ethics and the individual in business;
b) Ethics in the organization or corporate ethics; and
c) What leaders of business can and must do in their unending efforts.

ETHICS AND THE INDIVIDUAL

One strongly held view (it had the support of Aristotle 2,500 years ago) is that the ethics in an individual is entirely the result of upbringing and family background. They, therefore, 'cannot be changed when he becomes an adult. And yet, today, more than ever before, there is widespread recognition that ethics in business deserves special attention. No fewer than five hundred business schools all over the world have included the subject as part of their MBA curriculum, and in many, it is a core requirement. Every year in the past few years, *Harvard Business Review* has carried articles on the theme. Innumerable seminars and conferences are held precisely to consider the impact of ethical considerations on the behaviour of the individual. In the US, in particular, several issues have gained increasing attention—thanks to an unrelenting pursuit of individual rights. Some of these are:

- Equal opportunities for women and minorities;
- Rights of the individual to 'blow the whistle' on unethical practices;

- Right not to be asked questions about one's age in job applications; and
- Of course, the recently renewed interest in ensuring freedom from sexual harassment at work.

No business can hope to make much headway in the West unless it addresses these ethical issues.

In India, the interface of the individual with the corporation has been dictated by other considerations. In the main, the differences from situations in the West arise from the fact that our markets for labour are not yet as fiercely competitive and there is still an apparent excess of supply over demand—even if the situation is fast changing.

This is all the more reason to provide sufficient guidelines and rules in the company to encourage the individual to act honourably and in the interests of the company. To expect an employee to tell white lies to a customer in order to close a sale, or suppress material facts, or take shelter under purely legalistic definitions, is to invite trouble for the company in the long run.

A top manager who condones less than ethical behaviour, even implicitly, runs a serious risk. Next time, he may be a victim of the same risk. What stops the employee, who is patted on the back for cleverly procuring the market plans from a competitor for a certain price, from doing the reverse for purely personal profit?

Unfortunately, not all businessmen take this view. They feel that competition is warfare, that all is fair in war, and, therefore, running such ethical risks is all part of the game. As the rank of such businessmen swells, with laudatory epithets such as street mart, hard-nosed and savvy, the image of business in the public eye, undergoes a major change, as it has done: from being creators of wealth and providers of opportunity, they become predators and exploiters of resources, including human ones. Sadly, this deteriorates further into the view that all business, eventually, is self-serving and market economists must be subject to rigorous constraints and controls.

FACETS OF BUSINESS ETHICS

Business ethics is not concerned with bribing and getting things done. In other words, a businessman does not become ethical simply by not accepting or offering bribes. That would be too reductive, and a narrow view of what, in essence, is applicable to every human act. It covers the whole gamut of activities including quality, keeping up promises, transparency and reporting of financial performance, not evading taxes and so on. I shall briefly look at six of these in detail.

HAWKING POOR QUALITY PRODUCTS

This ought to be against any businessman's dharma. It is the duty of every entrepreneur to ensure that he gives products of the highest quality to his customers. The pursuit of quality—whether by total quality management (TQM), total productive maintenance (TPM), or whatever method—is a lifetime engagement. There are no permanent benchmarks. One needs to surpass all benchmarks and break the records set by himself, as far as quality is concerned. It is an accepted fact that the quality of workmanship that we had in gold ornaments and household utensils in the past is far superior to what we have today. The reason is that the workmen in those days considered themselves as creators and not appendages to a manufacturing process. The goldsmith, the ironsmith and the carpenter were all known as *vishwakarmas,* meaning *creators.* Extending the same notion, the potters, the weavers and the cobblers are also creators. Poets, artists and architects are also creators. Every employee should then become a creator.

There was a Chinese carpenter who was asked to make a cabinet. He was a very skilled carpenter and so he made this beautiful cabinet which was supposed to go into the recess of a wall. When he finished the cabinet, he started polishing the back of the cabinet. So his apprentice asked him, 'Master, the cabinet is going to go into the recess of the wall and then cemented. Nobody is going to look at the back once it is in. So why are you spending so much time on polishing the back of the cabinet?' The man said, 'Yes, I know it is going to go into the wall—nobody would see it, but I would know. That is why I'm polishing it.' That is ethics. That is creation.

KEEPING PROMISES

This is something that is essential for survival in any business. It could be promises made to the customers, the employees, or the contractors. It is in the enlightened self-interest of entrepreneurs to honour the promises made by them, because business is built on trust and relationships which will get eroded the moment the entrepreneur is seen as lacking in integrity and honesty. In 1942, our company, TVS, ran a bus service in Madurai. Three hundred buses in fifty different groups. One of the guiding visions was that every bus will come to the busstop on time—every busstop, every day, every bus. Until it was nationalized in 1974, all buses ran on time, so much so, in Madurai people used to say, 'The time the bus comes to the busstop, you can adjust your watch.' That is keeping promises. The founders believed in honouring promises made to the customers. If only every transport corporation and airline service had kept up their time schedules, India would have turned out to be a better place to live in as far as transport is concerned.

WINDOW DRESSING OF BALANCE SHEETS

Many companies resort to window dressing to attract investments and fudge the balance sheet in order to cheat workers of their rightful entitlements—be it bonus or ex gratia payments or indulging in unethical practices. This is as much as a person who sells adulterated foods and medicines.

SUPRA-NORMAL PROFITS

This is something dear to monopolies and mostly attempted by the short-run or fly-by-night operators. For the long haul, it is essential that we share the benefits with all those who are part of the business. If we squeeze the suppliers too much, we can be let down in a critical situation. This is true with customers and also with employees. The objective of a business is not just to maximize value for shareholders but rather to deliver balanced value in a manner that benefits all stakeholders and society.

Let me give you an example—again from our company, a long time ago, during the war years. There was a time when TVS used to import oil engines, which were in great demand in India during the war. Though the market price was close to something like ₹18,000, TVS sold these engines to dealers for ₹10,000, because we imported them at ₹9,000. The dealers used to take these engines—buy them from us, take them out of the gate—and sell them at ₹18,000 , making a ₹8,000 profit; whereas the company made only a ₹1000 profit. But at the end of the war, when things became normal, everybody came back to TVS; nobody went to those people who sold it for ₹18,000. So, there is a price to be paid if you want to be unethical. It is a long-term price. Milking the customers can give benefits in the short run, but will end up ruining the relationship built over a long period of time. Relationships are more precious than short-term profits. Several studies in the US report that it costs six times as much to develop a new customer as it does to sell to an existing one.

Compliance with the Laws and Statutes

To be a good, clean, corporate citizen in the country in which it operates is a moral binding on any business. The laws, for example, prohibit theft, enforce contracts, set limits to advertising and re-enforce many moral norms. Flouting or circumventing laws is sometimes seen as a smart thing to do, but it is, in the long run, not the nicest policy. We must also remember that that which is ethical need not always be covered by law. Often the law underscores only the non-negotiable minimum.

Concern for the Local Community

In the area in which your factories and offices are located, it pays to develop a harmonious relationships. Apart from providing employment to people from the local areas around a new project site, every company can contribute to some social cause. A few organizations have instilled a sense of purpose that has become a hallmark of why they exist. They have transformed noble and lofty sentiments into heartfelt responses from their employees, their customers and their stakeholders.

One fairly sustainable distinction in the public mind is the company's civic and ethical character. All the research evidence suggests that it is much more difficult to duplicate an organizational culture and a way of operation than technology, strategy or even products or services. That is why culture and organizational capability are increasingly becoming important sources of organizational success, and ethical behaviour by organizations tops this list.

A large corporation is respected—even venerated, and sometimes feared or vilified—for its economic might. Many have turnovers greater than the gross national products of several developing countries in which they do business. Discomfort and suspicion about the wisdom of allowing trans-border corporations to do business freely is widely prevalent amongst the political leadership in these countries. Such sentiments get strengthened every time one witnesses the massive impact of foreign investment—as in Asia, in recent months. No distinction is made between established corporations and dealers in hot money. All become suspects until they are proved innocent. The interface between corporations and society is now multi-faceted and very complex. Technology, deregulation, instantaneous communication and size and scope all make businesses subject to global pressures. Standards do differ between countries as to what is acceptable in business conduct. It is well known that eastern countries—at least in theory—tolerate a much higher level of speed money, commissions and favours in kind than the rest of the world. It is all easy to say, When in Rome, do as the Romans do.' One can only too easily take shelter under customs and traditions and turn a blind eye to all forms of corrupting influences. Unfortunately, this turns out to usually be a one-way street.

The more one condones, the more one is expected to stretch the limits of acceptable conduct. Where do you draw the line? That is the uncomfortable question.

I have found that the only way that lets you work peacefully and with commitment to your goals, is to draw the line—very clearly and with great clarity and finality—even before you start. If you make your organization, as well as its partners and constituencies, know what you will tolerate and what you will not, you can live with your conscience. Once you give room to the perception that everything has a price, you cannot be surprised if someone bids for everything that you have built.

Being ethical as a business, of course, cannot be achieved by one person alone. The leader, the CEO, however, has the duty to spell out what the organization stands for—its beliefs, values and what it will and will not accept.

The leader must begin by uncompromisingly being a good law abiding citizen himself, and make it clear that he intends to lead a company that behaves as a good corporate citizen.

This demands, firstly, as a minimum, willing compliance with all the laws of the country, without exception. One has to pay one's dues. Next, one has to deliver what is expected by laws governing health, safety, environment, equal opportunity, consumer rights, employee welfare—just to mention a few.

Yet, one quickly recognizes that compliance is—by no means—everything. In fact, it's just the beginning. Companies that are conscious of their responsibilities, especially in a developing country, have always done more. They have tried to be ahead of what is demanded by legislation. It is interesting to recall that some of the pioneers of industry in this country belonged to this category. People like J.R.D. Tata were visionaries who offered to do for the country so much more than what was strictly called for in legislation or law. The Bombay Plan and the establishment of exceptional institutions of research and scholarship are but two of the many initiatives one can recall. Tata Steel was a new national benchmark in standards of employee and community health, welfare and security.

All this is mentioned only to underline the notion that ethical behaviour is all-encompassing, positive and proactive, and not some vague philosophy or idea limited only to a few people.

In the Western world, business leaders have had to contend with the rising crescendo of demands for greater transparency in all that business does. Beginning with the process of raising funds, to detailed division-wise finances in their annual report, to conforming to every new green lobby, agitation, and taking evasive action against consumer-led litigations, the CEOs have seen it all.

It is important to realize that no one can anticipate all ethical dilemmas. Business today is so complex and increasingly uncertain that the average manager's repertoire of responses cannot fully cope with the challenge of acting out of a written manual. He must, therefore, be free from the added anxiety of risking the displeasure of his boss. If he takes a particular step in keeping with what he sees as right and the proper thing to do under a given circumstance, he should be truly at ease with his manager's will to back him up. In the absence of this confidence, an organization will eventually fail to be fully responsible and responsive.

Companies such as IBM, Unilever, ABB and 3M make it abundantly clear what the guiding principles of their businesses are—they are all on the internet. They then have to hold themselves accountable to these principles. This is, indeed, a big step for the widely regarded, highly visible corporations to take, and one can take it only when the leadership is confident that the organization, and the leadership themselves, can 'walk the talk', as they say in America. I think it is time, in India, that we not only tell society what we stand for in terms of ethics—make it public, advertise in papers, put it on the internet—so that people have the right to ask and expect what we stand for.

For that, indeed, is the crux of the matter. The corporation, its management and all its functions are set in the context of society. As the standard of expectation of the numbers in society change and become elaborate, so, too, does the scope of ethics in the business world.

A SUMMARY

The nature of the relationship between ethics and business is both wide and complex and fundamental to doing business, whether today or 2001 years ago.

The dominant paradigm in business and management, of late, has been the primacy of the shareholder value. The total performance of the enterprise is measured, sometimes, by one number, denoting the economic value added. Of course, any thinking manager will agree even after a moment's reflection that this one number reflecting the creation of wealth over and above what would have been earned by an average firm is not everything. But it does give one simple yardstick to measure performance in a standardized way across industries and even countries. The business world, I believe, needs to have a similar agreed measurement to which the broad majority of thinkers and actors in the management field will agree, about what ethics in business should be. This is not an idealist wish, but, I think, a survival need.

9

Role of Business in Ecological Security: An Ethical Perspective*

AMRITA PATEL

It has been my privilege and pleasure to make the acquaintance of JRD's successor, Ratan Tata, whom I have met on a number of occasions. I have also studied with pleasure and considerable respect the 'Tata Code of Conduct', set out for the first time in a booklet as an *aide-mémoire* for every Tata employee. I believe the inspiration for this was Ratan Tata himself. It does him great credit and is an example that every corporate house should emulate. What has aroused my curiosity, however, is the extent to which it is, can be, and will be followed both in letter and spirit by Tata employees. It is one thing to commit such a code to paper; it is entirely another, especially in this day and age, to translate it truly into practice. I hope, most sincerely, that the Tata Code of Conduct will become—if it has not already—systemic to the minds and hearts of at least every officer of the Tata organization, even at the cost of profitability and growth, so that the organization comes to be looked upon as the pinnacle of business enlightenment in the all-pervading gloom of contemporary corruption. Such unshakeable adherence to ethical practice will demonstrate to all and sundry that, to use the old hackneyed expression, 'honesty is the best policy.' To introduce and establish the culture to make this possible will require not merely the steadfast example of all Tata chief executive officers, but strong, firm and sustained direction from every member of the higher echelons of each company of the organization to all employees, besides constant

*Oration delivered on 10 October 1999.

peer pressure and example. One sincerely hopes that there are men and women at the commanding heights of each Tata company with the strength of character to exorcize deviant behaviour, no matter the cost. I say all this in no way to act high priestess to the House of Tata, but more as a shipwrecked woman, afloat in a turbulent sea of corruption, who finds a lifeboat that by the grace of God chances her way, and prays desperately that the Almighty takes it ashore.

I have often been sorely tempted to persuade Ratan Tata to discuss this code with me to gain some insights into the circumstances that led the Tatas to frame what they have now explicitly enunciated. I discovered very quickly that while Ratan is undoubtedly a man of considerable substance, he is also a man of few words and cannot easily be drawn out!

With the level of corruption, and generally the loss of standards of morality, now evident in all aspects of the public life of our country, the subject of business ethics is of greater relevance today than at any time since India gained independence. Somewhere along the way, the larger purpose of government and business has been lost and their place taken by greed and venality. The credibility of public officials has descended to such depths that throughout the country, decent, articulate sections of opinion have come to despise the very political process itself. And as is well-established, the contempt of democratic politics sows the seeds of authoritarianism. Similarly, the contempt for buccaneering business is matched only by an acute sense of helplessness in the face of the burgeoning nexus between businessmen on the one hand, and the political and bureaucratic classes on the other.

The sense of service to the community and the country, in the best ethical sense of the term, seems peripheral—or at best incidental—to the pursuit of business instead of being central to it. With a few honourable exceptions, business appears to the lay public to be largely self-seeking with little or no concern for moral and ethical considerations. The way business is now conducted gives the impression that businessmen operate on the premise that the ends—namely, maximising profit and growth—justify the means. A no-holds-barred approach seems to be the name of the game. What seems important is not to be caught doing wrong; and if one is, the important thing is to have the cash to bribe oneself out. The baneful influence of this mindset appears also to have pervaded the country's administration—the bureaucracy—and its momentum is spreading like a plague and seems to be beyond control. It is those small, few and far between beacons of light and hope appearing like glow-worms in the spreading darkness, such as the 'Tata Code of Conduct', that bring some hope of the dawn of a new day to those frail voices of morality and reason which today pray for the restoration of a more just, humane and equitable society.

I paint this picture of gloom deliberately, and I believe rightfully from the evidence I see and hear, and I shall tell you why. While, as chairman of the National Dairy Development Board, it is my privilege to be associated with the largest of India's co-operative movements, I can only say that after thirty-five years of the closest involvement at all levels, from the grassroot-level upwards, this is often a cross that I also have to bear—because of the constant, intimate and all too often painful exposure it gives me to the ugly realities on the ground. Ours is a far-flung and widespread network encompassing a total membership of some ten million farmers located in over 97,000 villages covering almost every state of our country. This not only takes me to many parts of the country, but also brings me into close contact with our people in all walks of life—from dairy farmers to ministers, from village co-operative secretaries to chief ministers and ministers of states, from extension workers to chief secretaries, from village panchayats to bureaucrats at all levels in the central and state administration, from elected co-operative leaders to businessmen of every description—big and small. As I interact with them and look around at the landscape that comprises this wonderful country of ours, and look beyond, I now find myself assailed by another and much greater sense of apprehension—sometimes verging on despair at what is happening to this country of ours. I see a scenario emerging that encompasses a new and deeply disturbing dimension that portends a disaster of cataclysmic proportions. This disaster will surely occur if today's decision-makers remain insulated and oblivious in their urban ivory towers. If they fail to recognize the emerging crisis and act, each and every one of us will be affected—individually and collectively. It is imperative that decision-makers in all areas of socio-economic endeavour not merely appreciate the implications of this emerging crisis, but realize that the crisis and its causes lie at the core of the ethical concerns on which the whole of their social and business edifice and endeavours rest.

You will be wondering what crisis I am referring to. I can best describe it as an impending crisis of national proportions, arising from the accelerated destruction of the country's ecological foundation, which sustains our very existence. The repercussions of the damage done so far are already evident in varying degrees, the most obvious and critical being the growing water shortage, the widespread water and air pollution, the now annually growing phenomenon of flash floods and droughts, and the disastrous loss of topsoil estimated to be of the order of over six billion tonnes per annum—particularly from our highlands—resulting from the destruction of the country's forest cover which once blanketed and protected these areas.

To the uninitiated among you, a word of explanation may be necessary at this juncture. I start from the premise that all life on earth rests on biological foundations. Virtually everything that sustains the daily existence not only of human beings but of all forms of life on earth, stems from the existence and interaction of the myriad life forms which we, especially in the tropics, have the great good fortune to be endowed with. We have, over the centuries, largely overlooked the need to concern ourselves with the total matrix of the interlocking systems of life forms that constitute the foundation of our existence. It is, however, this web of life that sustains us; we humans are but a fragile strand in what constitutes the most intricate, complex but wondrous web of life. For the first time in human history, we are, today, able to gain holistic glimpses and understanding of this through the technological advances humanity has achieved, particularly in this century. The more I see and sense this all-pervading phenomenon, the greater is my conviction that maintaining the integrity and vitality of this fundamental phenomenon must define the morality, and in its expression the ethics, that must regulate and guide our contemporary business and set the limits of our business ambitions and pursuits. To make this possible, this must now, and hereafter, constitute the steel framed boundary of our economic pursuits and the value systems that guide our daily lives both individually and collectively.

This morality has, in various ways, long been enshrined in the religious concepts and practices of virtually every caste and creed. However, in the prevailing economic systems, with their relentless and an all-consuming pursuit of growth and profitability, this morality has paled to the point of insignificance and fails to be the guiding spirit in our daily lives and ambitions. In our finite world, business has failed to recognize that there are limits to growth and that all too often, profit becomes increasingly unprofitable to all but the fortuitously favoured few. If business is to serve the common weal, as it must—if it is to justify its own existence—it must take cognizance in its practices and professions of these inalienable truths.

To many, the concept of ecological security might well appear esoteric; an aberration that has little or no relevance to contemporary business pursuits and management, and certainly not to the morality and ethics of business. I wonder how many, if any of you, have ever been exposed to the realities of this concept or felt the impact of the increasing neglect, to take these into account in planning for economic development as a whole and business forecasting and practices in particular. Since the dimensions of the impending ecological crisis are so insidious and all-pervading, visualizing its myriad dimensions as discernible and accountable economic concepts that can guide business seems beyond the intellectual capabilities and commercial acumen of all but the most exceptional individuals among us. With the objectives of business now confined to growth and profitability, our blinkered and myopic vision of business opportunities of the future is largely limited to immediate commercial gain and similar short-term prospects measured in opportunities for profit. Growth, today, almost inevitably entails the unrestricted exploitation—the plundering—of our finite and renewable natural resources. The increasing scale of such exploitation grossly exceeds all definable limits of sustainable use. The rapaciousness such growth involves is not only undermining the ecological processes that sustain us in the mid and long term, but in the short term depletes, irretrievably, the resource base of our economic development. Our pursuit of myopic economic objectives compels us to employ technologies that multiply the destruction of the natural resource base that sustains the ecological balance critical to our existence. This cannot continue. This unthinking urge for growth must be moderated by a wider and longer-term perspective—one that recognizes the importance of confining our enterprise to meeting essential needs rather than promoting unrestrained and extravagant consumerism based on creating endless wants.

Those who promote ventures, of any description, that make extravagant and wasteful use of natural resources, or destroy the natural resource foundations of our ecological security, must be made conscious of the long-term implications of their actions. There are far too many examples of industries being established in locations that result in the ravaging of forests and of coastal belts so vital for marine life, and the large scale displacement of local rural and tribal communities. The power of money has leveraged politicians, the bureaucracy and even research institutes that conduct environmental impact studies, to bring them all into line. Tragically, even the spokesmen of NGOs and local communities have often been silenced or turned into false witnesses. One is left wondering whether, with the general loss of ethics and social conscience, it is possible for peer pressure from responsible captains of industry or other enlightened entrepreneurs to correct deviant business behaviour in the community.

A major fallacy of modern economic thinking is that wealth is created from the conversion of natural resources into cash. If there is one thing today that constantly depreciates in value, it is cash. On the contrary, in the circumstances in which we live, what progressively increases in value, besides strengthening our economic foundations, are our finite and living natural resources—in other words, the natural capital with which our country has been so richly endowed. The growth of the country's wealth is directly reflected in the growth of the country's renewable natural capital. The GNP of a country should more appropriately be referred to as the gross natural capital, which regrettably is unaccounted for in our country's annual financial budgets—a gross omission which makes these budgets seriously misleading.

In saying what I have, I need perhaps to elaborate on my concept of ecological security on which I place such vital importance. It is a conviction I have formed and one that I consider is incontrovertible. It is that ecological restoration, by its very nature, not only ensures more equitable access to economic resources and opportunity to all men, but also more adequate availability of sources of sustenance to all other life forms. The first beneficiaries from all efforts to bring about a state of ecological security will be the least-privileged sections of our society—our tribals and rural poor—as this effort will contribute progressively to sustaining what little remains of our rapidly diminishing biological diversity, thereby strengthening the biological foundations of our collective lives.

How do we commence bringing about a state of ecological security? Primarily this entails what our National Forest Policy so sensibly lays down, and I believe this was done more intuitively than by intent but with a remarkable premonition of the crucial role of forests. This is that one-third of our country should have forest cover on what could be called our uplands—that is, our mountains, hills and plateaux, which comprise some 40 per cent of the terrestrial area of the country. It is from there that all our river systems emerge and where the maximum precipitation of rain takes place. It is, therefore, the major source of supply of our fresh water. With true forest cover, and, I must emphasize, not man-made monoculture or polyculture plantations, not only will precipitation significantly increase but there will be far greater water percolation into our soils, thereby recharging sub-soil water sources as well as the deeper aquifers. Such an approach will also drastically reduce the tremendous annual loss of topsoil we now suffer, strengthen our food security as nothing else can, and improve the intrinsic nutritional value of the food we produce by reducing the need for fertilizer, pesticide and artificial irrigation. If carried out rationally on a national scale, this would raise the subsoil water table, which has fallen so precipitously in recent decades, throughout the country and thereby restore the output of the innumerable tube wells that have been sunk in the country, a great many of which are now defunct. Sources other than forests can readily satisfy the need for timber, fuelwood and fodder, but that is another story.

However, it is in addressing all this that our most serious and fundamental problem lies. As I see it, the political support required will be forthcoming only when the relentless advance of this impending crisis denies us the necessities of our daily livelihood. At that juncture, we will in every likelihood find ourselves resorting to technologies that might mitigate our immediate predicament but soon create for us a situation beyond redemption.

It is my belief that it is still possible to initiate a process of ecological restoration leading to ecological security. But time is rapidly running out. In a few years from now, the difficulty in doing so will be infinitely greater, indeed it will require more than our entire GDP to meet the cost. The approach I have outlined is based largely on the exposure I have had, and insights I have gained as the chairman of the National Tree Growers' Co-operative Federation, an organization committed to revegetating wastelands of the country through structures managed by the rural communities directly affected.

Much as I would like to do so, this is not the occasion to elaborate at greater length on how the ecological security of the country can be brought about. My purpose in mentioning it is to reinforce the emphasis I place upon the morality of the ecological dimension forming more than just a casual intellectual curiosity of the business community. Instead, it must now emerge as the anchorage not only of the morality of the business mindset but shape the policies and practices it must follow, however far-fetched this might seem to those obsessed with today's norms of business objectives and theories of business management and practice.

The Dairy Board is responsible for enhancing the production of milk in the country to meet the increasing national demand. As its chairman, I find myself confronted with a serious dilemma and the constant need to ask myself fundamental questions. How far can, and should, the dairy industry go—how much milk can, and should we produce? Today, low-yielding and unproductive animals by the million are simply put out to graze, increasingly on vegetated revenue and forest lands. We recognize all too well the damage to the country's vegetative cover, particularly to the forests, that such cattle are causing. There are finite limits to the carrying capacity of our land. We have, to date, managed to some extent to minimize the competition between man and animal and animal and its environment. While I would like to believe that the Dairy Industry can continue for a while to grow without causing even greater damage than we are to what remains of the delicate ecological balance of our country, we need to take the greatest care in doing so. There are, I repeat, limits to growth—whether we like it or not. We must determine where these limits lie and firmly reject the temptation to grow at a pace that threatens to cross them. At the same time, the dilemma assumes greater dimensions when one considers the fact that for millions of our landless, small and marginal farmers, milk is the only or main source of livelihood. However, I do believe that ecological restoration can, and will revive the biological productivity of our resources, and by doing so, will provide sources of livelihood to our marginal farmers that today are not available. When one looks holistically at our land resources, we see that of the 328.7 million hectares which comprise the geographical area of the country, some 100 million hectares are already officially declared as wastelands and therefore, considered biologically unproductive. This, fortunately, is not the case. Tragically, mismanagement of our land resources is progressively increasing the extent of our wastelands denying thereby nourishment to a growing proportion of our already a billion population. Unless we reverse this trend, the food security of this country will soon be in serious jeopardy. The Dairy Board is committed to increasing milk production through stall feeding, by encouraging village communities to revegetate the wastelands around the villages to raise fodder and refrain from sending their cattle out to graze instead to cut grass and browse and take it to the animals. We are counting on the innate wisdom of our farmers, who recognize all too clearly the long-term benefits of revegetating our barren lands. And we hope this will support efforts to bring about the required change in land use, particularly current cattle grazing practices. Clearly, however, many marginal farmers will not find it possible to live with the restraints that must be imposed and will have to find alternative means of livelihood, hopefully that ecological security will make possible.

Worldwide, more so in our highly populated country, we have reached a point in our existence where we need to seek solutions based on true sustainable development that rests alone on ecological security. This can only come about through a fundamental reassessment of the very value systems and lifestyles we follow and reorient economic development, as Father Thomas the director of XLRI so aptly puts it in his introduction to the institute's 1999 prospectus, to quote him, 'to the cause of service to society and the establishment of a new world order of justice and faith in humanity.'

At ground level, sustainable development has now become an issue between the so-called developing and the developed nations—that is those with moderate or meagre standards of living, and the others indulging, by average world standards, in lifestyles that deplete our natural resources at a totally unsustainable rate. Surely justice demands the latter assume an equitable share of the responsibility in maintaining the world's ecological balance, including the burden of environmental protection by reducing their consumption to sustainable levels. Instead, they aspire to ever-increasing standards of living while using every possible means to persuade the rest of the world to emulate their example! It is estimated that 18 per cent of the world's population lives lifestyles that exploit 80 per cent of the world's resources.

I have noted with special interest one of the Tata Codes that states, 'a Tata company shall be committed to prevent the wasteful use of natural resources and minimise any hazardous impact of the development, production, use and disposal of any of its products and services on the ecological environment.' Though this features somewhat low down in the list of Tata's Code, I am hoping very much that the Tata's will treat it with the seriousness that it deserves. To do so and make this particular Code effective, will of course, depend on the nature of each individual industry, and require a thorough and imaginative field study of the ecological impact of its activities. I would like to take the liberty of urging the Tatas to set up a kind of Nature Conservation and Environmental Protection, Research and Audit Centre charged primarily with the responsibility of examining the operations of each of their companies and determining what changes are necessary in their ways of functioning, to minimize, preferably eliminate any adverse ecological impact they have on their immediate and more distant environment. In addition, and this is even more important, determine as an act of enlightened self-interest, ways in which each company can contribute to strengthening the ecology in and around the locations in which they operate. This will set an example that other industrial groups should follow. In fact, a pioneering venture of this nature could quickly provide professional consultancy to other industries, and, imaginatively developed, soon become self-sustaining, and even profitable. I would urge my friend Dr Irani to bring this suggestion to the attention of the Tata's and persuade the Group to put it into effect. If I may venture to suggest, it should be headed by an experienced environmentalist rather than a technologist. Well-conceived and sincerely implemented, the impact of such a development on the morale of the Group, as well as its public image in this decade of the Environment, could be considerable. It would be well worth the effort and investment. It would represent an outstanding demonstration of the Group's enlightened sense of social responsibility and broad-based contemporary ethical concerns. I foresee it could have a dramatic effect on the Group's business mindsets and operational norms, leading to basic preconceptions of approach to the ways business is and should be conducted. While not intending here to sound pessimistic, I am reminded of the Italian statesman, Nicollo Machiavelli, who said:

'There is nothing more difficult to take in hand, more perilous to conduct or more uncertain in its success than to take the lead in the introduction of a new order of things.'

If the Tata organization will dare to stand up and be counted, and assume the responsibility for introducing such a radically new approach to business ethics and conduct, and succeeds, they will make history and be a catalyst for change that would lead to sustainable development in the truest sense of the term. It would give shape and content to the most appropriate expression that I have yet heard used, and which I consider embodies the totality of the concept of sustainable development that should be the fundamental inspiration hereafter for every code of ethics adopted by business. The expression is, 'Ecological security is the foundation of equitable and sustainable development.' No other definition, I consider, can stand the test of rigorous scrutiny—certainly none of the definitions trotted out by a number of international economic and financial institutions, including the World Bank. The Tatas have been pioneers in many fields of human endeavour. Here is a challenge befitting their stature and reputation and, most of all, their capacity for foresight and their vision of the future.

Well established and appropriate institutions have an important role to play in establishing standards of ethics in society. It has been my good fortune to have been associated for my entire professional life with what I have come to believe is a very ethical form of institution: the co-operative. The very nature of the co-operative as an institution is—or should be—the microcosm of a healthy harmonious society. Each member of a co-operative—just as the member of a polity—is expected to surrender short-term individual gain for the greater long-term good of the group and every one of its individual members. As improbable as such behaviour may appear to be, there are millions of farmers who do, in fact, accept it and who, I believe, have benefited greatly from having done so. It is the basic value of such institutions—co-operation that unites all in purpose and action—that we should promote, encourage, nurture and support; these are institutions where the lessons of ethical, value-based behaviour are learnt and reinforced.

Each of the ten million farmer members owns a small share of his co-operative. Landless, small and marginal farmers constitute over 60 per cent of the membership of dairy co-operatives. Today, more than ₹5,000 crore flows back annually to the ten million members of the dairy co-operatives. The benefits, therefore, reach far more small farmers than it does the wealthier rural population. More importantly, the distribution of profit is equitable. Another principle of co-operation, perhaps less understood, is that it limits return on equity. When co-operative members invest in equity, they are building a business that they realize will benefit them to the extent that they patronize it. They are not investing for a direct immediate return.

Ethics is based on our need to create a society in which common rules of behaviour toward one another and to our environment leads to a fundamental harmony in which individuals and society can advance. Everyday, we are compelled to make choices that either conform to or negate these rules. Such rules often present difficult choices in which conflicting values pull us in different, often opposite directions. But in a democratic society it is the sum total of our individual choices that define not just our society's ethical standards, but in the final analysis, determines its future.

May I make bold to ask each of you to reflect—as I have often tried to reflect myself—on where the causes of the apparent regression in our own society's ethical values and standards of conduct are to be found? Is it in our poor that we see a breakdown of values? Or do we find that this erosion of values stems from amongst the haves and not the have-nots? I doubt that anyone would disagree that it is the wealthy and well-to-do that are responsible. Those who have the wealth, the benefits of education, of health, of access to the material goods and services that are supposed to contribute to the 'quality of life'—it is this part of our society that has abandoned the values of their forefathers and places society at risk by destroying the mutual confidence that is the foundation of a healthy polity.

But why then has our society's elite descended to such depths of immorality? Why does honest ethical behaviour no longer draw more than passing attention? Should it not be the norm? Should we not, rather, be dismayed when we see unethical or dishonest behaviour and react more assertively against it? Instead, we now seem to take it for granted. Is this not particularly strange, given the strict moral norms that our major religions enjoin upon us? Is it not particularly strange, given the sacrifice and the extraordinary high moral standards that the father of our nation, our founding fathers and freedom fighters observed? We are a people with an old civilization, deeply grounded in the morality of the world's major religions, born a free nation through the only example of independence gained through shaming the oppressor by acting ethically at every stage of our fight for freedom. Yet, today we all agree that we have abandoned the age-old spiritual values that are the essence of our heritage.

What we see, what we read, what we hear all suggests that the institutions which should be the guardians of morality, and which should encourage and nurture ethical behaviour, have failed in large measure. The risk—the worst risk of all—is that it should lead to cynicism. For it is cynicism, if it is allowed to persist, that becomes the fertile soil for deep-rooted corruption and dishonesty, and if it once takes hold, becomes difficult to eradicate short of authoritarian rule or revolution.

It is easy to catalogue the evil around us. It is far more difficult to offer solutions. But lest we fall victims of the slough of cynicism and its attendant ills, we should seek ways in which to restore morality in public service and private thinking.

Ethics is ingrained in all of us—indeed, all but genetically programmed through the processes of a long-lasting civilization. This can, and is, however, being quickly overwhelmed by aggressive 'frontiersman' cultures. Such cultures lack the underpinning of a long civilization of cultured, socially responsible behaviour based on living in symbiotic harmony with the natural environment. It is leading us to succumb to the human weaknesses of unrestrained self-advancement and indulgence in the fulfilment of every conceivable material and carnal desire. This is the situation that is rapidly emerging today, and is largely the cause for the loss of ethics among the affluent of our society and the rapidly growing numbers who are relentlessly urged by Western culture and its materialistic ambitions to emulate them. No greater courage, determination and foresight are required than to restrain ourselves from the suicidal inducements offered to create unlimited markets. Yet, without each of us marshalling the courage to resist, it will be the ruination of every one of us and the institutional structures we have so assiduously built, as well as our future generations.

To conclude, I would like to make three points:

Firstly, as I thought about what I should say about the ethics of business today, I was convinced that ethics begins with a fundamental respect for our fellow men. If there is a divinity, it must be intrinsic to all living beings. We must, therefore, respect and express in thought and deed that which is divine in all of us. If we accept this as a beginning then ethical values will progressively take possession of us and soon pervade all of society. I must respect the spiritual values that are a part of others by being truthful to them and being honest in my dealings with them. I must also respect the physical being of others. When faced with ethical dilemmas, I must attempt to resolve them not by trying to ensure that I do the least damage, but that I do no damage, and contribute to the greatest good.

Secondly, I must have confidence that however bleak things may seem to be, there is still evidence that there is a place for ethical behaviour in today's world. A manifest desire is still evident today in our urban middle class in India, as most of us here are, to work for organizations that have a reputation for ethical values and practice. The thousands of individuals who seek, every day, to do what is right, all confirm our desire to be ethical. We will not be alone.

Thirdly, we must act. Gandhiji once said, 'Be the change you want to see in the world.' He also said, 'There is enough for everyone's needs, but not for their greed.' If we want the world to be ethical, if we want our society to invest its energies and talents in building a better life for all of us, then we must each face ethical questions with the courage of our convictions and the facts now evident to all of us and must act by doing what we believe is right. It is acceptable to err in judgement on ethical issues, but not to err in intent and practice. Be, therefore, the change you want to see in others in the world.

We need to remember our own scriptures. We must ensure that equity and justice prevail. Besides, we have an inter-generational responsibility. We are trustees of the welfare of not only those in our country who are starving and unsheltered, but also of future generations. But this will not be possible without—and most importantly—caring for Mother Earth and her very capacity to sustain us all. Viewed from a worldwide perspective, humanity today has gained a stranglehold on the globe's natural resources, both finite and renewable. We must not fail to sustain and use these with caring, moderation and concern to ameliorate not only the privation of those less fortunate than ourselves, but also all other forms of life—over which we have recklessly gained 'dominion' by exploiting several species to extinction and thereby fulfilling, to the extreme, the edicts of Christianity's Old Testament. We have, therefore, failed so far not only in our all-encompassing role as trustees of the Earth, but as exemplars to future generations of society, a responsibility that has been inexorably thrust upon us. We have not just failed—we will have been false to the most sacred of all missions that could have devolved upon any generation of humanity in the past.

As Mikhail Gorbachev, the president of the former USSR and now president of Green Cross and Green Crescent (an international NGO formed by a resolution passed at the largest ever international conference in Rio de Janeiro in 1992, to co-ordinate global environmental initiatives) said, 'The crisis of civilization that we see today is a crisis of the naive belief in the omnipotence of humanity.'

Let me end by saying it is my belief that contemporary man stands today at the crossroads of human history, at a great divide. Unless we of the current generations can pause and take stock of ourselves, our resources and the power we now command, and with a sense of destiny recast the value systems that have made for human progress since the dawn of civilization, we may set in motion forces that will destroy the matrix of the systems of Nature that hold our world as we know it together.

Would that each one of us concerned with ethics in our private and professional lives be missionaries in this cause and find it in our heads and hearts to carry this torch for the rest of our lives, and ensure that we can pass it on to the generations of our fellow beings who follow in our footsteps.

10

Globalization and Corporate Ethics*

ROBERT F. DRINAN

The world is entering a century with unprecedented chances for peace and progress. Humanity now numbers over six billion people—a number that could possibly double in the next century.

Progress in the economic status of humanity has been startling since 1950, but there are still eight million people—half of them children—who are chronically malnourished. In addition, illiteracy is not declining and may even be marginally worse. Many diseases like polio have declined sharply, but other catastrophes like AIDS are now worldwide plagues.

Despite the unsettling and somewhat frightening state of the world, there is evidence everywhere of a new and universal feeling that the world's 190 countries and their major private corporations and non-governmental organizations should agree upon and implement high ethical standards for their conduct.

This feeling reflects the centuries-old standards of decency along with the golden rule adhered to by every religion in the history of the planet. This feeling is deepened by the growing awareness that we have just finished what is, in all probability, the bloodiest century in world history. The twentieth century brought on two world wars, the first and only use of the nuclear weapon, and mass slaughters in Africa and the Balkans.

But in the last hundred years we have also witnessed three important developments: (1) the evolution of a world code of ethics

---

*Oration delivered on 21 December 2000.

for business; (2) a similar movement to promote honesty and openness in government, especially in those nations which are experiencing the emergence of free and fair elections; and (3) a global commitment to internationally recognized human rights as synthesized by the final statement of 172 nations at the World Conference on Human Rights in Vienna, in 1993.

Let us talk together about these welcomed developments. They are closely interwoven, and are indeed inseparable. All three must be observed if the new century is to experience the rule of law.

ETHICAL STANDARD FOR CORPORATIONS

It is a truism that multi-national corporations—like citizens everywhere—have an inherent ethical duty to act like good citizens. Increasingly, corporations recognize and seek to fulfil their moral obligations. Citicorp, for example, with nearly 90,000 employees in ninety different countries, adheres to and communicates key ethical standards in several ways.

Your own country has many such examples. The most noteworthy perhaps is the Tata Code of Conduct. It states clearly what it stands for:

> The Tata name represents more than a century of ethical conduct of business in a wide array of markets and commercial activities in India and abroad. As the owner of the Tata mark, Tata Sons Limited wishes to strengthen the Tata brand by formulating the Tata Code of Conduct, enunciating the values which have governed and shall govern the conduct and activities of companies associating with or using the Tata name and of their employees.

Codes promulgated by corporations and regulatory bodies continue to multiply. Some companies like Nike, General Motors (GM) and IBM, want to be seen as 'socially responsible' and issue codes governing all types of activities by their employees.

In am interview that J.R.D. Tata gave to a correspondent of *The Economic Times,* he categorically states that Jamshetji Tata and his approach to being a good corporate citizen has been the major influence in his life. He says, and I quote:

> The prime influence in my career in Tatas, was certainly that which was inspired by Jamshetji Tata. Jamshetji was a towering personality in every sense, and above all, he was a man of vision. At a time when the British were skeptical about Indians setting up a steel plant, Jamshetji never had any doubts whatsoever. Even though there were several vicissitudes, TISCO emerged as the largest entity in the country. The same could be said about its entry into the power generation business and also hoteliering. I don't think anyone was on par with Jamshetji as an industrial visionary. But that is not the sole reason why I have been an admirer of Jamshetji. The major reason was his sense of values—sterling values—which he imparted to this group. If someone were to ask me, what holds the Tata companies together, I would say it is our shared ideals and values as a corporate citizen, which we have inherited from Jamshetji Tata.

In recent years, the Sullivan principles for South Africa were uniquely successful in ending the Apartheid. The MacBride Principles for Northern Ireland effectively sought to deter corporations from conducting business in that nation until they observed human rights. Codes urging the termination of business with Burma are among dozens of aspirational statements exhorting corporations to seek an ethical norm superior to business as usual.

Other codes of conduct for corporations have been issued by the Interfaith Center on Corporate Responsibility in the United States and its counterparts in the UK and Canada. These normative statements make it clear that corporate leaders anxious for business growth should not make plans without looking at the faces and lives of those oppressed by poverty.

It is undeniable that the leaders of multi-national businesses want to be good corporate citizens. A multiplication of codes and declarations echo the aspirations of business schools everywhere. The Harvard Graduate Business School, along with virtually all schools of this nature, give extensive and intensive instruction in business ethics.

XLRI has been the pioneer in providing a core course of instruction on ethics in business in India. Father William Tome, the former director of XLRI and an eloquent proponent of ethics in business, has ensured that the vision of the founders of XLRI, for itself and for its service to the nation, is best realized by this course on ethics. Fathers Theo Mathias and Cyriac have kept alive this spirit and made it into a living tradition of XLRI.

It is not just one core course that makes the contribution of XLRI unique. It is the overall approach of the whole Institute, in its teaching, training, research and publishing, that brings home to the students as well as to the managers who come here for training that ethics in business should be a way of life.

This wholehearted commitment of XLRI, to adhering to and propagating ethics in business, has been duly recognized by all the leading industrial houses of the country, and in a special way, by the Tata companies. It is this recognition that led the Tata Sons and its then chairman, J.R.D. Tata, to set up the Foundation for Ethics some ten years ago.

Perhaps the best-known of the codes for corporations was drawn up in Caux, Switzerland, as a result of the meetings held each year in Caux by leaders of the world business community. Subtitled 'Business Behaviour for a Better World,' the Caux Principles express standards for improving economic and social conditions.

The Caux Principles are grounded in the ethical ideals of the Japanese concept of *kyosei* and the more western concept of 'human dignity.' *Kyosei* means living and working together for the common good, in ways that enable cooperation and mutual prosperity to exist with healthy and fair competition. Human dignity refers to the sacredness of each human being as an end, not simply as a means to the benefit of others.

The preamble of the Caux Principles sums up the moral and ethical standards that are the essence of the worldwide aspirations for universal ethical norms for corporations. The preamble states very firmly that 'laws and market forces are necessary but insufficient guides for conduct.' Corporations must be responsible for their actions and policies. A 'commitment to shared prosperity' is essential in the operation of a corporation, especially since 'business can be a powerful agent of positive social change.'

The preamble ends by affirming the 'centrality of moral values in economic decision making.'

The seven broad principles of the Caux Declaration synthesize all of the major moral and ethical values which are contained in the ever increasing number of reaffirmations of desirable business practices.

The first principle makes it clear that a corporation has 'a role to play in improving the lives of all of its customers, employees and shareholders by sharing with them the wealth it has created.'

Corporations must be 'responsible citizens' from whom competitors can expect a 'spirit of honesty and fairness.'

Corporations should contribute to human rights, education and welfare. Corporate behaviour should be characterized by 'sincerity, candour, truthfulness, the keeping of promises and transparency.'

Corporations are also required to protect and where possible, improve the environment. This last warning expresses the spirit of the Caux Principles: 'a corporation in the exercise of its vast power, must be guided not by the law alone, but by the "centrality of moral values in economic decision-making."'

Business entities are also reminded that 'their own behavior, although legal, may still have adverse consequences.'

The third section of the Caux Principles endorses several specific ethical directives as to how corporations should treat customers, employees, investors, suppliers, competitors and communities. The concepts of openness, fairness and human dignity permeate the statement.

Those who are sometimes critical of the behaviour of some corporations will be edified at the commitments made by the adherents to the Caux Principles. They include a pledge to support 'human rights and democratic institutions' and to cooperate 'with those forces which are dedicated to raising standards of health, education and work place safety.'

While studying the Caux Principles, one has to ponder upon what the world would look like if most multi-national corporations followed them. Understandably, the world would be much better off, but corporations would still be hindered by the political forces that hinder democracy and repress human rights. In addition, corporations are increasingly subject to sudden scientific discoveries that make their products obsolete. Corporations are also subject to developments in world trade beyond their control. When the World Trade Organization is fully operational, corporations may be able to foresee their activities on the world scene better than they can at the present time. But the directors of global corporations will always need to deepen their commitments to the moral and ethical principles in the Caux pronouncements.

Another eminent source of corporate ethics is the Interfaith Declaration that originated in 1993. Drafted with Jews, Christians and Muslims in mind, the Interfaith Declaration concentrates on those values which are central to the Abrahamic religions. They include justice, fairness, love for others, stewardship for natural resources, honesty and integrity.

An inspection of both the Caux Principles and the faith-based Interfaith Declaration may suggest to some observers that, ultimately, an ethic for the global village may need more than a secularistic approach. That is the conclusion of Father Hans Kung's writing in the volume *International Business Ethics,* edited by George Enderle. Father Kung, a world renowned Roman Catholic theologian, wonders whether materialism or a non-religious ethic can resolve the world's social problems without the prophetic messages of Judaism, Christianity, Islam, Hinduism and Buddhism.

Father Kung relies on the 1993 Declaration of the Parliament of the World's Religions, which stresses the golden rule and urges all business executives to respect life and the age-old directives to deal honestly and fairly. In an eloquent statement, the authors of the *Declaration Issued by the Parliament on the World's Religions* plead for a sense of moderation instead of an unquenchable greed for money, prestige and consumption. The statement warns that in greed, 'humans lose their soul, their freedom and their inner peace.'

Some observers of the international scene are sceptical about the value of pronouncements concerning ethical norms. After all, the hundred largest multi-national corporations account for one-third for the world's direct investment. These gigantic entities deserve credit for enhancing global productivity and economic growth.

They are nonetheless an inextricable component of the worldwide maldistribution of resources.

The ongoing forces of globalization may seem at times to negate the force of ethical norms. Events unfold with unplanned impact on everything. The world, for example, will end up with three currencies—the US dollar, the euro and the yen. The present 175 independent currencies will be tied to one of these three. Will monetary issues tend to displace political sovereignty? Will these forces make economic and social planning difficult, if not impossible? Will governments and local economic units be so anxious for new markets that they will neglect human needs and environmental concerns? Will governments fear marginalization if they do not make compromises to win the favour of monetary blocs and the largest of the transnational corporations? Concern for business ethics may be something that can be engulfed by economic and global forces beyond the control, or even the anticipation, of individual governments.

One of the emerging issues in world law is the capacity of victims in one nation to sue a multi-national corporation in its home country. The victims of India's Bhopal disaster sued Union Carbide in the US courts. Texaco was sued by a group of Amazonian Indians for environmental damage in Ecuador. And Shell Oil is the defendant in a suit brought by victims in Nigeria; the case rests on the contention that Shell Oil is an accessory of the government of Nigeria.

The world has been scrutinizing multi-national corporations since their emergence after World War II. These vast entities seek to operate in all of the hundred new nations that emerged from the ashes of colonialism in the years 1945–1975. But the ambitions of these companies to bring resources to the two billion people who reside in those newly independent countries cannot be realized unless these nations are substantially free of political corruption. It is to that closely related topic that we now turn our attention.

THE GLOBAL NEED FOR STABLE AND HONEST GOVERNMENTS

A group named Transparency, Inc., an international anti-corruption coalition headquartered in Berlin, has opined that while there were pockets of corruption in the underdeveloped nations thirty years ago, there is now a form of corruption that is thoroughly entrenched in the global marketplace. George Moody Stuart, the chairman of the British chapter of Transparency, Inc., stated in 1994 that corruption in the governments of the developing world is now the rule rather than the exception.

Corruption is a strong word. It denotes the persistence of bribery, with all of its demoralizing consequences, to those who give and those who receive the bribes. When it is known by the citizens of developing countries that the government officials receive bribes from foreign corporations, they despise everyone in the transaction. This, of course, poisons the atmosphere and leads to the cynicism that is the inevitable consequence of institutionalized corruption.

A book written by Richard DeGeorge and published in 1993 by Oxford University Press entitled *Competing with Integrity in International Business,* grapples with the complex problem facing corporations that desire to preserve integrity while operating in a corrupt environment. Techniques to be used include adherence to sound ethical principles and persistence in patience, perseverance, publicity, honest reporting and courageous conduct.

Corporations seeking business in underdeveloped countries have tangled moral dilemmas to resolve. Is the dominant purpose of the corporation to return profits to its shareholders? Or are there larger purposes going beyond the maximization of profits? This thorny question is explored in the 1999 *Journal of Business Ethics* from page 319 to 334.

Pervasive bribery and other forms of corruption may be painfully present in developing countries, but the tide of world opinion against those businesses appears to be rising. Since 1983, the biennial International Anti-corruption Conference (IACC) has become the premier global forum for networking and cross-fertilization for corporate and government executives who are anxious to curb corruption. The Attorney General of India is one of the nine top executives of the IACC.

The statement of the IACC issued in Lima in 1997 signals a new clarity and a deeper commitment to the phasing-out of corruption in its myriad forms. The Lima Declaration, the work of over 1,000 citizens from ninety-three countries and all the continents, affirms that corruption violates the rights of the poor and vulnerable, undermines democracy, thwarts the rule of law, retards development and denies society the benefits of free and open competition.

The final declaration at the IACC in Durban in 1999 was even more explicit and sweeping than the statement from Lima. Attended by 1,600 participants from 135 countries, the conference characterized corruption as one of the most debilitating legacies of the twentieth century. The Durban conference reaffirmed and strengthened the Lima gathering's denunciations of corruption. Corruption 'deepens poverty, debases human rights, degrades the environment, derails development and destroys confidence in democracy and the legitimacy of governments.'

In its desire for transparency, accountability and integrity, the Durban pronouncement praised the Organisation for Economic Co-operation and Development (OECD) convention against the bribery of public officials in international business transactions. Praise was also offered to the United States Foreign Corruption Practice Act, which disallows tax deductibility for bribes given by the US corporations to foreign officials or entities.

The Durban conference recognized the holistic nature of the problem and made a plea to every sector of society to offer its services. An appeal was made to curb the levels of money-laundering and to facilitate the 'return to developing countries of monies looted by their leaders.' A special note of gratitude was expressed for the anti-corruption efforts of the Organization of American States (OAS). Support was also offered to actions of the United States that would criminalize all forms of corruption. The hope was expressed that the World Trade Organization would play a key role in the struggle to abolish corruption.

It is uniquely encouraging to view the vast array of global activities designed to help corporations everywhere fulfill their ethical aspirations. The directives of the Caux movement and the worldwide efforts of Transparency, Inc. offer solid evidence that new and profound efforts are underway to set high ethical standards for businesses and for governments in the new century.

Business schools, corporate leaders and political officials all around the world are following closely the interwoven forces, which after the horrors of forty years of the Cold War, want to foster a form of capitalism, which will bring economic decency as well as political stability to the world's poor and vulnerable.

The task is almost insuperable. But it cannot be evaded or avoided. The globalization of virtually every facet of human existence requires—and indeed compels—corporations and governments to develop, as rapidly as possible, a system that distributes the world's goods in equitable ways so that the fifth of humanity that now lives in circumstances unworthy of the human condition can, in the future, obtain dignity, decency and justice.

Those who are developing ethical standards for business and those who work at the global conference in Lima and Durban to create norms of public morality will continue to struggle with the best moral guidelines they can discover. But those individuals will readily admit that they need some globally accepted spiritual standards on which their work can be based. These groups can profitably point to the basic moral tenets of the world's religions. But they need more than the private creed of believers around the world. They need some norms which are universally accepted as binding and have some juridical applicability. Business ethicists and government reformers feel the need of some international norms which will find acceptance from the world's 190 nations, and most especially, from the juridical systems of these nations.

These are few such international norms, but the global moral revolution surrounding internationally recognized human rights comes closest. The United Nations and the Universal Declaration of Human Rights, along with the score of human rights conventions issued by the United Nations, increasingly offer the world the opportunity to anchor its aspirations in the achievements of an amazing array of newly adopted juridical safeguards, agreed to by the vast majority of nations in the global village.

An evaluation of those new guarantees could bring hope that the deep desire for a new regime that outlaws governmental corruption will be rooted in the norms of what is rapidly becoming customary international law.

HUMAN RIGHTS: THE ULTIMATE SOURCE OF BUSINESS ETHICS

During the darkest days of World War II, the allied nations—the United States, the UK, France, China and the USSR—agreed on the outlines of the Charter of the United Nations. That document—unlike the League of Nations—inserted the term 'human rights' on five different occasions in the Charter of the United Nations. The Universal Declaration of Human Rights, adopted on 10 December 1948 by all of the countries then in the United Nations, spelled out the political and economic rights which are the heritage of every being. For the first time in the history of humanity, nations made a contract with each other, and the world, with a solemn pledge that they would individually and collectively work to guarantee basic minimum standards of economic well-being as well as the right to literacy, health and economic stability.

The Covenants of Economic and Political Rights unfortunately separated in the 1950s because of the Cold War, but were accepted in 1966 and entered into force as a customary international law in 1976. The economic rights now agreed to by some 130 nations are clearly expounded and now the birthright of every human being.

The political rights indicated in the UN Covenant on Civil and Political Rights (CCPR) are well-defined. Freedom of speech, religious liberty and the right to procedural due process along with equal protection are increasingly taken for granted. The right to an open and fair government, the right to vote and the right to be free of exploitation by domestic and international corporations, has, as a result of recent international law, become rights that eventually should be routine.

The economic rights also indicated by the United Nations Covenant on Economic, Social and Cultural Rights (CESCR) are now emerging as obligations under customary international law. These rights are as specific as the rights to housing and health. There are United Nations entities that monitor the compliance of all the signatories to the several human rights treaties of the United Nations. Each nation is required to report, at stated times, its efforts to fulfill the pledges it made to carry out the objectives of the political and economic covenants of the United Nations.

As a result, a body of knowledge is being gathered as to how the members of the United Nations are behaving. That accumulated knowledge has not yet come to the attention of the world in ways which would embarrass nations and induce them to improve their performance.

There is also, now available, a comparative rating on how nations conform their conduct to international norms of human rights. Just as we all know the rates of infant mortality, average longevity and literacy in all nations, we will soon be able to judge nations as to how well they comply with the pledges they have made to observe internationally recognized human rights.

In addition, the nations of the earth are now much more sensitive to the human rights of newly identified groups, such as the indigenous (200 million in the world) and the mentally and physically handicapped.

A new and powerful acknowledgement of the universality of human rights occurred at the United Nations World Conference on Human Rights held in Vienna in 1993. After the collapse of the Soviet empire in 1990, the United Nations decided to invite all of the members of the UN to come together to reformulate the legacy of human rights laws, which the family of nations had received from the United Nations Charter and the Universal Declaration of Human Rights. As a delegate at the Vienna conference on behalf of the American Bar Association, this writer witnessed the evolution, over nine long days, of the magnificent declaration on human rights signed by the 172 nations present at the Vienna gathering. The affirmations made by the United Nations and its subsidiary organizations over the past forty-seven years were enlarged and re-endorsed. The Vienna declaration, moreover, can be categorized as a customary international law, since it is the contemporaneous acceptance, by the community of nations, of the human rights agreed to in the Vienna codification.

When corporations, governments and non-governmental organizations reaffirm and follow the Vienna declaration, they are not appealing to some higher statement of ideals made by the United Nations or the forty-eight nations that sponsored the Universal Declaration in 1948. The family of nations in the year 2000 can and must proclaim its allegiance to the global statement made in Vienna in 1993, because this declaration is world law, binding on every sovereign nation on the planet.

There is, therefore, a new and compelling link between all nations and all corporations of the world. A reformulated and broadened charter of human rights is now the law of the universe. It is a beautiful reaffirmation by every nation—indeed of all the people of the earth—of the fundamental moral and ethical priorities of humankind.

The United States was one of the principal architects of the Vienna conference. America, however, has not been a model with regard to its obligations under the Human Rights Covenants of the United Nations. The United States has not ratified the Covenant on Economic Rights or the Covenants on the Rights of Women and Children. Nor has America ratified the Inter-American Covenant on Human Rights. The United States is also, in my judgement, seriously delinquent in its duties because of its refusal to ratify the International Criminal Court—a plan designed to create a permanent Nuremberg.

The United States Congress did, however, proclaim its devotion to internationally recognized human rights when the US Congress in 1975 enacted Section 502b of the International Foreign Assistance Act. That section makes it illegal for the United States to give economic or military aid to nations where there has been a persistent pattern of conduct that denies internationally recognized human rights.

My vote for the bill in Congress reflected the deep desire of all Americans at that time to make a ringing affirmation of the country's devotion to human rights. In Jimmy Carter's presidency (1977-1981), the United States, as never before and never since, emphasized the majesty of human rights and their supreme place in the ideals and values that bind all nations together in their quest for the rule of law.

The law that contains Section 502b also created the annual State Department report concerning the conditions of human rights in every nation in the world. Each year, that 2,000-page document reveals the abuse of human rights in every nation of the world. The assessment seeks to be objective, but the report chronicles all of the major violations of human rights in the world.

The enhancement of ethics and the elimination of governmental corruption can be accelerated if all nations and all corporations could be guided by the vast accumulation of information about human rights around the world.

Some will ask whether the concept and the language employed to describe human rights can be understood and followed by the whole world. The answer is a resounding 'yes.' The framers of the United Nations and the authors of the Universal Declaration of Human Rights agreed that their ultimate concepts about God and the divine origin of law may have been different. But the moral concepts they introduced into the United Nations and the Universal Declaration of Human Rights had a universal appeal to believers and non-believers. The United Nations Charter and the Vienna Declaration appeal to people of all faiths and of no faiths. These documents assume that everyone believes in the fundamental dignity of all persons, their inalienable rights and their claim to be treated equally.

As a result, there can be no major differences between the East and the West or between the people of Europe and the citizens of Asia. There are truths and moral values which are ascertainable and applicable to all the six billion people in the universe, all of whom were made in the image of God.

We are, therefore, entering a century when, for the first time in the history of the world, humanity is bound together by a common understanding of the nature and binding force of internationally recognized human rights. The Vienna Declaration of 1993 has formalized the moral and juridical nature of the ethical and humanitarian ties which unite the entire world.

We will need clarifications and reaffirmations of the Vienna principles. But the solidarity of the sovereign nations and the moral truths they hold in common were made clear in Vienna. The enforcement of these norms is far from perfect. But the coming together of virtually all the countries of the earth in a joint statement with regard to their obligations and their aspirations maybe looked back upon as one of the epochal events of the twentieth century.

The Vienna Declaration reaffirms both the political and economic rights that the world has inherited from the United Nations. In the years to come, the centrality of economic rights will become clear and more demanding. Basic justice and fundamental equality are egregiously violated when at least one-fourth of humanity is denied access to food, education, housing and medicine, which are the birthright of every human being. World law has now placed an obligation on national and international governmental entities to eliminate these basically unjust situations.

Corporations of the world are also bound to do their part in making the vision of the Vienna Declaration attainable. After all, corporations are licensed by nations to carry out their mission of furthering the economic needs of human beings everywhere. Corporations are quasi-public in that they are creatures of the government. More and more corporate executives want to carry out their mission in ways that are compatible with world law and global aspirations.

It is unrealistic to think that the mandates of the Vienna Declaration are self-executing. The beauty of those mandates has to be re-announced all the time. Those who violate them must be rebuked by constant efforts to mobilize shame. World opinion must be elevated so that governments and multinational corporations understand their ethical duties and carry them out.

It is probably Utopian to think that the evils and tragedies which we remember from the twentieth century will decrease in number and frequency in the next hundred years. Global law, however, is now here and it is different. For the first time in history, massive dishonesty authorized or condoned by governments cannot be concealed and is known almost instantaneously to the world. There is no place for corrupt governments to hide. If they become known as 'pariah nations', their people will be vulnerable and their trade with foreign nations will be crippled. Hopefully, soon there will be in place a system of international sanctions so formidable that most nations will comply with the promises and pledges they made when they became members of the United Nations.

It seems clear that business and government leaders in the next twenty years will face problems that will seem incomprehensible and insolvable. Instantaneous worldwide communications, hundreds of people desperate and determined to improve the lot of their families, and unresponsive governments will certainly complicate the problem of bringing justice and dignity to more than six billion people. There will also be the clash of cultures, inter-religious tensions and even wars, along with the terrors of AIDS and possibly other plagues.

World law can seek to channel and conquer these intractable problems. But law is a feeble instrument if there are no clear and consistent moral values by which the underlying clashes can be resolved. The most urgent task, therefore, for national and international leaders is to formulate a moral and ethical consensus, which will form the basis for the resolution of complicated and unjust differences. The problem will be new and probably unprecedented in the history of modern times.

The first temptation when we face these problems is to hope that silence and inaction will make them disappear. But we know that without individual and collective action, global catastrophes will descend on us. Millions will migrate, seeking food for their children. Environmental disasters will occur, threatening the entire future of the human race, and people will resort to violence and war, recurring in ways that will be worse than in the last hundred years—which was possibly the bloodiest century in history.

Let us therefore come together seeking a moment of wisdom and grace. Nothing can ever be the same in our lives again, once we recognize how challenged we are. We have shared an opportunity to contemplate, together, the challenges that the providence of a loving God has sent into our lives, and which cannot be set aside.

We must learn and we must act. Accurate knowledge of global problems comes only with sustained study and reflection. These problems are more difficult and complex now than at any other time in world history. They are not only local or even regional, but they involve the whole human race. And they cannot be postponed or ignored. They are imperious, involving, quite literally, the fate of the planet.

The business community is at the core and the centre of every action that will succeed or fail in bringing peace and justice to the world in the next fifty years.

Full and accurate knowledge of what humanity needs over the next two generations is an essential requisite, if the disasters are to be avoided and some semblance of peace and prosperity is to come. The acquisition of that knowledge requires patient and intelligent study and meditation. Business and government leaders must understand issues like global warming, soil erosion, persistence of illiteracy and the clash of cultures.

But business and government leaders must also act on the knowledge which they acquire. They will be required and expected to act in ways that are courageous and indeed heroic. The heads of corporations and the presidents of governments are—whether they desire the role or not—men and women chosen by destiny or divine providence to act boldly and bravely to bring peace and justice to humanity, which is, as never before, crying out for food, fuel and fellowship.

The pressing demands on those who rule society will, in all likelihood, become more demanding in the near future.

Let us hope and pray that government leaders and corporate directors will bring enlightenment and a sense of fairness to those who depend upon them. And let us thank God for our time together on this memorable occasion. In seeking to bring justice to all the children of God, we are carrying out a task almost as old as the human race. Hammurabi expressed it well in the first code of law of the world, 2000 years before Christ.

He opened his set of laws with these words:

'The purpose of law is to protect the powerless from the powerful.'

11

The Past and Future of the Environmental Movement: Its Social and Ethical Perspectives*

RAMACHANDRA GUHA

Anyone who has some familiarity with the history of our country and feels for its future, must feel the need to pay homage to J.R.D. Tata, who stands with the likes of Mahatma Gandhi, Rabindranath Tagore, Jawaharlal Nehru, B.R. Ambedkar, M.S. Subbalakshmi, Baba Amte and a few others, as an Indian of exemplary integrity and courage, whose life has ennobled our land.

All Indians must feel the urge to publicly salute the memory of J.R.D. Tata. The topic I have chosen—the past and future of the environmental movement—immediately brings us into the domain of ethics. In at least three distinct (if inter-related) ways, the environmental movement has contributed to vital ethical debates of our times. First, it raises the question of how we, as humans, deal with other species on this Earth that we share with them. Second, the environmental movement asks us to be more attentive to the rights of the less fortunate members of our own species, so that the fruits of nature and its workings are not unfairly exploited by one class of humans. Third, it asks us to be attentive to the rights of future generations of humans. For, as has been well said, we were not bequeathed this earth by our ancestors, but have inherited it for our children. These then are the three great ethical questions raised by the environmental movement: equality between species, equality within a single generation and equality between generations.

---

*Oration delivered on 29 November 2001.

I am not a philosopher, so I will not explore these questions through an abstract analysis based on logic and reason. Rather, I will adopt the mode I am most familiar with, which is that of historical narrative.

There is a widespread belief that environmentalism is a phenomenon peculiar to the rich nations of the North, a product of the move towards 'postmaterialist' values among the populations of North America and Western Europe. In a series of books and essays published over the last twenty years, the political scientist Ronald Inglehart has argued that environmentalism is central to this shift 'from giving top priority to physical sustenance and safety, toward heavier emphasis on belonging, self-expression, and the quality of life.' A corollary of this thesis is the claim that poor countries cannot possibly generate environmental movements of their own. Consider these statements by three senior scholars:

'If you look at the countries that are interested in environmentalism, or at the individuals who support environmentalism within each country, one is struck by the extent to which environmentalism is an interest of the upper middle class. Poor countries and poor individuals simply aren't interested.'[1]

'It is no accident that the main support for ecological policies comes from the rich countries and from the comfortable rich and middle classes (except for businessmen, who hope to make money by polluting activity). The poor, multiplying and under-employed, wanted more "development", not less.'[2]

'Only the maligned Western world has the money and the will to conserve its environment. It is the "Northern White Empire's" last burden, and may be its last crusade.'[3]

The argument that environmental concern is a product of prosperity, a 'full-stomach' phenomenon so to speak, effectively rules out the articulation of environmentalism in the poorer countries of the globe, who, it is said, are 'too poor to be green.' However, the post materialist thesis flies in the face of vigorous environmental struggles in countries such as Brazil, Malaysia, Thailand and Venezuela. Moreover, these struggles have often arisen amongst the poorer sections of society—peasants, pastoralists, fisherfolk, forest tribals and rubber tappers.

The post-materialist thesis is also decisively refuted by the Indian experience. The environmental movement in this country is now at least a quarter of a century old. Its origins lie in the Chipko Andolan of the Central Himalaya, a movement that began in April 1973 as a struggle against commercial felling, but then turned to the rehabilitation of the hill ecosystem. Chipko was representative of a spectrum of natural-resource conflicts that erupted in different parts of India in the '70s and '80s: conflicts over access to forests, fish and grazing resources; conflicts over the effects of industrial pollution and mining; and conflicts over the siting of large dams.

Chipko, it must be stressed, is merely the best-known of a series of nature-based conflicts in contemporary India. These conflicts are played out against a backdrop of visible ecological degradation, the drying up of springs, the decimation of forests and the erosion of land. This has led in turn to acute resource shortages, and hence to the clash between competing claims—be it of peasants and paper mills over forest land, or of country boat owners and trawlers over fish stocks. Where 'traditional' class conflicts were waged in the cultivated field or in the factory, these struggles are waged over the gifts of nature, such as forests and water, which are gifts coveted by all but increasingly monopolized by some.

These conflicts take place over different resources and at different spatial scales. In numerous individual hamlets, the shrinking area of village commons is fought over between pastoralists searching for grass and labourers seeking to bring land under the plough. At the other extreme are conflicts that extend over several thousand square miles and involve two or more states—such as the building of the Sardar Sarovar Dam on the Narmada River, which shall provide electricity and water to Gujarat, while rendering homeless 100,000 peasants in upstream Madhya Pradesh. Analysts of social conflict in India have, however, tended to focus on conflicts over caste and religion. Nature-based conflicts have, comparatively speaking, been ignored, although they impact millions of people and have the potential to destabilize the political order. In the Northeast, for example, secessionist movements have originated in a sense of ecological deprivation, due to the fact that the region's rich oil, timber and mineral resources are exploited by the central government and put to productive use in other parts of India.

There has thus been an unmistakable material context to the upsurge of environmental conflict in contemporary India; provided by the shortages of, threats to, and struggles over natural resources. These conflicts have sparked a lively, nation-wide debate on the state of the environment and the sustainability of different technologies, ideologies and social systems. Indeed, the environmental movement in India has contributed to a profound rethinking of the idea of development itself. Intellectuals sympathetic to the movement have fashioned a critique of the industrial and urban bias of government policies, urging that it give way to a decentralized, socially aware, environmentally friendly and altogether more *gentle* form of development. Development as conventionally understood and practised has been attacked on a philosophical plane, but critics have been forthcoming with nose-to-the ground, sector-specific solutions as well. In the realm of water management, they have offered to large dams the alternative of small dams and/or the revival of traditional methods of irrigation, such as tanks and wells. In the realm of forestry, they have asked whether community control of natural forests is a more just and sustainable option when compared to the handing over of public land on a platter to industrial plantations. In the realm of fisheries, they have deplored the favours shown to trawlers at the expense of country boats, suggesting that a careful demarcation of ocean waters, by allowing indigenous methods sufficient play, might allow the renewal of rapidly depleting fish stocks.

Since it began—in or about the year 1973—the environmental movement has passed through three broad phases. The first stage has been described by one scholar as the 'struggle to be heard'. This lasted through most of the seventies. Social action groups struggled to give greater visibility to the problems of deforestation, soil erosion and water shortages, problems that affected millions of people in the countryside. However, for quite some time, the political system in India met these protests with a resounding silence.

The second stage, corresponding broadly with the '80s, saw the concerns of environmentalists being energetically taken up by the media, and less energetically by the political system and the State. The damage caused to the human health and well-being by industrial effluents, as well as the serious scarcity of water and fuelwood in the countryside, was conclusively demonstrated by scientific studies and investigative reportage. Slowly, the establishment responded to the evidence of environmental abuse. Departments of environment were set up at central and state levels, while attempts were made to forge a more ecologically sensitive forest policy.

However, in their desire to make the public and politicians more responsive to their agenda, environmentalists were often guilty of overstating their case. They spoke in alarmist and even apocalyptic language, predicting death, disease, the collapse of national sovereignty and the extinction of Indian culture, if their views did not immediately become State policy. This, as well as the radical transformation in global geopolitics wrought by the fall of the Berlin Wall, has in recent years generated a major anti-green backlash.

This third phase was willed along by propagandists on the other side and by the advocates of free market capitalism, who interpreted the collapse of the Soviet Empire as the end of history. It was now being said that there was a single successful economic model—the American one. The rest of the world, India included, needed to remake itself in the image of the American consumer. Only the environmentalists dared point out that there existed natural constraints to the globalization of a consumer society. The average North American household has two cars and two houses, and uses more energy and materials than a hundred average Bangladeshi households. Does the Earth have the capacity to sustain the replication of the American model in all other countries of the globe?

These questions were all brushed aside in the euphoria generated by the end of communism, a buoyancy reinforced in India by the promises held out by the programmes of economic liberalization. There is thus at present a tremendous backlash against the environmentalists. They are frequently and routinely attacked as the major impediment to the successful 'Singaporization' of the Indian society. Every summer, when the mercury touches 48 degrees Celsius in north India and the air-conditioners break down, prominent columnists in New Delhi blame it all on Medha Patkar. Indeed, the precise timing of the printed attacks on one of the most famous Indian environmentalists can almost be predicted from the weather reports.

Holding Medha Patkar responsible for the electricity crisis is to conveniently wish away the problems of theft, mismanagement, poor maintenance and antiquated technology that truly lie behind the shortages of power in India. It is also to ignore the fact that environmental campaigns have, for the first time, brought to centre stage the 'victims of development,' the poor peasants and tribals who have thus far had to unwillingly make way for the dams, steel mills and highways that dispossess them while benefitting others. Indeed, old-style public sector socialism and new-style market liberalization are akin in some crucial respects. Both have intensified social inequalities as well as devastated the natural environment.

The similarities, in an environmental sense, of orthodox models of socialism and capitalism were recognized early on by Mahatma Gandhi. As early as 1928, he had pointed to the unsustainability, at the global level, of the Western model of economic development. 'God forbid,' he wrote, 'that India should ever take to industrialization after the manner of the West. The economic imperialism of a single tiny island kingdom (England) is today keeping the world in chains. If an entire nation of 300 million took to similar economic exploitation, it would strip the world bare like locusts.'

Two years earlier, Gandhi had claimed that to 'make India like England and America is to find some other races and places of the earth for exploitation.' As it appeared that the Western nations had already 'divided all the known races outside Europe for exploitation and there are no new worlds to discover,' he pointedly asked: 'What can be the fate of India trying to ape the West?'

Gandhi's critique of modern industrialization has, of course, profound implications on the way we live and relate to the environment today. For him, 'the distinguishing characteristic of modern civilization is an indefinite multiplicity of wants' whereas, ancient civilizations were marked by an 'imperative restriction upon, and a strict regulating of, these wants.' In uncharacteristically intemperate tones, he spoke of 'wholeheartedly detest(ing) this mad desire to destroy distance and time, to increase animal appetites, and go to the ends of the earth in search of their satisfaction. If modern civilization stands for all this, and I have understood it to do so, I call it satanic.'

At the individual level, Gandhi's code of voluntary simplicity also offered a sustainable alternative to modern lifestyles. One of his best known aphorisms, that the 'world has enough for everybody's need, but not enough for everybody's greed,' is in effect, an exquisitely phrased one-line environmental ethic. This was an ethic he himself practised; for resource recycling and the minimization of wants were integral to his life.

Gandhi's arguments have been revived and elaborated by the present generation of Indian environmentalists. Their land is veritably an ecological disaster zone, marked by excessively high rates of deforestation, species loss, land degradation, and air and water pollution. The consequences of this wholesale abuse of nature have been chiefly borne by the poor in the countryside—the peasants, tribals, fisherfolk and pastoralists who have seen their resources snatched away or depleted by more powerful economic interests. For in the last few decades, the men who rule India have attempted precisely to 'make India like England and America.' Without the access to resources and markets enjoyed by those two nations when they began to industrialize, India perforce relied on the exploitation of its own people and environment. The natural resources of the countryside have been increasingly channelized to meet the needs of the urban industrial sector; the diversion of forests, water, etc., to the elite has accelerated processes of environmental degradation even as it has deprived rural and tribal communities of their traditional rights of access and use. Meanwhile, the modern sector has moved aggressively into the remaining resource frontiers of India, the Northeast and the Andaman and Nicobar Islands. This bias towards urban-industrial development has resulted only in a one-sided exploitation of the hinterland, thus proving Gandhi's contention that 'the blood of the villages is the cement with which the edifice of the cities is built.'

The preceding paragraph brutally summarizes arguments and

evidence provided in a whole array of Indian environmentalist tracts. The criticisms of these environmentalists are strongly flavoured by morality; by the sheer injustice of one group or country consuming more than its fair share of the earth's resources, and by the political imperative of restoring some sense of equality in global or national consumption.

An analytical framework might dispassionately explain these asymmetries in patterns of consumption. This framework is an elaboration of arguments first advanced by Madhav Gadgil and myself in our book, *Ecology and Equity*. Derived in the first instance from the Indian experience, this model rests on a fundamental opposition between two groups, termed omnivores and ecosystem people, respectively. The two groups are distinguished above all by the size of their 'resource catchment'. Thus omnivores, who include industrialists, rich farmers, state officials and the growing middle class based in the cities (estimated at an excess of hundred million), have the capability to draw upon the natural resources of the whole of India to maintain their lifestyles. Ecosystem people, on the other hand—who would include roughly two-thirds of the rural population, say about four hundred million people—rely for the most part on the resources of their own vicinity, from a catchment of a few dozen square miles at best. Such are the small and marginal farmers in rain-fed tracts, the landless labourers, and also the heavily resource-dependent communities of hunter-gatherers, swidden agriculturists, animal herders and wood-working artisans, all of whom are stubborn 'pre-modern' survivors in an increasingly 'postmodern' landscape.

The process of development in independent India has been characterized by a basic asymmetry between the omnivores and the ecosystem people. A one-sentence definition of development, as it has unfolded over the last fifty years, would be: 'Development is the channelizing of an ever increasing volume of natural resources, through the intervention of the state apparatus and at the cost of the state exchequer, to subserve the interests of the rural and urban omnivores.' Some central features of this process have been:

1. The concentration of political power/decision making in the hands of omnivores.
2. Hence, the use of the State machinery to divert natural resources to islands of omnivore prosperity, especially through the use of subsidies. Wood for paper mills, fertilizers for rich farmers, water and power for urban dwellers, are all supplied by the State to omnivores at well below the market prices.
3. The culture of subsidies has fostered an indifference of omnivores to the environmental degradation caused by them, aided by their ability to pass on its costs to ecosystem people or to society at large.
4. Projects based on the capture of wood, water or minerals—such as eucalyptus plantations, large dams or open-cast mining—have tended to dispossess the ecosystem people who previously enjoyed ready access to those resources. This has led to a rising tide of protests by the victims of development: Chipko, Narmada and dozens of other protests that we know collectively as the 'Indian environmental movement'.
5. But development has also permanently displaced large numbers of ecosystem people from their homes. Some twenty million Indians have been uprooted by steel mills, dams and the like; countless others have been forced to move to the cities in search of a legitimate livelihood denied to them in the countryside (sometimes as a direct consequence of environmental degradation). Thus has been created a third class of ecological refugees, living in slums and temporary shelters in the towns and cities of India.

This framework, which divides the Indian population into the three socio-ecological classes of omnivores, ecosystem people and ecological refugees, can help us understand why economic development since 1947 has destroyed nature but also failed to remove poverty. The framework synthesizes the insights of ecology with sociology, in that it distinguishes social classes by their respective resource catchments, their cultures and styles of consumption and also their widely varying ability to influence State policy.

The framework is analytical as well as value-laden, descriptive and prescriptive. It helps us understand and interpret nature-based conflicts at various spatial scales: from the village community upwards, through the district and region, then on to the nation. Stemming from the study of the history of modem India, it might also throw light on the dynamics of socio-ecological change in other large, developing 'Third World' countries such as Brazil and Malaysia, where, too, have erupted conflicts between 'omnivores'[1] and 'ecosystem people', and whose cities are likewise marked by a growing population of 'ecological refugees'. At a pinch, it might explain asymmetries and inequalities at the global level too. More than a hundred years ago, a famous German radical proclaimed, 'Workers of the World, Unite!' But as another German radical, Wolfgang Sachs, recently reminded this writer, the reality of our times is very nearly the reverse—the process of globalization whose motto might very well be 'Omnivores of the World, Unite!'

Why then, is a philosophy of economic development relevant to the requirements of the twenty-first century? Consider two well-known alternatives already prominent in the market place of ideas:

1. The Fallacy of the Romantic Economist, which states that everyone can become an omnivore, if only we allow the market full play. That is the hope and the illusion of globalization, which promises a universalization of American styles of consumption. But this is nonsense, for (although some businessmen and economists will resolutely refuse to recognize it), there are clear ecological limits to a global consumer society, to all Indians or Mexicans attaining the lifestyle of an average middle-class North American. Can there be a world with one billion cars and an India with two hundred million cars?
2. The Fallacy of the Romantic Environmentalist, which claims that ecosystem people want to remain ecosystem people. This is the anti-modern, anti-Western, anti-science position of some of India's best known, neo-Gandhian environmentalists. This position is also gaining currency among some sections of Western academia. Anthropologists, in particular, are almost falling over

> themselves in writing epitaphs to development, in works that seemingly dismiss the very prospects of directed social change in much of the Third World. It is implied that development is a nasty imposition on the innocent peasant and tribal, who left to himself, would not willingly partake in enlightenment rationality, modern technology or modern consumer goods. This literature has become so abundant and so influential that it has even been anthologized in a volume called (what else!) *The Post Development Reader*.

This last point can be made more effectively by way of an anecdote. Some years ago, a group of Indian scholars and activists gathered in the southern town of Manipal for a national meeting in commemoration of Mahatma Gandhi's 125th birth anniversary. They spoke against a backdrop of a life-size portrait of Gandhi, clad in the loincloth, which he wore for the last thirty-three years of his life. Speaker after speaker invoked the mode of dress as symbolizing the message of the Mahatma. Why did we all not follow his example and give up everything, to thus mingle more definitively with the masses?

Then, on the last evening of the conference, the Dalit poet Devanur Mahadeva got up to speak. He read out a short poem in Kannada, written not by him, but by a Dalit woman of his acquaintance. The poem spoke reverentially of the great untouchable leader B.R. Ambedkar, and especially of the dark blue suit that Ambedkar invariably wore in the last three decades of his life. 'Why did the Dalit lady focus on Ambedkar's suit?' asked Mahadeva. 'Why indeed, did the countless statues of Ambedkar put up in Dalit hamlets always have him clad in a suit and tie?' he asked. His answer was deceptively and eloquently simple. 'Now if Gandhi wears a loincloth,' said Mahadeva, 'we all marvel at his tyaga, his sacrifice. The scantiness of dress is, in this case, a marker of what the man has given up. A high caste, well born, English educated lawyer had voluntarily chosen to give up power and position and live the life of an Indian peasant. That is why we memorialize that loincloth.'

However, if Ambedkar had worn a loin cloth that would not occasion wonder or surprise. He is a Dalit, we would say—what else should he wear? Millions of his caste fellows wear nothing else. It is the fact that he has escaped this fate, the fact that his extraordinary personal achievements—a law degree from Lincoln's Inn, a PhD from Columbia university, the drafting of the Constitution of India—have allowed him to escape the fate that society and history had allotted to him that is so effectively symbolized in that blue suit. Modernity, not tradition; development, not stagnation; is responsible for this inversion, for this successful and all too infrequent storming of the upper caste citadel.

Going back to sustainability, let me now attempt to represent the story of Dr B.R. Ambedkar's suit in more material terms. Consider thus these simple hierarchies of fuel, housing and transportation.

Hierarchies of Resource Consumption

Fuel Used	Mode of Housing	Mode of Transport
Grass	Cave	Feet
Wood	Thatched hut	Bullock cart
Coal	Wooden house	Bicycle
Gas	Stone House	Motor scooter
Electricity	Cement House	Car

To go down any of these lists is to move towards a more reliable, more efficient, more long-lasting and generally safer mode of consumption. Why then would one abjure cheap and safe cooking fuel, for example, or quick and reliable transport, or stable houses that can outlive one monsoon? To prefer gas to dung for your stove, a car to a bullock-cart for your mobility, a wood home to a straw hut for your family, is to move towards more comfort, more well-being and more freedom. These are choices that, despite specious talk of cultural difference, must be made available to all humans.

At the same time, to move down these lists is generally to move towards a more intensive and possibly unsustainable use of resources. Unsustainable at the global level, that is, for while a car expands freedom, there is no possibility whatsoever of every human on earth being able to possess a car. As things stand, some people consume too much, while others consume too little. It is these asymmetries that responsible politics would seek to address. Restricting ourselves to India, for instance, one would work to enhance the social power of ecological refugees and ecosystem people, their ability to govern their lives and to gain from the transformation of nature into artefact. This policy would simultaneously force omnivores to internalize the costs of their profligate behavior. A new, environmentally sensitive development strategy would have five central elements:

1. A move towards a genuinely participatory democracy, with a strengthening of the institutions of local governance (at village, town or district levels) mandated by the Constitution of India, but aborted by successive central governments in New Delhi. The experience of the odd states, such as West Bengal and Karnataka, which have experimented successfully with the panchayat or self-government system suggests that local control is conducive to the successful management of forests, water, etc.
2. Creation of a process of natural resource use which is open, accessible and accountable. This would include a Freedom of Information Act, so that citizens are fully informed about the design of the State, and are better able to challenge or welcome it, thus making public officials more responsive..
3. The use of decentralization to stop the widespread undervaluing of natural resources. The removing of subsidies and the putting of a proper price tag will make resource use more efficient and less destructive to environment.
4. The encouragement of a shift to private enterprise for producing goods and services, while making sure that there are no hidden subsidies, and that firms properly internalize externalities. There is at present an unfortunate distaste for the market among Indian radicals, whether Gandhian or Marxist. But one cannot turn one's back on the market; the task rather is to tame it. The people and environment of India have already paid an enormous price for allowing state monopolies in sectors such as steel, energy, transport and communications.

5. This kind of development can, however, only succeed if India is a far more equitable society than is the case at present. Three key ways in enhancing the social power of ecological refugees and ecosystem people (all of which India has conspicuously failed in) are land reform, literacy—especially female literacy—and proper healthcare. These measures would also help bring population growth under control. In the provision of health and education, the State might be aided by the voluntary sector, paid for by communities out of public funds.

These are the elements of a new strategy that the Indian environmental movement might wish to canvass for. At the moment, however, the green movement is very much on the defensive. Whereas in the '80s, it looked as if their ideas might even translate into effective State policy, they are now the favourite scapegoats of non-performing politicians, avaricious industrialists and a consumer-driven media. How long will this situation last? What does the future hold for the environmentalists?

In its countrywide implications, the 'environmental problem' is in every bit as serious as the 'Kashmir problem' or the 'balance of payments problem.' Yet it has been poorly recognized by the intelligentsia and insufficiently acted upon by the political class. However, as we move into the twenty-first century, the future of India as a sovereign nation might come to centrally depend on how its people manage their natural bounty, on their success in distributing its fruits equitably, on the institutions they create (or re-create) for the purpose and on the promptness with which they can take pre-emptive or ameliorative action against environmental degradation.

Looking into my crystal ball, clouded over by the Bangalore smog, I can see three alternate paths for the Indian society, vis-*à*-vis the environment. The first, and in the short-term, the most likely response, is to simply ignore it. Under the imperatives of economic liberalization, India will continue to follow the path that is best described not as 'business-as-usual' but as 'more-business-than usual.' Despite its other merits, what a programme of liberalization cannot do is to successfully tackle ecological degradation. In fact, more 'business-than-usual' will most certainly mean the rapid exhaustion of natural resources, a greater pollutions of the waters and atmosphere, and, in consequence of both of these, a renewal of struggles conducted by or on behalf of the victims of environmental abuse.

If present trends continue, therefore, there will both be an acceleration of environmental degradation and an intensification of social conflict. This will place an enormous burden on the Indian political system, which will find it impossible to moderate these conflicts.

Let me now speculate outrageously. In October 2017, says my crystal ball, the old order shall collapse under the weight of massive social unrest, and an extremist green group will capture power in New Delhi. Like the Bolsheviks in Russia a century before, a small but fanatical sect will fill the political vacuum, to take charge of a society on the brink.

In his 1975 novel, *Ecotopia,* the California writer Ernest Callenbach develops just such a scenario for the western United States. An 'eco-fundamentalist' party comes to power and initiates a series of radical measures. These include the abolition of the motor car and of materials such as plastics that cannot be recycled. On the positive side, the revolutionaries institute a full-fledged Ministry for Organic Farming. The commissar for schools, meanwhile, makes first-hand knowledge of the wild an integral part of the curriculum. No one who cannot identify a hundred species a piece of birds, plants, animals and insects is allowed to go on to a college education.

Some Indian environmentalists might find this utopia attractive. For there are indeed some fanatics in the movement, who, like the Bolsheviks of yore, are completely intolerant of dissent. These folks might look longingly at the prospect of Green Communism. They would think, perhaps first of all, of constructing our own indigenous Gulag, the place where they would exile all those who disagreed, however mildly, with them. This Indian Siberia would most likely be the Thar Desert, the camps for dissidents to be built in the close vicinity of Pokhran, the air thick with natural dust and unnatural radioactivity.

The making up of such blueprints is a pleasant way of spending a Sunday afternoon; but there is, in fact, little likelihood of a successful political coup by a gang of Green Bolsheviks. In any case, an environmental revolution of this kind would come to grief far quicker than did the Soviet experiment. India is far too variegated a country to be successfully ruled by authoritarian means.

There could however be a more moderate route of environmental reform, a third possible path indicated by the crystal ball. Let me develop further the analogy with the history of European socialism. In the late nineteenth century the socialist movement split into two contending camps. One stood for violent revolution—it captured power in Russia, with what results we know only too well. The other tendency envisaged a more peaceful transition to the egalitarian society. Political parties professing a faith in 'democratic socialism' were to come to power, through the ballot box, in several European countries. These included the Labour Party in England and the Social Democratic parties of Germany and Sweden. While in power, these parties crafted the 'Welfare State', an institution which history will judge more kindly than the Soviet style command state.

In the late twentieth century, democratic green parties are making rapid strides across Western Europe. Thus in a united Germany the environmentalists are not only vocal but also politically powerful. Over the past decade, the Green Party has participated in various provincial governments. Now, after the September 1998 elections to the Federal Parliament, the Greens find themselves in a ruling coalition with the Social Democratic Party. Although the junior partner in the alliance, the Greens have three cabinet positions, including the high-profile post of foreign minister.

Perhaps the potential of this kind of 'Red-Green' alliance is even greater in this country. Here environmental degradation affects a far wider spectrum of the population, and especially the poor. As our final scenario, therefore, we have an 'eco-socialist' party winning the sixteenth General Election, an election held in early May 2011 with the results announced at the end of the month. This party will assume office on the 5 June 2011, which is World Environment Day.

In the best traditions of Indian politics, the new ruling party will both have an elaborate name and a crisper acronym by which it shall be known to its cadres and followers. It shall be called the Samajaur Pariyavaran Sudhaar Dal, the party of social and environmental reform, SPSD for short—or better still, Sapsidie.

On winning power, Sapsidie would set into motion a far-reaching process of political decentralization. Thus Sapsidie cadres will forge local institutions for the more efficient and sustainable management of forests, pastures, wells and tanks. Once these institutions are in place, the rural economy will be invigorated. One might even witness a stream of 'reverse migration', that is, from the city back to the village.

Sapsidie shall also make imaginative use of new technological opportunities. Its first act on coming to power shall be the renaming of the DRDO. The Defense Research and Development Organization would be transformed into the Decentralized Rural Development Organization. The reconstituted DRDO will work on converting rifles into ploughshares and Agni missiles into Surya solar power plants. These new units would provide a cheap, accessible, non-polluting and renewable source of energy for irrigation, small-scale industry and domestic users.

Moving to other spheres of economic life, the politics and policies of Sapsidie would ensure that those who destroy the environment are made to pay heavily for it. Where a Green Bolshevik would close down paper factories, indeed all factories, Sapsidie would allow them to function while empowering local communities to impose punitive fines, if they were to release untreated effluents into the soil, air, or water. In the world of Sapsidie there might yet be large dams, but those displaced by them would be given proper compensation and the choice of irrigated land in the command area of the project.

In a political system so obsessively focused on the short-term, my speculations might be laughed out of court. Nonetheless, the facts of environmental abuse will quietly, insistently make themselves felt, for ecological degradation does tangibly affect the vast majority of India's population. Numbers are vital in a democracy, and a new political formation might in time crystallize around a platform of environmental and social renewal.

This new formation called Sapsidie—or any other name—will

stand between the two extremes of more-business-than-usual—which, environmentally speaking, is a case of doing too little too late—and of Green Bolshevism, which is to do too much too soon. In time, people will come forward and outline the steps we need to take towards social and environmental renewal.

REFERENCES

1. Thurow, Lester Carl. *The Zero-Sum Society*. Basic Books, 1980.
2. Hobsbawm, Eric. *The Age of Extremes: a History of the World*; 1914-1991. Abacus, 2000.
3. Bramwell, Anna. *The Fading of the Greens: the Decline of Environmental Politics in the West*. Yale University Press, 1994.

12

Ethics and Media*

MARK TULLY

Journalism in Britain, you may be surprised to know, is one of the professions which enjoys the lowest esteem, along with politicians and bookmakers. We are held in low esteem and yet people are crowding to get into journalism, and I think these two things say something about the state of journalism. I think we have a reputation of being scandal-mongers, drain inspectors, sensationalists, parasites and even vultures. And as a journalist, you do sometimes feel like a vulture. When you go to the scene of disaster, you literally feel like a vulture which has come to gorge on the flesh of those who are suffering from the disaster. And you feel like this for two reasons: One, because you know that by going there you are going to write stories, get into the newspapers, get on to television screens and get heard on radio networks. You know, therefore, that for you, the disaster is a story, and a story is what you are all about. And all too often, in modern journalism, journalists fall into the trap of thinking that the story is less important than we are, or that it is our story, not that of those who are suffering from the disaster. And here is another reason why you feel uncomfortable and parasitical when you go to a disaster. You go out and see the victims of the disaster and then return to your hotel, send in your stories, and there you are, comfortably tucked up in bed or comfortably sitting on a bar stool, having left behind all the people who are suffering from the disaster. I remember feeling this particularly strongly after a cyclone in Bangladesh, when we were not even able to get out of the helicopters

*Oration delivered on 17 December 2002.

to actually see what happened on the ground. All we could do was fly safely over the islands where the cyclone had struck, and then go back to our hotels and file our stories. So, I do believe that there is some justification in the low esteem in which we are held, and I do believe that it is extremely important for all of us journalists to retain a sense of unimportance. A sense of the fact that we are the people who tell the stories of others, and to avoid that dreadful habit which we have of standing around bars and saying, 'this is my story' or 'do you remember my story of so and so...'

Why is that important? Well, because I think we do have influence. If we did not have influence, it would not particularly matter whether we were ethical people or not. But because we have influence, it is important that we ourselves be ethical. We all write for some organization, broadcast for some organization, make films for some organization, and so, organizational ethics—as well as personal ethics—are important.

But let me start with personal ethics and say that for my money, as I have already suggested to you, the most important ethical quality, the prime ethical quality, is humility. A part of humility is to listen and to learn. It's very easy. I know that as a journalist, to think that you know more than the person you are interviewing, to arrive with a whole lot of facts, and to think that you are there to floor him, to out-talk him, to get him to make mistakes, is your job. I do not believe that is the job. I believe it is the job of the journalist to learn and then to set out what he has learnt in the stories he writes or the broadcasts that he makes. I believe that it is absolutely essential that journalists should, as I say, realize that stories are not their stories, but the stories of the people they are talking about. How often do journalists covering a disaster describe to you the real heroes of the disaster—the survivors? All too often, they are just shown as impersonal faces, and their names are, quite often, not given. When you see on television or hear on the radio someone saying, 'this man has survived but his daughters have been killed' or something like that, the man's name isn't even given. Whereas, what we should do as journalists is to portray the people who survive the disasters as the heroes. In the case of the Bangladesh floods, there would be no point in all the stories we tell about relief supplies—and all too often, I am afraid we are tempted to tell stories about our own countries' relief supplies—if people had not had the courage to survive that disaster, to find some way of living until the relief supplies came in, and then to go on living. And I can tell you from the sights I have seen—it requires no mean courage to do that. It should be the humility of the journalists, to pay respect to those people.

In humility, also, we should realize our limitations. We journalists are far too fond of saying, 'we have the right to tell the truth.' Well, the truth is not quite as simple as that, and it is certainly not as simple as a newspaper article or a television broadcast. Whose truth are we telling? Everything is edited. No one can report everything he or she has seen or heard. We can only do our best to report accurately what we think is important in what we see, hear, or understand. But if we lay claim that we are telling 'the truth', then once again we are guilty of hubris and of arrogance, and that is the worst ethical quality that a journalist can have.

I also want to stress the other great virtue of a journalist—to be balanced. I am not trying to say that it is not our job to get as near to the truth as we can within our limitations—that would be an unbalanced thing to say. I am saying that we must not have the arrogance to think that we are telling the whole truth. We must realize our limitations. And we must make sure that in order to be balanced, in order to get as near to the truth as we can, that we have listened and have found out as much as we can do of the facts. I am extremely suspicious of the modern television habit of journalists standing on the spot, being interviewed by television news readers. I think to myself—how have these journalists had time to find out what is happening, if they are spending all the time talking to the news reader? On top of which, I believe that when you are talking off the top of your head, you cannot do your job as well as when you sit down to write a story or put a film or a radio package together. Because when you do that, you do have time to re-read, to alter, to look at the package or film, to see whether you can improve on it, whether you have got things wrong. If you are talking off the top of your head, you do not have time to do that. I also believe that the journalist, by standing there in that way, is intruding in some sort of way. There is too much of the journalist's personality coming over and not enough of what he is talking about. You haven't bought the television set to see the face of journalists, although too many journalists think that is what you have bought the television set for. You bought the television set to see scenes of what has happened and the faces of those people who are directly involved in it.

I think one of the dangers of television in particular, but the media in general, is that we are being led by technology rather than using technology as our tool. Why do you see so many journalists being interviewed on the spot? Because it is so easy to do now, and therefore everyone in the journalistic trade thinks, 'Oh, this is wonderful, we've got this technology of satellite telephones and satellite video links, therefore, we must use it all the time.' In my view that technology should be used in a limited and thoughtful manner. We should not be led by technology.

We should, in humility, also always be very careful about saying that we know what is going to happen. Particularly when that can be very damaging. If you are asked, for instance, Will there be riots?' Well, it is extremely damaging if you say, 'Yes, I think there will be riots.' This is an obvious example. I'll give you a less serious example, which happened to me when I fell foul of the arrogance of thinking I knew what was happening, back in 1979. There was a big political crisis, and no one knew who the next prime minister was going to be. I thought and said on the BBC that I thought it would be Jagjivan Ram, but it turned out to be Chaudhary Charan Singh. I paid the price for this because when I went to see Choudhary Saheb, his house was surrounded by lots and lots of people, and as I approached, they all started shouting, 'Mark Tully murdabad, BBC murdabad,' because I had not prophesied their man was going to win. When we prophesy, we are all too often claiming greater knowledge, greater understanding, greater foresight than we actually possess.

Honesty and accuracy are, of course, very much part of the ethical needs of a journalist. Honesty and accuracy can sometimes be strained in the interests of getting over what is called a good story. If you want to soup it up, or as it is sometimes said, 'sex it up,' then honesty and accuracy can go to the winds. There is the temptation to see the worst in everything too. It is our duty to expose things which have gone wrong. But that doesn't mean two things. Firstly, it doesn't mean that whenever we do a story, we should look for what we call the 'dirt'. There are plenty of straightforward stories which need to be told straightforwardly, and there are plenty of what I would call 'good news stories'. One of our problems as journalists is to put across good news stories in such a way that people will listen to them or read them and be pleased to read them.

We need to avoid sensationalism because sensationalism is a distortion of the truth. I am concerned about some of the coverage again of disasters, accidents, and that sort of thing in India. I do not think there is sufficient concern for the relatives of the dead, the relatives of those who have been hurt. I do not think myself that the showing of dead bodies on television is necessary or instructive and I think that, were I to have a relative who had died in an accident, I would certainly not want to see his or her body on television. Were I to have a relative who died I would not want television people coming up to me and asking me what I felt about it and trying to provoke me into blaming the railway company or the airline company or whoever was involved in the accident. I think that in India, as indeed in Britain, we need to have the humility and the sensitivity, when we cover disasters, to imagine ourselves in the place of the bereaved and those who are grieving.

Another problem which we journalists have is that we are tempted to be sensational because we want to get our stories on the air, we are tempted to look for the dirt because we want to get our stories on the air, and we are tempted to promote fights, because we want to get our stories on the air. The last, I think, is a particular danger of television journalism. The game is given away by news programme called the 'The Big Fight'. I don't think that we gain anything by putting two people, whose positions are known to be at opposite poles, on two chairs and getting them to fight with each other. I do not think we learn anything from that, and what do we lose out is so terribly important—we lose out the voice of moderation, which is there everywhere. We know that in Gujarat there were terrible riots. But we know that there were millions and millions of Gujaratis who had nothing to do with those riots, who were ashamed of those riots. We know that there were many politicians who were neither going to bitterly attack the BJP, blame everything on them, nor on the other hand totally support the BJP and Mr Modi. We know that there were informed discussions to be held about those things—but how often did we see them on television? Why is it that the media tends to present the most extreme Muslims as the representatives of the Muslim community, and the institutions like the Vishva Hindu Parishad (VHP) as representatives of the Hindu community? There are millions and millions of Muslims who would have nothing to do with figures who preach extremism, such as, for instance, the Shahi Imam of Jama Masjid in Delhi, and there are millions and millions of Hindus who are not members of the VHP. Theirs are the voices also, which need to be heard. But for reasons of sensationalism, we seem to believe, as journalists, that what is required is to make people fight and that everyone wants to see a punch shot. Everyone wants to see the 'Big Fight' as the news channel seems to think. In my view, that is boring and uninstructive, and it is one of the reasons, incidentally, why although I am a journalist, I really don't watch very much television. The other is because the news is much more comprehensive and detailed on the radio, but that's a different matter.

Now having said all that about the personal ethics of journalists and how I believe journalists need to be ethical if they are going to have the right influence—if the influence which they undoubtedly have is to be rightly exercised—I now want to go on to what in this hall, in particular, is a slightly more controversial subject. As I said, if we are to influence for the good—if we are to be ethical journalists— then we need ethical institutions within which to work. And one of my great concerns about journalism is that with the growth of proprietorial journalism, it is the pressures of business in what I might say, in a pejorative sense—and I'm not saying that all business pressures are pejorative—that journalists are under. What is the main concern of a Rupert Murdoch or a Conrad Black? It is the bottom line. The bottom line is, sell as many copies as you can, get as many viewers as you can—the more copies, not only the more circulation, but the more adds, the more viewers, and the more you can charge for them. So, there is inevitably a tendency to appeal to the lowest common denominator, to publish or broadcast what will appeal to the largest number of viewers, the largest number of readers. And as a result of this, what happens is that the advertising manager and the circulation manager become more important than the editor, and they start to dictate what should go in the newspapers. Now you might say that this is a legitimate thing that papers and television stations should be in the private sector. And here I want to say a word about something which you may think is heresy in this hall. I believe that the entrepreneurial spirit is essential. I believe that business has a great deal to its credit and we owe a great deal to business. But I do not subscribe to a theory which seems to be abroad still, and which is used often to justify the sort of organizations in the media which are totally commercially oriented. That theory is that the business way of doing things is the only way to do things. I just simply do not believe that. I remember I was appalled when the prime minister of Britain, Tony Blair, after his first year in office, said that in order to be businesslike, he was going to present an annual report of his government. Politics and business are not the same thing. And there are many other things which are not the same thing. Therefore, I think to apply business standards, and business ethics and business everything else to journalism and to leave out all other considerations, is wrong. There are other ways of managing institutions and organizations than on the principles of business. I would like to refer here to the BBC which was charged by Lord John Burke, when he became director general, with being inefficient, bureaucratic, not knowing where money was going, and all the rest of it. He was going to introduce business ethics, accounting and other practices into it. Well, in the first place, his criticism was a travesty of the truth. Alasdair Milne was dismissed as director general when director of the television service had brought in a multi-million-pound budget within 20,000 pounds every year. The independent television companies that John Burke came from used to run around the country with television crews of about fourteen people. The BBC used to have crews of three people. And I know from my own experience, that the BBC was a well-run organization, that accounting procedures were always being updated. Alasdair Milne appointed as his deputy director general, for the first time, an accountant, and yet we were told in the BBC that no, you are unbusinesslike, you have to be run as a business. And what was the best result of that? Well, I think if you ask anyone in the BBC, it was the proliferation of managers, the bureaucratization of the organization. And I'll just give you one example. The services which used to be broadcast to this part of the world, Hindi, Bengali, Urdu and other South Asian Services, were headed by two remarkable people, both of whom had PhDs in Indian history, both of whom had spent their lives in broadcasting to this part of world, but both of whom were pushed aside because they were not considered to be very keen on spreadsheets and things like that. They were replaced by people who put management first. And that was the surrender of the ethos and principles of the BBC to a business ethos. Now you may say that I am speaking against the business ethos. I'm not, I'm trying to be balanced. If I were to do that in this hall, it would be a very unwise thing to do, anyhow. But, what I'm trying to appeal for, is that in things like journalism, we cannot simply apply business principles. Broadcasting is not biscuit making.

I remember a lovely story, which is a bit unfair, but illustrates the narrowness which can come into some people's minds when they think that everything must be done in a business-like way. It was a story told by the Bishop of Leeds, about a company manager who sent his management consultant to a concert. When the management consultant came back and was asked how he had got on at the concert, he said, 'Well, in an orchestra I discovered that there are first and second violins. Why should there be first and second violins, surely the second violins must be redundant?' And then he said, 'Many of the instrumentalists don't play their instruments for much time. So, surely there could be multi-skilling and they could be told that you play the trumpet one minute and the saxophone the next minute, and the tuba after that.' And then he went on to say, 'There are lots of very short little notes called quavers—they are very, very short indeed—so why are they not marked up to the nearest big note?' And at the end of it all, he said, 'If Schubert had applied these principles, then his unfinished symphony would have been finished.' The unfinished symphony is one of the best-known compositions in Western music. Now that as an example is, I agree, a very limited view of business. So what happens then when business predominates in a journalistic organization? Well, as I said, managements are then out to find what sells, and what sells is sex, scandal, sensation and celebrity, if you look at the British Press. And where are the ethics there? What impact does selling those have on society? They promote, in my view, two very unethical instincts—call them by the old fashioned word if you like, vices—two vices, greed and egotism. The opposite of humility, which I concluded was the prime virtue of a journalist. Greed is—we have to accept it—at the heart of consumerism. If there is no greed, people will not consume. And what the media, when they become too commercial, are trying to do is to promote sales—their own sales—and therefore, they are indulging in consumerism, which is in my view indulging in promoting greed. An obvious form of greed which they sell particularly in Britain, I regret to say, in order to increase their circulation, is sex, and they sell that in such a manner as to promote sexual greed. Celebrity, I have also talked about. There are endless columns about celebrities, and I find myself in an awkward position here because I don't want to be seen as a celebrity in those terms, but I'm always finding myself rather uncomfortably being interviewed, whereas my job as a journalist is to interview. What is it that the celebrity, the cult of the celebrity promotes? It promotes egotism because what you are really saying is that these are the successful people, this is what you should be like, and they are successful because they have gone all out for something for themselves. The cult of celebrity does not take into account the fact that in society, where competition is dominant, there are losers as well as winners. How is the society to cope with the losers if its underlying ethos is that life is all about being a celebrity and being successful? And yet, that is what is sold by the media when they become too commercial. Spinoza once said, 'The things which mean to be judged by their actions deem the highest good are riches fame or sensual pleasures. Of these, the last is followed by satiety and repentance, and the other two are never satisfied.' And those are the three goods which—when it becomes too commercial, too business oriented—the media is selling. So, in a sense, the atmosphere, the ethos they are selling is an atmosphere of either permanent repentance or permanent dissatisfaction.

So, what is the answer? Well, I believe, in India and in Britain and in many other countries, that the answer lies in having competition between the commercial broadcasters and public service broadcasters. I believe that public service broadcasting can and should stand as a rock to withstand commercial pressures and, very importantly, to show what broadcasting can be. Public service broadcasting does not mean what you have in India, sadly. It means independent corporations, neither commercial nor government controlled. The BBC and the Public Broadcasting Service (PBS) in America have demonstrated how possible it is to have these corporations. But there is a danger for these corporations too, and that is the trap which many people feel that the BBC is falling into in Britain. Instead of competing by trying to do better, more ethical, higher standard broadcasting, what they try to do is win ratings wars with the commercial services. In other words, they try to outdo the commercial services in being commercial, and that is the worst possible thing. It is a total failure of public service broadcasting. But if it is genuine, independent public service broadcasting, then it provides a place where ethical broadcasting can take place and where it can be demonstrated to the public that you do not have to have commercial ethics and commercial principles to broadcast efficiently. If the media are to be ethical, we then have to have organizations like the BBC in order to protect a section of the media. And I think it is a sad reflection on India, which is a great democracy, that the government has not yet given full autonomy to All India Radio and Doordarshan.

I have said some things against business. I could be well accused of being arrogant, the opposite of the humility which I said we should espouse. But I had great respect for my father, who was a businessman, and of course, I have respect for my two sons, who are businessmen.

As I said at the start, we need the entrepreneurial spirit and India above almost any other country has learnt what strangling entrepreneurial spirit, by the license-permit raj, can do. So I'm not advocating everything should be in public service. I am not speaking against business, or business ethics, or business ways of doing things. I am saying two things which I think, for all of you who are going into the world of business, are important. Firstly that in the context of the media, and indeed in the context of everything else, you too must not be arrogant. You too must not think that you have all the answers. You must realize that sometimes your answers are suitable for one company, one organization, and one type of business, but not necessarily for everyone. And secondly, I think that you must realize that nothing stands still—that the present triumph of what you call liberal economics and of the market isn't going to last forever. I well remember that when I was a young man we thought that anyone who was not a socialist was immoral; and it took a long time to understand the problems created by socialism. When those lessons were learnt the pendulum swung the other way, until it almost became axiomatic that if you were a socialist you were a fool.

I believe time will change things and I believe we will get back to a business ethos as well as a journalist ethos where consumerism is tempered, where it is realized much more clearly that there are many other issues involved in any transaction, in any organization, in any area of life than the bottom line. In J.R.D. Tata, above everyone else, you have a businessman who rejected the idea that the bottom line was the be all and end all of everything—a businessman who realized the impact of business on society and realized also the duty of business to society.

I hope I realize the duty of journalism to society. I hope I realize my duty to society. But, I also realize the dangers to journalism of an over drastic application of what I might call the present doctrines of liberal market economics, and of the exaltation of the bottom line above everything else.

13

Corporate Governance and The Church's Contribution*

TELESPHORE P. TOPPO

'Corporate governance is a very contemporary topic as it continues to hold the attention of business houses, governments and corporate management. No other word, perhaps, with the exception of "Liberalization" and "Globalization", seems to dominate our day-to-day discourses and much of contemporary scholarly writings.'

Summing up the year 2003, *The Economist* gives us this neat account:

'Like 2002 and 2001 before it, 2003 has been a year in which the scandals have dominated the business headlines.'[1]

After recounting the tales of Heath South—an American medical services company, Ahold—a Dutch grocer, Boeing, and Parmalat, the write-up goes on to say:

'Each new story appeared against a constant background of complaints about bosses being paid far too much. On top of these were trials, and talk of still more trials, of errant executives connected with, among many others, Tyco, Credit Suisse, First Boston, Credit Lyonnais, Mannesmann and of course, Enron and World.com.'[2]

Our own business journals and newspapers have kept us on line with the recent crimes against corporate governance in our country. The broadcasters have given us detailed analysis of the sordid deals and scams that sunk a bank, a co-operative, a mutual fund and other such financial institutions in our country.

---

*Oration delivered on 9 February 2004.

WHAT IS CORPORATE GOVERNANCE?

All who write about corporate governance agree that corporate governance is about power and how it is controlled and exercised.

In the words of Mahatma Gandhi, the Father of the Nation, 'corporates should consider themselves as trustees of the poor and of public resources.'

The Harvard Business Group set out to look into this issue, and the Cadbury Commission Report that advocated broad changes in the structure and power of corporate teams, addressed themselves to the most glaring aspect—namely, the abuse of corporate power and the consequent destruction of well-established industrial and trading houses of business.

There is no need to labour on the point that this is indeed an issue of grave importance, not only to businesses but also to economies of nations and of the whole world.

THE BASIS OF THE PROBLEMS

In view of the growing importance of corporations, society is faced with three major problems. First, the growth in corporate size has brought an increasing separation of control from ownership. In large firms, the shareholder and nominal owner no longer exercises effective control. Actual control rests with management, which tends to be self-selecting and responsible only to itself.

Second, the size of many corporations gives them economic power, a development that permits escape from the discipline of the competitive market. Large corporations have substantial control over the prices charged for the goods they produce. Despite all attempts at control, they manage to dictate prices that are most favourable to their profits.

Finally, society has not been wholly successful in making certain that corporate performance serves the public interest as well as the interests of owners and managers. The laws governing the corporate house laws may prevent the emergence of outright monopoly, but they do not guarantee fair and equitable business competition.

These problems, present in the domestic economy, have become more acute with the growing number and power of multi-national corporations. The multinationals, many of which are trans-Atlantic, are business firms whose sales, workforce, production facilities and other operations are worldwide in scope. They represent the latest development in the continuing growth of corporate organizations. Their power to create wealth on a worldwide scale means that multinationals are likely to remain a dominant force shaping the world economy far into the future.

RESPONSES TO THESE PROBLEMS

In response to the first problem, organizations have been taking special care to bring in the voice of the shareholders in their decision making process. Recent researches have shown that firms that have stronger shareholder rights are the ones that have higher profits, higher sales growth, lower capital expenditure and fewer corporate acquisitions. Greater transparency of transactions and accountability have corrected, in some measure, the abuses brought on by self-seeking boards of directors.

In response to the second problem of the size of organizations and consequently, their freedom from the controlling forces of a market economy, the investors as well as managements have discovered the importance of social responsibility and self-control through business ethics. Market forces are not the only ones that should affect the production and distribution of a commodity; self-control and perception of ethical standards too have a role to play. Thus, we see the growing importance that corporate ethics has acquired over the past decade or so.

In response to the challenges that multinationals face, the concept of the corporate citizen is advocated—which brings in a wider sense of responsibility for local and global issues. What is good for the Mother Company is also made good to the national and local investors.

So, within the broader framework of corporate governance, we have corporate ethics, corporate accountability and corporate citizenship—all of them seeking to shape the future of organizations and make them not only profitable, but also viable in the long run.

These ground realities are well recognized by some of the successfully run companies, such as HDFC.

'I have run the company as if I owned 100 percent of the stock, although I don't own even one-fourth of 1 per cent. Although I had a number of opportunities to become my own boss, I never had the courage. I am a salaried person with a job. My mindset has not changed. I wanted to be a bank employee and that is what I am. I got the opportunity to promote a bank without owning it,'[3] said Deepak Parekh, the chairman of HDFC.

In another place, he goes on to say:

> The challenge to investor confidence in listed companies caused by recent events in the international capital markets has brought corporate governance issues under the spotlight, both in the international markets and in India. Serious financial manipulations in the corporate arena have intensified the focus on how businesses are managed. Our world is changing and forces are influencing corporations to compete globally for customers, suppliers, alliances, employees, assets, capital and shareholders. This makes it all the more important that companies follow the corporate governance route building market confidence.[4]

But we do know that not all Indian companies are run ethically and honestly, like HDFC. Analysing the lack of corporate governance in Indian companies, Sachendra and Lakshmi Smitha, in their paper, *Adherence to Corporate Governance in Practice: Experiences from India, USA and Australia*, give the following reason:

> The reasons for the lack of adequate corporate governance in India have much to do with how the Indian legal system has emerged. The budding Indian entrepreneurs, at the time of the Indian independence, were not very comfortable with the restrictions imposed by the Government of India. The penal rates of taxation have resulted in a culture of avoidance, which went up to evasion in many Indian companies. Unable to sustain it in the righteous way,

> companies were forced to try and gain special business advantages by bribing the officials. Bribery generated unaccounted money. In order to get away from the risk of possessing this unaccounted money, people started making political donations. People who accepted political donations got elected into law-making bodies and failed to take strict action against errant companies. As a result, the economy lost tax revenues and corporate non-governance began at the highest level.[5]

Today, in the changed scenario of lesser and lesser government control, the Indian companies need to re-think their strategies of doing business and bring in a measure of corporate governance that would make them acceptable all over the trading world.

Changes are taking place slowly. I learnt that the Confederation of Indian Industries (CII) initiated the process of reflecting on corporate governance in the late 1990s. It released its version of an Audit Committee. The Securities and Exchange Board of India (SEBI) set up a committee under Kumaramanglam Birla to look into ways and means of protecting the investors' interests. That committee made twenty-five recommendations, nineteen of which were mandatory and enforceable.

Even today, steps are being taken to plug the loopholes in the Companies Act and ensure ethical and transparent interactions to govern the way we do business.

It is obvious that there is still more room for improvement. Non-government agencies, the academic world and public-spirited citizens need to keep a close watch over industry and help it run in a way that enhances its reputation and improves the bottom line of profits.

As far as my knowledge goes, enough number of companies abroad, such as AXA Asia Pacific, BHP Billiton, National Australia Bank, Walmart stores, General Electric, Microsoft, Johnson and Johnson, and companies such as Infosys Technologies, WIPRO, Hindustan Lever, TELCO, TISCO, Hindalco and Ranbaxy Laboratories, to mention a few, are prime examples to prove that good corporate governance is also good business strategy and can bring about increase in profitability in our country.

As the write-up in the 30 December 2003 *The Economist* concluded:

> This flow of scandal is likely to continue into 2004, not least because legal proceedings in current cases are far from over. It will be easy to conclude that standards of corporate behaviour remain as bad as ever, and that the typical chief executive would be more appropriately employed on a chain gang. That would be a mistake. Whisper it softly, but there are plenty of reasons to be optimistic about how the world's big companies will conduct themselves in future.[6]

It is against these optimistic views of the corporate world in 2004 that I would like to set my views on what the church can contribute to good corporate governance.

Over the years I have spent as a pastor for my people and a leader among my brothers and sisters, I have received insights on authority, power, exercise of power and the value of power to do good. It is some of these insights that I intend to share with you. I realize that these may not sound very erudite or clever, but they are the fruits of a lifetime of study and living.

I shall describe two great events that took place recently, and though they are of disparate importance, they affected me deeply and also gave me insights into corporate governance. I refer to the beatification of Mother Teresa on 19 October 2003 and my being admitted to the ranks of the cardinals of the Catholic Church on Tuesday, 21 October 2003.

MOTHER TERESA'S POWER

On that Sunday morning in October 2003, as I stood with the thousands of pilgrims that had assembled to witness the beatification ceremony of Mother Teresa, I recalled the words of the BBC commentator commenting on the funeral of Mahatma Gandhi. I found it strangely appropriate for Mother Teresa.

'The object of this massive tribute (Mahatma Gandhi) died as he always willed, a private man, without wealth, without property, without office or title for office. He was not a commander of armies, nor a ruler of vast lands. He could not boast any scientific achievement or artistic gift. Yet, men, governments and dignitaries have joined hands to pay honour to this brown man who led his country to freedom.'[7]

Can't one truthfully say the very same words about Mother Teresa?

Blessed Mother Teresa was indeed a very powerful person. She headed a religious order that numbered some 4,500 members, operating out of 710 houses in 133 countries around the world! Speak of a multinational company!

She did have access to power at all levels. Doors were opened to her and she treaded the corridors of power as confidently as she walked the streets of Calcutta (Kolkata now). Heads of states, corporate chairmen, world leaders, spiritual gurus, wielders of power through politics—all bowed to her and came to her aid so that the poorest of the poor may have their dignity, at least in death.

Would her terms as superior general, with all its powers over the members and their homes and institutions, be described as a form of corporate governance? Could we apply our analysis of corporate governance to her style of functioning? What was the difference between her counterpart and herself in the secular world, both acting as the CEOs of their organizations?

I intend to consider carefully these and other questions. Suffice it now to say that Blessed Mother Teresa of Calcutta was a corporate governor par excellence!

CARDINALS IN THE CATHOLIC CHURCH

The other event that affected me personally and deeply was my admission to the College of Cardinals in the Catholic Church on 21 October 2003.

The *Simon and Schuster New Millennium Encyclopedia* has this entry under 'Cardinal':

> Highest dignitary in the Roman Catholic Church after the Pope, whose elector and councilor he is. The Cardinals are appointed by the Pope and constitute the Sacred College. The Pope is not obliged to consult them, but does so as a matter of course. The Cardinals are chief members of the Sacred Congregations of the papal

> government. They meet in the consistory or assembly, over which the Pope presides. They enjoy extraordinary privileges and honours.
>
> Within the vast scheme of the hierarchy of the Church's administration, the Cardinals occupy a very important place. As bishops, they are responsible to the church given to them. As Cardinals, they share with the Pope the responsibility over the whole church. They are called upon to exercise this responsibility through their collective counseling and individual exercise of authority.

What is the nature and purpose of their authority? Could they be compared to the members of the board of directors of conglomerates? could their exercise of power be analysed and understood by the same principles that you would apply to secular directors?

These issues need an answer and I intend to take them up together.

POWER AND THE CHURCH: A HISTORICAL OUTLOOK

From the dawn of history, we see power at work in all human interactions, sometimes controlling, sometimes compelling, but always being part of the interactions. The central concern of study then was how this power is delegated and shared with others, especially for the sake of the 'good life' of all.

THE ANCIENT PHILOSOPHERS

Plato in his *Republic* attempted to reconcile moral theory and political practice. He presents an ideal State, or more accurately, an ideal Greek polis or city-state, as modelled on the three elements of a human soul—namely, the appetitive, the spirited and the philosophical. Accordingly, his ideal city-state consisted of three distinct groups: a commercial class formed by those who are dominated by their appetites; a spirited class—administrators and soldiers responsible for the execution of the laws; and the guardians or philosopher-kings, who would be the law-makers. Because Plato entrusted the guardians, a carefully selected few, with the responsibility for maintaining a harmonious polis, republicanism is frequently associated with ends or goals established by a small segment of the community presumed to have a special insight into what constitutes the 'common good.'

Aristotle's *Politics* provides another republican concept, one that prevails in most of the Western world. Aristotle categorized governments on the basis of who rules: the one, the few or the many. Within these categories he distinguished between good and perverted forms of government—monarchy (good) versus tyranny, aristocracy (good) versus oligarchy—but the main difference being whether the rulers governed for the good of the State or for their own interests.

Thus, we see how power and its exercise were viewed as the basis of all political theories.

THE BIBLE AND ITS VIEW OF POWER

The Bible speaks of generations of people in Israel being held together, first by charismatic leaders such as Moses and Joshua, later by prophets like Elijah and Elisha, and still later by kings such as Saul and David, and Solomon and Hezekiah.

While granting monarchy to Israel, God warns them of the dangers of having kings lording over them. But the people remain adamant, and so God gives them kings. When they turn out to be faithless, God sends out prophets like Isaiah and Jeremiah, and Ezekiel and Daniel.

In the New Testament, Pilate makes a challenge to the captive Christ: 'You will not speak to me? Remember, I have the authority to set you free and also to have you crucified.' Jesus answers, 'You have authority over me only because it was given to you by God.' (John 19:11).'

This notion that all authority is derived from God and is to be exercised in accordance with his laws became the basis of authority in the Christian era.

From the very beginning, the Church became a dominant force in Western society. By the end of the fourth century, Christianity was recognized as the preferred religion; indeed, after an edict by Theodosius in AD 392, as the only legitimate religion.

Christianity influenced Western society in various ways. The civic and social centres were still civitates or city-states, including the surrounding countryside. It was in these administrative centres that bishops settled and exercised their influence. In AD 550, there were 120 civitates in Gaul, each with its own bishop. Roman territorial divisions were maintained (diocese and province) as well as Roman administration and Latin language. Furthermore, the bishops inherited the office of the advocate of the poor (defensor civitatis), which gave Episcopal courts the right of litigation of all kinds. Once again, we see that the power given to rulers was to be exercised for the good of all.

THE GOOD KINGS

The Church recognized those who ruled the land for the good of all and praised them. Power or exercise of power was not seen to be bad in itself. Thus, it honoured kings, queens, administrators and architects of empires. As Ronald Knox comments on King Edward:

> When we venerate Saint Edward, we venerate a failure. We do so advisedly. Not because success in life necessarily falls to the grasping and the unscrupulous, so Christians should mistrust that success itself as a sign of rascality. Nor that there have not been great saints who were also great kings, great statesmen and great warriors—Saint Oswald, Saint Dunstan, Saint Joan of Arc. But because we will not let ourselves be blinded by the lure of worldly success so as to forget that true statesmanship is exercised in the council chamber, and the true warfare fought on the battlefield of the human soul.

He continues to say, 'But this is certain, that true satisfaction came to them and true success crowned them only in so far as their ambitions were for a cause, not for a party; for others, not for themselves.'[8]

Thus, the Christian ideal of service to the people, service to the poor, slowly enters into governance and changes the whole image of it.

THE CONCEPT OF STEWARDSHIP

One of the most valuable insights that Jesus left behind for his followers is that of service.

> An argument broke out among his disciples as to which one of them should be thought of as the greatest. Jesus said to them,

> 'The kings of the pagans have power over their people and rulers claim their title, 'Friends of the People'. But this is not the way it is with you; rather the greatest one among you must be like the youngest, and the leader must be like the servant.' (Luke 22: 24-26).

It is this notion of service to others, even to the extent of giving oneself completely, that underlies the lifestyle of all great Christians. And it is this ideal that the Church offers to all the corporate personnel for their own fulfilment.

This service concept is based on one's perception that the gifts, talents and powers one possesses are from God and are given for the betterment of others. We are stewards of God's wealth, power and gifts. We are to use them to serve all his children.

BLESSED MOTHER TERESA AND HER SERVICE OF THE POOR

Blessed Mother Teresa drew her inspiration from the teaching of Christ, who said, 'Whenever you did this for one of the least important brothers and sisters of mine, you did it to me! (Matt. 25:40).' Indeed, in the poor she saw Christ and served Him through them. The result was spectacular: her governance of her Order, her dealings with the high and the mighty as well as the poorest of the poor, and above all, her very self, transformed and became glorious.

CARDINALS AND THEIR SERVICE OF THE CHURCH

Once again, the service that the Cardinals of the Catholic Church render to the Pope and through him to the whole Church makes them special and important people.

Having been admitted to the College of Cardinals and being aware of the serious and sacred responsibilities going with this appointment, I feel more humble than ever before. I feel that in every forum I am given access, including that of the corporates, I should carry the divine message of compassion so desperately needed in purveying equity among our masses.

SOME APPLICATIONS

When position and power become an opportunity to serve, and when service becomes the main thrust of corporate governance, then one can see how powerful it is. Corporate governance begins to express itself in terms of corporate responsibility to all its stakeholders. Commenting on the *Fortune* magazine's list of 'The World's Most Admired Companies', the writers of the lead article have this to say:

> Gone from the All-Star list are former favourites such as AOL Time Warner and Duke Energy, whose vaunted plans to make money in energy trading didn't pan out. Newcomers to the All-Star list, such as Unilever and Emerson Electric, were rewarded for delivering solid products—and financial results. The fight to quality was also a fight to cash: Nice guys who finish last in profits or performance get punished. Home Depot, for example, was the worst performing stock on the Dow in 2002. No wonder its most admired ranking also took a dive, falling from fifth to the seventeenth place in the list.[9]

Besides productivity, other necessary measures of governance, such as pruning the workforce and retraining them for better placement within the organization, also become well accepted. The trust of the employees in their employers, of the shareholders in the management, soars high and attracts loyalty and commitment. Greater sensitivity and transparency of interaction bring about understanding and make changes acceptable.

CORPORATE GOVERNANCE IN CIVIL LIFE

If the ideals of corporate governance are put into civil administration, then there will be greater concern for the governed and a greater appreciation for the governing. Recognizing the true needs of the people on whose behalf they govern, the administrators and bureaucrats could bring about greater changes and make them fully accepted.

But when big dams drain rivers, when forests are destroyed and the people are deprived of their livelihood, how could that be called true governance?

Denying the rights of the tribals to maintain and celebrate their way of life could by no means lead to success and fulfilment. We need to understand their basic aspirations and then fulfil them. Then the corporate governance would be a happy one.

His Holiness Pope John Paul II has rightly urged the proponents of globalization and industrialization to promote 'development with a human face.'

Which means that humans, especially the most vulnerable sections, should not be neglected.

CONCLUSION

When people approach us, we must be ready to say, 'What can I do for you?' It's good for us to remember the words of Lord Jesus, 'I have come not to be served but to serve.'

True leadership, whether in governments, civic bodies or organizations, manifests itself in genuine corporate governance. If we want corporate ethics, we need to ensure personal ethics. Will it not be good to derive inspiration from the guiding principles envisaged by Infosys, the flagship of India's IT industry? It says, 'The softest pillow is a clear conscience, when in doubt, disclose; don't use corporate resources for personal use, put long-term interests ahead of short-term ones, and share wealth with employees.'

I believe that human behaviour is not indifferent to God; he has a stake in it. We should not do whatever we like. Even though it is not always easy to discern good from evil, it remains true that we must ever search for what is best.

Recently I went to pay my respects to our President, Dr A.P.J. Abdul Kalam. He conveyed to me his views, which I want to share with you. He said that our country could forge ahead only if all its citizens base their lives on spiritual, social and moral values. He also stated that we need to build a more humane society that respects freedom, equality and justice. To achieve this, we are to follow the path of non-violence, mutual respect, love, tolerance and co-operation in a country that is characterized by a multiplicity of religions and cultures. We, as true Indians, will do well to make our own with this sound, presidential guidance. The corporate sector should set the pace and lead us on.

These last three words ('lead us on') take us back to the prayer meetings of Mahatma Gandhi, the Father of the Nation, who loved to hear the famous song of Cardinal Newman (1801–1890):

Lead kindly light, amid the encircling gloom,
Lead thou me on;
The night is dark, and I am far from home,
Lead thou me on.
Keep thou my feet;
I do not ask to see the distant scene;
one step enough for me.

REFERENCES

1. *The Economist.* 20 December 2003, p. 14.
2. Ibid.
3. *Corporate Governance and Corporate Citizenship Challenges for Business and Management Education,* ed. Ravindran, p. 116
4. Ibid., p. 120.
5. *Adherence to Corporate Governance in Practice: Experiences from India, USA and Australia,*Sachandra, B.V.N. and Smitha, L.T. in *Corporate Governance and Corporate Citizenship,* pp. 142–143.
6. *The Economist.* 30 December 2003, p. 15.
7. *Gandhi* a film by Attenborough.
8. Knox, R Sermon at the church of St. Edward the Confessor, Golders Green in Breviary, vol.III. pp. 437–438
9. *Fortune.* 10 March 2003, pp. 3032.

14

Tourism in Developing Countries: Neocolonialism or Nation Builder*

JAMES J. SPILLANE

INTRODUCTION

One of J.R.D. Tata's great achievements was being the first Indian in history to pilot a plane, in 1932. At that time, he surely could not have envisioned the impact of the airplane on the Indian and global society. As Peter Drucker so eloquently pointed out in his famous management book entitled *The Age of Discontinuity*, new industries can suddenly spring up and have far-reaching impacts on economies and society in general. Many of these industries, such as steel, chemical, pharmaceuticals and petroleum, have brought untold benefits to people everywhere. Unfortunately, these industries have also caused serious damage. Facing such moral dilemmas has fostered an interest in business ethics. The terrible tragedy in Bhopal on 4 December 1984—almost twenty years ago—is perhaps the most famous example to date.

Since the mid-1980s industrial systems in the advanced capitalist economies have undergone a profound transformation from Fordist to post-Fordist modes of production (Harvey, 1989). Upadhya and Rutten (1997) point out that this transformation has been characterized by two seemingly contradictory tendencies: the increasing centralization and monopolization of capital by huge transnational corporations, and a flourishing of small businesses at the other end of the scale.

*Oration delivered on 29 November 2004.

The changing nature of industrial systems in advanced capitalist economies has implications for developing countries, which makes it necessary to examine changing intra- and inter-firm relationships between enterprises operating at different scales in developing economies.

On this 100th anniversary of J.R.D. Tata's birth, a new industry has risen to prominence, especially since the Second World War—the global tourism industry. Many feel that it is now the largest industry in the world, especially if its formal and informal sectors are included in the definition. Today, some 240 million people are reported to be working in this truly global, yet very local industry. Governments applaud its ability to create jobs, earn foreign exchange, provide much needed infrastructure, preserve and promote cultural heritage, and even promote international peace and understanding. Critics, however, are quick to point out the low quality of the jobs created, the ultimate leakages of the foreign exchange earnings through imports, the degradation of ancient and sacred cultures (symbolized by the highly profitable international sex industry), and the frequent targeting of tourists by terrorists. For them, instead of being a nation-builder, it has become yet another form of the dependence of developing countries on rich nations. In short, it is neocolonialism in disguise. In the attempts to reconcile these strongly opposite views, there is plenty of work for business ethicians working in the rapidly expanding area of tourism studies. The well-being of its many stakeholders is involved in its critical decisions.

The tourism sector is expanding on a global level and this expansion results in an organization of international tourism that S. Britton (1989) conceptualized as a three-tiered hierarchy. At the apex are those tourist companies that have their headquarters in the metropolitan market countries and that dominate international tourism. At the intermediate level are the branch offices and local associates of these transnational companies organizing most of the international tourism in developing countries. Finally, at the base lie those small-scale tourism enterprises of the destination area that are marginal, but dependent upon the transnational companies

(S. Britton, 1989). Many governments of developing countries give priority to large-scale investments in tourism, as they expect tourism to contribute significantly to national income and employment. The growth scenarios in tourism, developed by government agencies, are fed by the projections of economists in terms of profits and multiplier effects. However, liberal economic models often overstate the direct benefits of tourism expenditures. It has been pointed out that large-scale transnational enterprises are often not as effective in increasing foreign exchange earnings and job opportunities as originally believed. This is because there is significant economic leakage due to the purchase of foreign supplies and labour and to the channelling of profits out of the developing countries. In poor states, tourists frequently pay for imports, creating massive leakage that undermines the validity of some basic economic analysis of the value of tourism for developing countries (S Britton, 1989; Leheny, 1995; Rodenburg, 1980).

In 1999, there were an estimated 2.4 million visitors to India, and this rose to 2.6 million in 2000-2001 (S. Singh, 2001 p. 51). This is remarkably low for a country as vast and culturally rich as India, with over a billion people. Surely international tourism is one of the untapped riches of India. Tourism is a crucial foreign exchange earner for the country, and it also stimulates the economy by boosting employment. Tourism officials claim that the lack of adequate flights to India, coupled with lacklustre marketing policies, is severely hindering tourism growth. Poor infrastructure within the country itself is another significant impediment. Infrastructure improvements intended for the tourism sector would surely benefit the whole of Indian society as has been the case in many developing countries.

In the late 1990s, most tourists to India came from the UK, followed by Germany, the USA and then, interestingly, Sri Lanka. Although not a foreign exchange earner, domestic tourism still has a positive effect on the economy. In 1999, approximately 160 million Indian people travelled within India; some hundred million for religious reasons.

The symbol of Indian tourism is surely the Taj Mahal, which this year celebrates its 350th anniversary. It is one of the world's loveliest buildings and perhaps the greatest monument to love. As one of the Seven Wonders of the World, the monument is breath-taking, both day and night. The white marble mausoleum was built by the grief-stricken Mughal emperor Shah Jahan in memory of his beloved wife Mumtaz Mahal, who died in childbirth in 1631. It took over 20,000 craftsmen from India and Central Asia about twenty-two years to complete the monument, at an estimated cost of about $60 million today. In recent years, there has been growing concern about the damage that atmospheric pollution is causing to the Taj. Acid rain, produced by the sulphur dioxide from vehicle emissions, is discolouring the famous white marble and eroding the fine carving and inlays. In an attempt to reduce pollution, new industrial developments were banned from a 10,400 square kilometre exclusion zone around the Taj Mahal in 1994 and motor vehicles are now prohibited in the four-kilometre area surrounding the monument. Sunset is an extremely impressive time to see the Taj, as the white marble first takes on a rich golden sheen, then slowly turns pink, red and finally blue with the changing light (Sugita Katyal, 2004 p. 19).

TOURISM DEVELOPMENT IN INDONESIA

One developing nation that has experienced the ups and downs of tourism development is Indonesia—the largest Muslim country, the third largest democracy and the fourth most populous nation in the world. In the late 1960s, when it foresaw the depletion of its huge petroleum and natural gas reserves (it is now a new importer of petroleum), the strongly centralized military government in Jakarta selected tourism as one of its primary sectors for development. Through foreign direct investment (especially in the form of multinational chain hotels and travel agencies) as well as government-sponsored promotion techniques culminating in the highly successful 1991 Visit Indonesia Year campaign, the Indonesian tourism industry boomed in the late 1990s. Unfortunately, these fortunes rather suddenly took several turns for the worst. First came the unfavourable international publicity from the rioting and civil disorders leading up to the dramatic fall of the Suharto government in May 1997. Then the 11 September 2001 terrorist attacks disrupted the entire global tourism industry. As recovery slowly but surely began, the tragic bombing in Bali on 12 October 2002 again gave Indonesia unwanted publicity and frightened away foreign visitors. As a final blow, the SARS epidemic had a profoundly negative impact on the whole of East Asia's tourism industry.

Despite all these setbacks, the Indonesian tourism industry today is much stronger and more mature as a result of its collective creativity, flexibility and innovation. A new and important player came onto the stage of Indonesian tourism—the domestic tourist. Through, clever promotional campaign aimed at filling idle capacity with domestic tourists, but especially through the efforts of perhaps millions of small- and medium-sized tourism enterprises, the industry now employs some twelve million people and has dramatically reduced its dependence on tourists from Western countries. The foreign tourists are now coming from the Southeast and East Asia regions and a gradual process of empowerment of the indigenous labour force in tourism has taken place. Moreover, the domestic tourism industry has become a key player in the efforts at decentralization of political power and giving greater political autonomy to the islands outside of Java and Bali. These two islands contain about 65 per cent of Indonesia's 220 million people.

There are three conflicting views of tourism: advocacy, caution and adaptability? Such analysis is quite similar to the Hegelian trilogy of the thesis, antithesis and synthesis. These ideas will be applied to the experience of Indonesia. An attempt will be made to show that if tourism in a developing country shifts away from an overemphasis on foreign visitors to a more balanced one that includes domestic tourists, there is hope that modern, well-planned and well-conceived tourism can indeed be a nation builder, rather than neocolonialism. Hopefully, Indians at all levels of society can profit from this Indonesian experience. These two huge countries have many things in common, including cultural heritage. After all, Indonesia does come from the Greek word meaning, 'Islands of the Indies.'

THE ROLE OF TOURISM IN ECONOMIC DEVELOPMENT

There are many major constraints to economic development facing developing countries today. These include balance of payment deficits, high unemployment, a fragile ecosystem, the depletion of scarce, non-renewable natural resources, as well as the social and political instability that results from them. Consequently, they are always looking for new and creative ways to improve economic and social welfare. One example is the tourism sector, which is currently receiving a lot of attention from development economists. Using standard economic concepts such as foreign exchange, balance of payments, gross domestic product, multiplier, employment absorption and redistribution of income, economists have produced a guarded optimism about tourism as an economic activity. There are many links in the long chain called the 'tourist product', so many stakeholders are involved.

One tourist product of special interest to developing countries is cultural tourism, because these countries possess a great deal of the world's rich cultural heritage. Many of the ancient wonders of the world and the birthplaces of great religions are all located in developing countries. These ancient civilizations are often culturally richer than materially and technologically modern nations.

FOUR PRINCIPAL APPROACHES TO TOURISM

The past studies can be divided into four chronological (yet co-existing) groups, each representing an approach to tourism. The advocacy approach represents the early writings, which deal with tourism's economic benefits. Among other things, this includes its potential to support diverse economic activities, to generate jobs, and to earn foreign exchange needed for development. This approach reached its height in the 1960s and brought unprecedented national and international attention to tourism. But since it was a one-sided perspective, it led to the emergence of a cautionary approach. This second group of writings, appearing mostly in the 1970s, either questioned or totally rejected the advocacy position. It argued that tourism can result in many socio-economic disbenefits; generating mostly seasonal or menial jobs, resulting in economic leakage, commodifying the culture as well as promoting prostitution and the sex industry. Thus, tourism, especially mass tourism, caused conflicts of many sorts.

As the two approaches stood by their respective positions, an adaptency approach found a niche to fill. It recognized that the earlier positive (advocacy) and negative (cautionary) views on tourism focused solely on its impacts. It was felt that these influences can be controlled in general, by promoting alternative forms of tourism development—or in particular, by adapting tourism to its host destination. This new approach took both nature and culture as its combined context. It favours such strategies as small-scale development, controlled tourism, sustainable tourism, life seeing tourism and ecotourism.

The adaptency approach tried to alert people to the obvious dangers of mass tourism and proposed alternative forms of tourism development as a solution. These adapted forms of tourism try to respect the relationships between the host and the guest in the tourism interchange. It comes under a variety of new types of tourism. They include such things as agritourism, appropriate tourism, balanced tourism, community-based tourism, compatible tourism, cottage tourism, ethnic tourism, farm tourism, festival tourism, gentle tourism, green tourism, indigenous tourism, life seeing tourism, nature tourism, paratourism, people-to people tourism, recreation tourism, responsible tourism, rural tourism, sensible tourism, small-scale tourism, soft tourism, sport tourism, and sustainable tourism. Ecotourism is the latest version, which has gained international popularity—both in concept and practise—during the last few years. The year 2002 was proclaimed the Year of Ecotourism by the World Tourism Organization (WTO). While these types focus on the tourism activity, other types are based on the type of tourists. The long list of examples includes anthropological tourists, business tourists, charter tourists, culture tourists, domestic tourists, drifters, elderly tourists, nostalgic tourists, pilgrim tourists, pleasure tourists, recreational tourists, spiritual tourists and youth tourists.

As the three approaches continued with their respective thrusts or orientations, it gradually became evident that by focusing on tourism's impact and forms, only a fragmentary view on tourism is attained. To understand tourism, it is necessary to also study it as a whole or as a system. This emerging line of thinking led to the formation of a knowledge-based approach. Having benefited from the earlier perspectives, it opts for a systematic treatment of tourism and considers it as a multidisciplinary field of investigation. It favors importing theories and methods from fields related to tourism and then aiming at cumulatively forming a knowledge-based foundation. This approach keeps an open mind about the works of the other three and selectively incorporates their contributions with its own. It does this without losing sight of its ultimate goal of the formation of knowledge on tourism, and its advancement to frontiers beyond. For example, the field of business ethics has contributed the concept of 'stakeholder' to help in the evaluation of the impacts of modern tourism on the economy and society in general.

In light of this concept, the tourism industry is today generally divided among three main actors:

1. those who seek satisfaction or welfare through their travels (tourists or guests)
2. those whose lives and places in society become the medium for its practice (residents or hosts)
3. those who promote and accommodate it (tourism businesses or brokers).

Literature on tourism attempts to discuss how each of these three (host, guest, and broker) groups define themselves as one group, or in relation to one another. It also notes the cultural forces and perspectives which influence their relationship, as well as suggests ways which would enlarge the concept of tourist welfare from its apparently unilateral (tourist-centered) view to a multilateral strategy—making tourism beneficial for all: guests, hosts and brokers. With the passage of time, tourism has gradually evolved into a business, a trade, an industry, a mega-industry, and now a phenomenon of untold dimensions.

These three distinct populations (guest, host, and broker), their forms (group and subgroups) and forces (cultures and subcultures), among other things, are at work due to tourism. Significantly, they do not happen in isolation—it is tourism which, by juxtapositioning them, sets the stage for a 'tourism theatre of operation.' It is a unique mix of these forms and forces, which—combined with tourism infrastructure and superstructure—become the backdrop and stage front in what is today called 'community based tourism.' While the picture capturing these forms and forces still appears manageable, the reality is that their relationship—and hence how they constitute tourism—is different from destination to destination. Each host community features a unique combination or pattern (whether in quantity or quality, in degree or kind, in dominance or submission, etc.), with an equally unique dialectic relationship between and among them. Therefore, while the 'ingredients,' 'recipes,' or 'menu' remains about the same (at least in names) across the universe of destinations, in each case, the outcome would be different. In this sense, there is no such thing as tourism, but tourisms (Jafari 1983).

Along these same lines, many other concepts and applications have emerged from tourism research. These include advancing knowledge in relation to physical and social carrying capacity, cultural commercialization, tranquilization of the arts and artifacts, economic dependency, tourist ghettos, local vs. multinational tourism developments and controls, resident vs. tourist use of community's resources, planning for tourism's growth and development, and many more.

To conclude, research-based strategies must be developed in order to foster harmonious co-existence of the three (host, guest, and broker) populations. Each must recognize its place in the system and observe their corresponding rights and duties. Such an informed form of tourism responds to the needs and expectations of the guests and hosts, without making the host prisoners to the guest's welfare. Freedom of traveling and responding to various needs of the tourists cannot be at the expense of denying freedom to others.

NEW MORAL TOURISM AND BUSINESS ETHICS

Any treatment of the knowledge-based approach to tourism would not be complete without including the growing field of business ethics. J. Butcher (2003) has pointed out that the moralization of tourism is a product of the disillusionment of modern societies. It is manifested in a search for the elements that new moral tourists deem to be missing from their lives: community, a sense of spirituality and closeness to nature. Ethical consumption ends up moralizing about exaggerated problems between people, hosts, and cultures. However, it neglects an assessment of the social inequalities that characterize relationships between nations. It must therefore be accompanied by the insights of business ethics, especially the key concept of stakeholder analysis. For example, many non-governmental organizations (NGOs) have adopted ethical brands such as ecotourism as an exemplary form of sustainable development. However, this reflects profoundly low horizons with regard to the potential to address poverty and inequality.

New moral tourism is tourism that is justified less in terms of the desires of the consumer and more from the perspective of its perceived influence on the natural world and on the culture of the host. In economic terms, mass tourism seems self-evidently vitally important. However, it has increasingly been discussed as a cultural and environmental phenomenon. But this does not mean it is automatically destructive. This emphasis on tourism as a cultural and environmental problem informs the moralization of tourism. The moralization of tourism involves two mutually reinforcing notions:

1. Mass tourism is deemed to have wrought damage to the environment and to the cultures exposed to it. Hence, new types of tourism are proposed that are deemed benign to the environment and benevolent towards other cultures.
2. This ethical tourism is deemed to be better for tourists too. It is more enlightening, encouraging respect for other ways of life and a critical reflection on the tourist's own developed society.

New tourism is both an appeal to a certain sense of enlightenment about one's effect on others and an environmental imperative. The new tourist is the 'thinking tourist.' She or he is more educated, more independent, more flexible and more green. New tourism considers the environment and culture of the destination visited to be a key part of the holiday experience. Advocacy is the key feature of new tourism. New Moral Tourism is a pervasive agenda for governments, companies and NGO's. For example, Agenda 21 for the Travel and Tourism Industry reflects an impulse for the education of tourists.

An important question is involved here. If the new tourists propose to protect nature from the excesses of development, how do they address the poverty and inequality arising from a dearth of development in many parts of the world? Ecumenical antipathy towards tourism has long been a common theme. But criticism of tourism today is less conservative and religious, and more radical and secular. There is an emphasis on changing the consumptive patterns and the behavior of holiday makers in favor of holidays that are deemed benign to the environment and benevolent to the culture of the host. Some tourism organizations have even produced ethical codes of conduct.

Projects based around preserving the environment are, in truth, unlikely to help in liberating people from poverty. As a result, some people have questioned the importance of new tourism. They observe that package holidays remain popular in spite of the assault on their ethical credentials. New tourism is estimated to remain below 10 per cent of total tourism for the foreseeable future. Nevertheless, new tourism is a prominent moral agenda. One can argue that new moral tourism can reflect a distinct disillusionment with family, people at work, people in the neighbourhood, and perhaps humanity. The new moral tourism may even be seen as an alienation from modern life. The mass tourist enjoys conviviality, crowds and people! The mass package tourist can lay claim to being more 'people oriented.'

Because there is little room for critical insight in the name of tolerance for diversity, new moral tourism can become a stifling etiquette that presents a barrier to discovery. On the one hand, mass tourism is often characterized by sameness and as being crude, destructive and modern. On the other hand, new moral tourism is characterized by being different and sensitive, constructive and critical of modern 'progress'. The self-conscious search for the 'backstage regions', which are those hidden from the less discerning tourist, is characteristic of new moral tourism. Sustainable development is development that meets the needs of the present without compromising the ability of future generations to meet their own needs. Sustainability has always lacked conceptual clarity and has been interpreted in different ways. Sustainable tourism has tended to develop increasingly as a socio-environmental category, with an emphasis on people as well as an effect on development of ecological processes. There is a profound sensitivity towards cultural change.

Today, tourism is becoming increasingly moralized. Consumer choices over what kind of holiday one prefers are transformed into moral choices, seen as having significant consequences for one's host and also for oneself. Historically, the extension of tourism has always been subject to criticisms—usually from those who wanted to preserve its benefits for themselves. It is easy to see this as a common brand of elitism with the more privileged trying to differentiate themselves from the uncultured masses. Thomas Cook criticized the sheer snobbery of the critics of tourism of his day. The origin of the word 'travel' is 'travail', meaning work, and traveling at the time of the Grand Tour required great endeavor. Business ethics can help overcome this dilemma.

The propensity to turn in on itself and to become self-critical is an important new characteristic of the new moral tourism. To be a traveller is to take an interest in the local culture, while the tourist is passive. A traveller is a thinking tourist. In general, for travellers, getting there is likely to be at least as important as being there. New moral tourism has tended to broaden the scope of what is to be criticized. There can be no fixed dividing line between mass tourism and new moral tourism today, as the latter's criticism of the former has increasingly turned in on itself. New moral tourism is not just critical of others but is self-critical too. New moral tourism is a fluid, moralistic perspective rather than a defined set of products or activities. The two overarching assumptions of new moral tourism are that environment and cultures are fragile in the face of growing numbers of tourists.

A key concept is 'carrying capacity'. It is the maximum use of any site without causing negative effects on the resources, reducing visitor satisfaction or exerting adverse impact upon society, economy and cultures. In fact, development itself, including tourist development, can actually transform the carrying capacity. Some forms of 'sustainable tourism' advocated by new moral tourism are designed to leave indigenous societies as they are—culturally authentic, but unfortunately grindingly poor. When too many people seek out the beauty of a remote place, it ceases to be remote and loses its beauty. Perceptual limits on tourism—at least those perceived by the host societies—cannot be understood outside the broader context of development and prospects for development. The present controversy over the use of the Taj Mahal is a good example of this problem. More people may pose environmental problems, but they also create possibilities for resolution of these problems at greater levels of development and with more opportunities for people as a result. More people help finance a solution than simply pose an environmental problem.

Hedonism, which was once a virtue of tourism, has now become a threat. Sex tours to developing countries is a primary example. In place of spontaneity, caution and wariness are characteristic of the new moral tourism. Freedom from tourists is pitted against freedom to travel. The critics argue that we should mould our desires, and indeed our lives, around what they consider to be environmental limits. The preservationist emphasis not only protects the people from the outside world, but also from any prospect of material development. In a sense, the code makers treat tourists and travellers like children, who are unable to think and act as autonomous adults. The new emphasis on ethical tourism implies a need for moral regulation at the interface of the tourist and their host. Before going on holiday, one should 'environmentally audit oneself'. However, the attempt to provide guidelines for individual conduct during holidays can be misguided. The advise offered is often derived from a particular ethical outlook. It is often one that stresses the pre-eminence of nature over development and is then a universal set of rules for all. Like other codes in business ethics, many feel that no rules or codes can be applied to every specific situation. They need to be general and flexible. Individuals may decide differently in different circumstances for a variety of reasons—these are matters for consideration and debate. To try to regulate these decisions by drawing ethical guidelines is a very challenging and difficult task. The insights of business ethics are helpful.

The cultural critique of modern tourism which views tourism as the destroyer of cultural diversity misses the social context of the poverty and inequality that many tourists come across on their travels. Reflected in the promotion of cultural diversity and environmental conservation is an implicit acceptance of the status quo with regards to the broader inequalities that characterize the world we live in. Perhaps the most striking criticism of mass tourism is that it constitutes domination or even colonialism or imperialism in the developing countries. Social class is rarely invoked in the moralized discussion of tourism.

Product choice is an important consideration in business ethics. Far from the discredited institutions of government, it is as consumers that we are apparently free to exercise our choice in the pursuit of a better world. For some people, buying a holiday, and how one conducts oneself abroad, has become a conspicuous expression of morality. Local lifestyle habits have now become globally consequential. In this way, globalization is often invoked to emphasize the interconnected nature of society. We are all bound together through the market. Ethical consumption reflects a very limited moral universe. Societies' problems cannot be addressed in the basis of consumption alone. Lifestyle politics means political solutions at the level of the individual in their daily lives. A pro-poor tourism aims to help the very poorest in rural parts of the developing countries by attracting tourists appreciative of the undisturbed environment. Tourism is sometimes suggested as a less damaging form of development by environmentalists who fear that developing countries may be committing 'ecocide' through logging and other activities that use up natural resources in their struggle to survive.

Proper development of tourism is a win-win situation.

Schemes that key into cultural tourism markets in order to engender development often make reference to this broader perspective of cultural conservation or enhancing the national spirit. Nevertheless, the relationship between tourism and culture is seen as being a fragile one. Tourism's role in maintaining aspects of culture is by making culture pay. The potential positive aspects of cultural tourism are building community pride, enhancing a sense of identity, encouraging revival or maintenance of traditional crafts, enhancing external support for minority groups and preservation of their culture, broadening community horizons, enhancing local and external appreciation and support for culture heritage.

Ecotourism is responsible travel to nature areas, that conserves the environment and improves the well-being of local people. The development of an ecotourism project depends on building a local constituency that has a vested economic interest in protecting their natural resources. When ecotourism is presented as a dynamic development strategy, it is important to point out that it offers relatively little in the way of benefits. If tourism is to have the greatest beneficial impact, then other related industries need to develop. Mass tourism is no *panacea,* but it is an industry. Like any other, it can and does improve the lifestyle of the people where it is located. Consequently, it is difficult to accept that small scale tourism has anything significant to offer to the development agenda. The conservation agenda that purports to offer development through nature-based tourism is rarely a matter of free choice for developing countries. North-South relations are characterized by an intense inequality in political and economic life.

In conclusion, tourism is being recast as an area for moral prescription and critical self-awareness. Unfortunately, this can become a recipe for wariness and personal guilt in an arena traditionally associated with innocence, fun and a footloose and fancy-free attitude. The root of the modern criticism of tourism is to see the relationship between people and nature as brittle. Hence, the relationship between host and tourist is regarded as adversarial. New moral tourists travel with a sense of a personal mission, as tourism is recast as philanthropy towards the hosts and a 'unique experience' for the tourist. However, the ire directed against tourism is misplaced. The growth of mass tourism has been a mark of real progress in modern society. Many can travel abroad for leisure, when only a couple of generations ago, foreign travel was a rarity for most people. New opportunities have opened up as holiday companies have expanded to even more destinations. This has not always been at the expense of those hosting the growing number of tourists.

In poor countries, the gulf between tourist and host is more marked. The best response is a call for more responsible and sensitive tourism. For the most part, tourists are ordinary people. While the moralization of tourism can apparently see only the differences between people, we should regard travel for leisure, for education or for business as part of a common culture. The moral baggage associated with travel now threatens to shackle a spirit of adventure for travellers young and old. As travel has become a focus of moral codes, something can easily be lost along the way if good business and ethical analysis is not involved. If travel is to really be a life expanding activity or a unique experience of any kind, then it has to rely on the individual consumer to make responsible choices.

DOMESTIC TOURISM VS. INTERNATIONAL TOURISM IN INDONESIA

Some interesting research has been done on tourism in developing countries. Previous works such as de Kate (1979) and North (1977), that evaluated the impact of tourism development in developing countries, showed that the positive economic, social, cultural and environmental impact of tourism development in host countries have been generally negligible. However, more recent tourism works such as Lee (1993) and Singh (1997) show that tourism impacts depend largely on the types of tourism developed, the travel motive of the tourist groups attracted, and their activities within destinations. Nevertheless, there is presently a dearth of empirical studies on the types of tourism that tourists value or prefer in many developing countries. There is also gross inadequacy of studies on tourist's values, activities or motivations for visiting destinations in developing countries, particularly Southeast Asia. Such inadequacies have resulted in speculation and unfounded beliefs on tourist attitudes and behavior, even in official publications.

In the case of Indonesia, which covers one eighth of the area around the equator and has 17,000 islands inhabited by more than four hundred ethnic groups, there is an enormous variety of tourist products that could be offered, especially in the areas of nature or ecotourism and cultural tourism. Some tourism works, notably Nielson (1984), Volkman (1982), McKean (1982), Van Dreven (1984) and Adams (1984), indicate that official tourism position in Indonesia may be inaccurate regarding the benefits of tourism. They show that tourists are having a great impact on the cultural and natural resources of Indonesia, and some of it is unfavorable.

In a related manner, stereotypes of foreign tourists as distinct from domestic tourists in their destination values, demands and motivations for travel are commonly held. They are used to differentiate the domestic from the foreign markets in developing country destinations (Lee, 1993, Singh, 1997). For instance, domestic tourists are believed to be more interested in and desirous to learn about the environment and are therefore more environmentally responsible than foreign tourists. However, Western studies such as Mosteller (1999), Greenwood and Moscardo (1999), Lubbe (1998) and Eftichaidou (2001), that compared domestic with foreign tourists in their use of destination environments, suggest that such stereotypes may not be accurate. Rather, foreign tourists are revealed as more interested and active in their use of destination environments and are also more caring and conservation oriented than domestic tourists. The same is true for cultural tourism, where foreign tourists frequently study beforehand and thus appreciate the cultures they are visiting.

Such conflicting positions suggest that empirical studies are needed to establish the types of tourism that are most desired or valued by tourists. They are also needed to verify whether differences exist between foreign and domestic tourists in their travel values, motivations and activities in destination environments in developing countries. Such empirical studies are particularly needed in Southeast Asia, as their continuous lack may heighten existing speculations and misconceptions on tourists' demands and activities. There is, therefore, the need for research to establish the types of tourism resources and activities tourists participate in, and their motives for visiting destinations in developing countries—especially Southeast Asia—which has been long neglected by tourism demand studies. Without such parallel non-Western studies, generalizations on these facets of tourists' attitudes and behavior may be hindered. Results obtained from the Western world cannot be applied directly to developing countries because of differences in environmental, economic and socio-cultural milieu.

INDONESIA AND ITS TOURISM RESOURCES

Indonesia is located in Southeast Asia astride the equator. It occupies a land area of almost 2 million square kilometres spread over some 17,000 islands and includes an exclusive sea zone area of 3.1 million square kilometres. Thus, the total area of Indonesia is over 5 million square kilometres with a population of 220 million people. As a result, it has one of the most diverse cultures in the world. However, the regional (inter-island) distribution of population in Indonesia is extremely unbalanced. The islands of Java, Madura and Bali account for just 7 per cent of the total land area but contain almost 65 per cent of the total population.

The country is characterized by the presence of several natural environments and cultural resources such as landforms, islands, rivers, lakes and beaches as well as rare species of animals, birds and plants. There are also several unique cultural resources that are associated with the ancient trade, shrines and sacred grounds, festivals and dances. Some of these date back to antiquity. Indonesia's new tourism promotion motto emphasizes that it is the ultimate in diversity.

Tourism was given little attention before 1969, when the government set up a special department devoted to it. Since then, considerable efforts have been made to promote the industry, and during the Second Development Plan (Repelita II) a master plan was drawn up for the development of tourism, with special emphasis being given to the islands of Sumatra, Java, Bali, Sulawesi and Nusa Tenggara. This eventually resulted in the ten provinces of North Sumatra, West Sumatra, Jakarta, West Java, Central Java, Yogyakarta, East Java, Bali, South Sulawesi and North Sulawesi being singled out as particularly important tourist destinations.

In these regions the government undertook to contribute to the development of potential tourist areas by providing infrastructure and general services, while calling on the private sector to establish the necessary hotel, leisure and entertainment facilities. While these measures had some success and substantial amounts of both foreign and domestic investment funds have been channelled into the hotel and tourism sector since the mid-1970s, the increase in tourist arrivals, though considerable, continued to fall below expectations until the late 1980s, when tourism became the third highest source of foreign exchange after petroleum and timber exports. Today, after the implementation of political autonomy and decentralization, each province, even down to the regency level, has a government office to promote tourism.

The prospect of declining export revenue from oil (today Indonesia is a net importer of oil), as well as the need to provide jobs for Indonesia's rapidly rising population (some 2.5 million young people join the labor force each year), gave rise in the early 1980s to a new appreciation of the value of tourism as a non-oil earner of foreign exchange and a labor intensive service industry. This caused a major review of all issues related to the growth of the sector. As a result, a number of shortcomings were identified and corrective measures were taken. Thus, on 1 April 1983, visa requirements were lifted for tourists from many countries. Several promotional packages were introduced by the country's international airline, Garuda Indonesian Airways, and its monopoly on flights to such important tourist destinations like Bali was lifted. This liberalization of the tourist arrivals did not keep pace with hotel construction and occupancy rates remained relatively low. By 1987, however, the impact of the tourism promotion efforts of previous years had begun to bear fruit. The Visit Indonesia Year in 1991 was considered a great success despite the fact that the year began with the first Iraq war in February 1991.

Tourist arrivals increased by an average of approximately 7 per cent per year between 1980 and 1986, while tourist spending increased by an average of approximately 13 per cent per year during the same period. Since 1986, the growth of the tourist industry has accelerated sharply, with the number of tourists visiting Indonesia increasing by 28.5 per cent to 1.06 million and tourist spending increasing by almost 62 per cent to $955 million in 1987. Of these arrivals, approximately 75 per cent entered Indonesia through the three main gateways of Jakarta, Bali and Medan. The number of star rated hotels increased from 281 (with 22,999 rooms) to 340 (with 26,931 rooms) between the end of 1986 and 1987. The growth of the tourist industry continued with the number of tourist arrivals rising to $1.29 million in 1988 and the value of tourist spending rising to $1,060 million.

Beyond the merchandise account, 1994 witnessed a strong growth in tourism. The number of tourist arrivals officially estimated to have risen from 3.4 million in 1993 to 4.4 million in 1994, and to have contributed some $4.6 billion to Indonesia's foreign exchange earnings in the latter year (AWSJ, 29 December 1994). This will have helped restrain the growth of Indonesia's traditional deficit on invisible accounts, which will have come under pressure from several sources. These include rising demand for trade related services associated with the increase in merchandise trade; higher net outflows of interest, profits and dividends (IPD) resulting from the continued growth and the deteriorating structure of Indonesia's foreign debt; and expanding foreign direct and portfolio investment (Sarwar Hobohm, 1995, p. 15).

Development of Tourist 1982-1987

	1982	1987
Tourist arrivals ('000)	592.1	1,060.3
Tourist spending ($ mn)	358.8	954.6
Hotel rooms ('000)	38.6	99.3
Travel agencies	426	506

People employed	113.9	390.0
Occupancy rate, star rated hotels (%)	54.4	48.5
Occupancy rate, non-star rated hotels (%)	33.8	28.9

Sources: Ministry of Finance, Nota Keuangan; Central Bureau of Statistics, Indikator Ekonomi.

However, the period from February to early June 1998, was one of the most tumultuous periods in Indonesia's economic and social history. A meltdown in the economy and devastating riots forced President Suharto's resignation on 21 May, moving Indonesia into uncharted waters. A key issue then became the development of new political laws and institutional infrastructure that would culminate in a general election in June 1999. New President Habibie oversaw the political transformation as an interim president. A stable political climate became a precondition for the return of confidence and capital. At the beginning of the transition, the economy continued to fall sharply—an uncertain and volatile backdrop to the political reform process—and extreme economic pressures made it difficult to maintain social order. (C Johnson, 1998 p. 3)

The economy was brought to its knees by a collapse in confidence and in the exchange rate. The government had sought help from the IMF in October 1997 and agreements on financial assistance and reforms designed to rebuild confidence were signed on 31 October (IMF I) and 15 January (IMF II) (Soesastro and Basri, 1998 pp. 10-26), but these attempts to restore economic stability failed for a variety of reasons. The IMF then reviewed its third program in the light of another sharp deterioration in economic and financial conditions. (C Johnson, 1998, p. 3)

As has been mentioned above, tourism plays an important role in the economy. At its peak, tourism brought $6.6 billion of foreign currency into Indonesia in 1997 (Jakarta Post, 1 May 1998). This has declined as a result of smoke from the fires of Borneo (Kalimantan) and Sumatra (even in the areas that have been affected), political tensions, social unrest and aircraft accidents. As a result, many international airlines reduced or halted flights to Indonesia in early 1998. Domestic airlines were decimated by reduced demand for air travel and by leasing or debt servicing costs of aircraft which were charged in dollars while revenue was in rupiah. Domestic flights were cut back, resulting in significant job losses. Hotels suffered reduced occupancy as international and domestic travelling declined. For example, occupancy in Jakarta was 30–40 per cent in the first two months of 1998, compared with an average of 75 per cent before the crisis (Jakarta Post, 27 March 1998).

Thus, Indonesia's economic collapse was the most profound to affect any significant market-oriented economy in decades. It is certainly far sharper than the recession of the early 1960s. Replacing President Suharto with President Habibie did not lead to a significant improvement in immediate economic prospects, although the resumption of external assistance by the international community did mitigate the extent of the collapse. Even so, the private sector, both local and foreign, remained wary about extending its economic activities (K. Evans, 1997, p. 5). Even today, Indonesia is still recovering from being the country hardest hit by the Asian financial and economic crisis of 1997-1998. Its real GDP declined by 13 per cent in 1998 as its banking and modern corporate sectors collapsed in the wake of short-term capital outflows, revealing fundamental structural deficiencies in the Indonesia 'miracle'. Restructuring and recovery were slow. Overall, Indonesia is lagging behind the other hand-hit Asian countries, despite growing faster in some years. Moreover, the recovery remains fragile and restructuring still has a long way to go (P.R. Deuster, 2002, p. 5).

However, in early 2004, macroeconomic stability had been restored and the economy is growing again, albeit only moderately. Almost without exception, macroeconomic indicators are favorable or improving. By way of a few examples, the exchange rate has been remarkably stable for the past several months; the international reserves position is very strong; public debt is looking much better; and the government's upcoming bond issue has received an enthusiastic international response (L.R. Kenward, 2004, p. 10).

In summary, since the fall of the Suharto government in May 1998,

Indonesia has been characterized by frequent political upheavals, religious crises and poor management of her economy and inadequate infrastructures. These problems were associated with the process of decentralization and political autonomy being given to the outer islands. Unfavorable international publicity discouraged foreign tourists from visiting Indonesia, especially since the global war on terrorism has branded Muslims as terrorists. This crisis has led to a dramatic decline in foreign tourist arrivals. However, recent political events, especially the peaceful, orderly and parliamentary first and second rounds of the presidential elections, have much improved the outside perceptions of Indonesia.

The new government of President Susilo Bambang Yudhohono went into office on 20 October 2004. It has indicated considerable interest in developing tourism aimed at attracting desired tourists markets using a more balanced approach than the Suharto government. The remarkable growth in domestic tourism during the last six years of political and economic crisis has created a need for information about this surprising development. Such information would shed light on the types of tourism resources that domestic tourists demand as well as their activities and motivations for travel. Such information is important in order to establish which destinations, environmental features and activities are also in accord with priorities in tourism development planning, programmes/projects and marketing.

TRAVEL MOTIVATIONS

Previous motivation studies exist in the West, mostly in Europe and North America. They show that people's motivation influences their destination values and choices of travel activities. These include Mosteller (1998), Dann (1988), Oh et al (1995), Iso-Ahola (1982); Plog (1991); Pyo et al. (1989); Moscardo and Percy (1986); Crompton (1979); McGehee et al. (1996); Uysal and Jurowski (1994); Muller (1997) and Moscardo et al. (1996). The more recent of these studies include Muller and O'Cass (2001); and Eftichaidou (2001). These studies suggest that leisure visits to destinations are multi-motive and that visitors differ in their travel motives. However, contact with local people/culture, change of scenery/getting away to a novel environment for sightseeing and social interaction are the most important travel reasons. Additionally, these studies show that destination selection and visits were linked to motives such as entertainment, sports, action/adventure and health.

In contrast, there is a dearth of studies on tourism motivation in the Third World, especially Southeast Asia. Thus, little is known concerning the travel motives of Indonesians themselves as well as foreign visitors to Indonesia because of paucity of studies in this direction.

However, studies by Moscardo (2001), Eftichiadon (2001), Greenwood and Moscardo (1999), and Lubbe (1998) in Western environments, indicate that domestic and foreign tourist differed in their travel motivations. First, foreign tourist display more interest and participate more in destination features and activities. Foreign tourists were also more interested in learning or experiencing the environment and are more critical of available tourism products. In contrast, domestic tourists fit stereotypes of visitors interested only in the sun, sea and sand (recreational/leisure tourism) and were much less interested in learning about the environment and local culture. Second, cultural context was shown in these studies to play a salient role in the destination selection and activities of tourists. Foreign tourists were more general and adventurous than local tourists in their destination choices. Additionally, while the dominant desire in destination choice by foreign tourists was appreciating and experiencing new environments and cultures, locals were more motivated to visit destinations where they felt comfortable with the language, culture and food.

Past studies that have examined the activities of tourists in their destinations abound in Western environments, mostly in North America, Western Europe and Australia. Sadly, the situation in Indonesia differs. These Western studies include Adams et al. (1975), Burch (1976), Field and O'Leary (1991), and Goffman (1971). Other more recent studies of this type include Moscardo (1992; 2001), Greenwood and Moscardo (1999), Woods (2000), and Oh et al. (1995). Among the important conclusions reached in these studies is that an individual's culture, social group or nationality does not adequately explain his or her tourism behavior and tastes.

Case studies on the types of tourism that attract priority values by visitors to developing countries in Southeast Asia are available in various publications by the World Tourism Organization (WTO). For the case of Indonesian domestic tourists, the major source of information is newspaper clippings from around the country compiled by the documentation section of the Center for Strategic and International Studies in Jakarta. The studies reveal that the range of destinations valued by visitors to Southeast Asia, including Indonesia, is wide. There are several classifications of these destinations. First are the destinations that offer standardized and fleeting encounters with the natural features or the culture of the locality visited. Second are destinations offering combined seaside beaches or mountain resorts, and leisure holidays. Thirdly there are resort holiday destinations offering brief side trips to specially created or preserved environments where indigenous culture may be experienced. These studies also show that the destinations most valued and patronized in Indonesia are nature- or wildlife-based and beach or mountain holiday destinations, especially the national marine and reserve parks. In some cases the natural environmental features that attract priority value from visitors includes a variety of wildlife, bird life, aesthetic landscapes, mountain views, clear sandy beaches and swift flowing rivers/waterfalls. In other locations, the almost all-year sunshine, the traditional Indonesian culture/heritage, and historic significance were destination features considered to be of high priority value to visitors.

THE ROLE OF SMALL AND MEDIUM SIZED ENTERPRISES IN TOURISM

Two good examples of Indonesia's beach and mountain tourism resources are Parangtritis beach near Yogyakarta and Tawangmangu mountain resort area near Surakarta in Central Java. They are good examples of the lively entrepreneurial spirit that has provided some inspiration for the Indonesian tourism industry, that is still in crisis. One blessing in disguise on this long series of disasters for the tourism industry was forcing it to rethink its overall tourism paradigm. Indonesia now needs to move its focus from international tourists to domestic ones. The amazing rise of low-cost Indonesian airlines is yet another positive sign of the enormous entrepreneurial talent in the small and medium sized enterprise (SMEs) that are part of what Indonesians call the *ekonomirakyat* (people's economy). As the nation moves through various crises in the tourism industry, a new paradigm emerged: concentrate more on small and medium tourism enterprises (SMTEs).

Today there is a consensus on the importance of SMEs to national economies and social well-being in both developing and developed countries. In China, these firms—of which there may be 30 million or more—are small but growing by perhaps 30 per cent a year, twice the pace of the economy, and produces 60 per cent of the GDP according to *The Economist* (9 October 2004 p. 69). Indonesia plans to create 20 million SMEs that will employ an estimated 100 million people by the year 2020, according to the new appointed Minister for Economic Coordination, Aburizal Bakrie. Today they are estimated to employ 80 million people and 86 per cent of them are concentrated in agricultural, estates, animal husbandry, forestry and fishing sectors. In the trade, hotel and restaurant sector, 75 per cent of the enterprises are small, 21 per cent are medium and only 4 per cent are large scale.

A broad variety of national and international programs and pilot projects exist today, stimulating the shift towards SMEs in general and towards tourism and hospitality SMEs in particular. These SMTEs are an integral part of the tourism and hospitality industry around the world. If the normal definition of SMEs as companies employing up to 250 people is used, then the vast majority of hospitality enterprises are small. In Indonesia, the National Bureau of Statistics defines a small enterprise as one having less than nineteen employees, a medium one as having nineteen to one hundred and a large one as having more than a hundred employees. (Bisnis Indonesia, 6 January 2004). There are significant perceived benefits of SME development, particularly from a macro-economic point of view, making them attractive to tourism and hospitality planners on national and regional levels.

In Indonesia, the establishment of a 'people's economy', one of the four areas to which social safety net expenditure will be directed, involves the dispersion of economic decision-making power to large numbers of Indonesians. Discussion of the 'people's economy' at the November Special Session of the MPR culminated in Decree No. XVI/MPR/1998 on Political Economy within Economic Democracy, which stipulates that:

- National economic development is designed to create a broad base of small and medium scale enterprises and to foster mutually beneficial linkages between cooperatives, SMEs, large companies and state enterprises. The implementation of economic democracy shall seek to avoid the concentration of economic assets and forces in the hands of a small number of people and companies. Cooperatives and SMEs, as the main pillar of national economic development, shall be given as much opportunity, incentive and assistance as possible, without ignoring the role of big businesses and state enterprises.
- National land use shall be organized in a just manner, and the concentration of land use rights and land ownership in the hands of a few individuals or companies shall be prevented in light of efforts to enhance the strength of cooperatives, SMEs and the people at large.
- Banks and financial institutions shall give top priority to co-operatives and SMEs while continuing to work within the principles of sound business management (L Cameron, 1999, p. 4).

The decree greatly strengthens the hand of advocates of an interventionist approach to economic policy as against the advocates of reliance on market forces, and could result in discriminating measures against Chinese Indonesian businesses (L. Cameron, 1999, p. 4).

Perhaps the foremost among them is the SMEs ability to generate needed employment. In developing economies the ability to create one's own job may be critical in stemming unemployment. In mature economies, the number of small company start-ups increases in times of recession. Hence, in both cases, the SME job creation capability may be critical to national and especially regional economic stability. SMEs are further credited with creating a more diverse economic structure. They are seen as significantly more flexible in adapting to the ever changing market environment. They stimulate competition and are thus an essential driving force behind innovation and quality improvements. Most importantly, they are applauded for their general contribution to stimulating an enterprise culture. Many major industries use them in their outsourcing practices.

Analyses of tourism have indicated that these economic goals of job opportunities, increased earnings, investment and entrepreneurship as well as harmonious social and cultural development are better served by small-scale hospitality projects as opposed to large, industrially scaled enterprises. With small and medium sized tourism enterprises (SMTEs), the communication with buyers or guests is more direct. This avoids trade intermediaries. The entry costs are lower. There is more local ownership and a higher reliance on locally produced goods and other services. This results in lower import leakages and thus a higher multiplier effect. SMTEs are less intrusive and give a more organic mode of economic growth. They are considered very much more in tune with sustainable development. Moreover, many countries, particularly Indonesia, today place considerable emphasis on local autonomy and regional development, particularly in terms of curbing immigration trends from rural, mountain or island communities, or revitalizing regions facing economic downturns.

Taking into account all the arguments favouring SMTE development, they obviously generate widespread political and social support. Many today acknowledge the indisputable fact that small tourism and hospitality firms do compete successfully in local, national and even international markets. Nevertheless, it is also a fact that failure levels for SMEs are quite high. Some studies conducted in the US and UK confirm that the rule of thumb of bank managers is that about one-third of SMEs are successful, one-third are surviving in a struggle that could go either way, and the remaining third should not be in this business in the first place. Consequently, SMTEs deserve more attention from the private sector, the public sector and civil society, especially universities. Some of the most significant challenges they face today have to do with management, marketing, human resources, productivity and finances.

Typically a SMTE is in the hands of one, or sometimes several, owners who have a major portion of their wealth and. metaphorically speaking, their lives invested in it. More often than not, ownership and management are not split up. Thus, the management of the company is very much subject to the psychological make-up, personal motivations, attitudes and prejudices of the owner(s). Their level of business knowledge and management skills may in all probability be incomplete. This has significant bearing on the operations of the company. Characteristically, there is an informal relationship between the owner(s) and the operating personnel. This is evident in terms of loosely defined duties and responsibilities, equally loose control of their execution and unstructured communication processes. If they exist at all, organizational structures are frequently developed around the owner's interests and abilities.

Management in small firms is primarily adaptive. Emphasis is placed on adjusting as quickly as possible to current demand in order to gain maximum and immediate short-term benefits. These firms tend to react to the environment, with the planning horizon being short-term. In fact, in the view of many small firm owners, a business plan is something done for the banks, but is peripheral to the task of running the business. In Indonesia, the majority of SMEs still do not apply standard reporting procedures in their accounting because of lack of knowledge about how to prepare a financial report. (*Bisnis Indonesia*, 12 January 2004).

Some research suggests that the marketing function in SMTEs is actually more dynamic than the general impression. These companies do some research into their customer's needs, or at least formulate promotional plans on a yearly basis and use market-oriented pricing. However, their marketing is still thought to be approached with over-generalized methods and techniques basically ineffective for selling small and highly individualistic products and services. Few have formal marketing strategies expressed in a marketing plan. Moreover, they lack the resources, both in terms of financial funds and know-hows, to overcome problems of market access, independent distribution and branding. These problems are inherent to small and dispersed companies.

After many attempts throughout Indonesia's history, one of the most radical decentralizations ever undertaken anywhere in the world is now fully under way. The decentralization is now facing a set of critical challenges. The most serious of these are the lack of equity in revenue sharing, mushrooming local taxes, fees and restrictions on businesses and trade, uncertainty relating to investment, lack of clear direction from the center on decentralization and monitoring, disproportionate increases in minimum wages, and a lack of local electoral reform to improve accountability. A survey ranked corruption as the fourth most significant reason for not investing in Indonesia, after economic uncertainty, high input costs and the business downturn (P.R. Deuster, 2002, p. 7).

Studies have further shown the hospitality industry in general to be relatively lax in employee development and training. The situation in small and medium hospitality enterprises is even worse. In an industry where chronic skilled labour shortages are experienced, ironically the owners show one of the lowest perceptions of training needs for both themselves and their staff. With a short timeframe and in the face of costly and time consuming training programs, human resource development is not a priority on their agenda. According to a recent Ministry of Manpower and Transmigration statement, the Indonesian government will require SMEs to implement an occupational safety and health program (OSH) in their companies, in a bid to curb the number of workplace accidents. Indonesia still ranks among countries with the worst occupational safety records, and is in fact the second worst in the world after Russia (*Jakarta Post*, 8 May 2004).

Finally, it can be argued that SMTEs are at a disadvantage because of their size. Being not only small but also dispersed, they do not enjoy the benefits of economies of scale. When the seasonality of the tourism business is added to the equation, the results are low levels of productivity and higher costs. This is the framework within which it is difficult to finance renovation or invest in technological improvements. Financial problems can be further exacerbated by banks, which consider SMEs high risk and low profit enterprises. Thus SMTEs merit intense credit scrutiny and very probably high interest rates. Thus, it should be no surprise that the uncertainties of operation faced by these small businesses make banks wary of lending to them.

On one hand, SMTEs are commended by planners for their spirit of entrepreneurship and innovation, their job creating opportunities, their involvement in local economies and their ability to offer individuality and personalization of service to their customers. On the other hand, these enterprises are often plagued by erratic management and poor human resource practises. They do not have the advantages of economies of scale in relation with suppliers or markets. This results in lower productivity and inconsistent economic performance thus generating further problems with financing. The key question facing the SMTEs today is how to integrate within the highly competitive framework of a globalized economy, the entrepreneurial innovative spirit with formalized management procedures, thus ensuring stability without stifling creativity.

Choosing the right strategy for cooperation is decisive for the economic success (and viability) of tourism SMTEs. Their cooperation can be horizontal (across the same branch, such as hotel accommodation), vertical (integrating complementary businesses jointly responsible for producing a quality product) or lateral (integrating diverse businesses involved in tourism) partnerships or strategic alliances. Whatever the model, the intention is to improve SMTE competitiveness and sustainability by improving access to capital, managerial know-how, markets and technology. At the same time, this will reduce costs and increase efficiency through economies of scale.

In conclusion, despite their small size, Indonesian SMTEs as a group have provided stable employment opportunities and support the integration of local economies in peripheral areas, especially during recession periods. Moreover, after the Asian financial crisis and the collapse of international tourism in Indonesia, they also enabled the infusion of domestic tourist expenditures at the local level and thus enhanced all types of multipliers both locally and nationally. More importantly, they reduce the gap between the rich and the poor which was a major factor in the fall of Suharto. Unlike larger chain-based organizations that were built during his regime, they are normally privately owned, family run, employ local people and purchase local goods and services.

Despite their small size, Indonesian SMTEs have provided stable employment opportunities and services from suppliers within the local economy. SMTEs also provide tourists direct contact with the character of the destination. The recent national Olympic games (PON) in Palembang, Sumatra in September 2004 was a fine example. It was an opportunity for all Indonesians to appreciate this distinctly interesting and enjoyable area of the country. There may be a wait of several years before the international tourists return to the Indonesian tourist paradise. In the meantime, it is better to concentrate efforts on upgrading Indonesian SMTEs as they continue to serve the growing and dynamic domestic tourist sector. The years following the East Asian financial crises of July 1997 proved that the people's economy is quite entrepreneurial. This experience was clearly shown in case of the tourism industry. As a result, Indonesia is now better prepared for the inevitable return of international tourists, especially those who are looking for adaptive forms of tourism.

CONCLUSIONS

As Peter Drucker so eloquently pointed out in his famous management book entitled *The Age of Discontinuity* (1969), new industries can suddenly spring up and have far reaching impacts on economies and society in general. On this 100th anniversary of J.R.D. Tata's birth, a new industry has risen to prominence—the global tourism industry. Many feel that it is now the largest industry in the world, especially if its formal and informal sectors are included in the definition. Today some 240 million people are reported to be working in this truly global yet very local industry. Some applaud its ability to create jobs, earn foreign exchange, provide much needed infrastructure, preserve and promote cultural heritage, and even promote international peace and understanding. Others deplore the low quality of the jobs created, its ultimate leakages of that foreign exchange earnings through imports, the degradation of ancient and sacred cultures (symbolized by the highly profitable international sex industry) and the frequent targeting of tourists by terrorists. For some, tourism is a nation builder, while for others, it is neocolonialism in disguise. Using the concept of stakeholder analysis, it is possible to find a middle road between these two extremes by emphasizing a balanced approach to tourism which is both adaptive and includes domestic tourism.

One developing nation that has experienced the ups and downs of tourism development is Indonesia—the largest Muslim country, the third largest democracy and the fourth most populous nation in the world. In the late 1960s it selected tourism as one of its primary sectors for development. Through foreign direct investment (FDI) and government sponsored promotion techniques, its tourism industry boomed until it was severely upset by a series of unfavorable events, both in Indonesia and around the world, in the late 1990s and early part of this century.

Despite all these setbacks, the Indonesian tourism industry today is much stronger and more mature as a result of its collective creativity, flexibility and innovation. The key roles were played by domestic tourists and the many small and medium sized enterprises in the tourism sector. Through a clever promotional campaign aimed at filling idle capacity with domestic tourists but especially through the effort of perhaps millions of small and medium sized tourism enterprises, the industry now employs some 12 million people and has dramatically reduced its dependence on tourists from Western countries. The foreign tourists are now coming from the Southeast and East Asia region and a gradual process of empowerment of the indigenous labor force in tourism has taken place. Moreover, the domestic tourism industry has become a key player in the efforts at decentralization of political power and giving greater political autonomy for the islands outside of heavily populated islands of Java and Bali.

Thus, the Indonesian case is a good illustration of the three conflicting views of tourism: advocacy, caution and adaptency. If tourism in a developing country shifts away from an overemphasis on foreign visitors to a more balanced one that includes domestic tourists, there is hope that modern, well planned and well-conceived tourism can indeed be a nation builder rather than neo-colonialism. Hopefully, India will be able to profit from this Indonesian experience since both of these huge countries have many things in common including cultural heritage.

REFERENCES

Aburizal Bakrie. 'Membangun UKM, Membangun Ekonomi, Indonesia' Kompas (16 August 2004) p. 13.

Adam A, Lewis P, Drake F. The Outdoor Recreation Plan (Wisconsin Development Series) Madison, Wisconsin: Department of Resource Development, pp. 11-21.

Adam, K.M. *Come to Tana Toraja, 'Land of the Heavenly Kings': Travel Agents as Brokers of Ethnicity* Annals of Tourism Research Vol. 11 No. 3 (1984) pp, 469-485.

Ali, M. 'Balinese Tourism Damaged, Not Yet Dead' *The Jakarta Post* (16 December 2002) p. 17.

Awaritefe, Onome Daniel. *Tourist Values, Activities and Motivation for Travel to Third World Destinations: Case Study of Nigeria* Tourism Review Vol. 59 No. 1 (2004) pp. 34-43.

'Bali to Operate Its Own Airline as Others Slash Flights' *Jakarta Post* (12 November 2002) p. 17.

'Bali Revival Costs Rp. 3.5 Billion' *Jakarta Post* (4 December 2002) p. 17.

Bird, Kelley. 'Survey of Recent Development' *Bulletin of Indonesian Economic Studies* Vol 32 No. 1 (April, 1996) pp.3-32.

Britton, S. 'Tourism, Dependency and Development. A Mode of Analysis' in Singh TejVir, H.L. Theuns and F.M. Go (Eds) Towards Appropriate Tourism: The Case of Developing Countries Frankfurt: Peter Lang Veriag, 1999 pp. 93-116.

Bystrzanowski, Julian (Ed.). Tourism as a Factor of Change: A Sociocultural Study *Vienna: European Coordination Centre for Research and Documentation in Social Sciences*, 1989.

Burch, C. 'Estimation of Net Social Benefits from Outdoor Recreation' *Econometrical* Vol. 39 (1976) pp. 813-827.

Cameron, Lisa. 'Survey of Recent Development' *Bulletin of Indonesian Economic Studies* Vol. 35 No. 1 (April, 1999) pp. 3-40.

Center for Responsible Tourism. A Code of Ethics for Tourists San Anselmo, CA.: Center for Responsible Tourism, n.d. Contours, 'A Code of Ethics for the Tourist Industry' Contours Vol. 7 No. 6 (1986) p. 12-13.

Crompton, J 'An Assessment of the Image of Mexico as a Vacation Destination and the Influence of Geographical Location Upon the Image' *Journal of Travel Research* Vol. 17 No. 4 (1979) pp. 18-24.

Dann, G. 'Tourist Motivation: An Appraisal' *Annals of Tourism Research* Vol. 8 No. 2 (1981) pp. 187-219.

Dann, G. 'Tourists' Images Formation: An Alternative Analysis' in Fesenmaier, D, O'Leary, T. and Uysal, M. (Eds.) *Recent Advances in Tourism Marketing Research London*: The Harworth Press, 1996 pp. 41-55.

De Kadt, E. *Tourism: Passport to Development?* New York: Oxford University Press, 1979.

Deuster, Paul R. 'Survey of Recent Development' *Bulletin of Indonesian Economic Studies* Vol.38 No.1 (April 2002) pp.5-37.

Dogan, H. 'Forms of Adjustment: Sociocultural Impacts of Tourism' *Annals of Tourism Research* Vol. 16 (1989) pp. 216-236.

Drucker, P. *The Age of Discontinuity* New York: Harper & Row, 1969.

Eftichaidou, V. 'A Multi-motive Segmentation of Urban Visitors: The Case of Liverpool' *Journal of Tourism Studies* Vol. 12 No. 1 (2001) pp. 2-19.

EIU, Indonesia: Country Profile London: *The Economist* Intelligence Unit, 2004.

Evans, Kevin. 'Survey of Recent Development' *Bulletin of Indonesian Economic Studies* Vol. 34 No. 3 (December 1997) pp. 5-36.

Field, S and O'Leary, T. 'Tourist Study in Economic and Geographical Adaptation' *Science* Vol. 23 No. 4 (1991) pp. 12- 21.

Fitri, Emmy. 'Balinese Call for Review of Tourism Policy' *Jakarta Post* (30 November 2002) p.17.

Fitri Wulandari. 'New Airlines Propel Domestic Market to Pre- crisis Level' *Jakarta Post* (25 November 2002) p. 17.

Foss, Brad. 'Bali Bombings Reverberate Throughout Travel Industry' *Jakarta Post* (20 October 20 2002) p. 13.

Goffman, J. 'Defining and Estimating A Tourist Zone' *Journal of Marketing* Vol. 5 (1971) pp. 21-32.

Greenwood, T and Moscardo, G. 'Australian and North American Coastal and Marine Tourists: What Do They Want? in Saxena, N. (Ed.) *Recent Advances in Marine Science and Technology* Seoul, Korea: Ocean Research Development Institute, 1999 pp. 253- 260.

Harvey, D. *The Conditions of Postmodernity: An Enquiry into the Origins of Cultural Change* Oxford: Basil Blackwell, 1989.

Hobohm, Sarwar. 'Survey of Recent Development' *Bulletin of Indonesian Economic Studies* Vol 31 No. 1 (April, 1995) pp.3- 40.

'InvestasiBaruFokuskeSektordengan Return Tinggi' *Bisnis Indonesia* (6 January 6 2004) p. 7.

'Investing in China: Milking It' *The Economist* (October 9, 2004), p. 69.

Iso-Ahola, Seppo E. 'Toward a Social Psychological Theory of Tourism Motivation: A Rejoinder' *Annals of Tourism Research* Vol. 9 No. 2 (1982) pp. 256-262.

Jafari, Jafar. 'The Scientification of Tourism' in Lecture of Keynote Speakers: International Congress on Scientific Tourism Alexandria, Egypt: Faculty of Tourism and Hotels, Alexandria University, 1992.

Jafari, Jafar. 'Sociocultural Dimensions of Tourism: An English Language Literature Review' in Bystrzanowski, Julian (Ed.) *Tourism as a Factor of Change: A Sociocultural Study* Vienna: European Coordination Centre for Research and Documentation in Social Sciences, 1989.

Jafari, Jafar. 'Towards Tourism Mitigation—Recognizing Cultural Forms and Forces Influencing Freedom for Traveling' in *The Freedom of Traveling in the Year 2000—Rights and Duties of the Tourist* St. Gall, Switzerland: Association Internationaled'ExpertsScientifiques du Tourisme, 1999 pp. 21-42.

Johnson, Colin, 'Survey of Recent Development' *Bulletin of Indonesian Economic Studies* Vol. 34 No. 2 (August 1998) pp. 3-60.

Kasali, Rhenald. 'Rebuilding Shattered Tourism' Jakarta Post (January 4, 2003) p. 6.

Kenward, Lloyd R, 'Survey of Recent Development' *Bulletin of Indonesian Economic Studies* Vol. 40 No. 1 (April 2004) pp. 9-35.

Lee, J, *Tourism and Development in the Third World* London: Routledge, 1993.

Leheny, D, 'A Political Economy of Asian Sex Tourism' *Annals of Tourism Research* Vol. 17 (1995) pp. 367-384.

Lubbe, B, 'Primary Image as a Dimension of Destination Image: An Empirical Assessment' *Journal of Travel and Tourism Management* Vol. 7 No. 4 (1998) pp. 21-41.

McGehee, G, Loker-Murphy, L and Uysal, M, 'The Australian International Pleasure Travel Market Motivations from a Gendered Perspective' *The Journal of Tourism Studies* Vol. 7 No. 1 (1996) pp. 45-57.

McKean, P.F. 'Tourists and Balinese' *Cultural Survival Quarterly* Vol. 6 No. 3 (1982) pp. 32-34.

Moscardo, G, 'The Tourist-Resident Distinction' *Journal of Tourism Studies* Vol. 3 No. 2 (1992) pp. 2-19.

Moscardo, G, 'Visitor Evaluations of Built Tourism Facilities: Pontoons on the Great Barrier Reef' *Journal of Tourism Studies* Vol. 12 No. 1 (2001) pp. 28-38.

Moscardo, G, and Pearcy, P, 'Tourist Theme Parks: Research Practices and Possibilities' *Australian Psychologists* Vol. 20 No. 3 (1986) pp. 303-312.

Moscardo, G, Morrison, A, Pearce, P, Lang, T and O'Leary, T, 'Understanding Vacation Destinations Choice Through Travel Motivation and Activities' *Journal of Vacation Marketing* Vol. 2 No. 2 (1996) pp. 109-122.

Mosteller, T, 'The Elusive Balance of Conservation and Experimental Contact in Cultural and Heritage Tourism' *Tourism Planning* Vol. 1 No. 4 (1998) pp. 1-14.

Muller, T, 'The Benevolent Society: Value and Lifestyle Changes Among Middle-aged Babyboomers' in Kable, L and Chiagouris, I (Eds.) *Values, Lifestyles, and Psychologics* Mahwah, NJ: Lawrence Erchaum Associates, 1997 pp. 299-316.

Muller, T and O' Cass, A, 'Targeting the Young at Heart: Seeing Senior Vacationers The Way They See Themselves' *Journal of Vacation Marketing* Vol. 7 No. 4 (2001) pp. 285-301.

Nielson, L.B. 'A Critique of Alternative Tourism in Bali' in Proceedings of a Worshop on Tourism in Chiang Mai, Thailand (April 24-May 8 1984) Bangkok: Ecumenical Coalition on Third World Tourism, 1984.

Noronha, R, *Social and Cultural Dimensions of Tourism: A Review of the Literature in English* (Draft Report of World Bank Working Papers, Second Section), 1977.

Oh, H, Uysal, M and Weaver, P. 'Product Bundles and Market Segments Based on Travel Motivations: A Canonical Correlation Approach' *International Journal of Hospitality Management* Vol. 14 No. 2 (1995) pp. 123-137.

Pardede, Raden. 'Survey of Recent Development' *Bulletin of Indonesian Economic Studies* Vol.35 No. 2 (August1999) pp.3-39.

Plog, S. *Leisure Travel: Making It A Growth Market Again* New York: Wiley, 1991.

Pyo, S, Mihalik, B and Uysal, M. 'Attraction Attributes and Motivations: A Canonical Correlation Analysis' *Annals of Tourism Research* Vol. 16 (1989) pp. 277-282.

Reyes, Damaso. 'Expatriates Organize Bali Recovery Tour' *Jakarta Post* (10 December 2002) p. 17.

Rodenburg, E. 'The Effects of Scale in Economic Development: Tourism in Bali' *Annals of Tourism Research* Vol. 7 No. 2 (1980) pp. 177-196.

Santoso, Dewi. 'SMEs Required to Apply Health and Safety Program' *The Jakarta Post* (8 May 2004) p. 7.

Singh, T. 'Review of Tourism in the Developing Countries' *Tourism Recreation Research* Vol. 22 No. 2 (1977) pp. 75-76.

Singh, Sarina et al. India (9th Ed.) London: *Lonely Planet,* 2001.

Sugita Katyal. 'Photographers Have All Angles Covered at Taj Mahal' *The Jakarta Post* (8 November 2004) p. 19.

Soesastro, Hadidan Chatib Basri. 'Survey of Recent Developments' *Bulletin of Indonesian* Economic Studies Vol. 34 No 1 (April 1998) pp. 3-54.

Smith, V. (Ed.) *Hosts and Guests: The Anthropology of Tourism* (Second Ed.) Philadephia: University of Pennsylvania Press, 1989.

'UKM Belum Pahami Standar Laporan Keuangan' *Bisnis Indonesia* (12 January 2004) p. 7.

Upadhya, C and Rutten, M. 'In Search of a Comparative Framework: Small Scale Entrepreneurs in Asia and Europe' in M Rutten & C Upadha (Eds) *Small Business Entrepreneurs in Asia and Europe. Toward a Comparative Perspective* New Delhi: Sage Publications, 1997 pp. 13-46.

Uysal, M. and Jurowski, C. 'Testing the Push and Pull Factors' *Journal of Tourism Research* Vol. 21 No. 4 (1994) pp. 844-846.

Van Dreven, K. *Tourism in Bali: A Closer Look at the Economic and Environmental Consequences* Diskussiestukken Geografisch Instituut No. 26 Utrecht: Rijksuniversiteit, 1984.

Volkman, T.A. 'Tana Toraja: A Decade of Tourism' *Cultural Survival Quarterly* Vol. 6 No. 3 (1982) pp. 30-31.

Waslin, Mike. 'Survey of Recent Development' *Bulletin of Indonesian Economic Studies* Vol. 39 No 1 (April, 2003) pp. 5-26.

Witular, R. 'Tourism: A Glittering Jewel in a Tattered Crown' *Jakarta Post* (27 December 2002) p. 15.

Woods, B. 'Beauty and the Beast: Preference for Animals in Australia' *Journal of Tourism Studies* Vol. 11 No. 2 (2000) pp. 25-34.

World Tourism Organization. 'Manila Declaration on World Tourism' in World Tourism Conference (Manila, 27 September–10 October 1980) Madrid: WTO, 1980.

15

Corporate Ethics and the Bottom Line: Why Fighting Corruption Matters for Business*

PETER EIGEN

I am the founder of Transparency International (TI), a global civil society organization dedicated to fighting corruption. It is a tall mission, and just a decade ago, people openly mocked my intentions, characterizing me as Don Quixote fighting the proverbial windmills. But that has changed; the world has changed. Today governments, businesses and societies are increasingly aware that fair, sustainable progress cannot be achieved as long as corruption is endemic.

Business education is an integral part of carrying forward these changes in attitude. Today's business students are tomorrow's decision-makers, and their ethics and attitudes towards accountability and transparency will define the future business climate.

J.R.D. Tata was a man who saw business, not just as an end in itself, but as a tool for economic development and for enriching communities. He had compassion and many of the innovations he introduced in worker safety and welfare were far ahead of their time and, incidentally, mirror the values enshrined in the UN Global Compact, which we will come to later. His story is proof that commercial success is not predicated on ruthless exploitation of man and environment.

He was a man guided by spiritual principles. But for those who think in terms of the bottom line only, there are perfectly rational reasons for business to espouse just and equitable practices. In short,

*Oration delivered on 26 November 2005.

it makes business sense.

Let me paint for you two scenarios. In one, business people accept bribes as inevitable. They simply see the cost and the legal risks as part of doing business and winning the right contract. In this scenario, business people pretend not to know what the systemic effects of their behaviour are; that they are distorting decision-making, especially government decision-making, so that it no longer serves the needs of the people but instead promotes poverty, inequality, disregard for the environment and human rights.

So that scenario, we might call 'indifference,' or even 'hopelessness.' But there is another scenario. In this one, business operates with a high level of integrity. Companies have and observe codes of conduct that strictly forbid the taking or offering of bribes. There are no hidden costs to doing business and contracts are won on the basis of quality and merit, meaning more value for money, and in the case of government, better services provided to citizens. In this scenario, there is a level playing field that encourages innovation and entrepreneurship and where officials are not paid to look the other way when the welfare of communities gets in the way of profit-making.

This scenario, we might call 'responsibility.' Which scenario do you prefer? It is a question that students and those already in the business world need to ask themselves. Do I want to contribute to the problem, or do I want to be part of the solution?

The problem of endemic corruption, is not a question of a few minor indiscretions. It is a multi-billion-dollar phenomenon that threatens the fabric of whole societies. The World Bank Institute estimates that one trillion US dollars are paid out each year in bribes.

Think about that number for a moment. That's greater than the gross domestic product of most countries on earth. And what that figure does not capture is the cost to society when the wrong decisions are made for greed and personal gain, when a road is built (or not built at all) so that politicians and bureaucrats can pocket bribes. The economic cost of the community, deprived of the road, is considerable.

Which brings me to another great citizen of India who we should remember today, although his name may not be so familiar to some of you. Satyendra Kumar Dubey, former deputy general manager of the National Highway Authority in India, was the winner of a Transparency International (TI) Integrity Award in 2004. It was, sadly, awarded posthumously. Dubey was overseeing a road project worth billions of dollars when he was killed in November of 2003, at the age of thirty-one. He was murdered after his name was leaked in connection with a complaint about corruption he had sent to the government and the road network authority.

It is a shocking case, but there was a silver lining. Dubey's death caused an outcry of condemnation and sympathy and drew awareness to the fact that, too often, public money is siphoned off from large government projects through corruption. And too often, officials react with indifference and resist when asked to justify their actions publicly.

Dubey's death has led to renewed demands for better whistleblowing laws. Cases like this should serve as alarm signals for all of society.

When the well-being of entire societies is at stake, then companies need to take heed because in cold, calculating terms—that is your future market and your future operating environment. Making a commitment to fighting corruption today ensures a fair and stable world tomorrow.

But truth be told, many businesses can't or won't think in the long term. Short-term profit maximizing has become something of a mantra in the business world. But do huge outlays in bribes help the bottom line? Does a web of deception support a healthy corporate culture? Does a corruption scandal help build a company's reputation? Ask Enron's managers, if you can find them! Reputational capital is real, that has been borne out time and again over the last decade, with any number of corporate scandals that have brought major companies to their knees or wiped them off the map entirely. This shows that codes of ethics and no-bribes policies are an integral part of watching the bottom line—not just a pleasant sideshow.

Far too often we have heard of managers manipulating results, deliberately creating opaque corporate structures, paying bribes, or shamelessly enriching themselves. But change is underway. The regulatory environment and business culture itself has become more attuned to issues of corporate citizenship, and of the added value of ethical behaviour. Organizations such as TI have played a key role here, to be sure, but we have also long recognized that we cannot fight corruption without working together with businesses and governments. But the competitive nature of business, and social acceptance of corruption, both pose serious obstacles to the emergence of an 'enabling environment' for ethical business that is conducive to responsible corporate behaviour.

The signing of the OECD Anti-Bribery Convention in 1999 was a major milestone for the anti-corruption movement and for the private sector, who wanted to play by the rules. It meant that most of the world's largest exporting countries were now committed to introducing explicit provisions into their national law, criminalizing bribery by their companies of foreign public officials, a process that is still underway today. At the same time, the tax deductibility of such bribes was outlawed in the OECD countries, a practice which until then had amounted to a state subsidy for bribing foreign officials.

In 2003, the UN Convention against Corruption expanded these principles to potentially over half of the world's countries and territories. It enters into force on December 2005 and means that all ratifying states, including, we hope and expect, India, will be bound to the same standards in matters of bribing public officials. The convention also introduces new measures to pursue cross-border cases of corruption and assist the recovery of stolen assets, to name a few but a few of the advances introduced by the convention. It will change the way international corruption cases, such as the Bofors scandal in the eighties, which involved Indian politicians, Swedish companies and Italian businessmen, are approached.

In Asia, processes are being put in place to support implementation of these international instruments, for example, the Asian Development Bank OECD Anti-Corruption Action Plan for Asia and the Pacific, endorsed by twenty-five countries across the region, including India.

These advances are also reflected in a new business environment. The UN Global Compact, a voluntary initiative with around 1,700 corporate members, including the Tatas, last year introduced anti-corruption and transparency as its tenth principle, complementing the existing nine in the areas of labour and human rights, as well as environmental sustainability. We at TI lobbied very hard for the inclusion of this tenth principle, and were heartened when a survey found that a full 95 per cent of all Global Compact members were for the addition. The World Economic Forum is also taking measures to address the issue of corruption from the perspective of international business.

This kind of large-scale awareness and willingness is a sea change. And although many detractors dismiss initiatives like the Global Compact because of their voluntary nature, we believe firmly that programmes such as the Compact or the Global Reporting Initiative are vital precursors to a new legislative environment, meaning that companies come into compliance of their own accord before new laws are introduced. Corporate Social Responsibility (CSR) programmes are also subject to similar criticism, that they are merely PR exercises, and admittedly they often have that element. But a word of caution—as such programmes become more widespread, civil society and the media become more adept at assessing them, meaning there had better be substance behind the words.

The Compact is also a perfect example of the type of action TI endorses, actors from different sectors coming together to pursue common goals. TI engages with business through industry sector work and with individual companies through its chapters and its secretariat. We lobby bodies and organizations that can help change company behaviour through contracting guidelines and debarment, such as the World Bank, development banks and export credit agencies, professional associations and initiatives such as the Global Compact.

But what exactly can business do? In response to the need for common anti-bribery standards in the corporate world, TI joined forces with Social Accountability International to develop with business and other stakeholders, a practical tool for companies to counter bribery.

The result—the Business Principles for Countering Bribery (see below)—provides a practical framework for implementing a no-bribes policy to deal with the many challenges businesses face domestically and abroad. And incidentally, the Tatas played a critical role in piloting and developing the principles.

Since completion in 2002, the Business Principles have become recognized as the no-bribes standard for industry. The principles have provided the basis to create sectoral no-bribes programmes under preparation by leading companies in the engineering and construction industry, in the context of the World Economic Forum in Davos. Two further industrial groups, energy, and minerals and mining, are also committed to developing a common no-bribes policy.

Along with some ninety other national chapters which form the backbone of the TI movement, TI India is at the forefront of mobilizing civil society and other non-government stakeholders to raise awareness of corruption and to advocate concrete measures to curb it.

TI India launched the Business Principles in India in August 2003, although the response of the private sector, I understand, has been moderate. This is bound to accelerate in the years to come.

TI has also widely employed a tool we call the Integrity Pact. It is a no-bribes pact signed by bidders on major public contracts, committing them to fair and transparent bidding, with appropriate sanctions, in case its terms are not observed. This has been heartily welcomed in many cases by companies, because it frees them from the dilemma of having to engage in illegal and expensive bribes in order to win a contract and by governments, because it has been shown to significantly reduce the cost of such contracts where it has been applied. Following an initiative of TI India, the Integrity Pact has been adopted by the Ministry of Defence for purchases of over ₹300 crores. It has also been adopted by the ONGC, Sardar Sarovar Narmada Nigam and Power Grid Corporation of India.

But it is obvious that merely having codes and initiatives on paper is not enough. What it comes down to, is the actions and decisions of employees and managers on a daily basis. Not only should a company's policies be clearly stated, they should also be actively and clearly communicated, both internally and externally.

The policies must be accompanied by staff training programmes, and backed up with whistleblower protection and appropriate disciplinary action, in the event of a breach.

It is also crucial that policies are extended right across a company's network of subsidiaries and include subcontractors in the supply chain. Board audit committees should take responsibility for conducting annual reviews of anti-bribery policies, and corporate annual reports should set out the state of anti-bribery compliance.

As well as regular engagement with stakeholders, a company must constantly assess potential risks facing its core business. For instance, a company active in a highly corrupt industry or a highly corrupt area must develop comprehensive programmes to protect its corporate reputation. Typical areas of vulnerability include subsidiaries and joint ventures, where fees must be restricted to actual services rendered, and where absolute compliance with the company's anti-bribery policies must be enforced. Problems with suppliers can be avoided through the use of fully transparent competitive procurement practices, due diligence of prospective contractors and ensuring that the award of sub-contracts precludes kickbacks.

The common thread here is awareness and action. Management may claim a commitment to transparency, but if they choose not to examine subsidiaries and partners for ethical shortcomings, they are essentially making themselves complicit in any final corrupt outcomes. That is why a commitment to transparency means a commitment to knowledge and to action based on that knowledge. If you find that a subsidiary that your company has acquired has a culture of bribery and extortion, you must act on that knowledge, on the basis of ethical responsibility but also, as we've discussed, on account of the risk to your bottom line. It is good business sense and good corporate citizenship at the same time.

In business, as in government, commitment to change needs to come from the top. CEOs and presidents need to be clear and vocal about the importance of ethical behaviour, which brings us back to J.R.D. Tata, a man who led by example and also had a sense for the potential of long-term change. Because I think, to some extent, this is what is often missing—that people fail to see themselves and their actions in a greater context, that the decisions they make have a knock-on effect on other people and that those decisions affect the world tomorrow and the day after. Fair and ethical choices in business amount to treating colleagues and communities with respect and with making the world a better, more just and more equitable one for generations to come.

BUSINESS PRINCIPLES FOR COUNTERING BRIBERY

Introduction

The Business Principles for Countering Bribery have been developed by a group of private sector interests, non-governmental organizations and trade unions as a tool to assist enterprises to develop effective approaches to countering bribery in all of their activities.

The Business Principles also give practical effect to recent initiatives such as the OECD Convention on Combating Bribery of Foreign Public Officials in International Business Transactions, the ICC Rules of Conduct to Combat Extortion and bribery and the anti-bribery provisions of the revised OECD guidelines for multinationals.

The Business Principles have been designed for use by large, medium and small enterprises. They apply to bribery of public officials and to private-to-private transactions. The purpose of the document is to provide practical guidance for countering bribery, creating a level playing field and providing a long-term business advantage.

The Business Principles

- The enterprise shall prohibit bribery in any form whether direct or indirect
- The enterprise shall commit to implementation of a programme to counter bribery

These Business Principles are based on a commitment to fundamental values of integrity, transparency and accountability. Enterprises shall aim to create and maintain a trust-based and inclusive internal culture in which bribery is not tolerated.

The programme is the entirety of an enterprise's anti-bribery efforts including values, policies, processes, training and guidance.

Aims

The aims of the Business Principles are to:

- Provide a framework for good business practices and risk management strategies for countering bribery.
- Assist enterprises to:
  - i. eliminate bribery;
  - ii. demonstrate their commitment to countering bribery;
  - iii. make a positive contribution to improving business standards of integrity, transparency and accountability wherever they operate.

Development of a Programme for Countering Bribery

An enterprise should develop a programme reflecting its size, business sector, potential risks and locations of operation, which should, clearly and in reasonable detail, articulate values, policies and procedures to be used to prevent bribery from occurring in all activities under its effective control.

The programme should be consistent with all laws relevant to countering bribery in all the jurisdictions in which the enterprise operates, particularly laws that are directly relevant to specific business practices.

The enterprise should develop the programme in consultation with employees, trade unions or other employee representative bodies.

The enterprise should ensure that it is informed of all matters material to the effective development of the programme by communicating with relevant interested parties.

Scope of the Programme

In developing its programme for countering bribery, an enterprise should analyse which specific areas pose the greatest risks from bribery.

The programme should address the most prevalent forms of bribery relevant to the enterprise but at a minimum should cover the following areas:

Bribes

The enterprise should prohibit the offer, gift or acceptance of a bribe in any form, including kickbacks, on any portion of a contract payment, or the use of other routes or channels to provide improper benefits to customers, agents, contractors, suppliers or employees of any such party or government officials.

The enterprise should also prohibit an employee from arranging or accepting a bribe or kickback from customers, agents, contractors, suppliers or employees of any such party or government officials, for the employee's benefit or that of the employee's family, friends, associates or acquaintances.

Political contributions

The enterprise, its employees or agents should not make direct or indirect contributions to political parties, organizations or individuals engaged in politics, as a way of obtaining advantage in business transactions.

The enterprise should publicly disclose all its political contributions.

Charitable contributions and sponsorships

The enterprise should ensure that charitable contributions and sponsorships are not being used as a subterfuge for bribery.

The enterprise should publicly disclose all its charitable contributions or sponsorships.

Facilitation payments

Recognizing that facilitation payments are a form of bribery, The enterprise should work to identify and eliminate them.

Gifts, hospitality and expenses

The enterprise should prohibit the offer or receipt of gifts, hospitality or expenses whenever such arrangements could affect the outcome of business transactions and are not reasonable and bona fide expenditures.

Facilitation payments

Also called 'facilitating,' 'speed' or 'grease' payments, these are small payments made to secure or expedite the performance of a routine or necessary action to which the payer of the facilitation payment has legal or other entitlement.

Programme Implementation Requirements

The following section sets out the requirements that enterprises should meet, at a minimum, when implementing the programme:

Organization and responsibilities

The board of directors or equivalent body should base their policy on the Business Principles and provide leadership, resources and active support for management's implementation of the programme.

The chief executive officer is responsible for ensuring that the programme is carried out consistently with clear lines of authority.

The board of directors, chief executive officer and senior management should demonstrate visible and active commitment to the implementation of the Business Principles.

Business relationships

The enterprise should apply its programme in its dealings with subsidiaries, joint venture partners, agents, contractors and other third parties with whom it has business relationships.

Subsidiaries and Joint Ventures

The enterprise should conduct due diligence before entering into a joint venture.

The enterprise should ensure that subsidiaries and joint ventures over which it maintains effective control adopt its programme. Where an enterprise does not have effective control it should make known its programme and use its best efforts to monitor that the conduct of such subsidiaries and joint ventures is consistent with the Business Principles.

Agents

The enterprise should not channel improper payments through an agent.

The enterprise should undertake due diligence before appointing an agent.

Compensation paid to agents should be appropriate and justifiable remuneration for legitimate services rendered.

The relationship should be documented.

The agent should contractually agree to comply with the enterprise's programme.

The enterprise should monitor the conduct of its agents and should have a right of termination in the event that they pay bribes.

Contractors and suppliers

The enterprise should conduct its procurement practices in a fair and transparent manner.

The enterprise should undertake due diligence in evaluating major prospective contractors and suppliers to ensure that they have effective anti-bribery policies.

The enterprise should make known its anti-bribery policies to contractors and suppliers. It should monitor the conduct of major contractors and suppliers and should have a right of termination in the event that they pay bribes.

The enterprise should avoid dealing with prospective contractors and suppliers known to be paying bribes.

Human resources

Recruitment, promotion, training, performance evaluation and recognition should reflect the enterprise's commitment to the programme.

The human resources policies and practices relevant to the programme should be developed and undertaken in consultation with employees, trade unions or other employee representative bodies as appropriate.

The enterprise should make it clear that no employee will suffer demotion, penalty, or other adverse consequences for refusing to pay bribes even if it may result in the enterprise losing business.

The enterprise should apply appropriate sanctions for violations of its programme.

Training

Managers, employees and agents should receive specific training on the programme.

Where appropriate, contractors and suppliers should receive training on the programme.

Raising concerns and seeking guidance

To be effective, the programme should rely on employees and others to raise concerns and violations as early as possible. To this end, the enterprise should provide secure and accessible channels through which employees and others should feel able to raise concerns and report violations ('whistleblowing') in confidence and without risk of reprisal.

These channels should also be available for employees and others to seek advice or suggest improvements to the programme. To support this process, the enterprise should provide guidance to employees and others with respect to the interpretation of the programme in individual cases.

Communication

The enterprise should establish effective internal and external communication of the programme.

The enterprise should, on request, publicly disclose the management systems it employs in countering bribery.

The enterprise should be open to receiving communications from relevant interested parties with respect to the programme.

Internal controls and audit

The enterprise should maintain accurate books and records, available for inspection, which properly and fairly document all financial transactions. The enterprise should not maintain off-the books accounts.

The enterprise should establish feedback mechanisms and other internal processes supporting the continuous improvement of the programme.

The enterprise should subject the internal control systems, in particular the accounting and record keeping practices, to regular audits to provide assurance that they are effective in countering bribery.

Monitoring and review

Senior management of the enterprise should monitor the programme and periodically review the programme's suitability, adequacy and effectiveness and implement improvements as appropriate. They should periodically report to the audit committee or the board the results of the programme review.

The audit committee or the board should make an independent assessment of the adequacy of the programme and disclose its findings in the annual report to shareholders.

Credits

The Steering Committee that produced this document comprised the following companies and organizations:

- Accountability
- The Conference Board
- Ethos
- European Bank for Reconstruction and Development
- General Electric
- Institute for Business Ethics, Universiteit Nyenrode l Norsk Hydro
- PricewaterhouseCoopers
- Responsible Business Initiative
- Rio Tinto plc
- SGS SA
- Shell International
- Social Accountability International
- Tata Sons Ltd
- Trade Union Advisory Committee to the OECD

Chairman of the Steering Committee (Feasibility Stage), Transparency International:

Laurence Cockcroft, Transparency International

Observer:
International Chamber of Commerce

The Steering Committee is grateful to the companies, organisations and people that submitted comments on the Consultation Draft:

- BP plc

- Cambridge University Press
- The Caux Round Table
- Crédit Mutuel l economiesuisse—Swiss Business Federation
- Ford of Europe GMBH
- France Télécom
- ISIS Asset Management plc
- General Motors Corp.
- GlaxoSmithKline plc
- Groupe Renault
- International Federation of Consulting Engineers (FIDIC)
- Société Générale
- Suez
- UBS AG
- Christine Parker, Professor of Law, University of New South Wales

The companies that generously allowed the Steering Committee to undertake Field Tests of the Business Principles were:

- BP Exploration (Caspian Sea) Limited, Azerbaijan
- Sika AG, Switzerland
- The Tata Iron and Steel Company Limited, India

16

All about Integrity, Values and Morals*

SUBROTO BAGCHI

What does the term 'integrity' actually mean? *The Roget's New Millennium™ Thesaurus* tells us that its synonyms are candour, forthrightness, goodness, honesty, honourableness, incorruptibility, principle, probity, purity, rectitude, righteousness, sincerity, straightforwardness, uprightness, virtue. The problem with the term is that it has many synonyms. As a result, we can be lost in the many possible interpretations. Sometimes, it is easier to understand what a term means by looking at the opposite of it. So, if you search for the antonym of integrity, unlike the many synonyms, you will find just one word. It is 'dishonesty.' So, integrity is the opposite of dishonesty.

Come to think of it, it is just an abstract concept. I sometimes wonder why only humans, and not plants and animals and other life forms, have to deal with the issue of integrity. And in men, why is it that the problem of integrity surfaces with more education, access to better amenities and greater material comfort? It is probably because animals live and die for themselves and, beyond passing on their genetic code, do not worry about hoisting their progeny on time. They'd rather vanish from the earth, than bribe someone so that their children can inherit it. So, I wonder, why humans have problems understanding the meaning of and practising integrity, when a baboon or an ant does not have to.

I think it has got something to do with intelligence. When we have intelligence without reasoning, when we have the power to think

*Oration delivered on 1 December 2006.

but are not blessed with the capability to contemplate, we cross the line. It is a disease of the mind that afflicts us, a disease that spreads without physical contact. If I am corrupt, there is a high chance that my child will be.

Among men, those who are more primitive, more rural, less affluent and further away from urban settings, are less likely to be thinking about integrity—they do not have to. They live in a state of innocence. Two hundred and twenty million people in this country live below the poverty line, they have no access to even the most minimum of health and sanitation and public services you and I consider our entitlement. They have waited for sixty years and would wait some more. They do not have the urgent desire to succeed at all costs. We cross the line because an intelligent urban mind decides to succeed at all costs.

I told you that integrity is an abstract concept. It is just an idea. There is a school of thought that says ideas are like genes. Genes have only one purpose—to replicate themselves. When they fail, a race can get obliterated. Some genes survive; some do not.

Just as genes replicate through DNA, ideas replicate through 'memes.' So, an idea like integrity requires what we will call 'memetic continuity.' Whose task is it to ensure the memetic continuity of the idea called integrity?

Traditionally, in this country, it has been the middle class which has, over the years, been the protector of the particular meme, the genetic equivalent of the idea called integrity. It is easy to understand that. The poorest of the poor have been in a state of poverty and innocence. To the rich and the powerful in any society, integrity is a very optional thing. So, it is the people in-between, who are intelligent and given to contemplation of what is right and what is wrong who have been the custodians. It is they who transmitted the meme from one generation to the other, because they had to 'uphold the values.' In that upholding of values, there was memetic continuity. I see that changing.

Today the same middle class lives in a scarcity mindset. In this country, historically, there have been fewer resources and significantly more claimants. Take school seats, hospital beds, sleeper berths in trains, jobs in the government offices, residential plots within municipal limits, engineering college seats—you name it—for everything, there has been a mindset of scarcity. That makes an intelligent man standing in a long queue afraid. He is gripped by the fear of losing out—the fear of the door closing just before his turn and someone saying, 'Go home; the quota is over.' So, he devises a way to succeed at all costs.

At that moment, the person contracts the disease.

The disease afflicts the mind. It suspends all reasoning and makes the individual justify the means for the end. Being intelligent, he conjures explanations that convince him, his family and friends that there is nothing wrong, everyone is doing it in any case and, it is a small price to pay after all! Soon, he becomes an expert at it and it even gives him a new power—the power to dominate. It becomes a game. It becomes an addiction that creates a high each time the individual gets the satisfaction of crossing the line, of 'buying out' someone.

Once, the chief executive of a world-class manufacturing plant in India was showing me around. I asked the man how he manages relationships with the government. He told me in a matter-of-fact tone that either people in the government listen, or when an individual does not, they simply buy the person out. There was pride in the statement. Like the pride of a hunter. Or, a hit man. Forty years back, that man who joined the public sector steel industry as a graduate engineer trainee, child of a middle-class home, young and probably innocent and he was inducted into the fraternity of the afflicted. He had the choice to opt out, but something in it gave him a sense of thrill and he has stayed back ever since. Today, he is diseased and will almost certainly pass on the disease to his children and many of those who come into mental contact with him. Why am I taking on the middle class with such harshness?

A couple of years back; we selected a young engineer to join MindTree. He was quite obviously a cut above the rest to have made it through our rigorous test. After working with us for two years, he decided to prepare for his masters. He wanted to prepare well, so he decided to take a couple of months off. At MindTree, we have provision for unlimited sick leave. After all, if someone is sick—he or she is sick. You cannot say, get well in a week because that is all the leave you have in your balance. So, he went to his hometown and sent in a medical certificate that he was very unwell. When the serious news reached us, someone in our People Function got worried enough to call the doctor to inquire about the well-being of the engineer. The flustered doctor spilled the beans. She was approached by the engineer, who asked her to issue a false certificate, and she had complied. I requested that the engineer be called to meet me. When I asked him why he did what he did, he replied, 'I did not realize I was doing something wrong.' I was stunned. He is one of the best educated people on the entire planet; as a computer science engineer, he is one of less than 1 per cent of all humanity, in terms of education and exposure. And he was telling me that he did not realize that he was doing something wrong!

I do not know why but I asked him, what his parents did. After all, he was at home with them for months and they would have wondered how he had managed such a long spell of leave. His reply left me speechless. He told me that both his parents were schoolteachers.

A couple of months ago, I received a letter from a state government official, seeking a job for his son. Usually in the IT industry, we do not get too many such solicitations because people by now know that without mathematical and logical reasoning capability, you do not go past the written test. When I saw the sealed envelope of the state, I did not quite imagine what was inside. Inside, there was the letter on the official stationery of the government. No sense of impropriety, no awkwardness. The man, not sure that the government's insignia would have sufficient impact on me, had gone a step ahead. He had stapled a packet of mahaprasad from the Lord Jagannath in Puri. This was the most audacious furthering of a personal agenda, putting the State and the Church together so that the son could get ahead.

My father had served the same state government for all his life. We were raised to a very different standard. When I was a four-year-old, a government jeep was allocated to him. It used to be parked in the garage of the government quarters. He would not ride the jeep to his office—he told us that the government had not given it for his commute to work. It was for touring the interiors. We were forbidden from sitting in it, except for when it was stationary. That man retired when I was in my eighth class and we came to live in my brother's quarters. He was a young IAS officer and was given a residential office. For the first time in our lives, there was a telephone at home. To me, the black rotary phone, connected to a manually operated exchange was mysterious and alluring. My retired father guarded it from my immediate elder brother and me so that we did not ever touch it. It belonged to the Republic.

When he was not guarding the phone, he was guarding the gate. His IAS officer-son was just about twenty-six-years-old and though he occupied the sub-divisional officer's bungalow, still needed his protection. So he would stand there to ward off the occasional favour seeker.

On one occasion, I have seen my retired father deal with one of them: a man with a large jackfruit and a big fish. He came and sheepishly wanted to leave his offering for the sahib. Father said very politely that he could not accept it, as he was a retired man. Perplexing logic. When the man persisted, father shouted at him, "Don't you hear? I am a retired man and cannot accept anything for the government anymore? If you must leave that thing, leave it as an offering to the mango tree out there.'

Away from the driveway, inside the compound was an old mango tree. Unable to get past the doorkeeper and left with the possibility of bribing the tree, better sense prevailed. The man left with his jackfruit and the fish.

From a little distance, the driver, the peon and the chowkidar saw the transaction. Governance was firmly etched in everyone's mind for such time as D.P. Bagchi IAS remained in the services of the state.

After 9/11, most of our clients started insisting on background verification check for people we recruit. Today, we have it as a mandatory process. Last year, we added a thousand people to the workforce. Of these, seven hundred joined us from other companies. Of the seven hundred, eighty people were asked to leave after coming on board because they had faked employment information. They did not have to. They had qualified through our recruitment tests, which mean that they were technically good. But, somewhere, someone had told them that it is quite all right to fake—a small gamble to get ahead in the race for an increment, a chance to go overseas, earn a few bucks more.

When we were just a year-old company, one of the senior most technical people, a man with a salary of $200,000 a year, had fudged his phone bills for all of a thousand dollars. He was competent at work and a very nice person to get along with. When we asked him to leave, many people were distraught. Where, they asked, is the role of forgiveness at work?

To us, breach of integrity is like dealing with cancer. Cancer occurs at a nanometre scale. It is a mistake in a molecule, an error in the DNA that programs our destiny. If you do not recognize that reality, one day that single cell replicates billions of time over till cancer colonizes the entire body and brings it down. Individually, each cell is no bigger than a nanometre.

We asked the man to leave for another reason.

Forgiveness would mean his continuance in the organization. Each time we would cross him in the corridor, meet him at the cafeteria and the conference room, our eyes would meet and he would know that we knew that he knew that we knew.

We did not want anyone wearing a MindTree badge walking around with a discounted self-esteem.

In our context, small is big. Just the way it is, in the context of India today.

This year, Transparency International (founded by Dr Peter Eigen) has come out with a report on petty corruption in India. Not the big scam. Not the heavy extortions—small, petty acts of bribery involving the citizenry and government officials. Like the nanometre-sized cancer cells, the nanometre-sized acts of bribery added up to a neat ₹21,068 crores a year.

I suspect that the number means very little to all of you here. So, let me tell you how much is ₹21,068 crores. What could it buy you? Look at these numbers here.

₹21,068 crores of petty bribery a year is:

- One-fourth of India's defence expenditure;
- 10 per cent more than the allocation for the Ministry of Human Resources;
- 20 per cent more than the total central government receipts from service tax;
- 33 per cent more than assistance for central and centrally sponsored schemes;
- Double of the plan expenditure on primary education;
- More than eight times of the allocation for the Ministry of Science and Technology;
- 90 per cent of the plan outlay of Indian railways;
- Twice the total external assistance (net of re-payments) that India received in 2005–06.

(This data has been taken from the Union budget and railway budget documents for FY06 and FY07).

If the quantum has not yet made sense to you, let me share with you the economics of the Golden Quadrilateral project. The Golden Quadrilateral network will connect Kolkata, Chennai, Delhi and Mumbai in a network of 5,846 kilometres of multi-lane roads. This highway will interconnect many major cities and ports. It will help in industrial growth in all small towns along it. It will provide vast opportunities for transport of agricultural produce from the hinterland to major cities and ports for export. This highway is expected to save eighty billion rupees per year through faster traffic movement, increased fuel-efficiency and improved trade.

For the golden quadrilateral and the north-south-east-west corridor combined, the funding requirements are estimated at ₹60,000 crores. Three years of petty bribery would be enough to deliver this project that would make the next seven generations of Indians remember us with gratitude for leaving them debt-free and more importantly, not infecting them with the virus that we have contracted.

No parent would want to pass on AIDS to their progeny. Why do we pass this one virus, deadlier in its impact because it can transmit even without physical contact and most often, infects a loved one?

Some time back, I was listening to three young Indians at a talk on integrity, organized under the aegis of CII's Young Indian forum. They spoke with innocence on the subject and I am grateful for that. Each speaker spoke eloquently about how e-governance was the key to making India conquer corruption. Listening to them, I slumped in my chair. Adults had obviously told them what to speak—they were standing in front of the audience, not to speak their mind, but to make their mark. Because the adults who had helped them with their speeches and had intelligently coached them to speak on e-governance, had not told them about the great Indian power to trivialize things. We trivialize things like no nation can. No one told them that e-governance is a just a tool. Computers are dumb things that can do routine things faster. So, you apply them in a dishonest society and they would make it even more dishonest.

The country does need e-governance, but what about character? Is there something like e-character? E-character that could substitute my lack of integrity so that the computer can do e-governance and the golden era could dawn one more time?

Unfortunately, there is nothing like e-character. Governance can be 'e-ed'; character can only be 'me-ed.' The system does not give me character—if at all, I give it character. Only my family can give me character. Without that, 'e' is an empty syllable.

I am not a social reformer. I am not a statesman. I am an ordinary Indian who has worked his way up doing the right things the right way. I do not know too much about things; I can only tell you what we do in our organization when we assimilate new MindTree Minds. Chairman Ashok Soota meets them in person and gives them a copy of the book, *All about Integrity*. And he explains to our people just four precepts:

- In business and personal dealings that affect business, we follow the rules. We use fair judgment where rules do not exist;
- When we are in doubt, we actively seek help;
- In moments of conflict, we do what is right and not what is convenient;

- Our conduct can stand public scrutiny at any time without causing us embarrassment.

Many years back, I met a young woman professional, who after many years of association, for some reason, decided to send a mail to me on a deeply personal subject. She wanted to tell about her past—to just share it with another human being, as part of her healing process. From her childhood, her alcoholic father had started physically abusing her. She was the victim of his drunken, sexual lust until she was grown up enough to protest. I was speechless. She had never shared this with anyone in the world except her husband, who must be a great soul indeed to have accepted her and loved her for who she was.

I knew her all along as an outstanding professional and an outstanding human being. She is a great mother and quite apparently a wonderful wife to her husband. Why am I telling you this story?

If ever life mistreats you and you are victimized, do not justify your loss of morality. Do not do unto others what wrong was done unto you.

Just because someone extorted money from you, held you at ransom and caused you a bruise or a bleed, do not do that to another human being. If ever life throws you in that situation, remember this story of a mother and wife who is healing the world and not spreading the wound. We have been endowed with higher intelligence so that we can see reason and choose our own path even when we are thrown into a dungeon.

Finally, I want to let you know that many times in life, you will wonder as to what you got by walking the right path. Your loved ones may even poke you from time to time, 'You talked about honesty, integrity and values and morality. While you lived all that, look at who got all the promotions and the good postings and all the material rewards?'

In this country, I find people who are dishonest and sometimes, effective. Then, there are some people who choose to be honest, but become ineffective. What good are they?

I do not believe in passive honesty.

You need to be honest and effective. If that entails struggle, it is the rite of passage.

People like J.R.D. Tata, Azim Premji, Narayana Murthy and Ashok Soota have proven that it is possible to be honest and effective even in a country like India.

At the same time, by leading a life of values, do not always expect the rainbow at the end of the journey. There may be no cheering crowds, no festooned high ground, no decorations—all these may still be for those who decided to walk a path in which the means justify the end.

If ever that conflict dawns in your mind, know that people like J.R.D. chose to be who they were, without regard to the end state.

17

Twenty-first Century Business Paradigm*

STEVEN J. SNYDER

INTRODUCTION

Back in 1980, when I was twenty-six years old, I read a book that had a tremendous impact on my life. It was *The Third Wave* by Alvin Toffler.[1]

In the book, Alvin Toffler talked about the major societal transitions: from an agrarian society, which he called the First Wave, to an industrial society, which he called the Second Wave and finally to the Third Wave—a post-industrial society.

The book was inspirational to me because for the first time, I could begin to visualize the impact that technology would have on the way we would work and live in the future.

Toffler's vision helped me begin to understand how computers would enhance our lives in the future—making us more productive and creative.

So, it is not surprising that three years later, in 1983, I found myself working for Bill Gates at Microsoft.

In my various jobs at Microsoft, I would continually hear Bill's voice—about how our products would help people reach their full creative potential.

As I think back on the last twenty-eight years, I realize how eerily accurate were Toffler's predictions about how technology would be a major catalyst for change. For example, Toffler talked about a collective social memory. Through the invention of what he called

*Oration delivered on 9 January 2008.

'new media,' he envisioned that the Third Wave Society would have total recall of virtually everything. He predicted that this information would become organized and would become available to us all. All we would need to do would be to ask a question and we could find the answer.

As I prepared for this talk, I was curious as to what ancient Indian traditions taught about environmental and social responsibility. So, I accessed the collective social memory—which we now call 'Google'—to see what I could learn. I found a long list of Vedic, Buddhist and Jain traditions teaching us to respect and honour our earth and the people who live on it. For example, Mahavir Jain said, 'One who neglects or disregards the existence of earth, air, fire, water and vegetation disregards his own existence which is entwined with them'[2].

Another topic also caught my interest. Back in November, as Indians all over the world were celebrating the festival of Diwali, an Indian friend told me—this is what your speech is really about—the victory of good over evil within every human being.

I again checked the collective social memory and learned about the many levels of meaning behind your festival of lights. I learned of the many stories of the origin of Diwali—as a harvest festival by some accounts, or as a victorious return from exile, by others.

This research made me even more curious. How is Diwali celebrated? What are the customs? What are the traditions?

To learn more, I asked myself: What would my sixteen-year-old daughter do if she wanted to learn about Diwali?

And so, I logged onto You Tube!

My initial search led me to the various cultural celebrations of Diwali in the United States. But, I wanted to learn more—especially about the customs in India.

So I refined my search criteria by specifying Delhi. And I saw videos of the lights, the firecrackers...and the traffic!

BUSINESS PARADIGMS

Perhaps no single voice has been as influential in shaping the philosophy of twentieth century business as Milton Friedman. A free market capitalist, Friedman warned that business should not distract itself with the well-being of society, instead should focus on its core responsibility—to maximize its profits.[3]

While it's true that this approach has propelled significant economic growth in the twentieth century, it also has several serious negative effects.

One bad consequence is the short-term myopia that occurs when this philosophy is put into practice. The pressure of making quarterly earnings targets often confounds the judgment of corporate leaders, who lose sight of longer-term considerations.

A second problem is with the philosophy itself. Leaders often become seduced by the power of money, and are lured into the moral point of view that greed is actually good.

A contrarian voice, albeit less pronounced, has been the voice of what I'll call traditional corporate social responsibility (CSR). This voice urges businesses to contribute to the well-being of society. However, this has often been translated into arbitrary and unfocused programmes of corporate philanthropy that have little to do with a company's core strategy.

The result has been sub-optimization at both levels. Advocates of Friedman's view often follow misguided policies that strive for optimal profits through the exploitation of other stakeholders. Meanwhile, traditional CSR zealots have funnelled money to increase social welfare without making a clear connection to long-term strategic advantage.

At the dawn of the twenty-first century, a fundamentally new way of thinking about business—a new business paradigm—is emerging. This paradigm is best articulated by Stuart Hart[4]. He asserts a collision between three worlds—the money economy, traditional economies and nature's economy. From this tension, he proposes a new synthesis—which brings together the best of the Friedman approach as well as the spirit of the traditional CSR approach. This paradigm rejects that businesses must make either-or tradeoffs—either generate profits *or* benefit society. Instead, it conceptualizes business as *interdependent* with society. The sustainability paradigm means that both business and society benefit over the long term.

There is research to suggest that this is possible[5] although it far from a sure thing.

So, how do we bring about this new business paradigm? We do it by both creating new companies, and by transforming existing companies.

Let me first give you a couple of examples of exciting new companies that have sprung up over the last several years.

Roshini International Bio-Energy Corporation (RIBEC) has begun to pioneer the production of biodiesel fuel through the plantation and harvesting of the Pongamia tree in the arid area of Andhra Pradesh. This benefits farmers because it boosts their productivity enormously. It is also good for the environment. This is a totally carbon neutral solution that transforms dry lands into green belts. And, it is economically good. It is profitable and scalable.

CoOptions Technologies Limited offers a financial services arbitrage solution—allowing primary agricultural cooperative societies (PACS) and their farmer customers significantly lower cost of capital by taking advantage of the 18 per cent lending requirement for public and private sector banks in India (much of which had previously gone unused). It does so by capturing and digitizing the credit history of the farmers as well as creating an automated lending platform that can be efficiently distributed. The result is a significant reduction in the cost of capital—again making farmers significantly more prosperous.

What about existing companies? To achieve the potential of the sustainability paradigm, companies will need twenty-first century leadership, twenty-first century technology, twenty-first century governmental institutions and the discipline of the triple bottom line.

TRIPLE BOTTOM LINE

The term 'Triple Bottom Line' is widely credited to John Elkington, head of the consulting firm SustainAbility, who first coined the phrase in 1994. Elkington was referring to three dimensions of accounting—economic, environmental and social.

In 1980, Toffler wrote this: 'Instead of the single 'bottom line' on which most executives have been taught to fixate, the Third Wave Corporation requires attention to multiple bottom lines—social, environmental, informational, political and ethical bottom lines—all of them interconnected.'

A number of different terms express the same concept, such as 'Sustainability Reporting' (a term used by the Global Reporting Initiative); 'CSR Reporting' (a term widely used in Japan); 'Corporate Responsibility Reporting' (a term used by KPMG); and 'Corporate Citizenship Reporting' (a term used by General Electric among others).

I did a Google search on these terms, and found that—at least as of now—the term 'Triple Bottom Line' is the most frequently appearing, with 683,000 hits. 'Sustainability Reporting' got 306,000 hits, 'CSR Reporting' got 73,100 hits, Corporate Responsibility Reporting' got 26,500 hits and 'Corporate Citizenship Reporting' only 904.[6]

I will refer to the Triple Bottom Line concept as 'Sustainability Reporting'—the term used by the Global Reporting Initiative.

The Global Reporting Initiative is quickly becoming the international standard bearer for this type of reporting. The initiative was started in 1997 as an offshoot of Ceres (a United States based coalition of investors, stakeholders and companies). In 2001, it was established as an independent organization. I might add that an executive from Tata Group, Kishor Chaukar, currently serves on the board of directors of the Global Reporting Initiative—signifying Tatas leadership in this practice.

One of the main functions of the GRI is to issue guidelines for Sustainability Reporting, and in November 2006, it issued 'G3'—the third generation of guidelines.

GRI's Sustainability Guidelines contain a forty-four-page summary document, supplemented with numerous protocols and sector-specific guidelines. The guidelines include principles that govern reporting decisions as well as the specific content that should be in the report. Included in a report should be an analysis of the company's strategy within a sustainability context, disclosures with respect to firm governance as well as specific economic, social, and environmental performance indicators.

It's important to note that the discipline of Sustainability Reporting is more than just producing a report. Instead, Sustainability Reporting is an organizational learning process that can dramatically advance a company's sustainability initiatives.

KEY ENABLERS

I will now describe five key enablers, which if properly managed, can drive an organization towards optimizing its sustainability strategy.

The first is through alignment of time horizons. As I mentioned before, a key problem with the Milton Friedman approach is that businesses become short-term, myopic. The discipline of Sustainability Reporting reinforces an important link between the short term and the long term. The G3 Guidelines encourage setting clear goals for all sustainability initiatives. Annual reporting fosters external visibility of these goals and promotes accountability for achieving stated outcomes. This helps prevent short-term profit pressures from overshadowing progress on longer-term environmental and social objectives.

A second enabler is through the facilitation of stakeholder dialogue. Research has shown that companies have serious gaps in engaging stakeholders in meaningful exchanges[7]. The G3 Guidelines explicitly call for an inclusive approach towards stakeholder engagement. The increased transparency results in enhanced collaboration which increases the level of trust between the company and its stakeholders. Out of this, new ideas might emerge—ideas that neither party may have thought about independently.

Building on these first two, a third enabler is the creative internal process that can occur when a company engages in the discipline of Sustainability Reporting. As externally committed goals are translated into internal corporate goals, organizations mobilize to achieve them. Stakeholder engagement brings new, creative ideas into the mix, and strategies are created to meet the goals. This triggers a whole host of additional processes: creating organizational structures; building skills; creating tracking, monitoring and incentive systems, etc.

Creativity and innovation can also be enhanced through external benchmarking activities. As more organizations produce Sustainability Reports, companies will have a wider palette from which to select innovative techniques for achieving sustainability objectives. This fosters the adoption of industry-wide best practices.

The Toxic Releases Inventory provides an interesting study of how these creative processes can work.[8] It is a glowing example of the old adage: 'What goes measured gets done.'

This inventory, which appears in an obscure section of the Superfund Amendments and Reauthorization Act—passed by the United States Congress in 1988—requires US manufacturing firms to report annual use, storage, transport and disposal of toxic chemicals to the EPA. This is virtually an honour system—there is hardly any checking or enforcement by the EPA.

The results are nothing short of remarkable. Within ten years of enactment, toxic emissions in the United States were reduced by more than 60 per cent. Furthermore, there were measurable and significant financial benefits. Rather than simply treating the toxic waste, companies creatively re-engineered their manufacturing processes to reduce toxic waste in the first place.

Another interesting dynamic took place. The 'worst offenders' were black-listed by environmental groups. This cacophony of pressure caused many additional companies to take action.

The combination of significant waste reduction, as well as positive economic outcomes for the firms, made this one of the most successful pieces of environmental legislation ever passed.

The momentum of the G3 Guidelines is another enabler. Over the past nine years, the guidelines have undergone three generations of development and tuning. G3, the most recent guidelines, issued in November 2006, have achieved a threshold of comprehensiveness and usability. These guidelines are a useful tool for companies embarking on the process. Furthermore, Global Reporting Initiative has increased its organizational outreach and support—and more consultants are coming up to speed to support the Sustainability Reporting process.

The Global Reporting Initiative now predicts that 1,750 organizations will file Sustainability Reports that conform to the GRI guidelines in 2008; up by a factor of three from just three years earlier. One illustration of this growing momentum is the fact that Sweden just announced last month, that G3 compliant Sustainability Reporting will be mandatory for all sixty-five government owned companies beginning in 2009.

As Sustainability Reporting continues to gain momentum, laggards will feel increased pressure—further accelerating the growth.

A final positive enabler is through what David Vogel calls Markets for Virtue[9]. Vogel argues that certain markets positively reward virtuous corporate behaviour independent of their economic impact. For example, companies included in the Dow Jones Sustainability Indexes (DJSI) or FTSE4Good Indexes are screened based on corporate citizenship criteria. It has been estimated that the market for socially responsible investing could be as much as $2.3 trillion in the United States[10] and €1 trillion in Europe[11]—roughly 10-15 per cent of the total investment marketplace. Through disclosure in Sustainability Reports, socially responsible endeavours gain prominence, allowing an organization to compete in this distinct market segment.

Another marketplace is the market for talent. Companies with positive social and environmental records can compete more successfully for those individuals who favour this type of employer. For example, a recent study of MBA students found that they would be willing to settle for 14 per cent less cash compensation in order to work for a company with a positive social and environmental reputation.[12]

Of course, the corporate reputation is also a factor among customers for many products. For example, one study in India found that 94 per cent of the Indian respondents said that they were more likely to favour companies with a reputation for ethical business practices when purchasing a product.[13]

CHALLENGES

Companies embarking on sustainability initiatives face certain challenges that may impede their progress towards the aims we have discussed. I'd like to talk about three potential obstacles—things companies need to be careful of, or else they might become entrapped in the quicksand of good intentions.

The first challenge pertains to systemic thinking. The G3 Guidelines suggest that companies frame their performance within an overall sustainability context—that is, how it affects conditions within the larger ecosystem: locally, regionally or globally. Often this involves looking either backward into the supply chain, or forward into how customers are using the products being produced.

Several companies do an excellent job of this. For example, Unilever, in its Sustainability Reporting recognizes the limited supply of clean water in many of the countries that it operates. Thus, instead of simply reporting its own consumption of water, it includes the water consumption of its suppliers and of its customers. It makes the commitment to keep its aggregate water consumption (including suppliers and customers) constant—even as it aspires to grow its operations in these regions.

Another example is the home furnishing retailer, IKEA. IKEA did a comprehensive study of their customers' travel patterns[14]. They found that two-thirds of the total systemic emission of greenhouse gases was due to customer travel to the stores. Thus, they embarked on a sustainability initiative to locate their stores convenient to mass transportation—and to encourage their customers to use mass transportation instead of their cars. They have convenient and energy efficient delivery, so customers don't have to carry their purchases on trains or buses. And, in their annual Sustainability Report, they track the percentage of customers using mass transportation—and how this has changed over time.

A final example is in automobiles. Here, I wish the manufacturers would do a better job of explicitly discussing their system-wide impact in their sustainability reports. For example, the lifetime greenhouse gas emissions from vehicles themselves far overshadow the greenhouse gas emissions to produce a vehicle. However, nowhere in the 143-page sustainability report does General Motors spell this out directly. You have to do a number of additional calculations to learn that each vehicle General Motors produces will discharge over *thirty-seven* times the amount of greenhouse gases during its life than General Motors discharged in the production of the vehicle.[15]

The need to look systemically is even greater in countries such as India, where car manufacturers must look at the effects of new cars on the transportation infrastructure—roads, highways, congestion effects, etc.

The G3 Guidelines do provide some guidance on determining the 'boundaries' of reporting. However, in my opinion, these guidelines are inadequate to adequately address the situations I have noted. Thus, further evolution of these guidelines is necessary to comprehensively account for the systemic effects inherent in a company's operation.

A second challenge has to do with alignment between sustainability initiatives and corporate strategy. If companies are not careful, certain aspects of the G3 guidelines may work against the desired results. For example, one of the G3 reporting principles is comparability—the ability to compare performance indicators across all companies, or companies in a given industry. Companies who let these generic performance indicators be their sole guide do so at their own peril. In addition to common metrics, companies should adopt key performance metrics that directly pertain to their specific business strategy.

There are two ways companies can align their sustainability initiatives with their business strategy. I'll call one 'adaptive' the other 'transformational.' Companies that use the adaptive approach hold their basic business strategy relatively fixed, and adopt sustainability approaches that fit directly within this strategy. In a moment, we'll see how Walmart falls into this category. In a transformational approach, companies engage in a creative exchange with their stakeholders out of which may emerge innovative new directions that alter or modify the strategic approach. We'll soon see that this is the path taken by General Electric as they embarked on a comprehensive journey towards a higher level of corporate citizenship.

The third challenge is building talent. Earlier, I mentioned Creative Internal Processes as a potential enabler that will help organizations achieve a sustainable business paradigm. The flip side of this is the challenge that organizations have in building the talent to foster these creative processes. Studies point that the lack of organizational skills as a key stumbling block in implementing sustainability initiatives.[16] If organizations are to move beyond the 'hype factor' and turn their sustainability reporting process into a dynamic organizational learning experience, they must substantially increase their organizational capabilities. They must align their talent strategy with their sustainability strategy. They must recruit talent that has the values and vision consistent with a sustainability paradigm and must integrate the talent into a workable organizational structure. They must engage in training and development. And they must create the right incentive systems that align with their strategies. These are significant challenges, indeed.

CASE STUDIES

To embellish on some of the concepts I've presented, I'd like to present two case studies: General Electric and Walmart.

General Electric[17] is one of the largest companies in the world, with revenues of over $163 billion. It employs over 3,19,000 people, and is recognized by *Fortune* magazine as the world's most admired company.

Let me share a little bit of corporate history. In 2001, Jeff Immelt took over as CEO from Jack Welch. In 2002, there was a shareholder initiative that would have required GE to disclose its greenhouse gas emissions. While it failed, still, it received a surprising 20 per cent of shareholder votes. In 2003, Immelt surprised investors, when, at the company's annual meeting, he announced that GE would begin to voluntarily disclose carbon emissions. In 2004, this first disclosure took place.

In 2005, GE launched an ambitious new programme—Eco imagination. It also published its first Corporate Citizenship Report (read Sustainability Report) that year. Finally, in 2007, GE published its third Corporate Citizenship Report.

GE's citizenship reporting has continually improved over the past several years. For example, the report now incorporates the new G3 Guidelines. It now reviews commitments made in the previous report, and discusses the progress made during the year in achieving these milestones. Furthermore, it articulates a new set of commitments moving forward. Also, an independent, external review process has been added. Instead of using an outside auditing firm, GE appoints an independent Stakeholder Report Review Panel to review the report. The panel is now in its second year, and GE reports on the changes it has made from the panel's previous recommendations.

GE is pursuing a powerful transformational strategy—using its stakeholder engagement process to guide its future direction. Let me give you two examples.

First, let's look at GE's approach of expanding into emerging markets. In 2000, GE received $10 billion in revenue from emerging markets or 8 per cent of total revenues. By 2006, this has blossomed to $29 billion or 18 per cent of total. By 2010, GE hopes that emerging market revenue will increase to $50 billion or approximately 22 per cent of total revenue. To accomplish this, GE has carefully listened to the needs of its emerging market stakeholders, and has embarked on a whole host of product innovations, including clean water, renewable energy and portable healthcare delivery systems. Rather than relying on a central R&D capability, GE has shifted to an off-shoring strategy—pushing its R&D out into the local countries where it intends for the products to be used. This shift has allowed GE to be more adaptive to local needs and usage patterns. Furthermore, GE has changed its sales and distribution policies to be more respectful of local customs. Also, as a part of the external stakeholder panel review, GE created a comprehensive statement of principles on human rights—which it is translating into local policies and operating procedures. Finally, GE has initiated programmes to help make local governments become more effective by strengthening the 'rule of law.' GE believes that by strengthening local legal processes it will create favourable conditions for long-term business development as well as the advancement of society.

The stakeholder engagement process can take some interesting twists and turns—as we learn from GE's $20 billion energy business. While there are some exciting new renewable energy innovations stemming from its Eco Imagination initiative, a significant portion GE's current energy revenues come from selling coal-fired power plants to electric utilities. As you know, coal-fired plants especially those not equipped with expensive new gasification capture technology are among the worst carbon polluters. Early in Immelt's tenure, GE's power utility customers began voicing concern with GE's new aggressive position toward disclosing and curtailing carbon emissions. Even some of Immelt's top lieutenants did not agree with the CEO's direction. Things got even stickier when Immelt decided to become a founding member of the USCAP (United States Climate Action Partnership), an industry group seeking US government action to limit greenhouse gas emissions. These limits would directly hurt the short-term financial bottom line of GE's top customers. Throughout this five-year journey, Immelt has done a masterful job of engaging key industry leaders in dialogue, allowing GE to take a leadership role in working towards a much needed change.

A second case example is Walmart[18]. With $345 billion in revenue and 1.9 million employees, it is the largest company in the world.

Walmart burst into the corporate responsibility scene when, in October 2005, in the aftermath of Hurricane Katrina, CEO Lee Scott announced his vision of twenty-first-century leadership. He committed to three key objectives: (1) to be supplied by 100 per cent renewable energy; (2) to eliminate all waste and (3) to sell products that sustain natural resources and the environment. In February 2007, he announced a strategy to go along with the vision—Sustainability 360. However, several months later there was a change in top leadership of the company's sustainability initiative. Then on 15 November 2007, the company released its first Sustainability Report.

To understand Walmart's sustainability strategy, you need to first understand its value chain. Walmart buys from over 60,000 suppliers, which supply its big-box retail stores, where over 176 million customers shop every year. The key to the value equation is simple. Low-cost purchasing from its suppliers means low prices for consumers. Thus, the essence of Walmart's value proposition is to drive costs out of its supply chain so that it can continue to drive down consumer prices.

Walmart's Supply Chain Initiative, which is the essence of its

Sustainability 360 project, creates a set of seven sustainable value networks (SVNs) to work with suppliers. These sustainable value networks are organized into product categories, such as jewellery, seafood, chemicals, etc. In addition, there is one global packaging initiative that addresses packaging waste throughout Walmart's entire supplier network.

The goals of these SVNs are to produce environmental-friendly products, create environmental friendly manufacturing processes and ensure that all suppliers respect basic human rights in their companies. To accomplish this, Walmart has created an elaborate supplier scorecard system—where it recognizes and rewards environmentally positive behaviour, and punishes behaviour which is less environmental friendly. Essentially, Walmart has adapted its corporate strategy to meet sustainability objectives. Walmart wields enormous power over its suppliers. To further its everyday low-cost strategy, it is using its leverage over its supplier network to continue to squeeze cost out of the system—all the while improving its system-wide environmental footprint.

As I mentioned, Walmart recently published its first sustainability report. But, while there is a lot of good news, there is also a lot of room to improve. First, it would be good to see Walmart move in the direction of the G3 Guidelines, as this would add significant rigour to the process. For example, some kind of independent review process rather than simply saying that management has reviewed the report and blessed it. Also, Walmart should address the issue of funding of political candidates. Despite its pro-environment public persona, behind the scenes, the record shows that Walmart gives the bulk of its political contributions to candidates who oppose environmental reforms.[19] The company would also do well to establish specific goals for its initiatives—similar to the way GE did. And, finally, the Sustainability Report should be revamped to achieve better balance especially with respect to the impact of its store location strategy. Of particular note, unlike IKEA, the Walmart sustainability report does not fully address the systemic energy footprint of customers travelling to shop at Walmart stores.

Despite these criticisms of Walmart, it's important to note that the initiatives at both GE and Walmart are significant steps in the right direction. Furthermore, when fully materialized both companies are likely to have ripple effects far beyond their company boundaries. GE is poised to influence the energy policy of the United States government, the design of power plants, better healthcare and clean water in developing countries, more renewable energy alternatives, and improved governmental effectiveness in developing countries. Furthermore, there will be a second order ripple effect as GE's best practices (as visible through their Sustainability Report) are emulated by other companies.

Walmart, on the other hand, is poised to have a profound effect on its 60,000 suppliers—improving the environmental and social impact of their processes and products. Furthermore, the second order effects will ripple throughout the suppliers' industries.

In short, both companies continue to prosper economically. But, in addition, they are both poised to deliver positive environmental and social outcomes as well.

PERSONAL VISION AND MORAL IMAGINATION

As we stand here today at the beginning of 2008, I can say that much has been done to advance the vision of sustainability as a business paradigm. However, as I said, the future is not predetermined. It will take the collective efforts of a global society to truly realize the changes that I have discussed.

At the beginning of my talk, I reflected on the past twenty-eight years for me and how Alvin Toffler's book *The Third Wave* was an inspiration for me. And, so, it is my hope to inspire each and every one of you to take action. The upside is enormous. If we are successful, then we could achieve, in the next twenty-eight years, a global civilization that has an abundance of resources. Poverty could be dramatically reduced. And the earth's resources can be replenished, and the damage that we've already done can begin to be repaired.

But if we fail to take action, I'm afraid that this will result in tragedy. If we fail to dramatically reduce our greenhouse gas emissions, we will transform this planet in ways that will make life for subsequent generations far worse than for it is for ourselves. If we fail to take action, hundreds of millions of people in India and other places around the world will continue to live in poverty.

In the end, it will be up to us. We will each express ourselves through what I call our ethical voice—the unique expression of a moral point of view via actions (or inactions). And, I believe that this is the true spirit of Diwali, and indeed, the spirit of J.R.D. Tata, whose memory I am honoured to celebrate here this evening.

Each of us must find that inner light, and we must shine it for the good of our global society and for the benefit of future generations.

As I said earlier, to drive us towards this sustainable business paradigm we require twenty-first century leaders, twenty-first[t] century technology, twenty-first century governmental institutions as well as the discipline of the Triple Bottom Line.

So, what actions are required?

For all of us, as citizens, we must require our governments to become truly twenty-first century governments. The United States must stop dancing around this greenhouse gas problem and take definitive action. Citizens of the United States must urge the United States Congress to pass the appropriate legislation to make this happen. And, we must all urge leaders in the United States, China and India to get together to find a workable global solution.

For leaders at Tata and other companies, it is my hope that you will go back to your jobs and think about how your work can achieve both economic benefits for your company as well as society benefits. Those of you at Tata have a distinct advantage here. Sustainability embodies the very fabric of your company's values. Many of you have been involved with Sustainability Reporting for quite a while. It is my hope that you will think how Tata can continue to raise the bar. You are clearly a role model for other companies. How will you continue to lead the way to make sustainability central to business throughout India and throughout the world?

New technologies are emerging every day that will allow people to escape poverty, to eat better, to live healthier and to use our precious resources more wisely.

Each of us should ask yourselves the question: What is your

vision for the next twenty-eight years of your life? In the year 2036, what do you want to look back and say about your life? How will you incorporate the spirit of Diwali and find that inner light to guide you in all that you will do to make this world a better place?

REFERENCES:

1. Alvin Toffler, *The Third Wave* (New York, New York: William Morrow and Company, 1980).
2. H. E. Laxmi Mal Singhvi, 'Environmental Wisdom in Ancient India,' Available at http://ecomall.com/greenshopping/eastgreen.htm. Last accessed on 30 December 2007.
3. Milton Friedman, 'The Social Responsibility of Business Is to Increase Its Profits,' *The New York Times Magazine*, September 13, 1970.
4. Stuart L. Hart, *Capitalism at the Crossroads: Aligning Business, Earth, and Humanity*. (Upper Saddle River, New Jersey: Wharton School Publishing, 2007).
5. Marc Orlitzky, Frank L. Schmidt, Sara L Rynes, 'Corporate Social and Financial Performance: A Meta-analysis,' *Organization Studies*, 24(3):2003, pp. 403-441.
6. Google search performed on 5 December 2007.
7. From American Management Association Webcast, 11 September 2007. Sustainability: An evolving business paradigm.
   Available at http://www.amanet.org/editorial/webcast/2007/sustainability.htm.
   Last accessed on 24 December 2007.
8. Andrew King, Michael Lenox, 'Exploring the Locus of Profitable Pollution Reduction,' *Management Science*, 48(2):2002, pp. 289-299.
9. David Vogel, *The Market for Virtue: The Potential and Limits of Corporate Social Responsibility* (Washington, D.C.: The Brookings Institution, 2006).
10. Socially Responsible Investment Forum http://www.socialinvest.org/resources/sriguide/srifacts.cfm.
    Last accessed, on 24 December 2007.
11. European Social Investment Forum http://www.eurosif.org/media/files/008_eurosif_pr_sri_study_2006. Last accessed on 24 December 2007.

12. Vogel, *The Market for Virtue,* p. 56.
13 Tata Motor Website.
http://www.tatamotors.com/CSR-0607/page-02.php.
Last accessed on 24 December 2007.
14. *The Greenhouse Gas Protocol. A Corporate Accounting and Reporting Standard,* p.31.
Available at: htp://www.ghgprotocol.org/. Last accessed December 24, 2007
15. General Motors emissions are calculated as follows: In 2005, GM produced approximately 9.2 million vehicles world-wide. Assume that each vehicle emits 371 grams per mile (based on averages from GM's US Vehicles). Then assume (conservatively) an average vehicle lifetime of 128,500 miles (based on US Department of Transportation estimates). This translates into aggregate lifetime emissions for vehicles produced in 2005 of 438.59 Metric Tons. Divide this by the 11.68 M Metric Tons consumed by GM in 2005. This reveals a factor of 37.55 times.
16. McKinsey & Company, Shaping the New Rules of Competition: UN Global Compact Participant Mirror, July 2007. Available at ww.unglobalcompact.org/docs/summit2007/mckinsey_embargoed_until020707.pdf
17. See GE website. See also, Kathryn Kranhold, 'GE's Environment Push Hits Business Realities,' *The Wall Street Journal,* September 14, 2007
18. See Walmart's Corporate Web Site. http://www.wal-martstores.com
19. *It's Not Easy Being Green: The Truth about Walmart's Environmental Makeover,* September 2007. Available at: http://walmartwatch.com/img/blog/enviro_white_paper.pdf

18

Atomic Energy in India—Emerging Scenario*

ANIL KAKODKAR

The Department of Atomic Energy (DAE) was established more than five decades ago. Its activities encompass research and development in areas relating to nuclear sciences and technologies, industrial-scale manufacture of critical raw materials, components, equipment and systems needed for Indian nuclear programme, production of nuclear power, and support of research, academic activities and services associated with nuclear energy and allied subjects within the country. In each of these areas, the required domestic infrastructure, including the human resources, has been progressively developed. A capability based on self-reliance has been acquired to take up newer challenges, as and when they arise.

The main drivers of DAE's activities have been: relevance to meet the national needs and priorities, and excellence by global standards. For a large country like India, it is considered strategically important to develop core capabilities in critical areas to reduce vulnerabilities to external pressures. Incidentally, technology denial regimes have been operational through a major part of the DAE's history. The achievements of DAE, in a wide range of fields, have to be viewed from this perspective as well.**

*Oration delivered on 30 November 2008.

**A large part of the lecture has been omitted.

19

A Few Anecdotes on Business Ethics: Factual Narrative*

TARUN DAS

I would like to relate a few stories, a few anecdotes, things which have happened in the last twenty to thirty years, which relate to values.

STORY ONE

It's 1985, and it's May. We have a forty-year-old prime minister. That's Rajiv Gandhi, and his first state visit has to be Moscow. So, he asked us, CII (Confederation of Indian Industry), then called AIEI (Association of Indian Engineering Industry), to take a CEO's delegation, a business leaders' team with him to Moscow. The Indian ambassador there, good man that he was, sent a teleprinter to the prime minister stating that he cannot bring a private sector delegation to the communist Soviet Union. That teleprinter, I understand, was trashed and eighteen of us went with Rajiv Gandhi to Moscow. He took us to every meeting, he took us to every function, he and Sonia Gandhi—she was also there—and he would introduce the delegation from the CII saying 'These are the outstanding people of the private sector who will change the shape of the country in the future.' I quote, 'These are the outstanding people of the private sector who will change the shape of the country in the future.' This is 1985. We didn't know that we would change the shape of the country in the future. The private sector was, by and large, handcuffed that time.

*Oration delivered on 20 November 2010.

Controls of all kinds. But here was a prime minister who had some vision. The young man who had an inkling of the future and told the world and told us and motivated us in the process of what we could achieve. So, a lesson of motivation.

STORY TWO

It's 1987. Rajiv Gandhi is still the PM. A man called Suresh Krishna from Chennai—Sundaram Fasteners TVS Group—becomes president of the CII. He spends the year driving me and my team mad. He spends the whole year travelling the country, reaching out to companies, reaching out to industries, communicating that we can be better, that we can be world beaters. This is the man who made his company the No. 1 vendor of General Motors, in terms of quality and reliability, year after year against competitors from around the world. In those days, it was unthinkable. By the way, this man got to know Ratan Tata in the CII Council, joined the Tata Steel board and, if I am not mistaken, is still on the Tata Steel board. And this is the man of values who then told us a story which we remember all the time and I want to share this with all of you. He tells the story of a carpenter. A carpenter who is building a cupboard. And he is spending a lot of time on the back of the cupboard, polishing it, cleaning it. Somebody asked him, 'Why are you wasting your time on the back of the cupboard? Nobody's going to see it. You've done a beautiful job on the front of the cupboard; you've done a great job on the side. Leave it; don't waste your time on the back.' He said, 'But I will see the back of the cupboard. I will know what the back of the cupboard looks like.' So, quality is in you. Quality is your own benchmark. Quality is your own standard. It's not what somebody else sets for you. So, as you go into the world and as you enter the world of business, or wherever you are, remember, quality comes from within. And don't forget the story of the carpenter, which Suresh Krishna always talks about.

By the way, many of my stories, fortunately or unfortunately, have a Tata connection. I have many other stories, but today, I thought I would come out with more of the stories which have a

Tata connection, considering where I am standing in Jamshedpur and the person in whose name the oration is being given.

STORY THREE

It's late '80s and early '90s. I get a call to go to Rashtrapati Bhavan. Great! The president of India lives there. I'd never been there. What is it all about? I don't know, just a phone call. And I'm told that the president would like to initiate a programme to help the disadvantaged to become entrepreneurs, to become micro-entrepreneurs through giving small loans, through giving a mentor, and would the CII take this on? How do you say 'no' to the president? It's not our business; it's something completely new to us. It's completely alien. We say yes. Who is the first chairman?—J.R.D. Tata. Who contributes to the corpus fund?—The house of Tatas. Others follow. And out of this is formed something called the Bharatiya Yuva Shakti Trust (BYST). It has a website. And, in the last nearly twenty years, thousands of disadvantaged people have been assisted to be self-employed. Fifty per cent of them are women; and would you believe it that the first people we assisted in the '90s are millionaires today. They are employing people. And have got dignity, self-respect and all of that. And in the formative years of this, all the board meetings were held in Bombay House on the fourth floor. Mr Tata was getting old. It was difficult for him to travel. So it was our privilege to go to Bombay House. To have these meetings under Mr Tata's chairmanship. And he took such meticulous interest, even at that age. And he laid the foundations of the Bharatiya Yuva Shakti Trust. And, for me to sit next to him as his secretary was just mind-blowing. From him, we learnt that business associations cannot just be business lobbies. You have to think beyond. Individuals have to think beyond their immediate interest and immediate focus. So, this was a big lesson from him, which then went on as a policy that we followed from Mr Tata's example—we set up other institutions and organizations in different areas so that the CII could diversify and spread its wings, through what I would call wholly owned or partly owned subsidiaries. But the inspiration for this, although it came initially from the president of India, but day-to-day, year after year, from Mr J.R.D. Tata.

STORY FOUR

It's the 1993-94 period. Liberalization had started. Competition had started. Pain had started. Restructuring was tough. There was a division in the CII Executive Board; it was called the Steering Committee at that time. Dr Irani will remember. Some industrialists who were prominent in the media wanted the CII to go slow on opening the economy. 'We will die; we will not be able to compete.' 'Tarun Das, you are selling out Indian companies to foreigners.' Ratan Tata was a member of the executive board. He attended meetings regularly. And, we faced a conflict. It's not that the Tatas were not going through pain. It was not that the Tatas were not going through competition. But he stood out single-handedly, turned everybody around, said that we must continue opening the economy, we must accept the challenge and we've got to restructure ourselves to be competitive. He won the day, we continued down that path. The people who opposed it backed off, and a country had been transformed in the process. So, lesson here, self-belief is self-confidence, moral of the story, fight for what you believe in, don't give up just because there are more people on the other side of the table saying something different from what you believe in.

STORY FIVE

India was a bad product in those days. Bad image. Reputation for bad quality. Foreign investments very slow to come. No confidence in the country at all. Can't believe this when you stand today and the whole world is—in spite of our challenges, our corruption and all that—the world is applauding India. We started taking missions of CEOs to the USA. We said 'Let's target the most powerful country in the world.' Five-member missions—all CEOs. We would only meet CEOs. We met the GE's, General Motors' chairmen, the Ford chairman, Allied Signals, etc. It took us one year to get to meet Jack Welch of GE, who over breakfast gave us a round of criticism about how bad India was. Today, GE's business in India is over three billion dollars and growing at 20-30 per cent a year. Each mission was led by the same man. We followed a consistent policy with the US. The leader would only be Ratan Tata. And he came and gave time, gave attention, gave energy and led every single CII mission to the USA, year after year. As we promoted India abroad, it was like a door to door sales job. The other part was, it was five members. We would always carry documents, literature, papers data to give to the CEOs and their top management team. How much can you carry? We had the leader of the mission, chairman of the House of Tatas, also carrying papers and briefcases and all of that. The humility of the man. The modesty of the person. No airs, no arrogance, ever. So remember that as you go through life, whatever your level of success is, if there is arrogance, you can fall the next day. But if you are humble and you are modest you keep your feet on the ground, then I think you're safe and you're secure for the future.

STORY SIX

HIV/AIDS is spreading in the country. The country is worried. The media is going to town. The government system is not effective. PM Atal Behari Vajpayee calls the corporate sector to South Block. Can you all supplement? Can you do something about HIV/AIDS? Can you work with the government, can you work independently, what can you do? Again, there is a division within the CII. It's not our business. It's government's business. Education and health is government's business. Why should we get involved? Overruled. An Indian Business Trust for HIV/AIDS is set up. To go beyond creating awareness, to set up care and treatment centres, which will give lifetime treatment to HIV/AIDS affected patients. Chairman of the Indian Business Trust for HIV/AIDS is again Ratan Tata. Going beyond the pale of normal business practices and again, the House of Tatas and the chairman coming in showing the way to the rest of the corporate sector, that we need to be engaged with the issues of the day in this country, even if we are not directly affected. The corporate sector's care and treatment centres in this country today are models. They're models for the rest of the world, they're models for the government and people come from long distances because they get good treatment there. They get drugs, they get good doctors, they get good nursing and all of that. They feel safe with the private sector. A huge message which is now spread across the world, saying that India is a model for care and treatment centres by industry, the leadership here is of a different kind, shown by the corporate sector.

STORY SEVEN

For the first eighty years of the CII's existence, the headquarters was Calcutta (now Kolkata). We came to Delhi in 1975, unknown, unheralded, small, in the jungle of Delhi. Mr Muthuraman referred to the challenges of corruption today, all kinds of challenges were there in those days also. And nobody knew us. But there was one man who we called on; who was at that time, Secretary - Heavy Industry, who took a liking to us. Who liked our vision, our mission that we were trying to build a different kind of an institution. His name was Mantosh Sondhi. He later became Secretary- Steel ministry. He recommended us for land, which we got in Lodhi Road in the centre of Delhi, without paying a bribe because of him. For two years after our building was ready, we couldn't get electricity connection because we couldn't pay a bribe to the electricity authorities. So we were operating in 45-degree-centigrade summer in Delhi with just pedestal fans because the building was not designed for ceiling fans. It was a great experience; all of us suffering together, sharing the pain, struggling, working, performing. Mantosh Sondhi became the guardian angel for us. Just because of the respect the people and the institution earned from him. When he died, we named the headquarters after him, it is now known as the Mantosh Sondhi Centre because of that. And by the way, after he retired from the government, curiously, he joined the Tata Steel board. He continued on the Tata Steel board till his death. Mr Sondhi followed J.R.D. Tata as chairman of the Bharatiya Yuva Shakti Trust, which I referred to earlier. So you keep coming back in different ways to the house of

Tatas and the people who are connected with the Tatas, because they have symbolized leadership—leadership with values.

STORY EIGHT

It's April 1997, 9 p.m. NDTV News headlines: 'The prime minister has resigned, the new prime minister will be sworn in the next morning.' It's our Annual General Meeting (AGM) the next morning. The prime minister has confirmed that he will address our AGM the next morning. We see this news. So what do we do? The president, the vice president and I, we go to Andhra Bhavan. The towering figure there, Chandra Babu Naidu, with all the leaders of the coalition parties, is discussing and agreeing that I.K. Gujral will be the next prime minister of India. He will be sworn in next morning. So we go to Mr Gujral, we break into the room, we break security, the three of us and tell him, 'You know you have to address our AGM tomorrow.' He says, 'How can I address the AGM tomorrow? I would be sworn in tomorrow morning.' 'After your swearing-in, sir, we will take you from *Rashtrapati Bhavan*, to Vigyan Bhavan to address our AGM.'

Miracles happen. This is another lesson of this story. He actually came. It was the first time in the history of India that a prime minister was sworn in in the morning and addressed a business association AGM on the same day. Why? Because we were determined. We didn't mind if we failed, it didn't matter if it didn't work out, but we were determined to try. When you try you can succeed. That was an amazing experience for all of us and we just felt that miracles can happen in very strange ways if you make that effort.

STORY NINE

It's 2006. I am no longer the Director General of the CII. I am free to join company boards or do whatever. I get a call from the chairman of Tata Motors. I guess you'll know who that is. Will I join the Tata Motors board? Can I think of saying no? It's so exciting to join the Tata Motors board. And of course, it's a yes. He takes the proposal to the board, gets it endorsed, and the paperwork was done for me to join. Then I get a call from the Prime Minister's Office. There are some things on which the prime minister wants you to help and work—skills development and some international issues in relation to the USA. What do you say? Can you say no? Do you say yes? Then I call the chairman of Tata Motors, who is in South Africa, which he visits regularly. I say this is the situation. It could actually be a conflict of interest, because in our country, fingers get pointed very easily if you are sitting on a private sector board and you also have access to government papers, documents, information, etc. He understood it immediately. We both agreed that I would accept and go ahead with the second and withdraw from the first. So I missed my opportunity of getting a Nano from the director's quota.

STORY TEN

Unfortunately, another story about the Tatas and the CII. But it teaches us about the values that people follow. About seven years ago, I think, the Tatas decided to set up an office in Washington, D.C. for the first time. Much needed, much overdue, they used to have an office in New York for a different purpose and there was a different objective to have an office in Washington, D.C. To take care of their interest there, the Tatas searched for the right man or woman (mostly men in the Tatas, I think, not many women). Internal search, external search. The executive director of Tata Sons focuses on the person who heads the CII Office in Washington DC. A lady; Kiran Pasricha. Calls her, wants to meet her. The conversation is about joining the Tatas to head the Washington office. So of course, I get a call in Delhi. What do I do? Can't afford to lose people, especially valuable people. So I call the chairman of the Tatas. He tells me a very interesting story. He says, 'I told my colleague that we want somebody who is like her, but I never said we want her. Matter is closed. Tatas will not take anyone from the CII.' Company after company, because they can afford to pay more, are always poaching good people from the CII. A company in the country which does not poach people from the CII is the house of Tatas. This is not the only example. There's another example of a young executive of the

CII who, by mistake or whatever, had approached the Tatas, was interviewed, was liked, but he was crucial to our plans. So when he came to me saying he's got this great offer from the Tatas to join, I made a second call. The same result. The matter was closed. This is the only house which follows the values of an institution which is serving you, serving the public, which cannot afford to pay by the industry standard, is a nonprofit. The Tatas will not poach staff from them. That policy has been followed by the Tatas consistently, year after year. That policy is not followed by many other corporates in this country, who are extremely well known and always in the media.

STORY ELEVEN

It's 1994. Finance Minister Manmohan Singh was struggling with liberalization. We used to go there for meetings from Monday to Friday every day. There was not a day when we were not in the Finance Ministry, working together on things to do to change the country. He was frustrated by the lack of consensus in Parliament amongst political parties. He told us that there is an organization in America called the Aspen Institute, which does leadership development, consensus building and international strategic co-operation building. 'Can you all study that? Can you see if there is something there which we can do over here which is like that?' So the seven of us go off to Aspen, Colorado. The head of the Tatas, New York, was a member of that team. What we saw was mind-blowing. In terms of the methodology that they followed, the techniques, the know-how that they had for shaping people's mind, for building consensus, for building shared understanding. We thought with the diversity of India, the challenges of India, this was something very relevant for India. We came back. We got two of the faculty from there to come to Goa and we had a five-day programme which was attended by people like R. Gopalakrishnan (executive director, Tata Sons), T.N. Ninan (editor, *Business Standard*), Rakesh Mohan (deputy governor, Reserve Bank), Jamshyd Godrej (chairman, Godrej and Boyce) and twenty CEO level people. I happened to bump into Ninan a few days ago. He says to me, 'You remember the Aspen programme you sent me to? That changed my life.' Out of that, it took us ten years of negotiation with the Americans to agree for us to set up Aspen India, to have access to all that technology and know-how, their readings, their internal papers and all of that. Because we don't pay royalty, we can't afford to. Aspen India is now six years old. But it came out of a vision of a person who was worrying about getting people together in India and keeping people together in India. Slowly, slowly its making headway dealing with political parties, police officers, IAS officers, foreign service officers, corporates, media, NGOs, etc., the entire cross section of Indian society is going through training programmes and sessions with teachers from the USA and teachers in India, whom we have trained in the USA, to change the future of this country in a small way. This is the dream of the then finance minister, now the prime minister which has come through.

Again, a story of going beyond the pale; an association like the CII going beyond its normal duties to create something which is an associate or subsidiary to do very specific work—that's a different face of the CII beyond just doing the business and economic related activities.

Suresh Krishna, Jamshed Irani, Jamshyd Godrej—all whom I mentioned—are some, but there are others who have given enormous time to doing things which are in the public interest. Not just in their company's interest. Not just in their sector interest. And, therefore, they have earned respect and trust. They've earned trust and respect from everybody. From the government, from outside, from the public, from the media. And as you go forward in life, you will find that the only thing you can take away from life and the only thing when you come to being seventy-one years old, you're thinking you're in the last percentile, basically what is that you want? Is it money? I would suggest to you, it is respect and trust. You need to have that and you need to work for that with integrity, with values. There are models, the models of J.R.D. Tata, the models of Ratan Tata, as I mentioned; but beyond that there are others who have done public service, who have earned respect and trust.

I think I have found in my life going through many crises, many challenges. Some of the worst challenges have been as chairman of

Haldia Petrochemicals, which by the way I became chairman of, because the chief minister of West Bengal and Ratan Tata asked me to be the chairman. The Tatas were our co-promoter at that time. But somebody up there looks after you. So don't ever feel all the time that it's your achievement, your doing, you've done a great thing, I think if you don't have someone holding your hand and watching over you then you're just not going to make it.

So even for ordinary people like me with an ordinary background who've had an opportunity, had the space, to do things, I think this factor of an invisible guardian holding your hand, watching over you is a very important thing.

The next ten years, irrespective of all the challenges, look like they are going to be great for India. 9 per cent to 10 per cent growth, if we can crack the inefficiency in the government systems: then it can go to 12 per cent per annum growth with huge opportunities for jobs, for self-employment, in India and abroad, growing and strengthening a competitive and confident corporate sector; a far cry from ten to twelve years ago when we were worried about competition from abroad.

So the world is in your hands. You can make what you want of it, but what I see of the young people of India is that they are the most talented of all the generations, past and present. I think my children are better than me. I'm already seeing that my grandchildren are better than my children. So I think the future of this five hundred million young Indians is going to shape an India which is much, much better than before. Because of technology, because of television, telecom and IT, I think we will create a more transparent society, so that we can deal with this cancer of corruption. But I think you will see huge attention given to it by the prime minister and others as we go forward, and I think you will see some changes in the way we deal with things.

20

Values and Ethics in a Volatile World*

LAXMAN NARASIMHAN

J.R.D. Tata is India's most distinctive business icon of the twentieth century. He was a visionary, a builder, an adventurer with an amazing zest for life and a humanitarian. Not only did he build world-class businesses, he also had material impact on India and its development, which will be felt for multiple generations to come. His impact is visible, be it in industry, as for example, in this city of Jamshedpur, or in Pune, where I come from. The impact is large in an area like education and research, particularly in the sciences, as in the Tata Institute of Fundamental Research or the Indian Institute of Sciences; or on the community, be it through the Tata Foundations or through the CSR activities of the various group companies. Increasingly, this impact is being felt around the world, as the group expands its presence worldwide.

JRD is the benchmark for global business leaders today.

These contributions from the Tatas have changed people's lives—mine for instance. I recall the time I was admitted to The Wharton School in the US and had little money to pay for it. I sat in Bombay House, nervously waiting for my interview for the J.N. Tata Scholarship. Mr Malegamwalla, then the person in charge of the scholarship, interviewed me for over an hour. He recognized the aspiration, overlooked the many shortfalls and empathized with the lack of resources. He was kind enough to recommend me for both the J.N. Tata Scholarship and the first Sumant Moolgaonkar Fellowship, telling me 'Go out into the world, but never forget India.'

---

*Oration delivered on 19 November 2011.

He changed my life.

After eighteen years spent living and working in many countries, I returned. As I landed in Delhi, I thought of Mr Malegamwalla and the Tata Trust that day in 1991.

'Go out into the world, but never forget India.'

Changing lives.

One life at a time.

In today's oration on 'Ethics and Values in a Volatile World,' I'd like to start off with a common definition of 'ethics.' The word 'ethics' comes from the Greek word *ethos*, which means 'the disposition, character, or fundamental values peculiar to a specific person, people, culture, or movement.' The definition points to two important implications:

- As cultures change over time, ethics change. It is therefore, a dynamic, not static concept.
- As we look across cultures, ethics by its very definition is a relativistic concept, not absolute—even if there is a base level of ethics consistent across cultures.

As examples, in every society of the world, 'killing' and 'stealing' are considered unethical. That choice is black and white—it is absolute.

But then, so is 'breaking the law'—the easiest way to define something as being 'unethical.'

But whose law? And which law? Breaking the law in any country is clearly unethical, as well as, as the definition goes, illegal. In most cases, it would also be socially unacceptable to do so. That is 'black and white.' Across countries, where laws differ in many cases, or where society's morals differ, it is not as black or white. It is a world of grey.

Let me demonstrate this through an example on values. Values define what we consider acceptable ways of working. They are often easier to break than the law. At McKinsey and Co., we live by fifteen values. Of these, 'Operate as One Firm' is a 'black and white' value. We hardwire this value by having one common committee elect our partners and another common set of committees evaluate them. Another set of values revolves around being 'non-hierarchical and inclusive.' How 'non-hierarchical' is interpreted in a hierarchical society like Japan is different in client settings from how it is interpreted in the US, even if it feels the same in internal problem-solving meetings.

It is therefore clear that there is a spectrum of grey in ethics and values beyond the 'black and white'. I will focus the rest of this address on that difficult 'grey'—not the black and white 'killing' and 'stealing', but the dynamic grey. It is this 'grey' that tests companies and its leaders.

I hope to address three central questions:

With what frame of ethics and values do we look at judgments, actions and responses in this grey world? How should companies and institutions manage in this world? How should individual leaders, particularly you who are students today and leaders tomorrow, respond?

I have three overall messages:

- First, global forces are transforming the world, making companies and some institutions more global and the world smaller and more connected.
- Second, these changes will challenge companies and institutions to consistently operate with a commitment to ethics and values, with significant downside potential, if managed poorly, and real upside potential.
- Third, at a personal level, leaders require an entirely new level of consistency, sensitivity and speeding their judgments, actions and responses in the 'grey' of the multiple operating environments they will find themselves in around the globe.

I hope, in this address, to raise questions for you to think about and to answer for yourself. No one else can answer them for you. After all, operating in the 'grey' is full of personal choices that test our individual characters.

Every single day.

FIVE GLOBAL FORCES ARE TRANSFORMING THE WORLD

We are in the middle of an era of unprecedented volatility and uncertainty. World leaders are challenged. As Roger Waters wrote in the wonderful Pink Floyd song:

'The paper holds their folded faces to the floor; and every day the paper boy brings more.'

In today's world it is more than the 'paper boy'. It's the TV channel. The online blog. The SMS. The WikiLeaks.

And volumes of it—enough to make your head spin and give you 'brain damage'. It is difficult simply to keep up with all that is happening, let alone respond to it. And as for those of you students looking out from in here, I can imagine how these unfolding—even scary—events are challenging what you are learning and what career choices you are considering.

Underlying the near-term tremors of the earthquake on the surface, are the five forces that will reshape the world in the medium to long term.

The first force is the rebalancing of the global economy. We are witnessing a fundamental shift of the economy due East. India and China make up about 25 per cent of the world GDP today, down from 50 per cent 2,000 years ago. This is changing as the developed world slows and the emerging and developing countries grow. Demographic shifts and urbanization will drive prosperity. Around 50 per cent of GDP growth over the next ten years will come from non-OECD countries. We expect one billion more in urban centres, with more than six hundred cities making up 60 per cent of the global GDP. Over half the consumption growth over the next fifteen years will come from developing economies. As average per capita income doubles, we will see more people come out of poverty over the next several years than ever before in human history.

The second force is the need for massive productivity increase in the developed markets. As these post-industrial societies age, as medicine makes rapid advances, they will need a multiple increase in their productivity to maintain the same relative lifestyle. This need presents multiple, ever-increasing opportunities for our Indian technology companies.

The third force is the challenge of an ever-growing networked world. Global financial flows in the world are growing at twice global GDP growth, while product flows are growing at 1.5 times global GDP growth. Distances are shrinking as technology and the media bring us ever closer, shrinking innovation cycles and bringing seemingly far-away worlds to our door. The massive digital explosion underway is further bringing us together.

The fourth force facing companies is that the planet is getting priced. McKinsey research expects a 30 per cent increase in resource consumption by 2020. This increase in consumption is not just for oil; it will impact all commodities: metals, water, food and other resources. Naturally, we expect that our researchers and companies will be ingenious: resource scarcity will drive fundamental innovation, much like what we are seeing in clean tech and water.

The fifth force facing companies is the increasing role of the market State. We witnessed a significant increase in the number of interventions by the State over the last five years. As the world works through this turbulent period, we fully expect the State to have an even bigger role.

These global forces will have a material impact on India and on Indian companies and institutions. India will be a top 5 economy in 2025. We expect 350 million more Indians to be urban. India will be one among the youngest populations in the BRICs—let alone the largest. We could have over a billion internet users by 2025. We expect a few Indian companies in the Global 50. Standards of living will improve and we fully expect to see a large number of Indians rise out of poverty.

COMPANIES AND THEIR LEADERSHIP WILL BE CHALLENGED BY CHANGE

These five global forces will significantly change the operating environment for companies, institutions and leaders. Companies, and institutions that matter, will be more global and operate in multiple cultural environments, each with their own norms. These changes throw up a few challenges:

- The increasing globalization of trade and migration will further make this operating environment more convergent —in other words, given this trend, what is acceptable will look more similar across countries, than different. Similarly, as distances shrink, and as technology, particularly social media, changes the landscape, there will be a further convergence of values at the average societal level.

- However, there will be forces that also drive divergence. As an example, the ability to form 'tribes' online around common interests, transcending cultures and geographies, will drive further divergence in values for some within the societies they physically live in, as opposed to virtually inhabit.
- As demographics change, and the population in some countries gets younger, as in the case of many Middle Eastern countries, these values will change over time.
- The explosion of the digital medium will shrink action and reaction time. Margins of error are narrowing and the impact of an error in one market will be felt in others.
- As the planet gets priced, and as resource companies search in more difficult areas for commodities, there will be many more flashpoints between the ethics of native residents and individual landowners and the needs of the global corporation.

Finally, the greater role of the market State across the world could mean greater regulation, and will mean greater interactions, cooperation and collision between corporations and governments around the world.

In such a world, we believe that ethics create value for business and society. Recently, McKinsey collaborated with Boston College, another fine Jesuit institution, and its Center of Corporate Citizenship to investigate the value of environmental, social and governance activities. We concluded:

> There are clear financial reasons to be ethical. Companies that excel in their social, environmental and governance programmes see improved performance in the dimensions that investors use to assess value: growth, return of capital, risk management, management quality, brand strength and the access to future growth opportunities.

> Over 77 per cent of the respondents of a survey felt that impact resulted from the options opened up through corporate reputation and brand equity, with over half suggesting that it was talent, and a third suggesting that it led to improved operational performance.
>
> Some sophisticated leaders, like Telefonica from Spain, have quantified the value of such efforts and can point to the differential economic value of such activities across geographies.

Such results should not surprise anyone. After all, companies need broad legitimacy in the societies in which they operate, if they are to sustain their long-term ability to create shareholder value.

Society depends upon big businesses to provide a set of critical economic and other benefits. This relationship forms the basis of an overarching contract between business and society. This social contract is under severe pressure, and the actions of corporations in some extremely visible instances are further reinforcing that pressure. The 2G scam in India is an example of such an instance.

In such a world, progressive businesses are realizing that they simply cannot ignore this contract. They are finding ways to move beyond thinking of these as necessary evils, but rather as a business opportunity that opens up new platforms for growth, performance and health. Interestingly, such companies are looking at quantitative and qualitative measures to demonstrate and communicate the value of such activities.

Yet, in 2009, the Edelman Trust Barometer showed that 62 per cent of the general public across twenty countries did not trust large corporations. In the US, that number was 77 per cent, the highest it has been for the ten years that this Trust Barometer has been run. It is, therefore, not surprising to see the movements we see unfolding in various cities around the world.

Additionally, what companies believe as consistent with their ethics or values will differ across geographies and over time. Let us imagine a hypothetical global Indian conglomerate in 2025. It operates in sixty countries, 35 per cent of its talent is global, drawn from over sixty countries. It is in three businesses, one of which gets most of its value from upstream natural resources in Africa and Latin America.

The other is a downstream business, headquartered in the US, with manufacturing plants in twenty countries. Its major competitor is from China. The final business is a consumer service oriented business providing services to developed markets with employees located in both the developed and developing markets.

The upstream business deals with governments in various African and Latin American countries. The downstream business, which sources from the upstream company and has a Chinese competitor, is governed in the US by the Foreign Corruption Prevention Act. The consumer services business is often challenged to lower costs by remote shoring labour; at the same time, the local governments need employment on shore. Its services are often rated online by end consumers in these various markets with very different expectations. Finally, the talent is sourced from these sixty countries with vastly different social mores.

What ethics and values will underpin this global corporation? Will it change between its operations in Nigeria as opposed to that in Russia or Brazil? How should it respond to Chinese competition that adopts aggressive competitive practices, inconsistent with what the FCPA allows, in a Middle East country, where such practices are overlooked and not considered illegal either in that country or in China? How will it think about intellectual property, when one of its competitors does not think of it in the same way? How will its talent respond to 'ethical rules' unacceptable in a few countries, but acceptable in others? How will this talent respond to mobility, when this context changes? What will happen if the company's actions in the consumer services business in one country are inconsistent with the promises made to customers in another? How will it respond to sudden changes—either driven through social movements, as the recent ones in India and on Wall Street, or through changes in law, as happened in Germany on corrupt practices in 1999?

Indeed, a complicated world.

A few reflections on what such a company can do:

Set a high bar for framing the company's approach in this 'grey' world. The higher the aspiration, the more challenging it is to consistently execute. Yet, in the long term, striving for this high bar is what makes institutions live for hundreds of years. While the positive impact is obvious, be prepared for a few individuals to disappoint. I know from recent personal experience at McKinsey that despite the highest aspirations, an individual or two can disappoint.

Adopt a 'top down' consistent set of values and ethical practices for their global operations. Such practices transcend what is legal or not in a particular geography. The objective is long-term performance and health, even if short-term returns are unclear. Given the forces of convergences, companies will be held accountable for how consistently they stick to these values across geographies, and across time. So, while there are relativistic differences, there must be a set of absolute ethics and values for the company.

Consider the example of Google in China. The commitment to free speech and personal privacy were occasionally at odds with what the government in China would have wished for. Google simply had to act to maintain credibility in the eyes of its core users in other geographies. Consider another example in the British media—and it is not the one you are thinking of, given all these wire-tapping scandals. The Guardian, which is owned by a trust, is an institution that stands out for its adoption of editorial principles, reflecting its position as an independent, unbiased voice.

In such a world, the hypothetical Indian global corporation cannot make decisions based on what its Chinese competitor does in Nigeria or the Middle East. It must choose for itself, what it wants to stand for in the long term. Over time, such a position will strengthen the 'soft power' for the company and for India, more broadly. As a result, we can expect that there will be fewer experiences for Indian companies similar to that Huawei is facing in India with worried regulators. One would hope for more of the welcoming response the Jaguar-Land Rover deal received in the UK, when Tata made the acquisition.

Embed these ethics and values deep inside the organization. During the financial crisis, it was clear that values had not percolated deep inside some of the financial institutions that are not around today. It led to choices down the line that were inconsistent with the perpetuation of a value-creating enterprise. For this Indian global conglomerate, as touch points with customers and stakeholders increase, as cultural complexities across the organization increase, and as institutions become larger and more difficult to reorient, embedding values into the culture of companies is most crucial. Cultural embedding is about actions. It is about role modelling. It is about reinforcing metrics and consequences. It is about language—not just what you say, but also, what you think. It is also not just about what line of business you are in. There are non-profits that do not have ethics and values embedded deeply inside the organization and banks that do.

PepsiCo stands out for 'performance with purpose', ITC with its movement on 'green' and 'environmental sustainability', and Hindustan Unilever with its activities in rural India. This hypothetical Indian global corporation must take actions in the sixty countries it is present in to live its values. The nature of the action will differ depending upon the business it is engaged in and the conditions of the local market; the actions though, will need to be consistent in spirit.

Engage and monitor consistent interpretation and compliance rigorously. Social media is transforming how we interact, engage and communicate. In a world with over a billion internet users being added over the next five years, social networking will be the route to the internet for a large number of consumers. For this global Indian conglomerate, its brand will be shaped by what is discussed on these sites. Our research says that the impact of these sites and word of mouth on the customer decision process is large. Customers want to engage with manufacturers. They want to share their thoughts. They want to see how manufacturers respond. They have control of the brands, not the manufacturers. Companies must invest to listen to what is being said about them and by whom and monitor compliance.

Respond quickly, firmly and consistently. Often, it is not just the violation that is the issue; it is how the response is handled.

> Watergate in the past, and recent events in the British press are examples where the response did not address, but rather, amplified the original violation.

A study in contrasts was how the spot-fixing scandal was handled in cricket. This scandal transcended nationalities. It was not just a South Asian issue. Many shrugged the scandal off—and in so doing, killed a piece of humanity in the cricket fans. Others did not shrug off the scandal, prosecuted the criminals and the guilty were convicted. It took time and it took the press to highlight this. In the US, it was difficult to watch how Penn State University handled the recent abuse scandal. For years, the coach had turned a blind eye to an egregious set of actions. The initial response was all about protecting the institution, which is high quality and values driven. Finally, the coach was fired, as was the president. It could have been done sooner. It could have been bolder. It could have made things better. But sadly, the handling of the issue aggravated it. In contrast, Johnson & Johnson's response to the Tylenol disaster in the eighties was a standout positive: bold, decisive, consistent and quick, with no regard for short-term economic consequences.

Such a decisive response will require potentially different organizational approaches. For the hypothetical global Indian conglomerate we have been discussing, it will require centrally-coordinated or centrally-led special structures to manage risk, audit compliance and respond to special events quickly.

> Dynamically alter, based on changes. As demographics change, and as the world both converges and diverges, what is expected of us might change. In some cases, these shifts change priorities. Globalization of companies provides an interesting example of how these changes in fact materially impact the values systems for companies. Listing in international markets drives significant governance changes, as companies look to harmonize how they are managed with international laws. As the race for resources continues, and flashpoints increase, companies will need to change what they do to access, develop and use these resources effectively and efficiently. For the global Indian conglomerate, how

it contributes to the capacity building of the countries in which it operates will be a critical determinant of whether it will, in fact, land some of these resource opportunities.

THE NEED FOR A RENEWED PERSONAL LEADERSHIP MODEL

This complex world will require a new level of personal leadership to lead organizations such as the global Indian conglomerate. Accountability is enforced every single minute of every day. The consequences can be large. The upside potential is significant as well.

What does the individual then have to embody? It is impossible to imagine that a worker or a manager will embody all of the individual themes. It can though serve as the basis for a framework from which to explore what you could be.

Five archetypes for you to consider, based on my personal experience seeing some influential client leaders in action:

The leader as the global, centred, champion with values consistent with those of the corporation: A Fortune 500 CEO I have observed closely, has the mental balance to understand what he sees and hears, and has the experiential and intrinsic judgment to consistently make good calls. He is truly global, and that shapes his judgment of first- and second-order implications of decisions made and helps him look beyond corners.

The leader as a tri-sector athlete: Future leaders in these types of companies must be comfortable operating at the intersection of the private, public and social sectors. This is particularly true in India, and we have some terrific CEOs, including some in this room, who recognize the increasing role of governments and regulation, and the debates being shaped by the social sector. Such leaders step up to the plate and play across these three sectors.

The leader as a storyteller: Leaders must stand for, and be able to communicate, their personal commitment to values and ethics. One client CEO recognizes that his credibility will be judged by what he says and does, and will erode, if these are inconsistent even once.

He is a wonderful story-teller and personalizes concepts through his stories. He teaches employees and associates what works and what does not. As the company operates in over a hundred countries, his stories are increasingly global.

The leader as a sensitive, dynamic listener: Leaders must be sensitive to the differences across markets. A client CEO I have observed closely is dynamic—always testing his assumptions on what he believes to be true. He recognizes that things are changing and he may be out of context with an increasingly younger, emerging market customer.

The leader as the consistent voice: In a recent instance, an executive in an industry was appalled that another was not removed by the CEO for a value transgression; they were in the middle of a large deal and this other executive was an important player in it. How then to 'commit' mind and body to the ethics and values, when things fail at that moment of truth? Consistency, particularly during difficult moments of truth, defines how these leaders can lead an ethical, values-based organization.

What does this mean for you, who are students and about to start your journey? It is hard to give you advice, even if one is in the profession of giving advice; a question that stumped even the consultant.

Let me, though, raise three questions for you to consider:

As you consider where you want to work, should you desire to be a global or Indian business leader, an entrepreneur, a social entrepreneur, a teacher or join a non-profit; what are your aspirations for the type of ethics and values you want your prospective place of work to have? Are you making potentially incorrect assumptions about who fits with your goals? Who does not? How will you define your personal ethical 'guard rails'?

How will you contribute to further elevating these aspirations of ethics and values in your immediate sphere of influence? What skill sets will you bring? What archetype will you be? How will you ensure that you will get the apprenticeship and global experiences necessary to develop this judgment to operate in this world of 'grey'?

As a future leader of an Indian conglomerate, a social entrepreneur, a teacher, a professor or a social sector leader, how will you help ensure India's image on ethical conduct is ever improving?

My father was an entrepreneur late in his life. Despite having been a very successful executive, success was hard to come by in business. I aspired to get into business with him. In fact, Tata Motors (or Telco as it was then known) was a customer. He sadly took ill when I turned nineteen. In the many conversations we had in his last days, when we knew the end was near, he said something to me which I shall never forget.

Quoting Einstein, he advised me, 'Try not to become a man of success, but rather a man of value.' Not just a person of success. Rather a person of value.

I think of him today, as I leave you all with that wish too.

21

Heroic Leaders: Who They Are and How They Live*

CHRIS R. LOWNEY

WHO ARE OUR LEADERS?

I'm sure you are, right now, thinking of very interesting names. But I wonder who is thinking of their own name? I guess no one.

We live in a culture that teaches us to be modest, and modesty is a beautiful virtue. But when it comes to leadership, I want to suggest that your modesty may be misplaced or mistaken because of our broken stereotype of leadership. We tend to associate leadership only with those in charge—like presidents, generals, chief executives and the like. We think of leaders only as people who are famous, rich, or celebrities, often obsessed with their status, the very opposite of humility. So, of course, it would be immodest to call ourselves leaders.

But the idea that leadership is only for chief executives is not the solution to any problems in business, politics, or society. It's part of the problem, and I want to suggest that if we understand leadership correctly, we will find that leadership is compatible with true humility and modesty, and that the very first people we need to think about as leaders are ourselves, and I will soon explain why.

And what do good leaders do to motivate those around them?

That was the second part of our experiment, and I know that people came up with wonderful ideas like decisiveness, vision, honour and so on. But I wonder who was thinking about this idea, articulated

*Oration delivered on 24 November 2012.

by one with wonderful leadership credentials. He said this, 'You must love those you lead before you can be an effective leader.'

The leader I just quoted was General Eric K. Shinseki, who until a few years ago was the chief of staff of the United States military. When I first heard that quote, it struck me as strange, coming from a military class that typically we associate with being tough and macho.

But maybe not out of place. Because the more I thought about it, the more I suspect that a general makes wiser choices when he loves those he must place in harm's way, and I also suspect that soldiers perform better when confident that they are loved and valued by those who have the horrible responsibility of sending them to face their possible death.

So, who is a leader? Well, we're *all* leading, well or poorly, all the time. And our claim to leadership is not our status in a school or organization, but simply the values that we choose to role model in our life and work.

This idea that 'everyone is a leader' certainly runs against stereotype. We don't think this way. But this is not a gimmick or something I've made up. If you look in the dictionary, you will find various definitions of leadership, but the definitions will always include this one: to point out a way, direction, or goal, and to influence others towards it.

Isn't it true that everyone in this room is doing those words all the time? You are pointing out a way or direction for your co-workers and associates by how you treat your colleagues, how hard you work, what you do with your money, whether you care only about yourself or about others also. In all these cases, you are leading: pointing out a way and having an influence on others, good or bad. Many of you are parents: can there be any more obvious act of pointing out a way and influencing others than the leadership that you are showing with your children every day?

Some of you are faculty and staff of this institution: your role modelling will likely be the most extensive example that young adult students will see of how adult human beings ought to behave and interact in a workplace. Alberto Hurtado, a twentieth-century Chilean Jesuit now considered a saint by the Catholic Church, once put it this way, 'In order to teach, it is enough to know something, but to educate, one must *be* something. True education consists in giving oneself as a living model, an authentic lesson.'

To realize our full leadership potential, we all need to get more explicit—more purposeful—about ourselves as leaders, about what kind of leaders we want to be, and about how we will project that in our families, workplaces, and the other arenas in which we interact.

To that end, I want to share some ideas about leadership drawn from research, personal experience and some examples close at hand here in Jamshedpur. For seven years, I was a Jesuit seminarian, studying to be a priest. Then for seventeen years after leaving the seminary, I worked at J.P. Morgan & Co. and was fortunate enough to serve as a managing director in three continents (and I might add, participate in some small way when Morgan launched its first joint venture in India, our first major participation in this thriving market). And, as it is my privilege to deliver the J.R.D. Tata lecture, I would also like to reflect my ideas through another prism, that is, the life and ideas of both the founder of this venerable group, Jamsetji Tata and of J.R.D. Tata.

And, so my friends, even if you find my thoughts of no particular value, I can assure you, after doing a bit of research on Google, that you will have participated in something completely unique by way of this lecture: I believe it is the first time in history that the names of Ignatius of Loyola, J.P. Morgan and Jamsetji Tata all appeared in the same lecture.

And why not? These three individuals long ago formed venerable organizations that still exist and that operate in dozens of countries: the Tata group currently has presence in eighty some odd countries according to recent corporate reports. Jesuits work in more than one hundred countries, but, to be fair, Ignatius of Loyola had a three-hundred-year headstart on the Tatas! To be sure, the mission of a religious order differs from that of an investment bank or from that of a diversified conglomerate; and of course, there are differences in business culture between the US and India.

But it is my conviction, after working in three continents, in both bottom-line driven financial institutions and devotedly charitable institutions, that great leadership is great leadership in every context. Management tactics may differ completely from one context to another, but there are some universal qualities of great leadership, and, perhaps controversially, I want to claim that there is something fundamentally spiritual about great leadership, and I want this evening to focus on three such leadership principles:

- Great leadership is focused on purpose greater than self; it is heroic.
- Great leaders are self-aware: they know their strengths, weaknesses, values and outlook of the world.
- Great leaders love those they lead; that is, they recognize each person as uniquely dignified, and they try to unlock the potential of their subordinates and colleagues.

LEADERSHIP AND HEROISM

I previously mentioned three remarkable individuals who changed history in some notable way, and we have grown accustomed to associating heroism with extraordinary acts like saving persons trapped in burning buildings, or saving comrades in a battle. But most of us will never have the chance to save someone in distress. Indeed, most of us cannot control the opportunities that life ultimately presents us: Ignatius of Loyola aspired to be a soldier until a battle injury forced him to consider a new path in life; and J.R.D. Tata's aspirations first to pursue his own military career, and later, to pursue an engineering degree had to yield to his father's urgings in other directions.

What these two controlled was not their life opportunities, but what we *always* control, namely: how we think, react and behave in the face of whatever opportunities life presents. We are gathered at a higher learning institution: teachers and staff here have no guarantee of making a profound, life-altering impact in a student's life; their heroism becomes manifest in their commitment to live and work as if they *might* make such a difference. And let's be frank. For most of us, the opportunities life presents will be small. Our heroism will not be won in one spectacular moment that others will watch on television. Rather, it will be the fruit of a lifetime of dedicated, conscientious effort, like that of teachers, parents, quality inspection officers in factories and building sites, nurses and countless other professions.

Above all, heroes devote themselves to a purpose greater than self. There is an anecdote, perhaps apocryphal, about the US President Kennedy in the early 1960s, who visited the space agency during the era when the US and Russia were racing to send a rocket to the moon first. And, as the story goes, the president, during his tour of the agency, met a janitor who was sweeping the floors, and, to be polite, asked what his job was. He supposedly replied, 'Mr President, I am putting a man on the moon.'

However overly romantic this anecdote may sound, everyone here knows that its point is sound: the teams that perform best are teams where people, if I may use some American slang, are willing to 'get over themselves' and appreciate that the organization does not revolve around them and their particular job. Rather, whether J.P. Morgan, the Jesuits, XLRI, or the Tata Group, organizations only succeed when individuals see themselves as participating in a mission greater than themselves and willingly invest some of their energy, talent, intellect, creativity and ego in purpose greater than self.

This sounds like a spiritual idea, and of course it is: every one of the world's great spiritual traditions champions the notion that we are here on earth to transcend ourselves. But it is also a *business* idea. Listen to Alan Mullally, the head of Ford Motor Company, a materially-oriented industry if ever there was one, as he describes his role in consummately spiritual terms, 'What I was really being asked to do was to help connect a set of talented people to a bigger goal... And so the higher the calling, the higher the compelling vision you can articulate, the more it pulls everybody in.'

In fact, listen to an example closer to home, as Jamsetji Tata explains his own philosophy of business, 'We do not claim to be more unselfish, more generous or more philanthropic than other people. But we think we started on sound and straightforward business principles, considering the interests of the shareholders our own, and the health and welfare of the employees; the sure foundation of our success... In a free enterprise, the community is not just another stakeholder in business, but is in fact, the very purpose of its existence.'

I talk about this principle of heroism not because it sounds nice, but because it goes to one of the great crises in the world of business: the struggle between self-interest and purpose greater than self. Some of you may be aware of the fascinating study conducted by the US university, UCLA, which annually interviews eighteen-year-olds across the country who are entering university. As students rank their values, more than 70 per cent of them now say it is very important to become very well off financially, and only some 30-odd per cent of them say it is important to develop a 'philosophy of a meaningful life'—proportions that have exactly reversed over the decades. We raise these students in a culture that celebrates conspicuous consumption, recruit them into industries like my former business—investment banking—that offers very lucrative pay packages, and we face real challenges nurturing 'purpose greater than self' players in a 'put yourself first' world.

Of course, in business, we need individuals who are ambitious and motivated to succeed in ways that result in superb performance, innovation and that inspires peers to raise their own performance levels. Without this element of self-interest, companies do not thrive.

But, at the very same moment, we need these same individuals to keep self-interest in proportion, individuals who are willing to struggle and fight for purpose greater than self, in family, in company, nation and community. But getting this attitude is a self-awareness task; it calls on us to become aware of our deepest beliefs. So let me talk briefly now about the importance of self-awareness.

GREAT LEADERS ARE SELF-AWARE

Every Jesuit in history, from the sixteenth century European founders to some 4,000 twenty-first-century Jesuits now working here in India, has participated during training in a month-long intense period of personal reflection called the Spiritual Exercises, during which the Jesuit is removed completely—from the workplace, from reading papers, watching television, talking with friends, or anything else that could deter from the intense introspection that becomes the Jesuit's only 'job responsibility' for thirty days. These guided meditations, which are probably the most widely used retreat tool in the Christian world today, were St Ignatius of Loyola's very practical attempt to translate into a systematic approach, the fruits of his own journey to religious and overall self-understanding. As far as Jesuits are concerned, this is a spiritual and religious experience, but the self-assessment that is taking place makes them a wonderful leadership training experience because each Jesuit is being forced to ponder: Who am I? Why am I here? What is worth doing in a human lifetime?

Anyone who has managed lots of people or worked in a human resources department—I did both at J.P. Morgan—has been mystified by the phenomenon of rising young stars who sometimes crash and burn even though they had the total package of technical skills, smarts, ambition and training. One school of thought attributes these spectacular flame-outs to lack of self-awareness. That is, they do very well when asked only to do straightforward tasks, like moving numbers around Excel spreadsheets. But they fail when asked to deal with ambiguous business problems that have no clear, exact answers; or to motivate and manage people through change and uncertainty.

And most business problems have no exact answers. Indeed, many strategic challenges have no perfect solutions at all. So we need individuals who have the good judgment to evaluate various imperfect alternatives and identify the best; and who have the courage to move forward without the mathematical certainty that their proposed strategy will succeed.

This lack of judgment and courage sometimes befalls very smart people who learn to 'do school' but never learn to 'do life.' 'Because school comes easily to them, they never face serious challenge, setbacks, or failure. They, therefore, never develop 'learning agility'—the ability to confront one's weaknesses, learn from mistakes, fail and persevere, and accept feedback from others, for example.

The long-time Harvard professor Abraham Zaleznik once noted how many successful executives were, in his words, 'twice born.' He was not referring to religious conversion, but observed that personal crisis like injury, alcoholism, or bankruptcy had buffeted these individuals early in adulthood and forced them to re-evaluate their lives and come to grips with who they were, what they stood for and what they wanted. His thesis—That the strength of character born of adversity, explained their long-term success by tiding them through life's subsequent challenges.

We might here recall Ignatius of Loyola's severe battle injury, shattering his life plans and dreams, leading to a profound conversion and self-reinvention. Or, we might also think of a young Jamsetji Tata watch his father's banking firm collapse, see his own future career dissipate with it, soon after embark on his first journey outside India to England, to be besieged there by his father's creditors, and, in the course of this jarring journey, to begin to perceive his way forward in the world as an industrialist.

Of course, not everyone will suffer a crisis that forces deep self-scrutiny upon us. But if we are to lead our own lives, not to mention to lead others, we need to make fundamental investments in knowing ourselves. Decades after the anecdote I just related, here is J.R.D. Tata, on his twenty-first birthday, writing to his father and in a painfully honest way underscoring that investment in one's self-knowledge is vital, 'One more year has fallen on my shoulders. I have been looking back and also deep inside myself with the merciless eye of conscience, and have been trying to find out whether during this last year I have gained in experience or wisdom. I haven't found out much yet!'

Let me connect this idea to the Jesuit Spiritual Exercises and self-awareness more broadly: if a crisis does not thrust a moment of self-scrutiny upon us, we need to find or manufacture some process for accomplishing this fundamental investment in our own self-awareness, using whatever spiritual or humanistic tradition we may follow. That is why, for example, students at great schools like XLRI learn not only technical skills like calculating present value or deciphering debits and credits, but likewise to scrutinize their own values, the morality of their actions and the broader purposes of human endeavour.

So we need to make a profound investment in knowing ourselves, and we also need to have some mechanism every day for keeping track of how we are doing. The Jesuit tradition teaches a wonderful little process that anyone here could begin using in less than five minutes a day. For the rest of his life after his month-long upfront investment, the Jesuit founder advised that Jesuits ought to take at least two short breaks each day—let's imagine that I take five minutes after my midday meal and another five minutes at the end of the workday. First, I remind myself of why I am grateful. Second, I call to mind some important objective or a personal weakness to be addressed. And third, I mentally revisit the last few hours and try to extract some learning that might help in the next few hours: if I have been distracted all morning, why? If I have not shown sufficient self-confidence in meetings, what could have been going on? Why have I not treated a colleague with sufficient respect or care?

The genius of this sixteenth-century practice becomes obvious when we consider the lives we are leading: floating along all day on a river of e-mails, phone calls, text messages, meetings and distractions without ever pulling back to take stock. I'm sure those of you who are managers have seen the fallout from these chaotic lifestyles as I have: the person who gets to the end of the day without ever getting to his or her #1 priority, or the person who has a meeting go badly at 8:30 a.m. and remains distracted all day, draining productivity. These are self-awareness problems, and we need to remedy them through self-awareness tools such as I described.

LOVE THOSE YOU LEAD

Let me now come to the third leadership principle I wanted to introduce, the idea about which people in large companies are sometimes most sceptical: What place could love have in a large company? First of all, I assure you that I did not wander the hallways of J.P. Morgan embracing my colleagues and telling them I loved them, nor am I suggesting you begin doing so here in Jamshedpur. But the founder of the Jesuits said that 'Love ought to manifest itself in deeds, not in words.'

So what kinds of 'deeds' might show the impact of love in a workplace?

How about this for starters: surely no chief executive who loved his or her employees would have recklessly gambled their livelihoods and pensions in order to enrich him or herself through fraud, as we have seen in too many companies in my home country, and, unfortunately, in yours as well. And surely no politicians or public servants who loved citizens would enrich themselves through corrupt use of government monies, depriving citizens of the basic human services to which they are entitled. These are perfectly legitimate examples: every great spiritual tradition teaches us that human beings have innate dignity, and, dignified human beings are entitled to just treatment simply because they are human.

But these foregoing examples make the case in a negative fashion, and I want also to develop a more positive perspective of what love could look like in a workplace. Listen to this idyllic vision for a factory zone, and I wonder if any of you will be able to guess its context: 'Be sure to lay wide streets planted with shady trees, every other of a quick-growing variety...Be sure that there is plenty of space for lawns and gardens. Reserve large areas for football, hockey and parks. Earmark areas for Hindu temples, Mohammedan mosques and Christian churches.' I hope that at least a few of you could recognize this quote. It is Jamsetji Tata, articulating his vision for the city of Jamshedpur to those who would be accountable for its initial construction. I trust you are familiar with his other labour market innovations, mandating shorter working hours, safe workplaces and provident fund contributions for employees at a time when these were common neither in India, nor in the West.

Decades later, J.R.D. Tata, describing his own management philosophy, puts into words the spirit that must have been behind Jamsetji Tata's vision, 'I am one who will make full allowance for a man's character and idiosyncrasies. You have to adapt yourself to their ways and deal accordingly and draw out the best in each man. At times it involves suppressing yourself. It is painful but necessary... To be a leader you have got to lead human beings with affection.'

I worked in investment banking for some seventeen years, during the era when my industry began to embrace and promulgate the so-called 'agency theory' of management, which posits that management's role, as agent for shareholders, is to focus on one consideration only: to maximize shareholder value. Managers are to make those investments which will provide optimal financial returns and ruthlessly slash expenses which do not.

How might we assess Jamsetji Tata's vision through the prism of maximizing shareholder value? Surely some analysts would tell us that space for lawns and gardens, not to mention fields for hockey, football, or houses of worship were completely extraneous to the firm's value maximization mission; allocations for provident funds, before this had been proven necessary to attract talent, would likewise be seen as squandering the firm's resources.

Well, shareholder maximization theories have, on the one hand, spurred admirable, laser-like focus on proper use of corporate resources. My spiritual tradition includes the parable of the 'good steward,' the manager, leader, or public servant, who understands he has been entrusted with resources, as a steward, to exercise wise and careful management of resources rather than squander them thoughtlessly. Agency theory reminds a manager to be conscientious of his role as a steward.

But the agency theory of shareholder value maximization, used in shallow or simplistic ways, has sometimes run amuck, leading to excessive preoccupation with short-term quarterly results, neglect of the long-term good of the firm and utter disregard for stakeholders beyond shareholders. Thus, some market analysts would be appalled at Jamsetji Tata's attention to parks and a pleasant working environment as a wasteful preoccupation that adds no shareholder value.

But I suspect Tata understood that he was not only treating his workers in a dignified way, but at the same time making investments that would have absolutely paid off in the long run. Let me use a few statistics from the US business environment to illustrate my point. In surveys of employees working in US corporations, the majority are unhappy in their work, 63 per cent report high levels of stress, only about 40 per cent say they trust their own senior manager, half of employees say they worry frequently about losing their job, and the work week in these unhappy, mistrustful places is now 20 per cent longer than it was one generation ago. Surely anyone could tell us that if this is the environment in which we are asking employees to perform, they cannot possibly be flourishing to their maximum productivity, and I suspect Jamsetji Tata understood that by giving employees humane working environments; they would be enabled to do their most productive work.

Hence, I do not make the case for a 'loving' work environment or, as J.R.D. Tata put it—'To be a leader you have to lead human beings with affection'—I am not making this case for soft reasons that will destroy shareholder value. Rather, I argue that we must create conditions in which each team member can flourish to his or her maximum potential, so that investors can realize a rich reward.

In fact, we ought to ponder the very notion of being a 'company,' as is the Tata Group, J.P. Morgan, or, believe it or not, the Jesuits. 'Jesuit' is a sort of nickname; when they founded their organization, they called themselves a 'company,' 'La Compañia de Jesus,' the company of Jesus. And the way they understood 'company' was likely closer to the word's etymological roots than the way we understand that word today, when its meaning has been almost completely hijacked by the connotation of a commercial enterprise. The word's Latin roots are 'cum,' that is, 'with or together,' and 'panis,' that is, 'bread.' So, etymologically, the word conveys an almost familial sense, the group of people who 'break bread' together, who give energy to and support one another, who are 'companions,' a word which comes from exactly the same root.

These early Jesuits, and perhaps too, Jamsetji and J.R.D. Tata, are challenging us to return our modern 'companies' to something nearer the word's roots, places where energized employees feel supported by the kind of companionship that enables them to deliver their best work and, in turn, provide best value for owner-shareholders.

We are gathered at XLRI, one of India's leading management schools, whose graduates will inevitably make a powerful impact on India's business culture, and it is no surprise that XLRI, itself part of the Jesuit tradition, champions exactly the kinds of ideas I have been speaking about. The school's mission includes, 'To enable aspiring managers to realize their full potential,' and the school's mission includes, 'An abiding commitment to improving the quality of life in organizations and society.'

Every pundit that I know of, whether they speak of business, political, or civic life, talks about the need for greater leadership. But though we all agree on the need, we have made very little progress. Indeed, in my country, the public is far more cynical and mistrustful of politicians and business leaders than we were one generation ago. We haven't made progress, in fact, we have gone backwards, in part because we're stuck with broken stereotypes of leadership that have to do only with status, position in a hierarchical chart, money, or power. Well, those in this room can teach society by the way we do business and the way we teach management, a unique, principled and workable model of leadership for the twenty-first century, based on the notion that everyone leads when role modelling values like those that I've outlined.

So, when asked to think of the names of one or two living leaders, and I hope by now you think of your own name first, when I say that we need competent, smart and virtuous people who can role model a way of leading for those who are on our teams, in our companies and in our communities.

22

Ethical Challenges for India Today*

PALLAM RAJU MALLIPUDI

On this occasion, it would be most appropriate to recall a few facets of Bharat Ratna J.R.D. Tata's legendary personality. What guided JRD. was the power of his conviction and not the fine print of law. I am reminded of a reply given by J.R.D. Tata when a professor of management asked him to share his philosophy of life with his students. JRD said, 'If I were to attribute any single reason to such success as I have achieved, I would say that success would not have been possible without a sustained belief that what I did or attempted to do, would serve the needs and interests of our country and our people; and that I was a trustee of such interests.'

JRD was one of the last of the great patriarchs of Indian industry, but to call JRD an industrialist is akin to saying Mahatma Gandhi was just a freedom fighter. JRD considered his leadership of the Tata group and his dedication to the cause of India as complementary, and he brought to the two undertakings, a rare dignity and sense of purpose.

Conducting the affairs of a business empire as diverse and complicated as that of the Tatas in the pre-liberalization era would, by itself, have been a prodigious task, but JRD had plenty more to offer. He played a critical role in increasing India's scientific, medical and artistic quotient. The Tata Institute of Fundamental Research, the Tata Memorial Hospital, the Tata Institute of Social Sciences, the National Institute of Advanced Sciences and the National Centre

*Oration delivered on 7 December 2013.

for the Performing Arts, each an exemplar of excellence in its field, were projects that would not have come to fruition without JRD's steadfast support.

Despite his very public persona, JRD was a shy and reticent man. He never hankered after honours, but was showered with them, to much bemusement on his part. On being told that the Indian government was thinking about giving him the Bharat Ratna, the country's highest civilian award, he is reported to have said, 'Why me? I don't deserve it. The Bharat Ratna is usually given to people who are dead or it is given to politicians. I am not prepared to oblige the government on the former and I am not the latter.'

I take this opportunity to salute JRD's vision and his ethical leadership. I would like to delve into three different facets that are linked to ethics in India today—Education, Business and Politics.

EDUCATION

Our ministry believes in the 3Es of Education Policy—expansion, equity and excellence. The first E is expansion—expansion of education. We achieved independence with just 17 per cent literacy, only 8.9 per cent of our women could read and write. We had just twenty-six universities in the entire country; 400,000 students in higher education in the whole country. Today, the transformation has been dramatic, we've gone from 17 per cent to 74 per cent literacy, women going to 66 per cent; we've gone from those twenty-six universities to close to seven hundred universities, from the 690 colleges in those days to 35,000 colleges today, and from 400,000 students to 20 million in higher education. Expansion from both the government and private sector has been vital in empowering the human resources of our country.

The second E is that of equity, reaching the unreached, including the excluded—people left out of education because of their gender, because of distance, caste, religion, language. That is where right to education (RTE)* has been able to form a bridge and we are sure

---

*Right to Education Act (RTE), is an Act of the Parliament of India enacted on

will transform the country.

RTE, along with now being a fundamental right is also an empowering right which equips citizens to secure other rights. Education gives people the ability to access information about their rights and government's obligations. RTE is proof of the government mainstreaming human rights perspective in policy.

The rights-based approach asserts education to be an entitlement and rightful claim of every citizen. The RTE looks at achieving the ideals of women empowerment, disintegration of artificial social barriers, abolition of child labour to the meaningful realization of decentralized democracy and distributive justice.

The RTE acknowledges the need for inclusion and explicitly establishes the normative responsibility for everyone and not just the government to contribute towards the goal of universal quality education for all of India's children.

After the implementation of the RTE, there has been remarkable growth in input indicators like infrastructure, teacher-pupil ratio, enrolment.

In the process of fulfilling these two Es, we have perhaps not paid enough attention to the third E—excellence. In coming years, the focus of the MHRD (Ministry of Human Resource Development) will emphasize on excellence. Achieving quality education is a step by step process, and considerable emphasis needs to be laid on each of the indicators. While it is easy to access the progress in terms of infrastructure, teacher-pupil ratio, enrolment, it is much harder and is bound to take longer to see the impact that these indicators will have on learning outcomes.

The Education Policy will continue to focus on the three Es of expansion, equity and excellence in education across all levels. Our vision is of providing quality education for all with special focus on marginalized and disadvantaged groups. But even if these 3Es are achieved, if we do not impart holistic education grounded in ethics,

---

4 August 2009, which describes the modalities of the importance of free and compulsory education for children between 6 and 14 in India under Article 21a of the Indian Constitution.

we may not see JRD's dream of India 'becoming a happy country' come to fruition.

Higher education must pay more attention to helping students understand how to lead 'ethical, reflective, fulfilling lives'.

Despite the importance of moral development to the individual student and society, one cannot say that higher education has demonstrated a deep concern for the problem of ethics.

BUSINESS

Business education

Even in business education, a strong ethics education can help counteract a narrowing worldview that often accompanies a student's progression through business school, supporters in academia say. I completed my MBA more than twenty-five years ago in the USA, where courses on business ethics were introduced at that point in time. But that did not stop the financial crisis from occurring and affecting the world. The danger is also that we only think about ethics when there's a major crisis.

More often, however, the subject is not treated as a serious responsibility worthy of sustained discussion and determined action by the faculty and administration.

XLRI

I am happy to learn that XLRI is the first B school in the country to introduce a core course on 'managerial ethics' for its programmes and that a medal is awarded to the best student in managerial ethics at the institute's annual convocation.

I am also happy to know that XLRI has moved beyond talk, and put into action the values it espoused. XLRI's mission on being a management school with a difference and uphold its commitment to inculcate a sensitive social conscience in future business leaders in the making has been demonstrated through its initiatives like the Annual Conference on Social Entrepreneurship.

While education is one aspect, it cannot only be left to educational institutions to impart ethics. A child or a student ultimately learns what he/she observes as part of society.

Ethics in business moves beyond just financial integrity and includes social and environmental responsibility. I'd like to draw your attention to importance of ethics in business through bringing JRD's example again: In a speech in Madras (now Chennai) in 1969, JRD called on the management of industries located in the rural areas or semi-urban areas to think of their less fortunate neighbours in the surrounding regions:

'Let industry established in the countryside 'adopt' the villages in its neighbourhood; let some of the time of its managers, its engineers, doctors and skilled specialists be spared to help and advise the people of the villages and to supervise new developments undertaken by co-operative effort between them and the company.'

In fact, many years later, JRD also included responsibility towards environment. Quoting him:

'I believe that the social responsibilities of our industrial enterprises should now extend, even beyond serving people, to the environment. This need is now fairly well recognized but there is still considerable scope for most industrial ventures to extend their support not only to human beings but also to the land, to the forests, to the waters and to the creatures that inhabit them. I hope that such need will be increasingly recognized by all industries and their managements, because of the neglect from which they have suffered for so long and the physical damage that the growth of industry has inflicted, and still inflicts on them.'

These concepts which JRD talked about many years ago are regarded as standard practices internationally—triple bottom line reporting and corporate social responsibility (CSR). The government has also promoted the importance of the business ethics and has made necessary amendments in the Companies Act, 2013. It is a first update of the country's corporate law in more than fifty years, aimed at modernizing it. One of the important provisions of the Act is including the allocation of 2 per cent of profits on CSR activities that promote poverty reduction, education, health, environmental sustainability, gender equality and vocational skills development. It is also advised that companies 'shall give preference to the local area and areas around where it operates.' India is the first country to mandate the CSR requirement.

I would encourage XLRI and the students to delve into this more and add to bridging the gap between industry and social responsibility through an ethical framework.

Most recent national rankings and ratings of B-schools in India have unquestionably placed XLRI among the top-most B-schools in India, and the very first and best among India's private B-schools. This is a superb accomplishment, and I sincerely congratulate the chairman and board of governors, the director, his administration, the faculty and the students. I believe there are over 2,400 business schools in India and are still proliferating. Given this highly competitive background, XLRI's achievements are still more laudable. I also understand some of its alumni have truly achieved national and international renown, and are ranked among the very best CEOs and professors in India and abroad. This is yet another landmark we are really proud of, and I once again commend XLRI for its great brand name and fame, brand identity and legacy. Our next hope is that XLRI will ascend to rank and shine among the top-most B-schools of the world.

POLITICS

Which brings me to the third aspect of my talk today—the world I inhabit—politics and the role ethics plays in it. Building on the traditions of the national movement, Indian leaders strengthened the foundations of democracy as they gave due importance to the institutional aspects of the democratic system and adhered to not only the forms of democratic institutions and procedures but also the spirit.

From an electorate of around 173 million in 1951, when India went to the polls for the first time under the Constitution, the number of electors will swell to nearly 800 million in 2014, out of which 150 million will be first-time voters. I hope many amongst you in the audience, will be among them. The fair and peaceful conduct of elections periodically with a large turnout of voters, with the participation of all groups with differing ideology and religious faith, is an indication of the acceptance of the framework of the Constitution and the growing political awareness among the people. These elections have demonstrated that the democratic urge is very deep-rooted among the people of India and their faith in a constitutional system of government very strong.

Jawaharlal Nehru was quite amazed at democracy functioning so successfully in India. On the last day of the second Lok Sabha, he could say with some satisfaction on the floor of the House, 'Democracy... is the hallmark of India at present. But democracy does not consist of 210 million people voting. Democracy, ultimately, is a way of life, a way of reacting to circumstances, a way of thinking and a way of putting up with the things we dislike even. And I think we have done fairly well.'

If we are to live in peace, prosperity and happiness, we must envision universal and humanitarian ideals and must strive to practise them in thought, speech and action. In ancient India, politics was regarded as a branch of ethics. Peace, justice and liberty for all were the prime purposes of politics.

Mahatma Gandhi recommended that politics should be a branch of ethics. Democracy is at stake if the loudest voice counts as the voice of wisdom, or when coercive pressures take the place of reason and persuasion.

In his address on 18 October 1951, Nehru laid great emphasis on the importance of the right means to achieve right ends. He said, '... [I]f in our eagerness to win the elections, we compromise with something that is wrong, then we have lost the fight already and it matters little who tops the poll...'

While there has been considerable progress on the economic front, there has been regression of the values in society and devaluation of institutions. Free, fair and effective democracy costs money. Parties need huge resources to sustain themselves, whether in office or in the opposition. Our counterproductive election laws have led to a proliferation of black money into the system to deal with the expenditure.

Therefore, across the board, parties have tried to cope by favouring candidates with black money and the networks and capability to expend those resources. Such candidates, whose political foundations are built on lawbreaking, typically hijack the political system for private profiteering. The rare few get caught and eventually convicted. This has led to deep cynicism in public opinion on politics in the country.

It is worth recalling that Mahatma Gandhi introduced the 'char-anna' membership for the Congress. Through small contributions he made the masses a stakeholder in swaraj. Similarly, we should enable individuals to contribute small sums and help free politicians from dependence on plutocrats and vested interests.

We must learn to contribute openly and hold our representatives accountable. We must explore different state funding formulae to encourage political participation. We must bring every aspect of the political process into the open. As more sections of society actively contribute and participate, the political system will undergo a transformation. We will see inclusive, empowered parties, citizen candidates and positive politics. Only that can rejuvenate our democracy and put it on track with the ethical framework of our nation as envisioned by our founding fathers.

CONCLUSION

An ethical framework of values should be instrumental in creating a generation of not mere managers but leaders that will take India to its rightful place in the world.

It is the need of the hour to nurture the next generation of India's leaders, whether in education, business or politics; in engaging their passions in the direction of India's growth, creating an Indian society that embraces values and promotes ethical leadership. And we do not have to look further than JRD as a role model as we embark on our journey.

23

Building Trust*

D. SHIVAKUMAR

Trust is declining in most countries, societies, companies and relationships. We live in an era of diminishing trust. Trust is diminishing for many reasons: the world is getting more selfish; the world is getting more materialistic; the measures of success are about money, there is a 'what's in it for me now' mindset; and trust is diminishing because decision-making favours short-term goals over long priorities. Trust is also dropping because consumers and citizens have more access to information and discriminate whether institutions and leaders are deserving of their trust.

A recent global Edelman survey surveyed trust amongst NGOs, business, media and government. Globally, trust in NGOs was the highest, followed by trust in business enterprises, followed by media and government. In India, the same study had business first, followed by NGOs, media and government. Here's the bad news from India, trust in three of the four groups dropped, with trust in the media dropping the steepest. Trust in government is dropping but trust in regulators, who are part of the government, is increasing. We need to introspect why consumers and citizens trust is dropping, and more importantly what do we need to do to win back their trust.

I will over the next twenty-five minutes attempt to answer the following:

- Why is trust declining?
- What is the cost of low trust? What is the benefit of high trust?

---

*Oration delivered on 29 November 2014.

- What can leaders do to build back trust?
- How does one build trust in a digital world?

Trust is declining because the words and actions of those who lead us are not trustworthy. We are scrutinizing our leaders much more closely today and every imperfection and transgression is under the spotlight. Trust is dropping because there is freedom in more countries today than before. Nearly half of the world's countries are free with a free media. A free and unbiased media takes no prisoners. Trust declines when we have doubts, when we have doubts, we withhold our commitment, when we withhold our commitment, we don't believe in the cause any more. There are so many vehicles and people who create fear, uncertainty and doubt about what's happening around us. Each fear, each uncertainty and each doubt chips away at trust. So, someone needs to show the way to better trust.

Trust is declining because people have choices in every sphere of life, from choosing a school, to a club, to a channel and to a newspaper. Choice forces people to pick something more on qualitative factors versus hard quantitative data. Most qualitative parameters finally converge to trust.

Trust is declining because values are not being practised. Values are like a lighthouse, they provide us direction to a safe shore in choppy waters. A value for me is something that one would die to uphold. We don't see enough examples of everyday practice of values. Trust is declining because we are not increasing inclusivity.

Trust is a two-way street; it involves two parties at a minimum. People involved should be thinking about what's in it for us versus what's in it for me, see the greater good and what we can do together. Intention that is purely self-interest, creates a culture of suspicion because the outcome will always be 'survival.' Mutuality and reciprocity are central to creating and sustaining trust.

In 2006, when the India mobile subscriber base was ninety million, a few of us believed that this could be nine hundred million in very quick time. In order to connect ninety million to nine hundred million, we had to open up the rural market. The rural consumer didn't want a sim card separately and a phone separately.

So Nokia needed to partner with Airtel. The two companies decided to run a thousand rural vans. The value of the rural drive got 60 per cent revenue share for Nokia and 40 per cent for Airtel. Airtel didn't bat an eyelid and continued to share a 50-50 cost sharing with Nokia because they knew that this would help them over the years. The trust the two companies built with this simple act has stayed even today.

When we discuss trust, very few of us ponder to think about the consequences of low trust. Trust is intangible and will not appear on balance sheets. Brand Trust reflects as goodwill, but trust in the organization or institution is not captured anywhere. A few studies have shown that a lack of trust slows down workflow, slows down decisions, and a lack of trust has a negative effect of about 10 per cent of GDP in any country. A trust deficit doubles the cost of doing business according to some studies. When there is a lack of trust, then every individual takes his own actions to get things done and that leads to large scale corruption and governance issues. Over time, this leads to social strife. This strife produces its own version of strong men and basic rights take a beating.

Lack of trust takes a society down a vicious cycle and recovery takes decades. The example of many countries in Africa is the best proof.

In an organization, trust is the glue that keeps the culture together. Trust in senior management keeps hopes alive, trust in senior management gets people to commit their best. Trust in senior management attracts good talent to the company. Despite all the benefits, few leaders spend time really thinking about this glue called trust. Warren Bennis said it best 'Leadership without trust is a contradiction in terms.'

Having spelt out the consequences of low trust, we should also look at the benefits of high trust. The benefit of high trust is that more people will do what's right versus what's convenient. They do so because they realize that this will benefit everyone. A good example of great trust is the relationship between airline pilots and the air traffic controllers. There are thousands of planes in the air. A pilot trusts the ATC to give him the right altitude and to keep him out of the way of other planes. The surprising part is that airline pilots and ATCs never meet in life. This trust has to be there because mistakes are costly as it is a life and death situation.

Sports is another great example of high mutual trust for a common goal. A team works to maximize the ability to score and everyone will pass the ball to the person who can maximize that opportunity.

In organizations, we always look at commitment scores of employees. Commitment scores of employees is simply the amount of discretionary effort that employees are willing to put in for the company. There is a direct co-relation between discretionary effort and trust in leadership or organization or both.

Trust impacts every line in an organization—the top line, the innovation line, the cost line and the profit line. Very few variables impact all lines the way trust does.

The best leaders know that building trust is critical to their success. We have seen Abraham Lincoln, Mahatma Gandhi, Martin Luther King, General Patton, Nelson Mandela and J.R.D. Tata himself. Franklin Covey said that trust is a combination of character and competence. Most leaders get the competence part right and spend time improving their skill set. However, very few leaders spend enough time thinking about their character and the impact it has on people around them. Organizations and leaders who are high on competence and low on character will not survive in the long term. Trust in a leader generates confidence and optimism in every sphere. Trust in a leader builds powerful ecosystems.

An authentic leader builds trust and hence we all seek and appreciate authentic leaders. Leaders build trust when they bring clarity to the table, they communicate with passion about the purpose. They consistently set a high benchmark and will not drop it to appease a few people. They connect emotionally with large bands of people. They have a high degree of commitment to do the right thing and agonize with their time and effort to do the right thing. They are always grateful for the chance to be the leader and show that in many ways to people, teams and corporations they lead.

I remember my time running the South India region for Unilever.

My personnel manager was Georgie Antony, an alum of XLRI, a great human being and a wonderful manager. We had a unionized staff led by the late K. Govindarajan (KG) and the long-term settlement came to a close on 1 May 1993. We had built a good, straight-talking, trustworthy relationship with KG and his team. We started the next long-term discussions on 2 May in the morning, and signed the new long-term settlement by 5 p.m. on the same day. A process that would normally take twelve to eighteen months in the company, took just eight hours. This one-day signing had never been done before and has not been done after. I believe the key to this eight-hour signing was a huge amount of trust between us and KG. And everyone was happy. The next day, every employee celebrated this by bringing sweets from home and sharing it in the office. The office resembled a sweet shop that day. This further added to the trust in the region.

As a leader, I realized that trust is an outcome and not a tick in the box; in fact, I realized that trust is an outcome of many ticks in many boxes.

A good leader never compromises on his vision, but compromises for his vision. That's what builds trust for him or her. Nelson Mandela is a leader whose vision was to unite South Africa; he compromised on various elements to ensure that the vision was realized. South Africa without the trust in Nelson Mandela, would have been a different story with a different ending. I know a number of people there. A friend of mine, Anthony, a white South African has named his daughter after Mandela.

Building back trust is far more difficult compared to building trust from scratch. People rarely give you a second chance. Leaders can build trust by being straight and honest with their stakeholders. Many leaders are economical with the truth, and invariably make the choice of disclosure on behalf of the recipients. I would argue that leaders need to be honest and leave it to their stakeholders to judge the importance and relevance of the information. That transparency builds more trust than selectively discussing information. The outcome of telling the truth is that you don't have to remember it. Truth-telling is a step ahead of whistle-blowing. A company where people tell the truth has little whistle-blowing. Ethics and good governance are foundations of building trust. Let me give you a personal example.

On 14 August 2007, Nokia announced a product advisory on the BL5C battery. Nokia didn't have to disclose this, but felt that it was the correct thing to do. Media went to town, labelling this as a 'bomb in your pocket.'

Nokia went to all stakeholders and explained the honesty of approach, that they were protecting consumers with full disclosure and not hiding anything from the consumer. The next two weeks were a nightmare, but Nokia's honesty won the day. A few months later, Nokia was voted India's most trusted brand, the very first technology brand in that list. Nokia has stayed in the list ever since and the key was the trust it built, by being truthful and addressing the issue in the best way. I was part of that team with Poonam Kaul and her team, and that trust award gave us more joy than anything else we achieved in Nokia.

Trust in a digital world is very different from trust in a physical world. For a start, the digital world has few rules and no boundaries. People are free to express what they want and in the words they choose. A thought with momentum becomes a cause in a digital world and we have seen examples of this starting with Tunisia. A Tunisian fruit seller who burnt himself over the harassment from the police, was captured on a mobile camera and went public. The dictator who ruled Tunisia for twenty-five years had to flee.

Trust built over years of toil can be burnt to the ground the way a forest is burnt to the ground with a small bush fire. A company can only build trust in a digital world if the company is humble, responsive and orchestrates the response from within the company to address stakeholders' concerns.

A digital world has given people and societies the right to information from sources they trust. So the role of information and how it is communicated is a crucial element of building trust. A digital world also judges you, your actions and words by the minute and trust goes up and down almost every day. Leaders have to be careful about what they tweet or blog in a digital world, and a lame excuse like 'this is my private view and not a public view or a company view' doesn't cut ice. We have seen commentators, leaders, etc. lose their credibility with poor comments. The memory in a digital world will come to haunt you for decades. This social hard disk cannot be erased.

Trust is about having faith, it is about not having to think. Trust is about being dependable, trust is a two-way street. The benefits of trust are immense and obvious; the consequences of poor trust are disastrous. I joined PepsiCo a year ago. As a new entrant into the company, I realized that I had to win the trust of the PepsiCo system, employees, ecosystem partners, etc. I started a weekly learnings note that goes out to the full company every Monday, I travelled half the month to meet people in the market, in the factory, so that they could experience me as a person and build their view of me as a leader. I collected feedback after every meeting to ensure that the direction I am setting with my team is clearly understood and more important, not misunderstood.

Trust is about showing concern for stakeholder interests. There is no better example than Jamshedpur. I have always seen Jamshedpur as a city of trust and Tatas as an institution of trust. Jamshedpur, the Tatas and the trust here for the Tatas is a wonderful example of all that I have said so far. This kind of trust is a bond that never breaks and everyone here associated with the Tatas and the XLRI should be proud and uphold that trust with every action you take. That legacy of trust will keep us all coming back to this JRD oration because we all believe that practising ethics is the start of the journey to build trust in relationships, companies and society.

24

Changing Role of the Media in Today's India*

SHEKHAR GUPTA

Having travelled quite a bit in Jharkhand during the elections and in Bihar during many elections now, I would say that if you blindfolded somebody and paradropped him into Jamshedpur, it'll be tough to think that he is in a city in Jharkhand or Bihar. Jamshedpur is a special place.

I'm especially honoured to be speaking about this very special institution as well, because I know its reputation and many of your graduates have been my colleagues and friends over the years, and I've seen them do very well in life. I speak at many educational institutions, but it is rare to see students cheer so enthusiastically when the teachers walk in. I also go to schools sometimes, and when the founder comes in, all the children have to applaud. But I can tell one applause from the other.

So here is an institution, where professors are rock stars and the biggest rock star is somebody who is holding the Chair of Ethics. I wish I can borrow that person for Indian journalism some time, to come and teach us and fix a few things. We face many ethical dilemmas now in our profession.

There is a simple mantra I follow about public speaking. When you have a captive audience and particularly, a hall full of people, you have one of two choices: either you call in a couple of interns, you give them some ideas to write a speech for you and you can read from it without making eye contact with the audience, or you can make eye contact with the audience and have a conversation.

---

*Oration delivered on 24 November 2015.

You have to endure many speeches and lectures. I don't know which is your favourite torture. But I thought that I will do the less lazy thing. By not reading from a written text but to speak with you as I look you in the eye, and try and answer some questions which I think assail your minds. We know the theme today: 'Changing Role of the Media in India.'

You have just indicated to me, by a show of hands, the following: About 25 per cent of you think that the media is playing a good role. About 80 per cent think that the media is playing a bad role in society today.

Your concerns are about honesty in the media and ownership of media. We'll talk about ownership. 'The media makes up our mind and doesn't let us think,' said one member of the audience. 'Lots of feedback...', 'More sensationalism,' 'Focus on the negatives...,' said others.

I think that the media needs a lot of help from colleges like this to help us do our branding properly and do proper marketing, otherwise *The Times of India* will vacuum-clean everything and the rest of us will be left with nothing. But you know, I can start with any of the points you raised but the point that you raised about the media becoming the story, that brings another story to my mind.

In 1991, you remember that the first Gulf War took place, and that was the Gulf War in which the Americans had come in. George Bush Sr had come in and Saddam Hussein was defeated, but not quite removed. So, I was covering that war in the strength of two—with me was a photographer from *India Today* magazine.

So, covering a war in a strength of 1+1 means that you have to be in every hot spot at the same time. You had to be in Baghdad in Al-Rasheed hotel when the bombs fell, you had to be in Saudi Arabia when the Scuds came in, it just so happened that we also made it to Jerusalem when the first Scuds fell. There was a big excitement as the first Scuds fell. All of us were trained in how to use our gas masks. The Israelis are very well-organized, as we got our accreditations and our badges, we were given our injections of atropine, that in case of a gas attack, this is what you do. In fact, I have a tough enough time getting a doctor to give me an injection, how would I give myself an injection? But we were trained to do that and we were set.

The night the first Scuds fell, all the journalists made it to the spot where one of the Scuds had fallen. One TV journalist was standing in front of it. And he said, 'Here I am standing, this is where the Scud fell last night, it did not have chemicals in it, it had a conventional warhead, this is one mile from the Israeli defence forces headquarters, that was the target, but the missile hit here.' That afternoon, at the usual briefing by the Israeli army spokesman, he said, 'Look gentlemen, I saw one of you standing in front of the missile impact site with a camera saying 'I am standing here a mile from the Israeli defence forces headquarters.' Remember the hotel you are staying in, the Hilton, is also half a mile from the Israeli defence forces headquarters. So, from today onwards, please do not try and become the story yourself. Because right now you will get some fame but the consequence tomorrow can be that you will get bombed. I'd rather that you write headlines instead of becoming mentioned in headlines.' So, that was a good lesson to learn. The journalist should not try and become the story, but you are right, very often journalists now try to become stories and that is indeed a problem.

But we are a very large, very diverse and very problematic country. This country is also a big challenge to govern. I've been a journalist for almost forty years because I started working very young, when I was in college. I have travelled to most parts of the country in these many years, as a reporter, to speak, to visit, on holidays. Still, it gives you an idea of the size and the diversity of this country that it's the first time that I am coming to an important place like Jamshedpur. So, you can imagine how difficult this country is to govern, and how difficult this country is for journalists to cover or to understand. I am thinking a great deal these days, about the past. Not just because I've grown to a certain age. My old friend Robert Blackwill, who was the ambassador of America to India and a professor at Harvard Kennedy School, used to say, 'Look, no matter how bad the times tomorrow, they'll be your good old days. So, all of us love to think about the 'good old days.'

But I am being forced to think a little bit more these days, because the *India Today* magazine where I've worked for twelve years, between

1983 and 1995 is turning forty next month. It has asked some of its former editors and senior people to write long articles about things they covered or the change that they saw in their times in India Today. I've been asked to write about two things: first, the Rajiv Gandhi phase; and second, about Bhindranwale problem and the rise of terrorism in India.

As I look back at it, only one thought comes to my mind—about how these stories would have panned out in the 80s had today's media been around. I ask myself often how many of the young people today have even heard the name of Sant Jarnail Singh Bhindranwale. Some who are clued into the study and pursuit of political events and general knowledge will know. But a majority of people will not. Bhindranwale was a man whose name was first mentioned in a newspaper when he was thirty-two years old. In 1978, it was a clash; a sect called Nirankaris, whoM the Sikhs resented because they thought that the Nirankaris claimed that they had a guru of their own. It was a very contentious issue. They were holding a congregation and the followers of Bhindranwale, who were basically very devout people, from a very conservative seminary, went to protest. There was a fight, thirteen of them were killed.

I used to work with the *Indian Express*, Chandigarh, at that point and I knew Punjab. I was brought up in Punjab, I went to Panjab University, I can speak Punjabi like my mother tongue and read and write, but I had never heard that name Bhindranwale. When he died six years later, he was just thirty-seven. Within six years, he'd become a phenomenon. He was completely illiterate, certainly knew no word of English, had no formal education. Even scriptures: he talked a little about them, and I don't believe that he was a great learned man on the scriptures. But he had one quality. He knew how to look you in the eye and make a point and convince you.

All my life as a reporter has been spent covering demagogues of the worst kind. You know the subcontinent is very good at producing very articulate demagogues, rhetoricians, who have the unique ability to pick up the grievances of a community, genuine or imagined, and build them into a persecution complex. We've had so many of them; Jinnah was one of them because he gave the Indian Muslims the sense that they could never be safe in India, so let's create Pakistan. I've seen some demagogues in Pakistan—Bhutto was one, although I haven't seen Bhutto campaign himself—the father Bhutto, not the daughter Bhutto. I think that talent has also declined through the generations. The shrillness has remained but the talent has declined. I've known the subsequent generations well, but not the old Bhutto.

But I met a man called Altaf Hussain in Pakistan, who is now in exile. He heads the refugee party in Karachi, which is like the Shiv Sena of Karachi. I have to say this with care, it's a much more successful and nasty 'mafia' than the Shiv Sena is in Bombay. It has guns, it shoots people, it kidnaps, it collects hafta from everybody. But he had the same ability. He could have a crowd of one lakh people and tell them complete lies and they will all go back believing him. In fact, if he would bend forward, the crowd will bend forward, if he'll bend backwards, the crowd will bend backwards. After his public meetings, women will bring their babies to be blessed by him. Soon they began calling him 'Pir Sahab' and there were stories that Pir Sahab fell sick so birds came through the windows of the hospital—I'd like to see a hospital which lets birds come in—to feed him medicine. He got mythologized. I've seen those types. I've seen those types in India as well. I mean there are many of them. Even now, I think Balasaheb Thackeray was one of them. He could hold an audience like that and tell them any lie he wished to and people would mostly believe it.

I've seen in Assam, the leader of the All Assam Students' Union, Prafulla Kumar Mahanta, when he was leading the agitation in 1983, but I've never seen one like Bhindranwale. Because his control over his audience, his sense of timing, his sense of what you wanted to hear; which if you were a likely follower, would impress you; which if you were a likely opponent, will scare you; or which if you were a journalist, will impress you, and also give you a good copy, is unmatched in history. God knows I've dealt with every character of this type in India's history for decades now, and the subcontinent's history, not just India's history. I've never found one with that talent.

I keep wondering what it would be like if he were to rise today, with today's 24x7 media. He died in 1984, much before independent

TV came to India. There was only Doordarshan at that time. If he was around today with 24x7 live media, which would make love to him 24x7, they will need nothing else for TRPs. They'll just need to have him there. And social media. And I'm sure his people would learn to use the social media just like how the ISIS did in the Middle East.

In fact, yesterday our defence minister said that ISIS uses the social media very well. Just sometime back, I had the US Secretary of Defense, the current Secretary of Defense, appear on my 'Walk the Talk' television show and he said, 'Look, the Al-Qaeda was a creation of Internet. The ISIS is a creation of the social media.'

I sometimes think that maybe I'd be better off as a fiction writer. I will write a novel imagining India with the rise of Bhindranwale in India, Prabhakaran in Sri Lanka, Altaf Hussain in Pakistan, etc., with 24x7 live media, everybody latching on to every single word of these people and calling it 'exclusive.' There is no way you will get them off the screens. And there is no way governments would be able to deal with that situation.

Now let us look at the method the government of India used in fighting Bhindranwale. One day they decided to send the army to Amritsar to assault the Golden Temple, they told all the journalists to leave. Everybody left. They put them in buses, foreign journalists, Indian journalists, three of us decided not to leave because under the Indian law, you can't tell an Indian journalist to leave, plus we had some 'apna bhai bandu (our brothers and friends)' with some army and police people so we were quietly allowed to slip away. Apart from me, there was the late Subhash Kirpekar of The Times of India, and there was also Brahma Chellaney, who you now see as a defence expert. He used to then work for the Associated Press. So we stayed on. But what did the government do? They shut off all communication from Punjab for ten days. No phones, no telegrams, no telex, obviously these were pre-internet, pre-mobile phone days. So, the state was completely cut off. It had many consequences—good or bad, and I will come to those because I'm using it as a metaphor for today's talk.

Such a thing is impossible today. There is no way you can cut off any part of the world now. When the Americans put prisoners in

Abu Ghraib in an occupied territory of Iraq pictures and videos of how prisoners were treated in Abu Ghraib prison got out of there. Saddam Hussein was such a prime target. He was arrested, he was locked up, even pictures of Saddam Hussein's hanging came out. So today, you're in such a transparent environment. Today, to imagine that you will be able to shut down an entire state and carry out an operation is an impossibility. Today, the media will be present in whatever you do. If the media like us will not be present because someone throws us out, then each one of you will be the media. All of you have telephones, all of you can make videos.

Besides my column called 'National Interest', I also write a series called *Writings on the Wall,* which I write when I travel through parts of India, particularly during elections. Bihar politics is the most interesting of all in India. We've done most of our travels in Bihar. We usually travel in a group of about twenty people. Although I have covered elections in Bihar since 1989, the first time we came as a group to Bihar was in 2005. Bihar had two elections in 2005. Almost anybody coming to a public meeting, to an election meeting, had bare feet, there was no footwear. By the time we came for the next election everybody had footwear. Most of them had cheap Chinese made flip-flops (hawai chappal).

By the time we came for the third election we found the walls in Bihar selling branded underwears like Rupa and Dollar, with their slogans. One brand was also called John Obama. So, it told you that people are going up the value chain. But what is the change that I saw this time in Bihar?, In every election rally, including at Lalu Yadav's and Nitish Kumar's, almost everybody was carrying a smartphone. They were holding them up and they were making videos. In fact, I took a picture and that was my display picture on my Twitter page for a couple of weeks. It just occurred to me that this country has changed. It has changed in a way where either it'll just break through and become the finest country in the world, or it will become the most unmanageable society/country in the world.

I say this because three things have happened to India. Let me digress a bit here, but not so much. George Shultz, who used to be the Secretary of State in America, gave a speech in the mid-70s, and he said—he did not use the word globalization—but he predicted oncoming globalization. He was a fine intellectual. He said that three things are making the world a much smaller place. These three things will change the world in a way we cannot imagine. These three things are the satellite, the microchip and the wide-bodied jet. All these made the world a smaller place and we got globalization.

I have similarly identified three such elements in India: One is the smartphone because now smartphones are available very cheap. Number 2 is the motorbike. Number 3 is the availability of cheap college education, even if it is of varying quality. I will tell you what it does for Indians. The phone gives you connectivity and access to the media. It also helps you become a part of the media. You can take a video; you can take a picture and post it. Number 2, the motorbike gives you mobility. You can go from place one to B, you don't have to wait. You don't have to envy somebody who owns a car or who owns a bike. Bikes are very cheap now. They are affordable. Number 3 is the college. The college classroom is a very equal place. You get connectivity, you get mobility and you get social equality.

Watching the film called *Masaan* made this light turn on in my head. That this India has changed. If in this India, boys and girls, young people get to know each other by sending a friend-request on Facebook, and meet in the classroom, where you don't know whose caste is what, by the time the parents start asking you your caste, it is too late. We are now becoming a country of 120 crore sovereign republics. Every individual has a mind of his or her own. Every individual has her own ideas, her own choices in terms of various issues, every individual decides who to trust, every individual decides who not to trust and every individual decides what to believe and what not to believe. Every individual can today verify for themselves. And that is what makes life so much tougher for us journalists. Today, among the people in this wonderful institution, which is full of people so well educated, privileged, either studying or teaching or living in Jamshedpur, and successful. These are not people who have many complaints and laments in life, they are not Meena Kumaris, the tragedy queen of '60s Bollywood movies. But the youth today are not Meena Kumaris, you are people thrilled with life, looking forward to doing better and better, and yet many young people have a dim view of the media. That's because people have access to a lot of information and they cross-check, which was not the case earlier in India.

Coming back to Bhindranwale, because I was writing about him on the flight so it's fresh in my mind. I call 1984 the most important year in India's independent history. And I will tell you why. Because 1984 is when Operation Blue Star took place. Mrs Gandhi sent tanks into the Golden Temple. 1984 is when she got assassinated; 1984 is when riots against Sikhs took place in Delhi and more than 3,000 were killed in cold blood, we covered that; 1984 is when Rajiv Gandhi took over and won the biggest mandate in India's history, 415 seats. 1984 is when the Bhopal gas tragedy took place, 1984 is also when the Indian army climbed and took over Siachen Glacier. Many of the young people today were not around in 1984. But all of them are still dealing with stories that started in 1984.

We see in the news these days that there are frequent protests in Punjab against a sect and desecration of holy books—that is the same as it was back then. The issue of justice in the Bhopal gas tragedy still festers, you've seen Siachen is still not settled, everything that started in 1984 continues. But think of what it would have been like if we had 24x7 media in 1984. I said initially that maybe that Bhindranwale would have been impossible to contain. With today's media, it's impossible for any government to have these luxuries or a corporate to have the luxury of the official version. Nobody wants to know. Because when 26/11 happens and Pakistani terrorists come to Mumbai, the chief of the Intelligence Bureau, the prime minister of India, the head of RAW, the head of NSG, the chief of police, the commanders of the terrorists—Zaki-ur-Rehman Lakhvi, Hafiz Muhammad Saeed—everybody has exactly the same information. Everybody is watching the same thing. Every journalist who is covering this. So those times have gone, so just as I think that maybe Bhindranwale would have gone out of control, would have been impossible to deal with him, at the same time I think maybe not. Maybe if we had the media and media coverage of that level and real professionalism, maybe that phenomenon would not have become as big as it was allowed to become because of the mythologies that spread all around him.

I was talking about mythologies earlier, let's talk about how mythologies—like Pir Sahib in Pakistan, women bringing their babies to be blessed by him, and the stories that birds were coming through the windows and feeding him grain for his quick recovery—are spread. Last year, I was travelling in Punjab during the elections. Again while writing the *Writings On The Wall* series, I read in some place that the Aam Aadmi Party in Punjab had gone and established contact with some of the remnants of the old Bhindranwale supporters, old Khalistani supporters. They were trying to win them over to their side, to get their votes, which I thought was a very cynical thing to do. Why the hell were they doing it? Then I read the name of a leader they were meeting. His name was Mohkam Singh. I said, 'I remember Mohkam Singh.' I used to know him when I used to often visit the Golden Temple during Bhindranwale's days. He was one of Bhindranwale's bodyguards. You can't miss him, tall, very impressive, two years younger than me. Very young, carried an AK, flowing beard, made-for-TV face—beautiful personality, aquiline nose, etc. So, I went to see him and found him. He was sitting under a portrait of Bhindranwale, carrying his stainless steel arrow, which was his trademark. And I said to him, 'How can you do this?' First of all he denied he ever carried weapons. The important thing I asked him was, what made you think of Bhindranwale as this mythical figure who can fight the might of the Indian army and win? He said, 'Sir, but he was an avatar of the tenth Guru.' So I said, 'He wasn't, and we know that, but what made you think that?' He just said, 'Didn't you see, our Guru, our tenth Guru had arms that were so long they hung below his knees.' So I said, but I knew Bhindranwale and even now we have pictures of him, it's not true. Yet they believed that. It did remind me of the fact that when I used to go to the Golden Temple a lot of people there said that. What I am saying is, that many of these mythologies were manufactured. If live TV was available then, if so much media was available then, these mythologies would not be built.

A lot that was done wrong by the government, by the army, the trauma that visited the Indian army, the mutinies that took place in the

Indian army—one of the biggest mutinies took place from Jharkhand, in fact from Ramgarh, where the Sikh Regiment has its centre, when a brigadier was killed—it all happened because there was no media. Because nothing reliable came out of Punjab, people believed every rumour, and I always say when nothing reliable comes out, then all rumours become true and the worst rumour becomes the truest.

In fact, after this happened, and these were funnily more open days in some ways because we had better generals at that time, I requested the army to let me go and cover the courtmartial of some of these mutinying soldiers who had been arrested. The courtmartials were being held in Jabalpur, so I came to Jabalpur, spent a few days and sat through the courtmartials. The story was the same. They were saying, 'didn't know what was going on in my village, I come from a small village in Punjab, everybody told me that my temple was destroyed, all young men had been killed, all children had been taken away, all women were being raped, so I had no way of checking.'

So once again if you had active media, it would have been a pest but it would have made sure: one, that no excesses were carried out; and second, whether they were carried out or not, people outside would have got credible information. No bad news is worse than unreliable news.

With so much experience, I can tell you that truth never hurts anybody. For the moment it looks bad, in the course of time, it is fine. The problem is, I know I can't just say public opinion is all wrong; the problem arises when you start manufacturing your own truth. Or you start picking up selective truth or you start picking up a little bit of the truth and exaggerating it. To cut a long story short, a very good example that a hyperactive media actually is very useful in very tough situations to unearth the truths which governments would otherwise like to hide from the media. Kargil is a very good example. Every single coffin that came back from Kargil had OB vans following it, so it became impossible for the Pakistanis to say that India lost 10,000 people, but they are hiding casualties. It's now impossible in India to hide casualties.

At the same time in Pakistan, because they were not covering anything, they were able to sustain a mythology for a long time that there was no fighting in Kargil. There is no Tiger Hill. Tololing is nothing. In fact, the story is, and it's true, that one day Mr Nawaz Sharif, who was then prime minister, got a call from his wife that '*Aapki to fauj keh rahi hai ki Tiger Hill to koi hai nahi. Main to yahaan dekh rahi hoon Zee TV ke upar media ke aadmi Tiger Hill pe aa gaye hai. Aur hamare faujiyon ki bodies bhi hain* (Your army is saying there is nothing called Tiger Hill. I am watching on Zee TV that media persons are descending on Tiger Hill. The dead bodies of our soldiers are also there.)'. So, because the media was present and the media was allowed to function, it actually became a force multiplier. If the army and the government had tried to make it a force multiplier, it would have never become a force multiplier. That would have become an instrument of propaganda. So, again what could be a big pain actually became an asset.

I will tell you where the problem arises, the problem arises when you have those two hours in the evening 9-11. When everybody comes home, you're fed up of your bosses, your teacher, whoever you work for, whoever tortures you through the day and you think the whole country is screwed up and my life is screwed up, so you switch on your TV and you're angry. So somebody starts shouting at all and sundry, and in a way you become a proxy for that person. Somebody got killed, somebody murdered, etc. You know it's a drama, nothing will happen. And everybody does it. I call it Raavan channels. Like the ten heads of Raavan. Each channel has ten heads. And you don't know which one is fighting whom sometimes. Even that's fine for me. But what worries me, and that also reflects on public opinion, is—how unwilling are they to stick to the facts? Or how willing are they to say sorry when they are not factual? And how much do they exaggerate facts?

So, I will quickly give you three examples of exaggeration which we have lived through and for which we are now paying the price. I'm cautious that I am saying it in a town that uses both iron ore and coal. But we all use the phone. Three big scandals rose during UPA-II. These were 2G, Commonwealth Games and Coal Scam. 2G started first in a way, with our very imaginative CAG putting the value of spectrum given away free in 2007 at 1.76 lakh crore. Now

I will put that figure in perspective. 1.76 lakh crore in 2007 was 4.4 per cent of India's GDP, 1.76 lakh crore in 2007 was $2 billion more than our entire defence budget, army, navy, air force, pensions, everything. Now could the value of this much spectrum be $2 billion more than our entire defence budget? Could the value of this much spectrum be 4.4 per cent of our GDP? Some kind of *hera pheri* (monkey business) was done.

Somebody broke the rules, somebody collected money, somebody is under trial and under the Prevention of Corruption Act, any government official will tell you that punishment is the same—whether you steal ₹10 crore or ₹10,000 crore. *Yahan America ki tarah nahi hai, ki 500 saal ki jail hoti hai* (It's not like America, that you are jailed for five hundred years.) But because it got set at 1.76 lakh, it had consequences. Similarly, coal: three lakh-crore scandal. Alright, but think that three lakh-crore was not even the market cap of all the companies using coal at that point. How could the value of these many mines be three lakh-crore? But it became part of the mythology and everybody spread it. Third, to me the most damaging as a sports fan, the 'scammification' of the Commonwealth Games. My big argument with Arvind Kejriwal—we are very good friends, we talk but we also argue and I fought with him when the India Against Corruption movement was on, and I think I was in the minority of one for some time.

If you read his book *Swaraj*, in the introduction to the book he called Commonwealth Games a ₹75,000 crore scam. Now give it a little reality check. Commonwealth Games took place in 2010, then the pound sterling was a little cheap. So this was about 9.5 billion pounds. In 2012, the Olympics took place in London. The entire cost of the Olympics in London was 9 billion pounds. So could the money stolen in our little Commonwealth Games be more than all the money spent in London Olympics where there was a mini city built? It's not possible. It's not to say there were no Commonwealth Games scams. Now what has happened? 2G cases are still floating; Coal - some cases are floating, some are not floating; Commonwealth Games nothing has happened. Not a single case has been filed against Sheila Dixit. A couple of cases against Suresh Kalmadi, which together amount to about ₹50 lakh, that's all. Because the CWG was given such a bad name that holding large games in India became a scandalous proposition. India, which had then acquired confidence having done one Commonwealth Games, two Asian Games, was to bid for the forthcoming Asian Games and maybe bid for Olympics, got cold feet, so we withdrew all our bids from our future games. So as a consequence, for another fifteen years, nobody will have the courage to hold one big tournament in India.

But the other two have had more far-reaching consequences. How many of you suffer from call drops? All of you use data, so you're constantly waltzing from left to right to get better signals, so you will get data because it's always buffering on your phones or other instruments. This is the direct consequence of the way we exaggerated on 2G. Because then the Supreme Court said auction, because the BJP and that government, helped by the media, had raised the bar so high that this much spectrum was 1 lakh 76 thousand crore, now every bit of spectrum auction must extract a price that seems to justify the size of that scandal, that seems to justify that myth. So government is now creating an artificial scarcity of both telecom spectrum and also of coal. Because with coal, you auction six mines, four mines, why don't you auction hundred mines at the same time? Because then the price will come down, then how do you say I got so much money? In fact, the money already committed will come to you over thirty years, that too if the mines are fully utilized, but nobody says that. In fact, its government's ministers are now happily saying *three lakh crore toh humaare pass aa gaya hai coal ke auction mein*, and the media is also saying that. So that is the problem with the media.

The problem is, today we are doing a lot of myth-making, and myth-making in collusion with the politicians, because it suits us—because it's a bigger story, because a three-lakh crore scandal is much bigger than a 30,000 crore scandal. Simple. This is distorting governance, this is distorting decision-making. I mean, look at this rape in Delhi. Horrible rape, the December 16 rape in the bus. It was a terrible incident. But to use the incident to generalize the entire environment about India—generalize an entire environment about working women in India, more and more women are going out to work now... To then pass this really terrible law on the streets, which has many sections that, at some point of time, Parliament will have to reverse. Because that law has many complicated things, it was passed under pressure, but all distortions were created by excessive pressure of the media and the inability of the ruling classes to deal with this hyperactive new media which is constantly in your face.

When seven people say that this is a fact it is very difficult for the eighth to refute it. I can give you hundred examples of where complete mythology has got cemented because everybody said the same thing. Anybody who said something different was seen to be an outlier or a liar or compromised or sold out. These are distortions which have come in. But I would say earlier, I used to apply the Kargil test to every situation, that if Kargil wasn't covered truthfully, would it have been better for India? Or would it have been worse for India? The answer to that was covering Kargil truthfully did very well for India. Similarly, I think now, had there been 24 hour media (I'm not saying we covered 1984 untruthfully) in 1984, would it have been a good thing or a bad thing? I think it would have been a good thing, because a lot of the excesses and a lot of the disasters, would not have taken place.

So I would take more troublesome media and more painful media any day. I know it's unpopular right now, but it's not the media's job to be popular.

Is the media now trying to produce and offer what the media thinks the audience would like to hear? That is a problem. In fact, at The Indian Express, which I used to edit, we were questioning the Anna Movement. Once Arvind Kejriwal came to meet me, something I have mentioned in the introduction of my book, he said that the line that your paper has taken on our movement, have you checked with your marketing department how this is selling with your audiences? So, a light went on in my head that these guys are smart, they have figured the weakness of the media. So, I said to him, 'Arvind, I'm not producing a Bollywood film that I have to net hundred crore on the first weekend, nor am I making a TV soap opera that I must get the audiences.'

News is what news is. 'All the news that's fit to print,' that is *The New York Times* principle. I can't decide news on the basis of what people would like to hear but yes, that's a problem. Foreign ownership of the media is least of the problems. In Indian media, only 26 per cent is allowed, I wish more was allowed because if more is allowed, more competition will come in, Indian monopolies will be broken. But for me, ownership is not even a problem—that the Indian corporates are acquiring the media. Reliance has acquired TV18, Aditya Birla Group has a sizeable share in the India Today Group. But what worries me is the phenomenon that you see in your state, which is, anybody with two mines or anybody with three building projects sets up a TV channel. So, any thug now has a TV channel. Because they have money, because they are not driven by the balance sheet of the media business; they use media as a special purpose vehicle for doing other things. They hire journalists at very high salaries so that gives them credibility and then they use that media to get their stuff done. Today, you look around the country, how many politicians, how many builders, how many mining barons, how many really not very nice guys now own the media. That is the worrisome part of the media. I don't know what the answer is. I think in the course of time, people will figure out who's coming from where, and I think those distortions will be set at rest.

Now, let me tell you a story about how controlled, controlled societies can be. This story is from the first Gulf War in Iraq. Any journalist going to those countries, Iraq, Afghanistan—I covered the Afghanistan War between 1989 and 1993...during the first jihad (the good jihad) when Americans were backing the Mujahideen, when Gulbuddin Hekmatyar was a nice guy—you could never go out alone. You always had a minder with you. The government said we are giving you an interpreter. An interpreter was basically an Intelligence guy, he helped also with language, but basically he kept an eye on you. Also, he kept you from doing something they didn't like. This was, I think the day three of the bombings in Baghdad, and our minder was a Mr Rashid, who was sitting in the front seat. My photographer and I were sitting in the back seat. We were driving past what looked like a huge, fresh ruin. This was one of Saddam

Hussein's many palaces, which were bombed the previous night. So my photographer Prashant Panjiar (playing a prank) said, 'Rashid, can you stop, I'll just take a picture.' So our interpreter or minder put his forehead in his hands and said, 'Habibi, by simply asking this question, you've already given me a headache.' So it was a very controlled society. This society did not last, everybody went unhappy, it got occupied and even today, it's a mess.

If the ISIS is growing, it's mainly because Iraq cannot be cohesive. Shias rule the country. Sunnis are not happy. The answer is: for a multi-cultural, diverse, large society, there is no solution but democracy, liberal democracy, and there can be no liberal democracy without politics, there can be no politics without politicians, and to keep an eye on all of this, you need the media.

In some phases, the media will be troublesome; in phases, the media will be compromised; in some phases, the media will be revolutionary; but I think at most points of time, the media will be a bit of everything. So if you ask me on balance, I also get very frustrated when I watch TV mostly, even sometimes when I write. It's an echo chamber, but at the same time, if I close my eyes and ask myself do I want to be like a country, like say Soviet Union used to be in the past or a country like Saddam's Iraq, or even a country like Mrs Gandhi's India during the Emergency, the answer will be no. It will be a much unhappier country.

Frankly, today I can come to you and ask you how many of you think media's role is positive or negative and 80 per cent of you say negative. If we did not have this freedom, I would not have been able to come to a hall like this and you will not be able to give me your honest opinion about anything. In fact, if I raise the same point, I don't want to embarrass your faculty and ask how many of you think the government is great or how many of you think that your government is not so great, you will quite freely raise your hands on one side or the other. So, these are freedoms to cherish and a noisy media is a part of these distractions, it sometimes irritates you, sometimes entertains you. At the end of the day, I think it's all a part of life.

25

The Place of International Law in Seeking Sustainable Development for India: Some Ethical Reflections*

FRANK BRENNAN

It is a profound and humbling honour for me to be invited to come to India for the first time in my life and to deliver the 25th J.R.D. Tata Oration on Business Ethics. Unfortunately, a family death precluded my coming to India for even an initial fortnight, in order to experience some of the wonders of your great country. I am a Jesuit, a Catholic priest, an Australian of Irish heritage, and a lawyer. So I know next to nothing about business. I am a one-week novice in India. I come from a religious tradition which has only a minority of adherents in this vast land. I come from a country which like yours, started the modern era under the colonial yoke of the British Empire. Unlike you, we gave no recognition whatever to the sovereignty or the land rights of the indigenous peoples. In our case, Aboriginal Australians had been the owners and occupiers of the land for up to 60,000 years. Eventually, six British colonies were federated to form the Commonwealth of Australia—an island nation continent. Nowadays, 28 per cent of Australians are born overseas. With 433,000 Indians now living in Australia, the number of Australian residents born in India has almost tripled over the last ten years. 46 per cent of Australians have at least one parent born overseas. And yet, or perhaps because of this, my nation has earned a particularly harsh international reputation, of late, for designing laws and policies aimed at ensuring that asylum seekers in our globalized world, that

*Oration delivered on 26 November 2016.

includes sixty million displaced people, do not reach our shores. Our prime minister recently boasted that our system for securing national borders was the best in the world. Suffice to say, it can be emulated only by those nation states which are island nation continents and which have mendicant island neighbours prepared to warehouse and process unvisaed asylum seekers, and which are sufficiently far from the world's major trouble spots that the asylum seekers are not in direct flight from persecution in the region, but rather are engaged in protracted journeys to seek more adequate protection, more transparent processing and a more benign migration outcome.

It is a tribute to the universal appeal of J.R.D. Tata and to the imaginative creativity of this oration's organizers that one of such a different religious, professional and national background might be thought to have something to contribute to your national quandaries about business and ethics in India at this time. I take heart that on receipt of the Bharat Ratna in 1992, JRD said, 'do not want India to be an economic superpower. I want India to be a happy country.' I daresay that JRD with his background and commitment to the establishment of the airline which was a precursor to Air India would be well pleased that the speaker for today's silver jubilee oration flew on the Air India Boeing 787 Dreamliner direct from Melbourne to Delhi in fifteen hours, and I was happy with the experience.

My thesis this evening is that, no matter what the economic, political and legal problems are confronted by modern-day India, these problems can be better addressed and answered by a consideration of the profound truths and insights of all the religious traditions represented in this country. An application of the key principles and norms developed in the international law of trade and human rights, helping to enunciate the realm of law, regulation and political accountability, enhancing public scrutiny, providing the right environment for doing business, and that no matter how well developed the regulatory machinery, no matter how elaborate the constitutional separation of powers and the legislative provisions for accountability, there will always be a place for and a value-add from the national culture, corporate ethos and personal character. Thus, there is a need to ensure that the national and ethnic cultures arc sufficiently open to international influences and sufficiently grounded in the goodness and the daily concerns of the ordinary citizen. There is a need to create the right corporate ethos and an appropriate business environment, particularly in a country which is still ranked 138th in the global ratings for ease of business investment. And, as J.R.D. Tata demonstrated by his own life, what a bonus it is for the country when even the most endowed and most privileged business leader is a person of sound character with a conscience dedicated to the common good and the national interest as well as to corporate profit and personal well-being.

To offer a very Anglo-Western perspective, might I suggest that there are learnings for all of us from Brexit and now, the election of Donald Trump. In these robust Western democracies with a strong commitment to the rule of law, there is a growing sense that the divide between the rich and the poor is becoming unbridgeable and that the gap between the technologically savvy and the not-so savvy is contributing to a sense of powerlessness, alienation and anomie such that an increasing number of citizens are convinced that the political, legal and economic system is fixed against them, with the result that they have lost all sense of agency and hope of full human flourishing. They have lost jobs in the wake of globalization and tariff reductions and they have abandoned all hope that they will enjoy the same job security and comfort as their parents. They sense that the major political parties and social institutions have conspired against them, failing to repel the forces of globalization which are corroding the old safeguards for employment, security and national identity. One certainty is that neither Brexit nor a Trump presidency is going to solve the most acute problems of those who voted for them. In the USA, those lacking the education and opportunity to participate in the new economy will gain little from Mr Trump's commitment to build a wall, to keep out Muslims and to re-ignite the fossil fuel economy. Even Mr Trump will eventually have to contribute to stemming the displacement of sixty million people on our planet and to reversing the drastic effects of climate change.

Many of the issues you confront in India are very different from those faced in societies like the USA and the United Kingdom. But what's common is a sense of the citizenry that there are global forces at play and global allegiances and agreements which can both undermine national integrity and identity, as well as contribute to national well-being and development, depending on how adept we are at riding the wave of internationalism while maintaining our national sovereignty. Ironically there is a growing understanding that some problems cannot be confronted adequately except with international co-operation and some national controversies can be more readily resolved by reference to international norms and processes with which the nation state agrees to comply as an exercise of national sovereignty.

Being a Catholic priest with a vow of poverty, living in an advanced country where most of my needs are provided by the State including adequate healthcare, good standard education and security, it is not for me to lecture business folk prescriptively in the developing economy of India on how to provide adequately for the world's poor. The most I can do is appeal to your finer nature and point to your great precursors like J.R.D. Tata. An outsider, I recall that J.R.D. Tata once wrote in reply to a letter by Prof Sahni, IIM Bangalore, who requested him to share his philosophy of life with his students:

> If I were to attribute any single reason to such success as I have achieved, I would say that success would not have been possible without a sustained belief that what I did or attempted to do would serve the needs and interests of our country and our people and that I was a trustee of such interests.

The World Bank acknowledges: India's economic and human development is one of the most significant global achievements of recent times. Your share of global GDP escalated from 1.8 to 2.7 per cent between 2005 and 2010. More than 53 million people have been lifted out of poverty here in India in that time—and that's more than twice the entire population of Australia. Between 2003 and 2013, your economy expanded at an average rate of 7.6 per cent, making you one of the ten fastest growing nations. The World Bank notes: Exports account for 21.5 per cent of the GDP, three times more than in 1990, and net inflows of foreign direct investment (FDI) make up another 1.6 per cent. Life expectancy has more than doubled between 1947 and 2011 from 31 years to 65 years. Adult literacy had more than quadrupled between 1951 and 2011 from 18 per cent to 74 per cent. These are great achievements, and yet you are still home to one-third of the global poor—four hundred million people. More disturbing: With population growth, the absolute number of poor people actually increased in some of your poorest states between 2004-05 and 2009-10, with poverty rates three to four times higher than those of the most advanced states—Haryana, Kerala and Punjab. When it comes to the great ethical challenge of striking an appropriate balance between poverty alleviation and climate change, you have some of the most difficult decisions to make when determining how much cheap electricity might be produced to lift people from poverty while making the planet less liveable for their descendants. The World Bank notes:

> An estimated 300 million people do not have access to electricity, while those who are connected to the grid must cope with unreliable supply. Sixty per cent of firms resort to costly backup power generation. The sector continues to be hobbled by a range of problems—among them energy demand that far outstrips supply, below market pricing of electricity, constraints in coal and gas supply that force generation stations to operate below capacity, and high rates of loss (technical, commercial, and financial) in distribution. The continued unreliability and poor quality of electricity supplied to firms and households sap investment and growth and reduce India's competitiveness.

Your quest for cheap coal to generate electricity is subjected to understandable scrutiny in Australia with the proposed development of Adani's Carmichael Coal Mine. Some think that environmental lawyers and environmentalists take a too restricted view of the complexity of the competing goods to be achieved. One of our leading Australian judges, and a great internationalist, Michael Kirby when paying tribute to graduates of a business school at a university graduation observed:

> You have more to teach judges and lawyers than we generally care to acknowledge. At least in business schools there is a self-conscious search for all the factors that influence important decision-making. There is a constant study of whether business decisions are effective or not. Commonly, in business, the market constitutes the final court of appeal. It tolerates little dissent. In the law, our decision-making tends to be more formal and less empirical. Correctives are often a long time coming.

Serving the needs and interests of our planet, in fact, just saving our planet, is the great contemporary challenge, while at the same time continuing to raise India's poor out of poverty. Those who are privileged with wealth, power and honours need to see themselves as the primary custodians of the planet and as key contributors to the relief of dehumanizing poverty. I note that your Prime Minister Mr Modi has twice addressed the General Assembly of the United Nations. In 2014, shortly after he became Prime Minister, he told the assembly:

> India is a country that constitutes one-sixth of humanity; a nation experiencing economic and social transformation on a scale rarely seen in history. Every nation's world view is shaped by its civilization and philosophical tradition. India's ancient wisdom sees the world as one family. It is this timeless current of thought that gives India an unwavering belief in multilateralism.

I don't know what success Mr Modi has had in calling for a World Yoga Day. I think the idea is still to take hold down under in Australia. But he has noted the need for the world to operate on three levels: the need for a change of personal lifestyles, national action and what he calls 'a beautiful balance of collective action—common but differentiated responsibilities.' Returning to the UN in 2016, he invited members to focus on the global public good and not just private returns. He said:

> The principle of common but differentiated responsibilities is the bedrock of our collective enterprise. When we speak only of climate change, there is a perception of our desire to secure the

> comforts of our lifestyle. When we speak of climate justice, we demonstrate our sensitivity and resolve to secure the future of the poor from the perils of natural disasters.

Often we wonder: What is the point of global conversations, such as these talk fests by the world leaders at the UN that result in no immediate outcomes? The fruits include the ongoing consolation that we can share our deepest insights with competent, accomplished individuals knowing that our uncertainties and limitations are not held against us, but are reckoned as part of the global calculus in discerning how we might start addressing big unresolved questions about sustainable and equitable economic well-being for all; the enthusiasm and optimism born of the realization that a meeting of minds can effect real change globally and with immediate consequences; the hope that in the face of enormous difficulties and problems we can translate the oft-repeated declaration 'They should do something about it', into the insight, 'We are they'; the satisfaction of knowing that together we can provide respectful space to drill down together doing the deeper thinking and the more critical self-reflection needed for us to return to our cabinet tables, our boardrooms and workplaces more grounded in the challenges and the means for meeting them; and the stimulation of realizing that there are still fundamental disagreements about the most basic issues underpinning sustainable, equitable economic well-being for all, including the requirement for continued economic growth and the necessity of reducing greenhouse gas emissions and other human contributions to the warming of the planet.

There is no international legal regime in place for the guaranteed protection of human rights and for the protection of the planet. But there is now a plethora of international human rights instruments to which nations are voluntarily a party. These instruments though not enforceable directly in domestic or international courts are persuasive. Increasingly there are optional protocol procedures being appended to key international human rights instruments allowing disaffected individuals to agitate their human rights complaints against their national government before an international disputes body. The procedures are usually perfunctory with matters being decided on the papers, but the media attention to some of these complaints assists focus the attention of governments on the complaints and there is jurisprudence developing. Also there is periodic reporting which is required of signatories to key international human rights instruments. And now there are the Universal Periodic Reviews (UPR) conducted under the auspices of the United Nations Human Rights Council (UNHRC). Member States provide a peer review of each other with each State coming under the spotlight once every four years. Despite the political correctness and the political point scoring in these exercises, over time they contribute to a culture of human rights.

Marking the sixtieth anniversary of the UN Declaration of Human Rights, the late and revered Irish poet Seamus Heaney wrote:

> Since it was framed, the Declaration has succeeded in creating an international moral consensus. It is always there as a means of highlighting abuse if not always as a remedy: it exists instead in the moral imagination as an equivalent of the gold standard in the monetary system.
>
> The articulation of its tenets has made them into world currency of a negotiable sort. Even if its Articles are ignored or flouted—in many cases by governments who have signed up to them—it provides a worldwide amplification system for the still, small voice.

There is of course no international legal regime for the comprehensive governance and regulation of commercial activity. But increasingly nation states are negotiating free trade agreements and other trade treaties. In addition to membership of the World Trade Organization, they are also committing themselves to a plethora of international dispute resolution procedures including conciliation and arbitration under the auspices of the Permanent Court of Arbitration.

Australia's last Solicitor-General, Justin Gleeson SC, who had a range of experiences before these international for a recently postulated some interesting questions:

> Every time we exercise sovereignty by assuming an international obligation, we have two further choices. One is to bind ourselves further to the international project by submitting to a binding dispute resolution mechanism, of the type which best suits the case. The other is to eschew the prospect of being able to be held to account for whether we have breached our international obligations. Do we turn the first way for trade obligations, in order to close the deal, but the second way for human rights obligations? Is that a principled way to proceed?
>
> What kind of future do we want for our country in our engagement with the international legal order?

The Australian Parliament, responding to the irrefutable health risk of smoking has instituted a ban on cigarette advertising and legislated for plain packaging of cigarettes. In Australia, you can still buy cigarettes. But they have to be held in locked cupboards by merchants. The packaging is plain with only graphic health warnings about the ghastly effects of smoking, including photos of collapsing lungs and gangrenous limbs. The Marlboro man on horseback is a relic in Australia. The Australian Institute of Health and Welfare reports: 'Daily smoking rates in Australia are among the lowest in the world. In 2013, 13 per cent of the population aged 15 and over in Australia smoked, compared to 20 per cent in the United Kingdom, 15 per cent in Canada and 14 per cent in the United States. Australia's rate was well below the average across 34 OECD countries (Organisation for Economic Cooperation and Development) (20 per cent).' There have been many contributing factors to the marked decrease of smoking in Australia, including steep and rising excises, prohibitions on smoking in public places and the plain packaging law. India's Ministry of Health and Family Welfare produced a fact sheet on the Global Adult Tobacco Survey for 2009-10, which found that 34.6 per cent of adults use tobacco in some form—47.9 per cent of males and 20.3 per cent of females. At least 14 per cent of Indian adults smoke.

It's still early days but the plain packaging legislation is thought to be having a marked effect on the smoking habits of young Australians and contributing to a marked decline in sales, dissuading young people even to give it a try. The tobacco manufacturers obviously think there is a real risk to their global sales if this sort of legislation is enacted in other countries. They are displeased. They first claimed that the legislation effected an acquisition of their property on other than just terms contrary to the Australian Constitution. When they failed in the Australian courts, they went on to claim before an international arbitration that these measures were an interference with free trade, contrary to various provisions of free trade agreements which Australia has voluntarily negotiated with other countries.

One tobacco producer Philip Morris tried to invoke some provisions of Australia's bilateral investment treaty (BIT) with Hong Kong to challenge the Australian restrictions on free trade and advertising of cigarettes. Australia has twenty-one such bilateral treaties including the one finalized with India in 2000. All up, there are now over 3,000 BITs which have been negotiated globally.

Philip Morris Asia Ltd, a company incorporated in Hong Kong, acquired a 100 per cent shareholding in Philip Morris Australia Ltd thereby obtaining an indirect interest in its subsidiary Philip Morris Ltd. This way the PM group thought they would be able to invoke the provisions of the BIT between Hong Kong and Australia. Ultimately they failed with the tribunal finding that the corporate restructure was engaged in specifically so as to invoke the provisions of the BIT and that this was an abuse of process.

The seat of the PM arbitration was Singapore with the consequence that the Singapore domestic courts could have been required to determine disputed questions according to Singapore domestic law including questions which had been resolved finally by the Australian High Court which were questions about the interpretation of the Australian Constitution.

Australia's Chief Justice Robert French has sounded salutary warning notes about the capacity of private parties involved in investor-state dispute settlements (TSDSs) to bring claims against countries which are parties to BITs or free trade agreements (FTAs). With a second bite of the cherry, even if they have failed in a challenge to the constitutional validity of impugned legislation in a nation's highest court, investors might try to claim in an international arbitration that the decision of the respondent state is a breach of a provision of the investment treaty to which the State is a party.

The Australian High Court had delivered a judgment in which it rejected challenges to the validity of the *Tobacco Plain Packaging Act 2011 (Cth)*. The tobacco companies had argued that the Act effected an acquisition of their intellectual property rights in trademarks, designs, copyright and get-up used on cigarettes and cigarette packaging. They argued that the acquisition, being uncompensated, was not on just terms. The Australian Court rejected their submission that the legislation amounted to an acquisition of property on other than just terms contrary to section 51 (xxxi) of the Australian Constitution. One of the majority judges observed: 'The extinguishment, modification or deprivation of rights in relation to property does not of itself constitute an acquisition of property.'

But for the abuse of process, it was possible that the Singapore tribunal, in the context of an argument about expropriation, could have been asked to form a view about the correctness of the Australian High Court's conclusion that there was no acquisition within the meaning of section 51 (xxxi) of the Australian Constitution. In an extraordinary development, an Australian retired High Court judge was on hand in Singapore to provide advice to, and evidence for, the tobacco companies questioning the correctness of the High Court decision, which, of course, was delivered after he had left the bench.

This case highlights the extent to which it may be possible in future for businesses to utilize free trade agreements in order to impugn even the final binding decisions of national constitutional courts of final appeal. Though in the end such procedures can be accommodated with notions of national sovereignty, there are many citizens and, dare I say it in the Brexit-Trump era, many politicians who regard such moves as inconsistent with national sovereignty.

If businesses pursuing their economic self-interest are able to utilize such international legal procedures, then what about marginalized and vulnerable citizens who feel that their basic human rights are being overlooked not just by governments and parliaments but also by the courts, including national final courts of appeal?

The American international lawyer Mary Ellen O'Connell

concludes her book *The Power and Purpose of International Law* with the observation:

> International law needs improvement, not demolition, because it remains the single, generally accepted means to solve the world's problems. These problems will not be solved by armed conflict or the imposition of a single ideology or religion. Through international law diverse cultures can reach consensus about the moral norms that we should commonly live by. People everywhere believe in law, believe in this alternative to force, as they believe in higher things. They want the power of law to be used to achieve the community's most important common goals. International law reflects that the international community's shared goals are peace, respect for human rights, prosperity, and the protection of the natural environment.

International law, statesmanship, moral leadership by civil society, including religious communities and religious leaders of various faith traditions can all contribute to a developing consensus about the moral norms that we should commonly live by, providing a leg up for those who are still living in poverty and securing our national borders while being responsive to our obligations to those less fortunate than ourselves because they find themselves on the wrong side of our borders plagued by persecution.

When considering the mission of international lawyers trying to humanize domestic laws and policies, especially those laws and policies which pay insufficient regard to the rights and liberties of the excluded whether within or outside national borders or which patently disregard the need to sustain the planet for future generations, I call to mind Martii Koskenniemi's prescient remarks:

> International law increasingly appears as that which resists being reduced to a technique of governance. When international lawyers are interviewed on the Iraqi war, or on torture, or on trade and environment, on poverty and disease in Africa—as they increasingly are—they are not expected to engage in hair-splitting technical analyses. Instead, they are called upon to soothe anxious souls, to

> give voice to frustration and outrage. Moral pathos and religion frequently fail as vocabularies of engagement, providers of 'empty signifiers' for expressing commitment and solidarity. Foreign policy may connote party rule. This is why international law may often appear as the only available surface over which managerial governance may be challenged, the sole vocabulary with a horizon of transcendence—even if or perhaps precisely because, that horizon is not easily translated into another institutional project. I often think of international law as a kind of secular faith.

None of us would want more realistic and more decent options in these most toxic of times to be forfeited simply because there is a new emerging fundamentalism being preached by the most respected high priests of international law. For example, in Australia, our debates about border protection and asylum often divide between those who claim that law and policy comply with the letter of the key international instruments and those who claim it violates the spirit of those instruments. None of us has a right to enter another country and all of us have the obligation not to return anyone presenting at our border to a situation of persecution, torture, or cruel punishment. Though I doubt the possibility of the European Union (EU) negotiating appropriate returns of asylum seekers to Libya in the foreseeable future, I continue to entertain the hope that Australia can negotiate appropriate returns to transit countries such as Indonesia for Iraqis, Afghans and Iranians and India for Tamils, so that Australia might then decently extend the hand of welcome to more of the world's sixty million displaced persons who might be issued with humanitarian visas for permanent settlement in Australia without the need for their risking perilous unvisaed voyages. For the moment, my country is failing to strike the right balance between human rights and the national interest. It is stopping the boats indecently, violating the human dignity of those being held in unsatisfactory conditions in Papua New Guinea, and on Nauru; and failing to ensure appropriate safeguards are in place for the return of asylum seekers to Indonesia. For as long as international lawyers claim there is no possibility of a legally negotiated regional agreement for safe returns—because they argue that asylum seekers have a right of entry to Australia to seek asylum—the Australian government, the Australian parliament, and the Australian courts will maintain, with impunity but with the occasional expression of outrage from international lawyers, a regime of returns insufficiently scrutinized for human rights compliance. The boats will continue to be stopped (no matter which political party is in power), but they should be stopped decently and in compliance with the legal regime enunciated by the EU which has to deal with a far more pressing issue but subject to the more searching supervision of the European Court of Human Rights and of the European Parliament which has greater sensitivity to the human rights of asylum seekers than do their more pragmatic Australian colleagues.

Pope Francis's encyclical *Laudato Si* is on the topic 'care for our common home.' Rupert Murdoch's international press network was quick to label it a 'Papal prescription for a flawed economic order' with their national newspaper in Australia declaring, 'The church should not belong to the green-left fringe.'

Pope Francis is not the first pope to address a social encyclical to everyone. Pope John Paul I addressed his 1988 encyclical *Sollicitudo Rei Socialis* to members of the Church and to 'all people of good will.' Pope Benedict XVI did the same with his 2009 encyclical *Caritas in Veritate.* In comparison with his predecessors, however, Francis has been more inclusive in the process of writing the encyclical and in the final content of the document. He quotes from seventeen different conferences of Catholic bishops. This was rarely done by his predecessors. He is at pains to indicate that he is collaborative and that he takes the principle of subsidiarity very seriously. He convened meetings of various types of experts including scientists, economists and political scientists. He is not afraid to indicate that the final product is something of a committee job with various authors.

Being the final redactor of the text, Pope Francis has felt free to interpolate some very folksy advice from time to time—from the need to use less air conditioning, to the appropriateness of consumer boycotts on certain products, to the desirability of saying grace before and after meals. He has also taken the liberty of inserting some very blunt, evocative images of environmental and economic devastation: 'The earth, our home, is beginning to look more and more like an immense pile of filth. In many parts of the planet, the elderly lament that once beautiful landscapes are now covered with rubbish.'

His concerns are not narrowly dogmatic or pedagogical, but universally pastoral. He knows that millions of people, including erstwhile Catholics, are now suspicious of or not helped by notions of tradition, authority, ritual and community when it comes to their own spiritual growth which is now more individual and eclectic. He wants to step beyond the Church's perceived lack of authenticity and its moral focus on individual matters or on content of faith, rather than depth of faith. He thinks the world is in a mess, particularly with the state of the planet—climate change, loss of biodiversity and water shortages, and with the oppression of the poor, whose life basics are not assured by the operation of the free market, and with the clutter and violence of lives which are cheated the opportunity for interior peace. At the conclusion of the encyclical, he describes the document as a 'lengthy reflection which has been both joyful and troubling.' Clearly, he wants all people of good-will to emulate him and to be both joyful and troubled as they wrestle with the problems of the age.

Pope Francis thinks the planet risks going to hell in a basket. He says he is 'pointing to the cracks in the planet.' Perhaps we should take heart from the recently deceased Leonard Cohen's observation, 'There is a crack in everything. That's how the light gets in.' This is the only home we have got. And the science is in. It indicates that climate change is real. The loss of biodiversity is real. Human activity continues to contribute adversely to both changes, though of course there are other causes. We cannot undo the other causes. We do have the power to change and to address some of the human causes. An untrammelled free market will not provide the solution, neither will untrammelled governments whether they be self-seeking and corrupt or populist and short-sighted. Pope Francis sees an urgent need for people to be well-educated, to be concerned about future generations, and to be focused beyond their national borders. He sees an urgent need for governments to abide by the rule of law. He sees an urgent need for markets to be regulated so that self-interest and economic imperatives can be better aligned to pay dividends for the planet and for future generations. He doesn't see how this can be done unless more people, especially those designing laws and regulations for government and economic actors, are integrated in themselves finding completion in a deep interior life marked by concern for neighbour and for creation as well as self. Francis calls us to consider the tragic effects of environmental degradation especially on the lives of the world's poorest. He says:

> The problem is that we still lack the culture needed to confront this crisis. We lack leadership capable of striking out on new paths and meeting the needs of the present with concern for all and without prejudice towards coming generations. The establishment of a legal framework which can set clear boundaries and ensure the protection of ecosystems has become indispensable; otherwise, the new power structures based on the techno-economic paradigm may overwhelm not only our politics but also freedom and justice.

Developing the culture, the leadership and the legal framework—These are the challenges to those of us who want to be intelligent contributors to truly sustainable development of India and the planet. Having noted, 'There are certain environmental issues where it is not easy to achieve a broad consensus', he concedes that 'the Church does not presume to settle scientific questions or to replace politics. But I want to encourage an honest and open debate, so that particular interests or ideologies will not prejudice the common good.'

Hailing from Argentina, he puts his trust neither in ideological Communism nor in unbridled capitalism. Like his predecessors Benedict and John Paul II he is unapologetic asserting, 'By itself the market cannot guarantee integral human development and social inclusion.' His concern is not to settle arguments about politics, economics or science. He makes no pretence to give the last word on anything. He is wanting to enliven the passion and the spiritual commitment of his readers who grasping the link between care for the earth, care for the poor and care for the personal interior life, will be motivated to work for real change.

Francis calls everyone to engagement in an honest and open debate, respecting the competencies of all, and inspired by the vision of St Francis of Assisi who is the model of the inseparable bond 'between concern for nature, justice for the poor, commitment to society, and interior peace.'

Like many, Francis is convinced that we need to phase out our reliance on fossil fuels—coal, oil, 'and to a lesser degree, gas'—progressively and without delay. I doubt that he would be a supporter of Adani Mining's proposed Carmichael mine in Australia which will be Australia's largest coal mine. He thinks any scheme for buying and selling carbon credits is deeply flawed. He is a great advocate for solar energy. But what is new is the integration of the scientific, the political, the sociological, the spiritual and the theological—an integration given the stamp of approval of the leader of one of the world's most significant religious communities. Granted that the Judeo-Christian tradition has done much to inculcate the notion that we humans are to subdue the earth, it is heartening that a pope has been able to say:

> The best way to restore men and women to their rightful place, putting an end to their claim to absolute dominion over the earth, is to speak once more of the figure of a Father who creates and who alone owns the world. Otherwise, human beings will always try to impose their own laws and interests on reality.

It could be even more helpful for us to move beyond the patriarchal view of God. It is not only the Church that has been complicit, but it has been complicit especially in ventures of colonization aimed at plundering the resources of indigenous peoples. Francis notes, 'Modernity has been marked by an excessive anthropocentrism.'

Where I find Francis truly prophetic, and this is where he grates the Murdoch press and the conservative Catholic think tanks in the West, is in his bold declaration:

> If we acknowledge the value and the fragility of nature and, at the same time, our God-given abilities, we can finally leave behind the modern myth of unlimited material progress. A fragile world, entrusted by God to human care, challenges us to devise intelligent

ways of directing, developing and limiting our power.

This provides the real challenge for those of you in India committed to sustainable development accelerating the alleviation of poverty for tens of millions of people, who have never known the basics of good health, education and housing. Of course, the real heresy of this pope in the eyes of the free marketers, who long presumed that the anti-Communist Polish Pope John Paul XI was their unswerving ally, is that he speaks of the need first to 'reject a magical conception of the market' and then to redefine 'our notion of progress.' He proceeds to utter the unthinkable, that 'the time has come to accept decreased growth in some parts of the world, in order to provide resources for other places to experience healthy growth.' This papal prescription is very difficult to reconcile with Christine Lagarde's often repeated IMF claim that what the world, and most especially the poor need, is strong economic growth across the board internationally. For example, Lagarde when speaking on 'Decisive Action to Secure Durable Growth' in April 2016 claimed:

> From a macroeconomic perspective, the first priority must be to secure the recovery and lay the foundation for stronger and more equitable medium-term growth. Overcoming the voices of despair and exclusion requires an alternative path—one that leads to prospects for more employment, higher incomes and more secure lives.

There are still fundamental disagreements about the most basic issues underpinning sustainable, equitable economic well-being for all, including the requirement for continued economic growth and the necessity of reducing greenhouse gas emissions and other human contributions to the warming of the planet. Pope Francis could well have had in mind some of our Australian Cabinet ministers, and dare I say, some of your ministers in the Modi cabinet, when he wrote:

> A politics concerned with immediate results, supported by consumerist sectors of the population, is driven to produce short-term growth. In response to electoral interests, governments are reluctant to upset the public with measures which could affect

> the level of consumption or create risks for foreign investment. The myopia of power politics delays the inclusion of a farsighted environmental agenda within the overall agenda of governments. Thus we forget that 'time is greater than space', that we are always more effective when we generate processes rather than holding on to positions of power. True statecraft is manifest when, in difficult times, we uphold high principles and think of the long-term common good. Political powers do not find it easy to assume this duty in the work of nation-building.

In October 2015, the *New York Times* columnist, Andrew Revkin spoke in Australia at a Global Integrity Summit. Revkin has been writing about science and the environment for more than three decades. Through his hard-hitting coverage of global warning, he has earned most of the major awards for science journalism. He is no papal groupie but he reported on being one of the experts called to Rome for consultations when the encyclical was being drafted. In his Australian presentation, Revkin particularly emphasized this paragraph from the encyclical:

> We need to acknowledge that different approaches and lines of thought have emerged regarding this situation and its possible solutions. At one extreme, we find those who doggedly uphold the myth of progress and tell us that ecological problems will solve themselves simply with the application of new technology and without any need for ethical considerations or deep change. At the other extreme are those who view men and women and all their interventions as no more than a threat, jeopardizing the global ecosystem, and consequently, the presence of human beings on the planet should be reduced and all forms of intervention prohibited. Viable future scenarios will have to be generated between these extremes, since there is no one path to a solution. This makes a variety of proposals possible, all capable of entering into dialogue with a view to developing comprehensive solutions.

Revkin was impressed at Francis's willingness to listen attentively to all views and to weigh the evidence. But we are left wondering whether Francis does take sides or not on the desirability of arresting economic growth at least in some countries, and of taking drastic action to reduce human impacts on the climate.

In his folksy style, Francis notes that 'sobriety and humility were not favourably regarded in the last century.' He calls us back to a 'serene attentiveness,' reminding us in a grandfatherly way that being good and decent are worth it. He calls us to an 'ecological conversion.'

The encyclical would be all the stronger if it conceded that the growth in the world's human population—from two billion when Pius XII first spoke of contraception to 3.5 billion when Paul VI promulgated *Humanae Vitae* to 7.4 billion and climbing as it is today—points to a need to reconsider the Church's teaching on contraception. The Pope is quite right to insist that the reduction of population growth is not the only solution to the environmental crisis. But it is part of the solution. It may even be an essential part of the solution. Banning contraception in a world of 7.4 billion people confronting the challenges of climate change and loss of biodiversity is a very different proposition from banning it in a world of only two billion people oblivious of such challenges. I don't think you would find any papal advisers today who would advocate that the planet's situation with climate change, loss of biodiversity, and water shortages would be improved if only all people of good will had declined to use artificial birth control for the last fifty years. I note that J.R.D. Tata had a lifelong concern about population growth. He used to speak of the 'desperate race between population and production.' He strongly disagreed with Nehru, who thought 'population is our strength.' JRD was committed to propagating methods to control India's population growth. He helped start what eventually became the International Institute of Population Studies. In 1992, JRD received the United Nations Population Award in recognition of his commitment to this task.

Joy filled and troubled, Pope Francis is inviting us to do something to change the market settings and political settings to modify the behaviour of all global citizens in the future, and he invites us to attend to our own Franciscan interior ecological conversion with our care for the vulnerable and 'an integral ecology lived out joyfully and authentically.' Caring for our common home begins at home. But that's only the beginning, and it will get us nowhere unless there be agreement and committed action posited on economic growth tailored to the well-being of the poorest and economic activity within markets and State regulation designed to reduce the human impact on global warming.

Religious leaders have a capacity to contribute to that amplification of the still, small voice, as of course do international lawyers and business leaders. So too do poets, folk singers and novelists. The concept of human rights has real work to do whenever those with power justify their solutions to social ills or political conflicts, only on the basis of majority support or by claiming the solutions will lead to an improved situation for the mainstream majority. Even if a particular solution is popular or maximizes gains for the greatest number of people, it might still be wrong and objectionable. There is a need to have regard to the well-being of all members of the human community, and not just those within the preferred purview of government consideration.

This month the 22nd session of the Conference of the Parties (COP22) to the UN Framework Convention on Climate Change has taken place in Marrakech, Morocco. The Paris Agreement now enjoys the support of 109 countries. In the wake of the failure to reach agreement at Copenhagen in 2009, world leaders from 196 nations succeeded in achieving the Paris Agreement with the pledge to keep global warming to 2 degrees Celsius or less and deliver through nationally determined contributions to reduce greenhouse gas emissions. But the Trump cloud now hangs over the agreement. Ban Ki-Moon speaking at COP 22 said:

> Cities, citizens and CEOs were crucial to mobilizing political support for the Paris Agreement. They are also among the most visionary' and ambitious actors building low-carbon, resilient economies that will prosper in a climate-changed world.
>
> Businesses can do more to seize the many potential opportunities. There has been tremendous progress. In the growth of renewables. In green innovations. In thriving public-private partnerships working to transform key sectors of our economy from land use and agriculture to sustainable transport.

Answering questions at his media conference on November 15, 2016, the Secretary General was upbeat claiming, 'The global business community is now fully on board and moving forward to decarbonize and lessen their carbon footprint.' In the wake of the Trump victory in the USA, this might be a little too optimistic. But at least there is now a universal appreciation that the Copenhagen approach was bound to fail, and that the Paris approach inviting nation states to volunteer achievable, internationally verifiable targets and encouraging business and civil society to play their role in the greening of the economy, is bearing fruit. Pope Francis delivered a message at Marrakech, welcoming the coining into effect of the Paris Agreement. He told COP22, 'Its adoption represents the important awareness that, faced with issues as complex as climate change, individual and/or national action is not enough; instead it is necessary to implement a responsible collective response truly intended to work together in building our common home.'

Pope Francis said:

> One of the main contributions of this Agreement is that of stimulating the promotion of strategies for national and international development based on an environmental quality that we could define as fraternal; indeed, it encourages solidarity in relation to the most vulnerable and builds on the strong links between the battle against climate change and that of poverty. Although there are many elements of a technical nature involved in this field, we are also aware that it cannot all be limited solely to the economic and technological dimension: technical solutions are necessary but they are not enough; it is essential and proper to take into careful consideration also the ethical and social aspects of the new paradigm of development and progress.

Coming from an advanced economy, I happily acknowledge that India's emissions per capita are comparatively low, being one quarter of China and one-tenth of the United States. Prime Minister Modi has been committed to harnessing solar power, such that every Indian household will be able to run at least one electric light bulb by 2019. Sir Nicholas Stern continues to espouse co-operative international action based on the idea of 'equitable access to sustainable development.' He suggests:

> Rich countries undertake a dynamic and attractive transition to the low-carbon economy in their own economies, taking the lead in terms of emissions quantity reductions, innovation, and providing strong examples, and of support for similar transitions in developing countries through collaboration in the areas of finance, technology and capacity building.

Stem, like many international opinion leaders in this field, has learnt lessons in between Copenhagen 2009 and Paris 2015. He now sees that 'looking for formal international sanctions within an agreement that have real bite may be a mistake.' He sees a greater need for 'routes and processes that can encourage both collaboration and ambition.' There is no substitute for building trust, enhancing the 'mutually supportive relationships between overall agreements at the international level and actions at the national, regional, city or firm level.' Kevin Rudd, the Australian Prime Minister who saw so many of his dreams go up in smoke at Copenhagen 2009 made the point prior to Marrakech 2016: 'The policy settings are generally now fine. The current level of financial investment in transformational infrastructure, technology, and renewable energy is not adequate. And ultimately, the planet does not lie.' Neither India nor Australia can do it alone when confronting a global issue such as climate change. And given the scale of investment, innovation, and technological development required for sustainable development, governments cannot do it without business being aboard, convinced and committed to real change.

India cannot disregard the effects on other nations when it adopts laws and policies for alleviating the poverty of the poorest of the poor. Australia cannot disregard the effects on other nations when it adopts laws and policies aimed at securing and even hermetically sealing its borders, or when it considers restricting the availability of resources for export such as coal, which might help provide electricity for India's poorest citizens. The development of national laws and policies needs to be contoured by sufficient regard for the principles and values enunciated in international law. Laws and policies cannot be fully integrated into the life of the community unless the lawmakers and the policymakers are finely attuned to all that is noblest in their cultures and in their religious and philosophical traditions. The implementation of good laws and policies, depends on the character of those who exercise political power as a public trust and on those who exercise economic muscle with a commitment to the common good and the public interest, not just of the nation state but also of the community of nations and the planet itself. Corporations will not be able to play their role unless there is greater attention paid to 'corporate culture.'

Nowadays high level managers and board members are expected to take greater responsibility for their company's 'corporate culture', which includes attitudes, policies, rules, courses of conduct or practices existing within the body corporate generally or in the part of the body corporate which authorize or permit tacitly or impliedly wrongful behaviour by company employees. Boards should now be very clear in articulating a corporation's core purpose, values and principles. They should readily review how their real corporate culture aligns with the ideal stipulated in key corporate documents.

In recent weeks, there has been a very graphic instance of the breakdown of corporate culture, in the mining giant Rio Tinto. On November 16, 2016, the RT board terminated the contracts of its Energy and Minerals chief executive and of its Legal and Regulatory Affairs Group executive. Having reviewed the findings of an internal investigation into 2011 contractual arrangements with a consultant who provided advisory services on the Simandou project in Guinea, the board concluded that the executives failed to maintain the standards expected of them under the company's global code of conduct. These executives had been closely involved in providing a $10.5-million payment to a consultant who had good access to the President of Guinea. Two days before the board terminated the contracts of two of its key executives, the CEO wrote to staff saying, '1 am fully aware that this week's announcement about Simandou came as a surprise and many people across RT are still shell-shocked. Some of us may be feeling that we are better informed by the press than by ourselves. Speculation is running in some quarters and some of what is being said strikes at the heart of the culture and values of our company, which for me, are fundamentally strong and vitally important.' After his dismissal, the Energy and Minerals Chief Executive published his own statement claiming, 'The treatment of me and my past and recent colleagues is totally at variance with the values and behaviours of the company to which I have devoted my professional life.' It was not as if the Minerals Chief Executive had failed to disclose to his superiors the details and purpose of the \$10.5-million payment which his superiors had approved with the then CEO signing off with the observation, 'Worth giving this a try, but also think about optics to the GoG (Government of Guinea).' The Minerals Chief Executive had told his superiors that the payment to the consultant was a 'very necessary step' for providing a good relationship between the company and the Guinea government, achievable because of the consultant's 'very unique and irreplaceable services and closeness to the President.' The matter has now been reported to the US Justice Department, the UK Fraud Office and the Australian Federal Police. It is a matter of international concern, warranting investigation by the anti-corruption authorities in multiple countries other than Guinea. For example, the 1998 amendments to the US *Foreign Corrupt Practices Act 1977* has expanded the reach of US law enforcement well beyond the actions of US firms. I think we'll be hearing a lot more about corporate culture or ethos, and the need for broad international agreement about attitudes, policies, rules, courses of conduct or practices which impact on big business wherever it is transacted.

Gone are the days when this sort of corporate breakdown would be investigated only within the board room, or within the cabinet room of the offended African government. And gone are the days when the invocation of 'national sovereignty' or 'the free market' will foreclose on options for international co-operation and international rulemaking, providing the safety net for the planet and the poor, and the scaffolding for universal respect for human rights and for best business practice. International law does not provide the answers for sustainable development in India. But there are piecemeal international developments which should assist Indian citizens and Indian decision makers at the Cabinet table and in boardrooms to make better decisions, informed by all that is best in your religious traditions, in your national cultures, in the corporate cultures, being true to the people's noblest sense of themselves and faithful to the character each of us is called to be and develop. Never forget Mahatma Gandhi's injunction, 'One must care about the world one will not see.' All things considered, I think J.R.D. Tata would be happy. I hope so, for the sake of the planet, for the sake of the poor and for the sake of our own internal peace. During his most recent appearance at the UN, Prime Minister Modi quoted from one of your ancient texts. Respectfully, I repeat those words: 'May all be happy, may all be healthy, may all see welfare, may no one have any sorrow.' May the planet be happy and healthy so that future generations might be spared much sorrow.

26

My Experiences with JRD and His Principles*

J.J. IRANI

I feel privileged and honoured at being invited to deliver this, the twenty-sixth J.R.D. Tata Oration. Privileged because I am aware that those invited to deliver this oration are carefully selected, and honoured because J.R.D. Tata played a very significant role in my professional life, and I look upon him as my mentor, who guided me through some difficult periods. As you saw, I followed J.R.D. Tata in coming here with a written speech. When it was decided that he would give the first oration way back in 1991 and he was a bit reluctant to do that, Sharokh Sabavala, whose idea it was by the way to start the orations, said, 'Don't worry, I will prepare for you a good text that would cover the forty-five minutes at your speed of oration.' So he came, like I did just now with the speech, he walked up to the lectern like I did just now and then he put the speech on one side and did not touch it for the next seventy-five minutes. Which I cannot do and everyone in that packed auditorium heard him out in pin drop silence. After the applause and the congratulations were over, JRD walked up to Mr Sabavala and myself, asked how do you think it went? I piped up and said, 'It was good Sir, but it was a bit too long. You spent seventy-five minutes and the audience was expecting forty-five minutes.' He then looked at me and with a twinkle in the eye said, 'Rubbish. I spoke for exactly forty-five minutes.' For him the time stood still; but I know for me that it cannot. The organizers have correctly insisted that the content of the oration should be non-political and also not commercially oriented.

*Oration delivered on 29 November 2017.

And therefore sometimes to select such a person becomes difficult.

JRD believed that before man could excel in any field (of endeavour) that person should be a good man. And a good man must have great credibility. Perhaps that belief was instilled in him through his early education in France and later in Japan where his father moved with his family in the course of his business. You know that in Japan, the Japanese think first of the country, followed by the company to which they belong, probably for a lifetime, and then only about themselves. This was exactly JRD's attitude also. Unfortunately it is not so at present in our country. JRD also always believed that before India became a great country, India should be a happy country. He always prevailed upon his friend Jawaharlal Nehru, that what we need in this country is the creation of wealth and also that the wealth is spread and available for the benefit of all concerned. Once when JRD talked about industrial progress in India, and the need to have a profitable industrial base, Nehru is said to have cut him short by exclaiming, 'Jeh, profit is a dirty word'. But JRD persevered and he continued his association with the top family and after Nehru was gone, he was a good friend of Indira also.

JRD's mantra was always to aim for excellence or even perfection and to never be satisfied with second best. He abhorred mediocrity. That drive was clearly reflected in his leadership of Air India. When JRD was the chairman, for more than a quarter of a century, Air India was counted amongst the top three airlines of the world. A distant situation from what it is today.

JRD never completed his formal education because he was called away to India from France to help his father and his family, before he reached twenty years of age. I think that lack of formal education at university level made him a great admirer of the 'ECOLE' system of education in France, which he had yearned for, and he was forever keen to inject that kind of education into India. He would talk to his colleagues about the need in India to have an establishment of the type they had in France. The Tata House did try and in 1988 we established in Bangalore (now Bengaluru) the NIAS (National Institute for Advanced Studies). It is a fine institution where reputed scholars from all over the world can come and pursue studies of their choice for a length of time, according to their wishes. But it is in no way comparable to the ECOLE system in France.

JRD was a very humane person. And there are ample stories of how he used to help people in distress. Like when he was driving through the monsoon rains in Bombay (now Mumbai), he saw a family getting drenched standing by the road. He asked his driver to stop the car, reverse and ask that family to join him in his car and deliver them to their destination. Such small acts of kindness were ingrained in him. And we, of course, noticed it most when we had that terrible tragedy in 1989 (on Founder's Day) on 3rd March—the birthday of Jamsetjee Tata has always been looked upon as Founder's Day and it was celebrated with great gaiety in Jamshedpur. But in 1989, we had a terrible fire. The unfortunate coincidence was JRD who used to come to Jamshedpur every year on that day was not with us in 1989. He was in Geneva and when he heard about the tragedy, he immediately rushed back and forty-eight hours later on 5th March he was with us. JRD insisted on visiting each and every family which had suffered a casualty; most of these being family members of our officers and kept on telling me repeatedly, 'Please Jamshed, ensure that they get the best treatment that we can offer, not only here but abroad and there should be no scarcity as far as financials are concerned.' We did try to do the best that we can, but I am not sure whether we matched his expectation.

Much has been written about him, by his biographer, the late Russi Lala, and others. To say something new and unique is difficult. So I will take the safe path and concentrate in this oration on my personal interactions with him—instances of my personal conversations, and my observations, which not many others could have shared, or are aware of.

JRD believed totally in the concept of trusteeship. This is a quote from Jayaprakash Narayan, who JRD respected.

'The concept of trusteeship fostered by Mahatma Gandhi received a much-needed fillip in Tata enterprises. After all what is this concept of trusteeship? Under it, all wealth is a social trust and every individual—the employer, the engineer or even the ordinary mistry—is a trustee entitled to its proper utilization for the common good. True to the ideas of its founder, the House of Tata has always prompted this concept of trusteeship and today more than 85 per cent of its profits go to trusts.'

In the same vein, JRD believed that 'every company has a special and continuing responsibility towards the people of the area in which it is located and in which its employees and their families live. In every city, town or village, large or small, there is always need for improvement, for help, for relief, for leadership and for guidance. I suggest that the most significant contribution organized industry can make is by identifying itself with the life and problems of the people of the community to which it belongs, and by applying its resources, skills and talents, to the extent that it can reasonably spare them to serve and help them'. Obviously most of you, if not all of you are residents are Jamshedpur, and if you look around you, you can see how his words have been put into practice.

FAMILY PLANNING

JRD was a great advocate of family planning and encouraged us to set up family planning centres across Jamshedpur and in all our outlying areas. One day he asked me whether, in addition to providing medical facility, we give an incentive to the person undergoing the procedure. Proudly I said, 'Yes, we give Rs. 200 to each individual.' He exploded, 'What! Only Rs 200. You should make it Rs. 5, 000 per head. It is the greatest service you can do for the nation. Far better than spending to increase production of steel.' Rs. 5, 000would have made us bankrupt! But to honour the chairman's enthusiasm, we did double the stipend to Rs 400per head!

PERSONAL PROBITY

He disliked any fuss made over his visits, and took pride in managing 'byself'. Once, by chance, I travelled with him from Bombay to Delhi. At Delhi airport, I tried to help him with his checked-in bag. As I saw it approaching us on the conveyor belt, I stretched out my hand to lift it, whereupon he smacked my outstretched hand with the curt remark, 'Jamshed, when I need your help I will ask for it.' He then proceeded to lift it and place it in a trolley he pushed himself towards the exit, with me following with my trolley.

On that very occasion there was another amusing incident. A flight from Kolkata had arrived at the same time and on it were some marketing executives of our marketing division. In those days of steel shortages, senior marketing staffs were VVIPs and they were always received by a hoard of steel traders and important customers with flowers and various other paraphernalia. This occasion was no different. Much to the embarrassment of our executives the traders and others fought among themselves to greet and get the attention of our officers. In turn they were embarrassed at seeing their chairman and dep. MD (yours truly) also exiting at the same time. Of course they had to greet us, which they did, very sheepishly. After we got into our car, JRD asked me what the fuss was about. On my explaining the situation he dryly remarked that may be some changes in location were due. Marketing division did not fall under my purview then, but over the next few weeks there were some changes, and those gentlemen from the marketing division found themselves transferred to Jamshedpur, where I took good care of them!!

JRD'S LIFESTYLE

JRD lived a very simple lifestyle. He and Mrs Thelly Tata lived in a rented house for all the years that they spent in Mumbai; maybe four decades or so. Their house belonged to a trust. Not a Tata trust, he wouldn't have that. They were tenants in that house. Whenever there was a chance for him to, shall we say, point out that we were over stepping on our personal lives, he would say so. He also wanted to establish his sincerity by his own example. His office in Bombay (it has now been reproduced by the way in the Tata archives in Pune) has been kept exactly as it was in Mumbai, it is a study in simplicity. To his office, of course, came, politicians, business leaders, people from abroad, people from Delhi because of his position he entertained all of them in his office. Some of his colleagues in Mumbai, felt that the faded curtains and the stale upholstery was not becoming of the chairman of the House of Tatas. So they kept on telling him to please make some changes. Of course, he would not let any of the companies do it. So under pressure from his colleagues in Bombay House, he finally relented and with his secretary in tow went on a shopping trip in the Flora Fountain area. He always carried a small red calculator. He had taken the measurements of how many yards of material he required. His secretary takes up the story that everywhere he went and liked something he would ask for the price per metre and after that he would use his calculator. Everywhere he muttered, 'No, too expensive'. This way it went on for three hours. Finally, they returned to the office after having bought nothing. He would not allow any of his companies to support the upkeep of his office. After his demise, his will confirmed that his personal wealth was next to nothing. You and I would laugh at the figure. He had, of course, his wealth with trusts bequeathed to various charities of his choice. But his trusts were sacred and not to be used for any personal preferences.

Whenever he came to Jamshedpur, he wanted to see something new. 'Show me something new'—that became increasingly difficult because we were not growing in the '70s and '80s. So one day, I took him to the water treatment plant on the river Kharkai where all sewage generated in Jamshedpur was collected, treated and then pure water fed back into the river downstream. When we went there, a bearer came up with two glasses of water. He said, 'But I'm not thirsty.' So I said, 'No sir, this is a custom in this part of the world and you have to drink the water otherwise they will feel offended.' So he gingerly took up the glass and drank from it. I did the same. After that I told him what that water was; where it had come from. That it was purified from all the sewages. He exploded, 'What! You made me drink that!' I said, 'Yes, but it's perfectly drinkable. Are you feeling ill or anything?' He did not reply, but for the rest of the morning he hardly spoke to me and I was wondering whether I would have my job by the end of the day. But I survived.

He had a tremendous eye for detail. He never tolerated any deviation from his penchant for perfection. Those of you who have been to our office in Jamshedpur would know there is a staircase which leads up to a landing where there is a bust of the founder.

He never used the lift. He always used the staircase. And he would always go to that bust and pay his respects. One morning there was a meeting in my office. So I was not with him as I was preparing for the meeting. My colleagues brought him up the staircase. On his way up he examined the founder's bust and kept on muttering that you people are dishonouring the founder, look at the stains on the bust and the imperfections which have crept in, you can't even look after the founder's bust!' He came to my office and one of my colleagues who came with him whispered this into my ears. So I quickly excused myself, went into the next room and phoned the man in charge of our model room. We used to have a man in charge who took care of such small imperfections. I told him, 'Please drop whatever you are doing, I'll give you two hours, I'll hold JRD in my office for two hours, you've got to clean up or patch up whatever is necessary on that bust.' So when the meeting finished, we again all trooped out, again went down the staircase, and I innocently mentioned to him, 'Sir, I was told that you found some imperfection on this bust.' He said, 'Yes yes yes! Jamshed, you can't look after these things?' and he wanted to point them out. He went to the bust but couldn't see anything, there were no stains, no dust, it looked really perfect, and then he felt under the statue and got wet paint on his fingers. He burst out jokingly of course and said, 'You're trying to fool an old man! You'll never succeed at that!' But he was happy that we had paid some attention to what he expected of us.

As you know he was a great aviator. He had India's first pilot's licence (No.001). It is still available for viewing in our archives in Pune. When he came to Jamshedpur he would fly our plane to put in necessary hours required to maintain his flying licence. There were at that time no Tata aircraft in Bombay. We had two or three aircrafts in Jamshedpur. So he would come to Jamshedpur and put in the necessary hours to maintain his licence. He did that religiously every year. In 1932, when he was twenty-eight years old, he had made a solo flight from Karachi to Bombay to start a postal service in the country. He had flown the plane single handedly on his own. All his colleagues were really taken aback when in 1982 he said that he wanted to repeat that historic journey, solo, at the age of seventy-eight. There was no point in trying to dissuade him. His mind was made up. Finally, his senior colleagues said that at least let a Tata Steel plane accompany you., He said what good would a plane flying half a kilometre behind me or in front of me be of any help if anything happens to my plane. But then he agreed to please his colleagues. So they took off. The historic flight was made from Karachi to Bombay. But he had obviously to first reach Karachi. So off he went to Bombay with the Tata Steel plane in tow. But the Tata Steel plane developed a snag and had to land at Ahmedabad and could not go any further. JRD flew on to Karachi alone and landed there safely, made preparations for his main flight in the reverse direction the next morning. He then asked for his overnight bag. Some personnel, shall we say very 'thoughtfully', had packed his bag in the Tata Steel plane. So here he was in Karachi, without a bag which was grounded at Ahmedabad airport.

He said, 'I told these people not to interfere with my plans; they did and now look what has happened. I have to stay overnight at Karachi without my overnight bag.' I don't know how he spent the night. But next morning he made the reverse flight. He would do all his calculations, his flight plans, his timings and so on, himself. As he was approaching Bombay he realized that due to favourable winds he would actually land half an hour earlier than what was the plan. Of course the plan was to give him a grand reception at Bombay on his arrival. VIPs were expected. So he didn't want to come in earlier. He started circling over Bombay, just to spend time because his view was that coming in late is bad but coming in early is equally bad. So he circled over Bombay for half an hour and then landed exactly at the correct time to the reception that was awaiting him at Bombay airport.

Air India as all know was his favourite baby. He had started the airline as Tata Airways and in the late 1950s it was nationalized and became Air India. But Nehru requested him to continue to look after it and he was happy to do so for many years. That harmonious relationship ended when Morarji Desai took over as the prime minister of India. Apparently, immediately after he took over a memo was sent to JRD inquiring, 'When are you going to stop serving liquor on Air India flights?' JRD replied immediately, 'Sir, we will do it immediately after you decide to turn Air India into a freight service. Because no passenger would fly Air India if we stop serving liquor.' After that there were many instances where things were not cordial between JRD and the prime minister of India.

One day, JRD went with a plan to buy new planes for Air India and he told the PM that we have come very far and I think we have made a good choice both cost wise and efficiency wise, we think that we will be going for these planes. Then Morarji exploded. He said, 'Jeh, you just recommend, I will decide which planes are to be bought.' JRD recounted the story to us with humour with a tinge of disgust. But in the end Morarji had his way. I think some of you might be aware that without even the courtesy of informing JRD, who had nurtures Air India since birth, in 1977 JRD was fired. We heard the announcement on All India Radio. As it happened that day he was in Jamshedpur. As usual we were meeting for dinner. All the senior officers had gathered very sombre mood. When JRD came and sat in his chair and we didn't know what to say. Finally, one person piped up and said, 'Sir, we heard the news. How do you feel about it?' Quietly he said, 'I feel as if my favourite child has been taken away from me.' So that was the way the government treated him somebody who had raised Air India to be one of the best airlines in the world. Far removed from where Air India is now.

There is also a story attached to his Bharat Ratna. He had already been awarded the Padma Bhushan and the Padma Vibhushan. In the late 1980, there was a move that JRD be awarded the Bharat Ratna. Then it was not like what we read in the papers now, of people being sponsored by sports group or art groups and the like. It was just decided by the government. One day, Mr B. G. Deshmukh who was then either the cabinet secretary flew down from Delhi to Bombay with the invitation for JRD. The PM wanted to know whether JRD would accept if the Bharat Ratna was offered to him. They didn't want the embarrassment of offering something and then the recipient turning it down. So JRD was asked and he said give me a day or two to think it over. We had a meeting before lunch time the next day and JRD said that look I've been asked by the government of

India to accept this honour, but as far as I know this honour is only given to politicians and it is also given posthumously. He said I'm not a politician and I'm not prepared to oblige the government of India on the second requirement. So there was a deathly silence in the room and then somebody suggested let's look at the list of people who have already been awarded this. Mr Deshmukh, who was the emissary from Delhi, was carrying the list. On that list, much to our relief, there was a person who was still alive and who was not a politician! That clinched the argument in our favour and JRD finally agreed to accept the honour which the government of India was planning to bestow on him.

He was very interested in technical development. As I said, his first love was Air India and I had often hoped that his second love would be Tata Steel. After I joined Tata Steel, that is also a long story, he requested me to go to Japan. Japan that time, in the '70s, was the place for modern steel making. New plants were coming up that were far ahead of the Europeans and the US. So he arranged for me to go to Japan and I spent four weeks there; Looking at almost all the plants there in existence. After I came back, he naturally wanted to discuss the situation with me. I came and told him quite frankly, 'Look, I think it was a very good trip but next time you please send your finance people. Because we technical people know what I saw, the blast furnace, rolling mills and so on. We knew these beforehand. What I would like to know from the finance people is how the Japanese managed to knock down plants which are just ten years old and afford to build new ones? Whereas our people here in Jamshedpur were always told by the head office in Bombay that sorry there was no money for your plans.' Mr Firoze Tarapore who was in charge of the modernization programmes of the Steel Co once told me that he had put up fifty proposals for Tata Steel to modernize, but not one of those had been accepted on the same grounds—that we had no money. I recounted that to JRD and said, 'Look unless we have some modernization, both you and I will be standing at the gates of Tata Steel selling tickets saying come and see the steel museum.' He laughed but the message went home. We did start in a small way. The blast furnace we bought from Portugal at a very low price. That got me into trouble because I was accused by the import authorities of trying to smuggle into the country a blast furnace! When the case came for hearing I remember the judge dryly remarking that up till now all cases of improper imports which have come to me were for diamonds and gold. I have never seen a case come up for smuggling a blast furnace. Which, by the way, were carried on three ships into the port of Paradip. I got away without a fine or imprisonment—and Tata Steel got a brand new blast furnace.

I always have an everlasting regret that JRD did not live long enough to see the Tata Steel that he had envisaged in his mind's eye. We were fully modernized by the end of the century. In fact, we were looked upon at that time as the lowest cost producer of steel. But JRD had passed away in 1993. But it was his idea. For example, cutting down the labour in the '90s, we had reduced our manpower strength by 50 per cent from around 80,000 to around 40,000. Through a very innovative plan which had been recognized in the world. I remember the day sometime in the '80s when our annual report showed that the wage bill had passed ₹100 crore, he threw up his hands and said, 'Gentlemen, what are you doing? We are spending a 100 crore on labour?' Three years later it had crossed 200 crore. I don't know the figure for today which must be in 1000s of crores. So, in the '90s we undertook a programme. Though he was not there then it was he who had pointed the way towards where we are now.

He was very meticulous and at the same time very polite in conveying messages. He had a little red diary and to remind himself he would open it and would pen those notes in. Towards the end of his tenure, we were hearing a lecture given by one of our very senior colleagues. Half way he expounded what we can do in Tata Steel and how we can expand it and so on. JRD took out his diary and wrote something in it. After he finished writing, he passed it to the person on his right and that person read it and then passed it on to me. I was absolutely amazed at what was written in it. He had written there in his own handwriting 'this person must be removed before he does all this damage!' By coincidence, that person was removed within a year or two. So this is how he controlled his vast empire.

He never had the need to have a show of hands.

When I joined Tata Steel, Tata's holding in Tata Steel was 3½ per cent. Mr G.D. Birla, JRD's friend, owned 5 per cent. But they were great friends. Every year G.D. Birla would sign on his proxy papers and send them to JRD saying, 'do what you want with it.' So with 8½ per cent in his pocket he did whatever he thought was necessary.

I would go on and on but I see that forty minutes are already over and I will conclude by saying this. He inspired all of us, all that Tata Steel is today is thanks to him and he will always be looked upon with awe. I hope that even from far he will keep looking at us benevolently, Air India first but Tata Steel not far behind! And all that he did was the result of his credibility. People even in the highest level of the government, and even outside India, knew that what he said was exactly what he meant. There will not be another one like J.R.D. Tata.

27

Ethics in Action: Corporate Social Responsibility in the 21st Century*

JENNIFER J. GRIFFIN

After considerable thought, I decided to speak on a topic close to my heart and crucial to the survival and re-birth of businesses across the globe—putting ethics into action. Far too often in headlines from around the world we, unfortunately, see violence, destruction of lives and livelihoods, questions about humane treatment of workers or immigrants. In short, businesses putting profits before safety,[1] before people. The positive impacts of treating people with dignity and respect; enabling others to do good and do well often gets lost. Sadly, one tree falling in the forest makes more noise than a thousand trees growing.

Tonight, let's focus on the positive, on putting ethics into action. Let's focus on what we as individuals and as employees or managers within organizations can do. India, in particular, with the Companies Act of 2013 makes for exciting times. It's a game changer. A game changer for India and potentially the world. While the Companies Act of 2013 specifies corporate social responsibility's (CSR's) certain activities[2] in theory, CSR is only limited by your imagination.

My own belief: I'm bullish on India getting it right. Why? Because it is in businesses best interest to get it right: to do good and do well. Building self-sufficient households within healthy, resilient communities requires vision, business acumen, disciplined investments, communication, funding, bold leadership and operational

*Oration delivered on 27 November 2018.

excellence to work across sectors with new and different partners. It will take a bit of imagination. It will require a shifting of mindsets. Nevertheless, working towards a more humane, just world is a worthy goal for business.

Certainly, there will the inevitable turmoil: sorting out where to invest money, undertaking lots of large and small experimental projects, pivoting, the inevitable dead ends and wrong turns, but eventually it will be sorted out. And, as Indian businesses learn, you will lead a global effort: showing all of us the impossible is possible.

Paraphrasing Al Gini my Loyola University Chicago colleague: making money is easy, making a difference is much harder.[3]

Tonight, I focus on putting ethics into action via a why-what-how triad. Why bother? What is CSR/ethics in action? And, in particular, how ethical leadership within businesses can give tangible evidence of putting ethics in action.

WHY CORPORATIONS? WHY NOW?

Pope Francis provided a partial response when addressing the US Congress in 2015:

> Business is a noble vocation, directed to producing wealth and improving the world. It can be a fruitful source of prosperity for the area in which it operates, especially if it sees the creation of jobs as an essential part of its service to the common good.[4]

So, why corporations? In part because large and small businesses are job creators with wages and importantly, dignity of work as direct benefits through employment. Indirectly, the benefits of employment in large corporations can be double or triply-felt across vast supply chain networks via distribution and retail ecosystems shown by a recent study to alleviate poverty in Indonesia.[5] This might mean re-skilling or up-skilling your own employees. Or looking further afield to your suppliers' employees, or the suppliers of suppliers' employees. You can just imagine the ripple effects, both positive and negative, large and small businesses can have across their networks.

Businesses can, and do, multiply positive spillover effects within local communities by transferring skills and expertise, incubating new businesses and encouraging other businesses to co-locate. Clusters of small and large businesses in urban and rural areas support artisans, farmers and skilled trades. Together they build soft and hard infrastructure: roads, telecom, information services, education creating shared prosperity.

As a colleague once explained to me: if you get off a plane or train meaning you have transportation, with cell phone service and access to an ATM you can create a business. Start a business or help others start businesses.

To address the question 'why now?', Father Raymond C. Baumhart, former president, Loyola University Chicago and the namesake of my endowed chair made this observation in his Harvard Business School dissertation, fifty years ago: No group in America is more influential than businessmen (and women). Their influence, for good or evil, enters every life and every home many times each day. If this influence is good, the nation is strengthened; if it is evil, the nation is weakened. The myriad decisions of businessmen (and women) will significantly determine our national health, ethical as well as economic

I think his insights still resonates today: in America, in India and around the world. The time is now!

For me, putting ethics into action, day in and day out, fundamentally depends upon the choices we as individuals make in how we choose to treat one another. It's our relationships with one another. It's the rules we choose to live by, once we choose to live together[7] in organizations, in businesses, in communities and within our family.

To paraphrase Aristotle, the key question to putting ethics into action becomes: How shall we live, and live well, together?[8]

Turning to organization, in addition to it being the right thing to do, for businesses there are often three additional reasons to put ethics in action: market motivations, government mandates and leadership.

WHY SHOULD CORPORATIONS BOTHER WITH CSR?

It's at the intersection of market motivation, government mandates and leadership that becomes the 'sweet spot' for businesses that get it right or the 'messy middle' for others.

Market Motivation

More than thirty years ago, my bosses' boss's boss asked me, a young chemical engineer working on a new polycarbonate process for GE Plastics: 'What's the business case?' I was the Dutch lead of a tri-country team, charged with changing a batch reaction to a continuous reaction. In charge of the lab scale, my team had gotten the chemistry right with all of the kinetics, heat/mass transfer details. We had increased productivity, increased yield and decreased methylene chloride, a greenhouse gas. We had a win-win-win! What's not to like?

Still, he asked: What is the business case? My response, with my engineer's hat firmly on, was: What do you mean? We can do this! A leadership argument.

Well, my answer did not carry the day. But he asked a good question. For three-plus decades, I have been learning about strategy and ethical leadership, to create narratives with current and future business leaders about win-win-wins.

What I've found? Strategy has two definitions. There is the traditional, classic definition: profits equals total revenue minus total costs.

The business narrative for prosocial, voluntary CSR goes something like this. Does this proposed CSR initiative increase price, develop new markets, create more demand and thus increase revenue while keeping costs contained and, in turn, increase profits?

Or, focusing on the cost side of the equation: CSR is a tax, a fixed cost, or a variable cost that will be a drag on profits. In short, it's a noose around the neck regardless of the benefits to others.

So, when you think about the Companies Act of 2013; what comes to mind? Is CSR a tax? A shake-down? Extortion of corporations by mandating charitable contributions? Or, yet one more responsibility on top of an already overloaded plateful of 'must dos'? That's certainly one why to look it from the costs/expenses side of the equation.

Alternatively, is the Companies Act an opportunity for innovation? For investment? For growing markets by doubling down on the company's values and putting ethics into action?

Let's dig into each of these mindsets a bit more closely. Imagine if you will, a two by two matrix[9]. Along the x-axis is corporate profits, harms and benefits. The y-axis is labelled 'Impacts on Others'. This could be employees, suppliers, customers, consumers, communities, just someone else other than investors. The scale is harms and benefits.

The upper right hand quadrant is the win-win: high returns and someone else benefits. That's the easy decision. Definitely invest. Help yourself and help others: decrease carbon, water, energy consumption; decrease packaging costs and save the planet while reducing costs and improving profits.

The bottom left-hand quadrant, what I call the 'parade of horribles'[10], is to be avoided: profits suffer and others are harmed. That's the lose-lose quadrant you want to stay away from. Sadly, many businesses come to CSR or to think about ethics from this backfoot stance. Newspaper headlines, a market failure and government intervenes. We'll talk about these government mandates shortly. But, let's keep examining the 2x2 matrix.

For me, as a strategist and ethicist, the most interesting quadrant, is the top left. When someone else benefits yet the returns are not there, yet, for the corporation. How do you talk about that? What's the narrative? It's a classic case of an expense. A cost centre. A drain on profits.

Alternatively, if someone else benefits, yet the company currently does not, this scenario is an investment. Imagine an investment in a greenfield site, an undeveloped community that will in time, with effort including transportation, roads, education yield fruitful benefits for the company and others.

So, when you think about CSR is it an expense? Yet, another cost? Or, is CSR an investment? An investment in your employees. An investment in building thriving and prosperous communities that are self-sufficient and resilient, transferring skills and expertise from engaged, motivated and productive employees.

Is CSR, for example, viewed as a differentiator for prospective employees of why to work for your businesses rather than the competitor just down the road? As an investment in building cross-functional teams to work together while sponsoring a local community: building housing, re-skilling or upskilling others, building leaders of tomorrow as a team with a common goal, for a higher purpose.

In short, putting ethics into action requires looking inside the firm as well as examining the plethora of demands from outside. Choose. Choose wisely. Choose, for example, based on the uniquenesses within your company: the location, logistics, comms or infrastructure. In short, doubling down on the inimitable intangibles.

So, ethics in action can be 'the right thing to do', yet the mindset matter. Do you consider it a cost or an investment? Now, let's turn to government mandates.

Government Mandate

Is CSR the government's job? Maybe it is. Yet aid isn't working.[11] And government regulation, by definition, means a market failure: businesses aren't taking care for some externality. Or, some unmet need is not able to be addressed directly through market mechanisms.

Alternatively, government action can provide seed money or incentives. Or in the case of the Companies Act of 2013 spark behaviour change by setting a minimal threshold of acceptable business behaviour.

Yet, with government mandates, companies can't comply their way to greatness. Compliance with legal norms merely becomes a minimal threshold. Yet, if we re-imagine government mandates as creating a level playing field, the differentiator among companies then becomes how your company will make an impact. All must pay. But the differentiation will be in the impact and the investments you, as ethical leaders, choose to make.

In other words, maybe it is in a company's best interest to make an investment, provide services, or maintain infrastructure. Businesses have the twenty-year, thirty-year, century-long vision and likely want to be in business that long. Father Baumhart's insights are relevant: business men and women are very influential, for good or for evil... affecting a nation's ethical and economic health.[12]

So, while governments and who is in power may come and go, when it comes to skills-building, long-term projects, or nation-building for example; maybe it is in a private company's best interest to win the bid; build the community's co-gen plants as well as build schools for the children living in the community. If designed to be resilient and self-sufficient, the communities, schools, computers and infrastructure can thrive long after the co-gen plant is built and the construction company leaves town.

These needs for employability, upskilling and reskilling exist around the world: Illinois Tool Works (ITW) in my hometown Chicago adopted a school, increased employability, created support networks and mentoring for plumbers, carpenters, construction workers and electricians.

With minimal thresholds set down by government mandates, the question, in my mind, changes to: What solution is your company providing? Within your communities? Within your nation? In other words, *if* you choose to act, or are mandated to act, what impact will your company's millions of rupees have on the local neighbourhoods, on the nation?

This is where ethical leadership comes into play.

ETHICAL LEADERSHIP

Leadership, and bold leadership, is part of the second definition of strategy. As you recall, the first definition of strategy is profits equals total revenues minus total costs. The second definition of strategy is: creating the future.[13]

Creating the future requires, in part, imaging a future in which we and our grandkids want to live in. Reflection and action to be bold enough to create that future. A future not just as individuals but as ethical leaders within an organization bringing to bear a vast array of resources: the scale, scope, relationships, technology, innovations, equipment and human ingenuity within businesses.

We don't have to look far for inspiration regarding ethical leadership. The 2017 compendium of XLRI orations by Father Abraham, and his co-editors, quote J.R.D. Tata as saying, 'Do not ask what is the "legal" thing to do, but ask what is the "right thing" we should do..... do not do only what is the right thing to do, but do it rightly, and for the right reasons.'[14] Getting the thinking, the talking and the doing aligned is part of ethical leadership.

Leaders also unleash the creative spirit of employees in the workplace by ensuring, for example, as J.R.D. Tata did when building TISCO: 'plenty of space for lawns and greens, large areas for football, hockey and parks, earmarking areas for Hindu temples, mosques and Christian churches.'[15]

Another example: a fast-moving consumer goods company built a railroad spur outside of St. Petersburg. Is that part of their core competence? No. Were they required to build it? No. Was it in their best interest to build it rather than wait for government? Yes. They built it. They maintained it.

And they allowed others to use the railroad spur, helping to build out the local market and gain access to a larger market, as a rising tide lifts all boats.

Similarly, what if we really listen to Amazon founder/CEO Jeff Bezos when he explained why earlier this year he raised minimum wages to $15 (nearly 1100 rupees per hour) for 300,000 workers: 'We listened to our critics, thought hard about what we wanted to do, and decided we want to lead.' Chose to lead. It is a choice. Leadership comes from within rather than an externally mandated tax.

So, if ethical leadership involves choices in how we create the future, together, my advice: Choose.

Choose wisely. Which takes us to the next series of questions: What is CSR? And what is it NOT?

WHAT IS CORPORATE SOCIAL RESPONSIBILITY?

I've written that CSR is a Tower of Babel,[16] it means different things to different people at different points in time. So, a rational response by a rational manager is to throw up their hands and wait. Wait until programmes are better defined, wait until impact is measured, wait until widespread agreement on outcomes, etc. In short, wait and keep waiting, as the business has got enough on its plate already.

Yet, as businesses are sorting out what to do; government or civil society organizations might define CSR and tell businesses what to do (for example, select among ten activities in Schedule VII of Section 135). Executives may not be so happy. They might feel put upon.

All too often acceptable business behaviours are defined by outsiders: the media, activists, governments, public opinion. This back-foot, 'parade of horribles' is seen in headlines taken from the *Financial Times* this past year:

- (The Federal Government) to hold public inquiry into (your industry's) misconduct (*FT*; Australia and banking)
- (Your company) says data woes extend into core business (*FT*: Kobe)
- (Your company's) shares plunge as scandal widens (*FT*: Kobe Steel)
- (Your company) pays the price for trampling on public trust (*FT*: Uber)
- (Your company) pays heavy price for customer carelessness (*FT*: United)
- (Your company) joins list of corporate misfires with poor handling of crisis (*FT*, VW)
- Why (your product) is no longer fantastic (*FT*: plastic)

From a strategic and ethical leadership perspective, my response is: shift the narrative.

Let me ask you what I ask all of my graduate and undergraduate students when they role play being CEO, chairman of the board, or managing directors: What headlines do you want to generate in 5-7 years? What type of company do you want to be known as? What impact do you want to have?

Here's some other headlines in the past year from the *Financial Times*:

- (Your country) learns to harvest its formidable solar power opportunities (*FT*, Chile)

- (Your) rivals take aim at (your) stream of success (*FT*, Netflix)
- (Your company) launches 'cutting edge' (initiative) (*FT*, Legg Mason, parental leave plan)

After talking about Why? And What? Let's now turn to how? How to tangibly demonstrate ethical leadership by putting ethics into action?

HOW TO DEMONSTRATE CORPORATE RESPONSIBILITY?

Yet, traditionally it is associated with philanthropy. Let's unpack the 'how' since intentions to do good are often undermined with implementation.

Historically: In many countries, CSR is equated with philanthropy.[17] Philanthropic foundations, corporate foundations, private giving are quite effective addressing social issues; initiating social businesses; and some very ambitious projects: Grameen Foundation, Gates Foundation, Carnegie, Siemens, Bosch, Rockefeller.....the list goes on. The Tata trusts, for example took a holistic, long-term view, to 'plant seeds out of which will grow the trees that will yield rich fruit for generations to come.'

Turning to corporate treasuries, however, *if* what a firm truly values beyond profits are *only* reflected in philanthropic give-a-ways from corporate treasuries then ethics-in-action can become a residual, optional activities, or an afterthought after, and only, profits have been made. That view is widespread in many organizations around the world.

Philanthropy has a more profound meaning than that of mere charity. Philanthropy's derivative is fil-anthra-pi; meaning 'love of mankind.'[18,19]

So, what if we shifted the focus to take a more ecumenical, broader view of how to tangibly demonstrate what a company values? Rather than focusing on the 5 per cent or the 2 per cent give-a-way; what about focusing on the 95 per cent or the 98 per cent, by focusing on how companies make their money.

Impacts: Ethics in action is on impacts of business. In general, there are four points of interaction between business and its many communities: financial; employees and in the workplace; products including supply/distribution networks; as well as information-based impacts through sharing platforms, for example.[20]

Financial impacts include disaster relief, impact investing, socially responsible investing, re-balancing portfolios, re-allocating resources as well as a cost/expense and investment mindset as we've already talked about.

Employee impacts, meaning treatment of employees including safe workplaces is often how many organizations start expressing CSR especially if firms are competing for top talent or a large percentage of net worth is based upon knowledge-workers or skilled artisans. Charitable activities for others or community outreach can fall flat when employees point out the hollowness of leaders' rhetoric in not matching the reality of day-to-day workplace conditions.[21] By extension, treatment of employees' families, or community organizations creates an ever-widening circle of impacts such as my former doctoral student did regarding poverty alleviation with the Self-Employed Women's Association (SEWA).[22]

Alternatively, ethics in action might emphasize becomes how profits are created by focusing on specific issues tied to your industry or needs of the nation-state. Aligning with issues, identifying uniqueness within your industry, or addressing needs of the nation-state. [23]

ISSUES-INDUSTRIES-NATION STATES

Issues: Unilever the Anglo-Dutch health and hygiene company under the leadership of CEO Paul Polman, for example, created a hand-washing campaign to improve health and hygiene with the ambitious goal of reaching billions of people before 2020. Supporters would say: what a great thing to address diarrhea, water-borne diseases and help this generation and the next generation to prevent treatable diseases. Antagonists would argue: oh, it's just a marketing campaign with free media exposure as they sell soaps, shampoos, dishwashing liquid and cleaning up surfactants.

The Yays and the Nays are both right: but the fact remains

the number of integrated programmes, mechanisms, resources including employees, technology, their value chain networks have created an ecosystem, a resilient ecosystem to address water-borne diseases. The best accolade might be: their competitors are (trying to) copying them. As you pull one thread, sorting out one issue, there will inevitably be innumerable issues attached and co-mingled. Of course, there's the next set of additional issues now: small sachets, landfills and water-borne pollution, for example, in adopting villages developed integrated programmes, building infrastructure and addressing multiple issues simultaneously. The outcomes are measurable: improving household wages, assuring access to clean water and education, enabling families to pull themselves out of extreme poverty while eliminating malaria. Local organizations are integral to local neighbourhoods and vice versa: healthy communities thrive with healthy businesses.

Industries: Alternatively, an industry perspective might have us focus on product impacts. For example, product impacts might entail mapping the economic, social and environmental impacts both downstream and upstream for goods and services. If a vertically integrated company such as petrochemicals, for example, do you gather information on your impacts. Do you know if money is made upstream (mining the ore) but its lost downstream (closer to the customer) with negative social/environmental impacts? Do you know if you are making money upstream (mining the ore) but are you losing money downstream (closer to the customer)?

Whereas banks, individually or collectively, might be addressing financial literacy at the individual household or business levels, plus micro-financing to accelerate start-ups and addressing creditworthiness and a whole host of requirements and permitting to move businesses from the informal sector. In the states, for example, there's a focus on impact bonds, impact investing, and the like.

Maybe you're in the logistics or ICT industries, being able to move product from point A to point B can be expanded, perhaps sponsoring hackathons or accelerators to help others get product from point A to point B, create appropriate designs, and take ideas from concept to consumer. The issues to be addressed are vase: plastic bottles, recycling; circular economy...

Nation-states: Bayer, a pharmaceutical company when trying to enter to Chinese market eventually won partial approval via its community health campaigns. It makes commitments to the Chinese government to address diseases and health outcomes.

Interestingly, J.P. Morgan Chase wants to smart cities and there are efforts afloat in India to do the same.

Yet, a word of caution: be quick to pivot. L'Oreal, a French cosmetics company, when it was expanding to other continents, for example, made quite a few investments in climate change in South America. But when asked, the communities weren't so interested in alleviating climate change they were keen to address other closer-to-home issues such as homelessness, nutrition, employability and the like. L'Oreal pivoted.

GOING FORWARD: WHAT'S NEEDED?

Putting ethics in action requires more than a checklist of activities; it requires integrated action starting with:

1. Tone at the Top.

While the Companies Act of 2013 and other CSR initiatives around the world have created incentives and penalties, I believe reliance on rules-based regulation can only succeed if these rules are matched with principled leadership for decency, honesty and respectability among corporate leadership.

Putting ethics into action won't happen unless corporate leaders talk the talk and walk the walk. Your leadership and your mindset matters. In short, is CSR a cost, an expense, a savings or an investment? As powerful role models, employee watch senior leaders carefully and imitate them.

As Peter Drucker famously said: Culture eats strategy for breakfast, every day.

2. Choose. Choose Wisely. Choose Impact.

Adam Smith had it right: division of labour and coordination/ integration are required.[24] We're fairly good at division of labour—look at the silos, the specialties, the proliferation of divisions, units and teams.

Yet we need to be dot connectors, too. Rather than not my problem, not my budget, not my vertical, change the question: How can we create impact? How do we solve this problem?

3. Big Bold Initiatives *and* Letting A Thousand Flowers Bloom.

In theory, scale doesn't matter. Yet, in practice scale matters quite a bit. Some (US AID, for example) might say collaborations with bold initiatives are the only way forward. [25] Yet, free riders and collective action issues cannot be wished away even when collaborating for a good cause with the best of intentions. In short, being in a collaboration is not enough to move the needle.

Perhaps we also need to re-define the scale of social issues.[26] Taking one small step at a time, working with one household or one community at a time with our feet firmly on the ground. In doing so, we can let a thousand flowers bloom: experimenting with trial and error, pivoting quickly with an eye towards to larger picture of impact.

Imagine if you will: a thousand lotus flowers, continually adapting, adjusting all the while blooming.

4. Trust Remains Essential.

Trust remains essential for businesses. With less reliance on traditional intermediaries and decreased trust in corporations, governments and institutions around the world there's a shift towards networks as well as local provisioning. Developing inter-dependencies, enabling self-reliance and self-sufficiency in others with resilient communities is more important than ever.

Last but not least,

5. Pick Your Partners.

Find folks willing to talk the talk and walk and walk with you. And, *if* you choose to purposefully combine ethical and economic leadership then hire and partner based upon trust on the willingness to learn, readiness to experiment with news ways of operating. In short, double down on the ampersand of creating profits and prosperity.

Having been down on this journey for more than 30+ years, most of it as an academic based in Washington D.C., being erroneously introduced at a keynote in Mexico City as a faculty member from the Jesuit University, I offer this unpaid advertisement: consider hiring a Jesuit-trained graduate.

What can you do when you choose to believe that ethics matters? I'd say: Hire a Jesuit-trained graduate.

Do you want leaders sensitive to their organization's impact on the environment and communities while also growing financial prosperity?

Hire a Jesuit-trained graduate. They live it and breathe it in ways that other institutions don't: J.R.D. Tata recognized this when he set up this annual oration twenty-seven years ago.

Final words: I look forward to following your progress in creating an inclusive, prosperous future: Be creative, be inspired and make a difference. Show us how to do good while doing well and make the seemingly impossible, possible.

REFERENCES

1. BBC News, 2013. BP oil spill trial told it 'put profits over safety'. 25 February.
2. The EU, for example, mandates a different set of reporting requirements.
3. Gini, A. 2007. *God Can Quote Me on That.* ACTA Publications.
4. Laudato Si, 129. *Washington Post,* 2015. Pope Francis's speech to Congress, September 24, 2015. https://www.washingtonpost.com/local/social-issues/transcript-pope-franciss-speech-to-congress/2015/09/24/6d7d7ac8-62bf-11e5-8e9e-dce8a2a2a679_story.html?noredirect=on&utm_term=.2558006382bd

5. Clay, J. 2005. *Exploring the links between international business and poverty reduction: A case study of Unilever in Indonesia*. Eynsham, UK: Information Press.
6. Baumhart, R.C. 1968. *An Honest Profit: What Business People Say about Ethics in Business*. Cambridge, MA: Harvard Business School.
7. Gini, A. 2006. *Why It's Hard To Be Good*. New York, NY: Routledge.
8. Aristotle, 350 B.C.E. *Nicomachean Ethics*. Translated by Ross, W.D.
9. Griffin, J. J. & Mahon, J. F. 1997. 'The Corporate Social Performance and Corporate Financial Performance Debate: Twenty-five Years of Incomparable Research'. Business & Society, 36(1): 5-31; Mahon, J. F., & Griffin, J. J. (1999). Painting a portrait: A reply. Business & Society, 38(1): 126-133.
10. Griffin, J.J. 2016. *Managing Corporate Impacts: Co-Creating Value*. Cambridge University Press.
11. Easterly, W. 2007. The *White Man's Burden: Why the West's Efforts to Aid the Rest Have Done So Much Ill and So Little Good*. The Penguin Press.; Yunus, M. 2017. *A World of Three Zeros: The New Economics of Zero Poverty, Zero Unemployment, and Zero Net Carbon Emissions*, PublicAffairs.
12. Baumhart, R.C. 1968. *An Honest Profit: What Business People Say about Ethics in Business*. Rinehart and Winston.
13. Andrews, K. R. 1971. *The Concept of Corporate Strategy*. Homewood, IL: Richard D. Irwin, Inc.; Ansoff, H. I. 1965. Corporate Strategy. New York, NY: McGraw-Hill Book Company.
14. Mascarenhas, O.A.J. D'Souza, D. and Abraham, E. 2017. (Editors) *In Memory of J.R.D. Tata: A Quarter Century of Ethics Discourses*, XLRI, Jamshedpur, India: J.R.D. Tata Foundation in Business Ethics, page 1.
15. Lala, R.M. 2007. *The Romance of Tata Steel. Penguin Press: New Delhi, India*: Penguin Press, p. 8. Quoted from Lala, R.M. 2004, *For the Love of India*.
16. Griffin and Mahon, 1997.
17. Griffin, J.J. 2004. 'Corporate restructurings: Ripple effects on corporate philanthropy', Journal of Public Affairs, 4(1): 27-43.
18. Lala, R.M. 1984. *The Heartbeat of a Trust: Fifty Years of the Sir Dorabji Tata Trust*. New Delhi, India: Penguin. pages xi - xii.
19. Ibid., page xiii.

20 Evans, 1965; Griffin, J.J. 2016. *Managing Corporate Impacts: Co-creating Value*. Cambridge University Press.

21. Ibid.

22. Trivedi, S. 2015.

23. Griffin, J.J. 2016. *Managing Corporate Impacts: Co-creating Value.* Cambridge University Press.

24. Smith, A. *Theory of Moral Sentiments*. Smith, A. *The Wealth of Nations*.

About the Contributors

Joseph M. Sciortino, former President and CEO of Sysco Food Services (headquartered in Miami, South Florida), was a highly regarded speaker and author on the subject of business ethics. Before Sysco, he spent twenty years as general sales manager of H.J. Heinz Company. He was a member of the boards of many charitable trusts. He served as a founding director of Covenant House of Ft. Lauderdale, and the Daily Bread Community Food Bank of South Florida. He was on the board of St. John Vianney Seminary and of Food for the Poor. Following his retirement in Daytona Beach, he continued to devote his life to his Catholic faith, to his family, to Church of the Epiphany in Port Orange and to philanthropy. He passed away on 1 February 2009.

Justice Bakhtawar Lentin was one of the most illustrious and respected judges of the Bombay High Court. He was called to Middle Temple, London, in 1950 to sign the Roll of Barristers of the High Court of Justice, King's Bench Division. He is particularly known for his relentless uncovering of the health department's gross negligence and corruption in the JJ Hospital case. The state health services, especially the food and drugs administration, was scathingly criticized for failing to protect the public from ruthless drug manufacturers. He started his career as an advocate in Bombay High Court in 1950. He practised in civil and criminal cases in the high court and in the city civil and sessions court. He held the position of judge and later additional judge in the city civil and sessions court in Mumbai. He served as the judge of Bombay High Court from 1975 till his retirement in 1989.

Dr Kenneth E. Goodpaster was a professor of ethics and business law. He taught graduate and undergraduate philosophy students at the University of Notre Dame throughout the 1970s before joining the Harvard Business School as faculty in 1980. At Harvard, he taught both MBA candidates and executives, alongside developing the second-year elective course, ethical aspects of corporate policy, as well as the first-year module, managerial decision making and ethical values. He authored two textbooks, *Ethics in Management* (1984) and *Policies and Persons: A Casebook in Business Ethics* (First Edition 1985, Second Edition 1991, Third Edition 1998). In 1990, Dr Goodpaster accepted the David and Barbara Koch Endowed Chair in Business Ethics at the University of St. Thomas. There he taught undergraduate, MBA and executive educational programmes.

His research interests range from conceptual studies of ethical reasoning to empirical studies of the social implications of management decision-making. This work has led to three books: *Perspectives on Morality* (1976), *Ethics and Problems of the 21st Century* (1979), and *Regulation, Values and the Public Interest* (1980). He has published articles in a variety of professional journals, including *Journal of Business Ethics, Business Ethics Quarterly* and *Harvard Business Review*, among others.

Fr Peter-Hans Kolvenbach, revered for his simplicity and moderation, was the twenty-ninth superior general of the Society of Jesus, from 1983 for nearly a quarter century. His relentless urge to grow in knowledge inspired him to earn a doctorate in sacred theology from the Jesuit-run St Joseph University in Beirut. He pursued linguistics from the Paris-Sorbonne University. Fr Kolvenbach also served as professor of linguistics at St Joseph University and as vice-provincial of the Jesuits' Near-East Vice-Province, which served the Society of Jesus in Egypt, Lebanon and Syria. From 1964 to 1976, he taught general and oriental linguistics in Hague, Paris, and then in Beirut, where he became professor of general linguistics and Armenian at St Joseph University. He served in that capacity until 1981, when he became rector of the Pontifical Oriental Institute. Fr Kolvenbach entered the Society of Jesus at Mariëndaal, the Netherlands, when he was only nineteen. He was ordained to the priesthood in Beirut in 1961. Fr Kolvenbach passed away at the age of eighty-eight in Beirut on 26 November 2016.

Tarjani M. Vakil, former MD and Chairman of Export-Import

(EXIM) Bank of India, was the first Indian woman to head a bank and a financial institution. Her style of working at EXIM Bank made her the highest ranking official in Asia. She revamped the banking sector through adoption of effective technologies and improved ethical standards of working. Her foray into the banking and financial sector was at a time when women were just beginning to consider the business sector as a career choice. In 1958, she joined the Maharashtra State Finance Corporation (MSFC), set up for financing small scale industries. After serving MSFC for seven years, she made a transition from the state level to the national level development bank, Industrial Development Bank of India (IDBI), in 1965. Her seventeen years in IDBI were spent in working in almost all the departments, including underwriting, disinvestment of shares on Stock Exchanges, project financing and monitoring, and export finance. She eventually left IDBI as Deputy General Manager and joined EXIM in the position of General Manager.

She has contributed immensely in the development banking sector in career spanning over forty years. She was declared Woman of the Year in 1996. In 1997, KPMG Worldwide Business recognized her as one of the top fifty women to prove their valour in the world of business.

Since her retirement in 1996, she has been on the boards of many companies. She has been the Non-Executive and Independent Director of Idea Cellular Ltd since 2 September, 2006; an Independent Director at Aditya Birla Nuvo Ltd since 27 July 2000; and an Independent Non-Executive Director at Alkyl Amines Chemicals Ltd since August 2005.

Prof Christopher Peter Frost is the former Head of Journalism at Liverpool John Moores University. He was a newspaper journalist and editor before joining academics some twenty years ago. His research interest inclines towards media ethics, given his extensive experience in the field. He has been a long-term member of the National Union of Journalists' (NUJ) Ethics Council and served on the UK Press Council as well. He was NUJ President in 1992 and a member of the union's National Executive Council for many years. In 1993, he chaired the union's Ethics Council, which debates journalism ethics and has a role in educating NUJ members. He has given evidence to the UK House of Commons select committee on press regulation on several occasions, and also at the high-profile Leveson Inquiry. He is a former chair of the Association for Journalism Education, which represents most schools of journalism in UK and Ireland higher education institutions. He has published widely and regularly speaks at international conferences. He is the author of the books *Designing Newspaper and Magazines* (2011) and *Reporting for Journalists* (2010). Prof. Frost has written innumerable articles and features, a couple of short factual books, as well as a number of papers on journalistic ethics, journalism and new technology, the Press Council and the Press Complaints Commission.

Suresh Krishna is the chairman and, till 11 May 2006, the managing director of Sundram Fasteners Ltd, which recently completed fifty years of manufacturing high-tensile fasteners. Krishna, a third-generation member of the TVS family, entered the business in 1962, when the TVS group was taking its first steps into manufacturing. Coming from a literature and science background, he apprenticed for six months in Lucas TVS and for about a year in Wheels India. He started Sundaram Fasteners in 1966 with only eight workers and a four lakh turnover in its first year of manufacturing. Krishna soon learned the ropes of the manufacturing sector. Under his astute leadership, the company, which had started its operations from a small industrial unit in Ambattur Industrial Estate, soon moved to its present location in Padi and has since expanded to multiple locations in India and abroad.

He has been on the boards of several leading companies and financial institutions. He has served as an independent non-executive director of Tata Steel Ltd, as a director on the Central Board of RBI and as a director of Tata Communications Ltd. He has won numerous awards and honours, including Padma Shri in 2006, Sir Jehangir Ghandy Medal for Industrial Peace from XLRI in 1991, Businessman of the Year award in 1995, and Ernst & Young's Entrepreneur of the Year award for manufacturing in 2001. The All India Management

Association conferred upon him the JRD Tata Corporate Leadership Award 2000.

Dr Amrita Patel, former chairman of National Dairy Development Board from 1998 to 2014, is a relentless development activist and passionate environmentalist. She was at the forefront of Operation Flood, the largest programme in the world aimed at using food aid for development. It was under her stewardship that the programme was implemented to promote, finance and deliver a variety of supporting services to a national cooperative dairy structure. The programme transformed the lives of millions of marginalized and small farmers, and milk producers. She has also contributed immensely to activities ranging from livestock development, disease control, vaccine production, R&D and policy review, to banking and finance, through her nomination on the boards of the Reserve Bank of India (RBI) and the National Bank for Agriculture and Rural Development (NABARD).

Given her grave concern for environment and health, she is on the boards of several organizations and trusts working in the area. She is on the boards of the Foundation for Ecological Security, Sardar Patel Renewable Energy Research Institute and Charutar Arogya Mandal Trust, among others. Dr Patel was conferred the Padma Bhushan and numerous other awards and honorary degrees, including the Dr Norman Borlaug Award, the Financial Express Lifetime Achievement Award, the Jawaharlal Nehru Birth Centenary Award for Nation Building for 1999-2000, and World Dairy Expo Inc.'s International Person of the Year in 1997, to name a few.

Fr Dr Robert Frederick Drinan, was a Roman Catholic Jesuit priest, lawyer, human rights activist, and Democratic US representative from Massachusetts. He was also a law professor at Georgetown University Law Center for the last twenty-six years of his life, from 1981 to 2007. His academic work and classes focused on legal ethics and international human rights. He served as dean of the Boston College Law School from 1956 until 1970, during which time he also taught as a professor of family law and church-State relations. In 1970, Drinan sought a seat in Congress on an anti-Vietnam War platform.

He went on to win the election to the House of Representatives, and was re-elected four times, serving from 1971 until 1981. He was the first of two Roman Catholic priests to serve as a voting member of Congress. Drinan served as a member of the American Bar Association (ABA) House of Delegates until his death and was chair of the ABA Section on Individual Rights and Responsibilities. In 2004, Drinan received the ABA Medal, the organization's highest honour for distinguished service in law. On 10 May, 2006, Drinan was presented the Distinguished Service Award by then Speaker *Dennis Hastert* and then Minority Leader Nancy Pelosi on behalf of the House of Representatives. He received twenty-one honorary doctorates during his life. Drinan died on 28 January 2007 in Washington DC.

Dr Ramachandra Guha is an eminent historian, biographer and cricket writer based in Bengaluru. He has authored several books. Some of his most well-known titles are *The Unquiet Woods* (University of California Press, 1989), a profound environmental history; *A Corner of a Foreign Field* (Picador, 2002), an award-winning social history of cricket; and *India after Gandhi* (Macmillan/Ecco Press, 2007), regarded as book of the year by several leading publications. His most recent book is *Gandhi: The Years That Changed the World* (2018), the follow-up to his acclaimed *Gandhi before India* (Knopf, 2014). He has also written numerous essays on environmentalism in the north and the south, which have been widely anthologized and translated. His essay 'Radical American Environmentalism and Wilderness Preservation' (first published in *Environmental Ethics* in 1989) has been reprinted in more than a dozen anthologies.

Dr Guha has also been a prominent figure in academics. He has taught at the universities of Yale and Stanford, and held the Arné Naess Chair at the University of Oslo. In 1997-98 he was the Indo-American Community Visiting Professor at the University of California at Berkeley. In the academic year 2011-12 he served as the Philippe Roman Professor of History and International Affairs at the London School of Economics. He has received several awards, including the Ramnath Goenka Prize for excellence in journalism, the Sahitya Akademi Award, and the R.K. Narayan Prize. In 2009, he was awarded the Padma Bhushan, India's third highest civilian honour. In 2008 and again in 2013, *Prospect* magazine nominated Guha as one of the world's most influential intellectuals. In 2014 he was awarded an honorary doctorate in the humanities by Yale University. In 2015 he was awarded the Fukuoka Prize.

Sir William Mark Tully is a celebrated former BBC journalist and author of several books on India and religion. His reportage of several major incidents in South Asia during his tenure won him honours like the Padma Shri, the Padma Bhushan, the Order of the British Empire and Knighthood. He was appointed the India correspondent for BBC World Services in 1964. For thirty years, he was the definitive voice on the sub-continent, covering politics and culture, reporting on disasters and despair. His reporting assignments included some of the contentious issues of the times, ranging from Indo-Pakistan conflicts, the Bhopal gas tragedy, Operation Blue Star (and the subsequent assassination of Indira Gandhi, followed by anti-Sikh riots), and the assassination of Rajiv Gandhi to the Demolition of Babri Masjid. He was elevated to the post of Bureau Chief in 1974 and held the post for twenty years till his resignation. After leaving the BBC, he worked as a freelance journalist and broadcaster based in New Delhi.

Some of the noted titles that showcase Mr Tully's profound knowledge and insight of the subcontinent are *Amritsar: Mrs Gandhi's Last Battle* (1985), co-authored with his colleague in BBC Delhi; *Raj to Rajiv: 40 Years of Indian Independence* (1996), based on a BBC radio series of the same name; and *No Full Stops in India* (1988), a collection of journalistic essays. His has written two collections of short stories, *The Heart of India* (1995) and *Upcountry Tales: Once Upon A Time in The Heart of India* (2017). *India in Slow Motion* (2002) was written in collaboration with Gillian Wright. Tully later wrote *India's Unending Journey* (2008) and *India: The Road Ahead* (2011), published in India under the title *Non-stop India*. Tully has also written *An Investigation into The Lives of Jesus* (1996) to accompany the BBC series by the same name, and *Mother* (1992), on *Mother Teresa*.

Telesphore P. Cardinal Toppo is former Archbishop of Ranchi and a former President of the Catholic Bishops' Conference of India (2004-08) and Conference of Catholic Bishops of India (2003-05). He is the first Adivasi Indian to become a cardinal. In 2002, he was honoured with the Jharkhand Ratan Award for his distinguished social work in the state. He was ordained a priest on 3 May, 1969. Cardinal Toppo studied at the Regional Major Seminary of St Albert's College in Ranchi. He holds a Bachelor degree from St Xavier's College, Ranchi, and a masters in history from Ranchi University. After his studies in Theology at the Pontifical Urbaniana College in Rome, he was nominated Bishop of Dumka on 8 June 1978 and in October, the same year, was ordained as Bishop. Cardinal Toppo served first as assistant teacher and then headmaster at the St Joseph's High School, Torpa, and later founded and also directed the Lievens Vocational Centre in Torpa. He was appointed Archbishop Co-adjutor of Ranchi on 8 November 1984. He was assigned the responsibilities of Cardinal-Priest by Pope John Paul II on 21 October 2003. He was elector at the 2005 papal conclave that elected Joseph Ratzinger as Pope Benedict XVI. He was again in the papal conclave in 2013, that selected Pope Francis. He is on the Elijah Board of World Religious Leaders. The board brings together some of the world's most prominent religious figures from Judaism, Islam, Christianity, Buddhism and the religions of India.

Fr Dr James J Spillane, is an American priest born at Brighton, Massachusetts in 1943. He entered the Jesuit Society in 1964 and was ordained a priest in 1976. His early assignments as a Jesuit priest were mainly teaching in universities in Jamaica, Colombia, Iraq, Iran and Indonesia. He spent the major part of his life working in Indonesia and later becoming a citizen of the nation. He has also worked as a consultant in Center for Building, Planning, and Housing at United Nations in New York (1970-72) and in the Center for International Studies at Massachusetts Institute of Technology (MIT), Cambridge (1974-76). He pursued his B.Sc. and M.A. in mathematics from Boston College and completed his PhD in international economics from New York University. He has taught international business and business ethics at Sanata Dharma University, Yogyakarta, Indonesia. He was the Chair Professor of Business Ethics at Milwaukee, Wisconsin, in the central United States in 2003-04. He has written several articles and books in English and Indonesian on international economics (especially Indonesian commodity exports), values and university education, and the role of tourism in the Indonesian economy.

Dr Peter Eigen, founder of Transparency International, is a relentless advocate of the global fight against corruption. He has made major contributions towards raising awareness of the diminishing effects of corruption on economic growth, social welfare and justice. Eigen has worked tirelessly to promote transparency and accountability in international development. From 1993 to 2005 he was Chair of Transparency International and later became the chairman of Transparency International's Advisory Council. Subsequently, Eigen was the founding chairman of the Extractive Industries Transparency Initiative (EITI) until 2011. During the same time, he founded the Berlin Civil Society Center and supported the creation of the Humboldt-Viadrina School of Governance. His work in the field of economic development as a World Bank manager of programmes in Africa and Latin America is highly regarded. Under a Ford Foundation sponsorship, he provided legal and technical assistance to the governments of Botswana and Namibia. From 1988 to 1991 he was the director of the Regional Mission for Eastern Africa of the World Bank. In 2001, Eigen received a first class medal of merit (Bundesverdienstkreuz 1.Klasse) from the President of the Federal Republic of Germany. In 2004, he was honoured with the Readers Digest European of the Year award and in 2007 with the Gustav Heinemann Award. Since 2007, Eigen has been a member of Kofi Annan's Africa Progress Panel. He is a member of the boards of the Columbia Center on Sustainable International Investment at Columbia University, New York; the Arnold-Bergstrasser-Institute, Freiburg; and the Humboldt-Viadrina School of Governance, Berlin. Eigen has also chaired the Board of the Stiftung Kinder-Hilfe and in 2011 joined the board of the German Doctors Association (Ärzte für die Dritte Welt).

Subroto Bagchi, co-founder and non-executive director of Mindtree, is one of the country's most admired entrepreneurs, business leaders and writers. He started as the chief operating officer at Mindtree, a software services company, after its inception in 1999. He served as the executive chairman of the company from 2012-16 and has been its non-executive and non-independent director since 1 April 2016. From 1999 to 2007 was the period when the vision, mission and values of Mindtree were being formulated and Mr Bagchi, as the COO, was at the centre of the entire process. He laid down the points of differentiation for the company on the lines of leadership development, marketing and knowledge management. Before starting Mindtree, Bagchi served in leadership roles in many other companies. From 1998-99 he served as the vice president of Product Realization, Lucent Technologies. He also worked with the leading IT services company, Wipro, where he structured the six Sigma initiatives as corporate vice president of Mission Quality. In 2006, he was ranked amongst the most influential business persons by *Business Today* magazine. In 2016, he was invited by the Odisha government to head the state's Skill Development Authority and set up a unified body that would guide, implement and oversee all skill development programmes in the state. He resigned from the post in March 2019. He is also a widely read business writer, having penned a number of books and columns for newspapers and magazines. Some of his highly motivating titles include *High Performance Entrepreneur, Go Kiss the World* and *The Professional.*

Steven Snyder, founder and managing director of Snyder Leadership Group, assists organizations and their executives to accelerate innovation, advance leadership capabilities and tap emerging market opportunities through his innovative methods. During his tenure at Microsoft, Snyder was highly appreciated for his distinctive ideas by Bill Gates. As a general manager, Snyder led the company's development tool business, strengthening its technology innovations. Along with computer scientists from the University of Minnesota, Snyder developed a pioneering technology called collaborative filtering. As co-founder and CEO of Net Perceptions, he successfully commercialized this invention to enable the real-time personalized recommendations that have become central to the online shopping experience with Amazon.com, the company's first customer. This won him the first ever World Technology Award in 1999 for contributing to the advance of emerging technologies for the benefit of business and society. Dr Snyder has taught business ethics at the Carlson School of Management and served as an executive in residence at the Center for Integrative Leadership at the University of Minnesota. He has also taught in the Executive MBA programme in Warsaw, Poland.

Dr Anil Kakodkar, former director of Bhabha Atomic Research Centre (BARC) and former chairman of Atomic Energy Commission, was the brain behind the designing and construction of Dhruva reactor. He has contributed immensely in the indigenous development of a large number of critical systems of Pressurized Heavy Water Reactors. Throughout his forty-five-year-long career he worked for the development of the atomic energy programme of India. His work focused on developing nuclear reactor systems to address the nuclear power requirements of the country. He was amongst the selected group of scientists involved in the first successful peaceful nuclear explosion experiment that India conducted on 18 May 1974 in Pokhran. Later, he played a pivotal role in the series of successful nuclear tests conducted during May 1998, again at Pokhran. Under his stewardship, India also demonstrated nuclear submarine powerpack technology. He has headed the boards of several educational institutes, including the Indian Institute of Technology, Bombay; Inter-University Centre for Astronomy & Astrophysics, Pune; and National Geophysical Research Institute, Hyderabad. He became the proud recipient of the Padma Shri in 1998 and the Padma Bhushan in 1999. He has also been conferred with many international honours for his exceptional work in the area of atomic energy. He is the recipient of Rockwell Medal for Excellence in Technology (1997). He is a member of the International Nuclear Energy Academy and the World Innovation Foundation, among others.

Tarun Das has spent a major part of his career in industry associations. He joined the Confederation of Indian Industry (CII) in 1963 and served as the director general and chief executive of CII from April 1967 to May 2004, and chief mentor from June 2004 till his retirement in October 2009. He was instrumental in promoting business co-operation internationally and was also involved with major policymaking groups concerned with Indian industry. Das has been on the board of many companies. He served as chairman of Haldia Petrochemicals Limited until July 2011. He was the chairman and independent non-executive director of ACC Ltd until January 2006. He was associated with John Keells Holdings PLC from 2000 until 1 July, 2016. He co-chaired the Indo-US Strategic Dialogue and Indo-US-Japan Strategic Dialogue. Das has received many accolades and awards for his contributions in the field of trade and policy making. He was awarded an honorary doctorate in science by The University of Warwick, UK, and has been conferred an honorary CBE by Her Majesty the Queen for his contribution to Indo-British relations. He has also been conferred the 2004 Singapore National Award (Public Service Medal) by the Singapore government for his contribution to strengthening economic ties between India and Singapore. The Indian government honoured his services through the Padma Bhushan in 2006.

Laxman Narasimhan is the chief commercial officer of PepsiCo and soon to be the CEO of Reckitt Benckiser from September 2019. He previously served as the senior vice president and CFO of PepsiCo Americas Foods based in Purchase, New York, which covered Frito-Lay North America, Quaker North America and PepsiCo's Latin America Foods. Prior to PepsiCo, Narasimhan was director and location manager of McKinsey's New Delhi office. He worked with McKinsey and held several positions around the world for nineteen years, until 2012. He had responsibility for consumer-facing industries in India, co-led the Global Consumer and Shopper Insights Practice and led McKinsey's research on the emerging market consumer. He has worked across multiple industries, including consumer, retail, energy, manufacturing, technology and healthcare. Previously, Laxman co-led the Global Retail Knowledge Council of McKinsey's Retail Practice. In addition to client service and research, Laxman has led assignments in the public sector, working on important policy issues, particularly in education and skill building. He is a trustee of the Brookings Institution, a member of the Council on Foreign Relations, a fellow of the Foreign Policy Association and is an Advisory Board member of the Jay H. Baker Retailing Center at the Wharton School, University of Pennsylvania.

Dr Christopher R. Lowney is a widely acclaimed writer and an influential public speaker and leadership consultant. Being a former Jesuit seminarian, his writings on business ethics and decision-making emphasize on adopting a Jesuit leadership style towards business and politics. His first book, *Heroic Leadership: Best Practices from a 450-year-old Company that Changed the World*, was ranked a bestseller and was named a finalist for the 2003 Book of the Year Award from *ForeWord* magazine. It has been translated into several languages. He has delivered leadership seminars and workshops in some two dozen countries on five continents. His most recent book, published in 2013, is an examination of the leadership style of Pope Francis. He is the former Managing Director of JP Morgan & Co. At Morgan, he was an investment banker to Fortune 1000 companies and, later, a managing director in Tokyo and Singapore, where he served on Morgan's Asia-Pacific management committee. Later, as a managing director in London, he served on Morgan's Europe, Mideast and Africa management committee. He currently serves as chair-elect of the Board of Catholic Health Initiatives, one of the largest healthcare systems in the US, comprising more than seventy hospitals. He is a holder of five honorary doctoral degrees from Gonzaga University, St. Louis University, the University of Scranton, the University of Great Falls and Marymount Manhattan College. Dr Lowney founded Pilgrimage for Our Children's Future, which funds education and healthcare projects in the developing world. He helped launch Jesuit Commons-Higher Education at the Margins, which offers university-level education in refugee camps.

Dr Pallam Raju Mallipudi is a former Minister of Human Resource Development (2012-14) under the UPA–II government. As one of the longest serving ministers in the defence portfolio, Pallam Raju has travelled the country extensively in the discharge of his duties and has also led many important delegations on multiple missions to various countries like UK, France, Norway, Singapore, Belarus, South Korea, Bangladesh, Mongolia, etc. and was an active participant in international forums like the Shangri-La Dialogue at Singapore. He has received many honorary doctoral degrees. The Institution of Electronics and Telecommunication Engineers (IETE) conferred on him its highest honour, the honorary fellowship, in July 2013 for strengthening the education systems of the country, giving greater focus to industry-academia relationships, advocating skills development and entrepreneurship amongst the youth, and promoting innovation and R&D amongst institutions of higher learning. He received an honorary doctorate from the Jawaharlal Nehru Technological University, Hyderabad, in 2008. He was conferred the Doctor of Humane Letters by Temple University, USA in May 2013.

D. Shivakumar is the Group Executive President, Corporate Strategy and Business Development, at the Aditya Birla Group. He has previously served as the chairman and CEO of PepsiCo India Holdings Pvt. Ltd. Before Pepsico, he was with Nokia for eight years, running India and then the Emerging Markets operations. He has played stewardship role to over thirty-four brands in his career across Unilever, Philips and Nokia. He is a growth manager, having established every brand and geographic footprint through innovation, new business models and ecosystem partnerships. Like a sagacious coach, he invests time and energy in nurturing skills in people. He writes regularly for business journals and publications on emerging markets, brands, consumers, leadership and followership. Mr Shivakumar also teaches in business schools across the world. Mr Shivakumar has been awarded many times for marketing, leadership, and turning businesses around. The one award that's dear to his heart is the Most Distinguished Alumnus award from his alma mater, IIM Calcutta, bestowed on him in 2011. He was one among nine people who got the Most Distinguished Alumnus award during the golden jubilee celebration of IIM Calcutta. His pioneering work in telecom has provided case studies for Ivy League Universities like Harvard, and ISB (Indian School of Business). He is an independent director on the board of Godrej Consumer Products Ltd and is on the board of governors of IIM Ahmedabad.

Shekhar Gupta, a veteran journalist and a distinguished columnist, is the former editor-in-chief of *The Indian Express*. He concluded his nineteen-year-long stint at *The Indian Express* in 2014 to venture into a news media start-up, Mediascape. As the editor-in-chief of one of the country's leading publications, he led the largest network of award-winning journalists. His highly influential columns have been translated into Hindi, Telugu, Kannada, Gujarati and Marathi. He hosts the prime-time interview show *Walk the Talk* on NDTV 24x7 every week. He has now started a second weekly show in Hindi, *Chalte Chalte*, telecast on NDTV India. During a thirty-eight-year career, Mr Gupta has reported on key Indian and international events, including the Nellie massacre in Assam, Operation Blue Star, the student uprising in Tiananmen Square, the fall of the Berlin Wall, the first Gulf War from Baghdad, the first jihad in Afghanistan, and the many twists and turns in Sri Lanka's troubled Tamil North during 1983-93.

Fr Dr Frank Brennan is a Jesuit priest and a professor of law at Australian Catholic University. He is the Adjunct Professor at the Australian Centre for Christianity and Culture, Australian National University College of Law and the National Centre for Indigenous Studies. He is the National Director of Human Rights and Social Justice for Jesuit Social Services, and Superior of the Jesuit community at Xavier House in Canberra. He has written several books on the rights of indigenous people and leadership in the church. His most recent books include *No Small Change: The Road to Recognition for Indigenous Australia*; *Amplifying That Still, Small Voice*; *The Quest for Leadership in Church and State*; and *Maintaining a Convinced and Pondered Trust: The 2015 Gasson Lectures*. He is an Officer of the Order of Australia for services to Aboriginal Australians, particularly as an advocate in the areas of law, social justice and reconciliation. He is the recipient of the 2013 Distinguished Service to Immigration Award from the Migration Institute of Australia and the 2015 Eureka

Democracy Award in recognition of his endeavours, which have contributed to strengthening democratic traditions in Australia. In 2009, he chaired the Australian National Human Rights Consultation Committee. Fr. Brennan serves on the board of the National Apology Foundation and the Advisory Council of the Global Foundation. His research interests include conscience and faith, human rights and the rule of law, and the rights of indigenous people and asylum seekers.

Dr J.J. Irani is the former Managing Director of Tata Iron and Steel Company. He joined Tata Steel in 1968 and rose to take over as MD in 1992, a position he held for nearly two decades. He is credited for turning around the steel giant and for modernizing the steel-making process. He has received a number of awards recognizing his contributions to Tata Steel and the industry. Prominent among them are the Metallurgist of the Year award in 1974 from the Ministry of Steel and Mines, the prestigious Platinum Medal in November, 1988, by the Indian Institute of Metals, Ernst & Young's Lifetime Achievement Award, 2001, for entrepreneurial success and the Twelfth Willy Korf Steel Vision Award from World Steel Dynamics and American Metal Market.

Dr Irani was appointed chairman of the Expert Committee set up by the Ministry of Company Affairs in December, 2004, to advise the Government on drafting new Companies Act. He was awarded the Padma Bhushan in 2007. He also played a significant role in strengthening the Indo-British partnership and was conferred honorary knighthood in October 1997 by the Queen of England. After his retirement as MD in 2001 he was appointed non-executive Director on the board of Tata Steel. Dr Irani was on the board of several other Tata Group companies, including Tata Sons, Tata Motors and Tata Teleservices.

Dr Jennifer J. Griffin is the Raymond C. Baumhart Professor of Business Ethics and Professor of Strategy at Loyola University Chicago's Quinlan School of Business (Chicago, IL). Engaged at all levels of learning (e.g. executive, doctoral, graduate, and undergraduate including online and experiential study abroad courses) Dr Griffin examines how organizations continuously co-create value. Annually, she leads corporate strategy, social impact, and strategy-oriented CSR workshops for Australian, Chilean, and US executives as well as periodically in Brazil, India and Lebanon.

Award-winning author of the Academy of Management 2017 Best Book Award, SIM Division, for her Cambridge University Press book, *Managing Corporate Impacts: Co-Creating Value,* Dr Griffin has received numerous research awards and grants. Among the research awards is the Best Paper Award (in twenty years) for a co-authored article, 'Corporate Social Performance and Corporate Financial Performance: Twenty-five Years of Incomparable Research.' It remains among the most cited articles in *Business & Society.* Her research is published in multiple disciplines: *Journal of Business Ethics, Public Administration Review, Business & Society, Group & Organization Management, Business Ethics: An European Review, Business & Politics, Corporate Reputation Review, Journal of Public Affairs,* and *Public Relations Quarterly,* among others. Co-author of several case studies on social entrepreneurship, she has written book chapters for the United Nations Principles for Responsible Management Education (UN PRME) series, the *Doing Well by Doing Good* series, the *Handbook for Public Affairs,* and *The Accountable Corporation* series, among others. Dr Griffin is an associate editor of *Business & Society,* the North American editor for *Journal of Public Affairs,* and senior editor of the *Oxford Research Encyclopedia.*

www.ingramcontent.com/pod-product-compliance
Lightning Source LLC
Chambersburg PA
CBHW030807310726
48980CB00006B/414/J
9789353335687